OXFORD HISTORICAL MONOGRAPHS

Politics and the Law in Late Nineteenth-Century Germany

The Origins of the Civil Code

MICHAEL JOHN

CLARENDON PRESS · OXFORD

1989

Oxford University Press, Walton Street, Oxford OX2 6DP

Oxford New York Toronto
Delhi Bombay Calcutta Madras Karachi
Petaling Jaya Singapore Hong Kong Tokyo
Nairobi Dar es Salaam Cape Town
Melbourne Auckland
and associated companies in
Berlin Ibadan

Oxford is a trade mark of Oxford University Press

Published in the United States
by Oxford University Press, New York

British Library Cataloguing in Publication Data
John, Michael
Politics and the law in late nineteenth
century Germany: the origins of the
civil code.—(Oxford historical
monographs)
1. Germany. Politics, 1814–1896. Legal
aspects
I. Title
344.302
ISBN 0-19-822748-5

Library of Congress Cataloging in Publication Data
Data available

Set by Oxford Text Systems
Printed in Great Britain by
Biddles Ltd., Guildford and Kings' Lynn

To my parents

ACKNOWLEDGEMENTS

I have incurred many debts in the course of writing this book. The first and greatest of these is to Hartmut Pogge von Strandmann who originally suggested that the German Civil Code might be important and subsequently acted as my doctoral supervisor. His combination of critical acuity, common sense, and enthusiasm for this project have been indispensable to its completion. I should also like to thank my doctoral examiners, Professor A. M. Honoré and Jonathan Steinberg, for their many helpful comments. I have greatly benefited from discussions with many people but would especially like to thank David Blackbourn, John Breuilly, Geoff Eley, Richard Evans, Ian Kershaw, Ross McKibbin, Tony Nicholls, Jim Retallack, Jürgen Thieme, and Walter Wilhelm. Werner Schubert deserves special mention for his uncommon generosity in lending me important research materials and providing working space in the University of Kiel. I should also like to thank Colin Matthew for reading the manuscript and making a number of helpful suggestions. The editors of the The Historical Journal and Past and Present kindly allowed me to use material which first appeared in 'The Politics of Legal Unity in Germany, 1870-1896', Historical Journal, 28 (1985), 341-55, and 'The Peculiarities of the German State: Bourgeois Law and Society in the Imperial Era', Past and Present, 119 (1988), 105-31.

Most of the research for this book was funded by the Department of Education and Science and the FVS Stiftung, Hamburg. A three-month grant from the British Council in late 1981 made it possible for me to consult vital materials in the German Democratic Republic. I should like to thank the staffs of the archives listed in the Bibliography and the librarians of the Staats- und Universitätsbibliothek, Hamburg and the Staatsbibliothek, Berlin-GDR. I am grateful to the Warden and Fellows of Nuffield College, Oxford, the Master and Fellows of Jesus College, Cambridge, and the President and Fellows of Magdalen College, Oxford, for providing me with the opportunity to transform a hastily completed doctorate into a book.

I should like to take this opportunity to thank the many friends who have had to put up with the German Civil Code for too long.

Alex Holdcroft not only read the manuscript and suggested many improvements, but also made life bearable while it was being written. My final debt of gratitude is to my parents for their support and interest. This book is dedicated to them.

M. J.

January 1988

ABBREVIATIONS

AcP	*Archiv für die civilistische Praxis*
ADB	*Allgemeine deutsche Biographie*
AH Lübeck	Archiv der Hansestadt Lübeck
BA	Bundesarchiv
BHStA	Bayerisches Hauptstaatsarchiv
CEH	*Central European History*
DJZ	*Deutsche Juristenzeitung*
EHQ	*European History Quarterly*
GLA	Generallandesarchiv
GstA	*Geheimes Staatsarchiv Preussischer Kulturbesitz*
HA Cologne	Historisches Archiv Stadt Köln
HStA	Hauptstaatsarchiv
HZ	*Historische Zeitschrift*
JMH	*Journal of Modern History*
JuS	*Juristische Schulung*
NStA	Niedersächsisches Staatsarchiv
NSUUB	Niedersächsische Staats- und Universitätsbibliothek
Quad. fior.	*Quaderni fiorentini per la storia del pensiero giuridico moderno*
SBRT	*Stenographische Berichte über die Verhandlungen des Reichstags*
StA	Staatsarchiv
ZRG GA	*Zeitschrift der Savigny-Stiftung für Rechtsgeschichte Germanistische Abteilung.*
ZRG RA	*Zeitschrift der Savigny-Stiftung für Rechtsgeschichte. Romanistische Abteilung*
ZStA	Zentrales Staatsarchiv

I.

Introduction

THIS book is intended as a contribution to the study of the development of German political culture in the nineteenth century. It seeks to examine the development and transformation of that cluster of traditions associated with liberalism, nationalism, and state formation which decisively affected the ways in which German society attempted to come to terms with the problems of modernity. As with most works on these matters, the shadow of 1933 lurks behind what follows, but I hope that it is satisfactorily distanced. The main subject of this study, the Civil Code (*Bürgerliches Gesetzbuch*) of 1896, was very much the completion of nineteenth-century developments rather than the harbinger of a new age. If there is a case for studying the Second Reich in its own terms without constantly looking over one's shoulder to the Third,[1] it is surely here.

This is not, then, a work of legal history in the common sense of the term. Emphasis is placed far more on the evolution of attitudes towards the legal system than on the details of specific legal developments. Naturally, it would have been undesirable and indeed impossible to omit all discussion of legal detail; such a course would have left the analysis unsatisfactorily detached from the issues which shaped the intellectual and political climate in which decision-makers had to operate. For that reason, the central sections of the book, which cover the period between 1874 and 1896, include detailed consideration of certain politically controversial areas of the civil law: land and inheritance law; certain aspects of freedom of contract; the law of associations, and so on. In this way it is hoped that important aspects of Germany's political development will be elucidated without overburdening the discussion with legal technicalities.

The question immediately arises as to why this particular subject should have been chosen as a way of addressing the broader themes which interest historians of nineteenth-century Germany. In the general

---

[1] R. J. Evans, 'Introduction', in Evans (ed.), *Society and Politics in Wilhelmine Germany* (London, 1978), 35-6.

works on the period, the work of legal unification in the last quarter of the nineteenth century is normally awarded at best a sentence or two.[2] Nor, with a few exceptions have contributors to the recent debates surrounding Germany's 'special path to modernity' (*Sonderweg*) sought to examine the legal system as an important component of the nation's political development. Where the law does enter the debate, it tends to do so in the form of comments about the class bias of the state in the application of the criminal law, particularly *vis-à-vis* the labour movement. The Bismarckian and Wilhelmine state's attitude to labour tends to be treated as a prime example of the failure of political modernization in Germany. The legal system thus becomes an instrument of the ruling classes or élites in their battle against threats from below. Where the German tradition of the rule of law (*Rechtsstaat*) is considered at all, it is usually in terms of its contribution to the survival of illiberal, authoritarian traditions in the practices of the state.[3]

The law cannot, however, be reduced to an instrument of the ruling class—a fact that is obscured by the concentration of much of the literature on the undoubted manipulation of certain sections of the law against particular groups in late nineteenth-century Germany. The very fact that attempts to curb Social Democratic or Catholic political agitation were commonly viewed as 'exceptional laws' (*Ausnahmegesetze*) prompts questions about the nature of 'normal' laws. Was it not the case that such exceptions were deemed necessary precisely because the standard principles of the legal system afforded insufficient means of protection? In any case, such considerations ignore the whole area of the civil law, which was arguably at least as important as the criminal law in reflecting the tensions of a rapidly changing society. The foundations of the civil law—contractual relationships, property rights, the family, and inheritance—are concerned with the basic institutions of modern society. Changes in those institutions—the rise of social-welfare projects, the growth of the tax-raising powers of the state, the

[2] See e.g. G. A. Craig, *Germany 1866–1945* (Oxford, 1978), 66; W. Carr, *A History of Germany 1815–1985* (3rd edn.; London, 1985), 122.

[3] See D. Blackbourn and G. Eley, *The Peculiarities of the German State* (Oxford, 1984), 190–4, 221–4; cf. D. Grimm, 'Bürgerlichkeit im Recht', in J. Kocka (ed.), *Bürger und Bürgerlichkeit im 19. Jahrhundert* (Göttingen, 1987), 149–88; H.-U. Wehler, *The German Empire 1871–1918* (Leamington Spa, 1985), 127 ff.; K. Saul, *Staat, Industrie, Arbeiterbewegung. Zur Innen- und Sozialpolitik des Wilhelminischen Deutschland 1903–1914* (Düsseldorf, 1974); cf. E. Kehr's important essay, 'Zur Genesis der preussischen Bürokratie und des Rechtsstaats', in Kehr, *Der Primat der Innenpolitik. Gesammelte Aufsätze zur preussisch-deutschen Sozialgeschichte im 19. und 20. Jahrhundert*, ed. H.-U. Wehler (Frankfurt, 1965), 31–52.

development of aggregate rights in property and labour law, and the extension of women's rights, to name but a few examples—are all central to the process of modernization. These developments were all, of course, related to the social and economic changes associated with industrialization. The civil law was the sphere within which attempts to regulate constantly evolving economic relationships took place. Indeed, much of the importance ascribed to legal unity in the nineteenth century derived from the belief that it would have a beneficial effect on economic activity. Statements about the civil law reflected opinions about the future of German society in the sense that they concerned the reconciliation of the common good with the explosion of private economic activity. By the late nineteenth century these matters had become the subject of highly divisive political controversies. The very nature of the common good, the definition of the social interests which claimed the right to special treatment by the state, became a central feature of the Wilhelmine age. A major goal of the present study is to explore the political ramifications of these controversies.

A second reason for considering these questions lies in the existence of a distinctive tradition of German legal thought and its contribution to the political culture of the country. Lawyers had a high profile in the major political movements of the day, especially in liberal nationalism. Moreover, the status of the law as an academic discipline was undoubtedly enhanced by the monopoly of senior positions in the bureaucracy that was enjoyed by trained lawyers. That meant that developments in academic jurisprudence directly influenced the attitudes of officials and politicians to an extent which was not equalled in other Western European countries. The abstract legalism of much of Germany's political culture in the mid-nineteenth century has often been noted, even if its exact relationship to the law faculties of German universities is still imperfectly understood. However, it is clear that the development of the positivist tradition in mid-century German jurisprudence was important in shaping the ways in which the relationship between the state and individual freedoms was considered. As we shall see, German civil-law jurisprudence was a principal factor in the development of a type of non-participatory, 'statist' liberalism, whose contours were by no means the necessary consequence of economic developments.[4] The

---

[4] See J. Breuilly, 'Civil Society and the Labour Movement, Class Relations and the Law', in J. Kocka (ed.), *Arbeiter und Bürger im 19. Jahrhundert* (Munich, 1985), 287–318; H.-E. Mueller, *Bureaucracy, Education, and Monopoly. Civil Service Reforms in Prussia and England* (Berkeley/Los Angeles/London, 1984); R. M. Unger, *Law and Modern*

4 *Introduction*

Civil Code was in large measure an expression of this particular type of liberalism.

The development of new ways of considering civil relationships was a prominent aspect of liberal reform. The first half of the century saw the completion of most of the crucial stages in the transition from a society of Estates (*Ständestaat*) to a modern civil society (*bürgerliche Gesellschaft*). The key feature of this transformation in the post-Napoleonic period was the establishment of a legal order founded on the formal equality of citizens and the breaking down of corporate restrictions on the individual's freedom of action. This meant, in the first place, the abolition of serfdom and the panoply of seigneurial rights which were a basic feature of the *ancien régime*. In the sphere of the civil law, it led to the elevation of individual freedoms—of contract, disposition of property, inheritance, etc.—to the status of fundamental norms. During the first half of the nineteenth century, these freedoms came to be seen as virtually absolute. In the inviolability of such freedoms at the hands of the state or fellow citizens lay an essential guarantee of personal liberty.[5]

These principles had established a dominant position in German jurisprudence before the period of national unification, and came to dominate the civil legislation of the various states. But by the 1860s it was widely felt that the adoption of such principles was not enough. The decades after 1848 saw a growing desire for 'legal certainty'—a notion which had a range of meanings in the German context. In the first place, it was associated with the demand for a *Rechtsstaat*, in which the state was legally obliged to treat its citizens in certain ways and could be brought to account if it did not. Second, legal certainty had Weberian connotations of calculability and predictability in economic activity: the citizen could only make rational decisions about his best course of action if he could predict with reasonable certainty the future application of the law. This second aspect might be considered analogous to the first, but with the emphasis placed on the civil relationships between individuals rather than on the state's powers. Third, the idea had a strong *territorial* aspect in that legal certainty was difficult, if not

Society (New York, 1976), 181–92. In general, see L. Krieger, *The German Idea of Freedom. History of a Political Tradition* (Chicago/London, 1957), 252 ff., chs. 7–9.

[5] See especially M. Riedel, 'Bürger, Staatsbürger, Bürgertum', in O. Brunner *et al.* (eds.), *Geschichtliche Grundbegriffe*, i (Stuttgart, 1972), 702–25; Riedel, 'Gesellschaft, bürgerliche' and D. S. Schwab, 'Eigentum', in ibid. ii (Stuttgart, 1975), 719–800 and 65–115.

impossible, to establish in states which did not possess uniform legal systems. In such cases, the problem was that the state's administration of justice was required to implement a network of different laws which undoubtedly hindered both the bureaucracy's pursuit of uniform government and the individual's ability to gauge the outcome of his own decisions.

There can be little doubt that these concerns provide much of the explanation for the movement towards codification in the nineteenth century. The problem of legal disunity existed to a greater or lesser extent in all the main German states. Excluding Austria, there were three major legal systems—the 'common law'[6] and the Prussian and French codes—in operation in Germany in 1815, and these systems frequently operated side by side in a single state. Moreover, local and regional 'particular' laws cut across each of these systems. In Prussia, for example, the *Allgemeines Landrecht* of 1794 had only subsidiary jurisdiction in relation to local law in the provinces of Pomerania, Brandenburg, Silesia, and parts of Saxony. Certain parts of the law which profoundly influenced the normal rhythms of society—for example, land law, family law, and inheritance law—were particularly affected by such regional diversities.[7] Reinhart Koselleck's research on the Prussian bureaucracy has shown the limitations of the unifying effects of the *Allgemeines Landrecht* and the ways in which the survival of provincial legal systems hampered the bureaucracy in the *Vormärz* period.[8] The same story could be told in stronger terms for states such as Bavaria, where failed codifications were a constant feature of bureaucratic attempts to solve this problem between 1815 and 1871. These difficulties were indeed greatest in those states (predominantly in the centre and south of Germany), where the effects of the territorial revolution of 1803-15 had been most profound. Legal insecurity, which had adverse effects on both government and citizens, was related to the political difficulties of integrating new territories into existing states. As

---

[6] The term 'common law' will be used in the Continental sense—i.e. as a translation of *gemeines Recht*, which was the German equivalent of the Latin *jus commune* and the French *droit commun*. In contrast to normal English usage, the term thus refers to the modified Roman law system, which was developed in the universities after the 'Reception' of Roman law in Germany of the 16th century; see F. Stier-Somlo and A. Elster, *Handwörterbuch der Rechtswissenschaft*, ii (Berlin/Leipzig, 1927), 685 f.

[7] See H.-G. Mertens, *Die Entstehung der Vorschriften des BGB über die gesetzliche Erbfolge und das Pflichtteilsrecht* (Berlin, 1966), 3 ff. Mertens estimates that over 100 different inheritance laws were in operation in Germany; ibid. 3 and n. 3.

[8] R. Koselleck, *Preussen zwischen Reform und Revolution* (Stuttgart, 1967), esp. 44-51.

we shall see in Chapter 2, codification was widely seen as a solution to both problems.

Codification was thus widely regarded as an integral part of the process of state formation, a view which bureaucrats borrowed from their eighteenth-century predecessors in their attempt to come to terms with the problems of the post-Napoleonic age. But if bureaucratic motives showed some degree of continuity, the intellectual and political context in which they were expressed did not. The closing years of the Napoleonic Wars saw the development of new legal doctrines which were in many ways defined by a hostility to the recently completed codes of the late Enlightenment.[9] These doctrines emerged as a reaction to the experience of the French Revolution, and were closely associated with contemporary intellectual movements such as political Romanticism and the rise of historicism. In the field of jurisprudence the dominant figure was Friedrich Carl von Savigny (1779-1861), a man whose influence on subsequent patterns of German legal thought would be almost impossible to overestimate. In particular, his views about the nature of the law, the role of the legislator and the possibility of codification coloured attitudes to these matters until the end of the century.

The immediate background to Savigny's work was the nationalist enthusiasm of the years after 1812, a period in which the demand for a national code to bind Germans together was commonly heard. Savigny is generally credited with success in demolishing the intellectual basis of the arguments in favour of such a code; throughout the century his name was cited by those who wished to attack the pretensions of codifiers.[10] Yet Savigny's legacy was ambivalent. In the political context of the Restoration, his views were welcome to conservative statesmen as an intellectual bulwark against liberalism, radicalism, and nationalism. As we shall see, it was generally adherents of one or more of the latter schools of thought who were at the forefront of the campaign for a code until 1848. As early as the 1840s, however, there were many calls for national codification which were based on Savigny's own theories, and after 1848 this became what might be termed the standard liberal/nationalist position. The implications of this for the way in which Germany's legal system was unified after 1871 were enormous, and will feature prominently in the following account.

[9] i.e. the Prussian *Allgemeines Landrecht* (1794), the French *Code Civil* (1804), and the Austrian *Allgemeines Bürgerliches Gesetzbuch* (1811).
[10] For a late example, see *Kreuzzeitung*, 4 June 1888.

From the start of the nineteenth century, codification was linked to nationalism. That connection was never simple, however, for it involved a range of problems concerning the territorial extent of sovereignty. Most politicians could agree that legal uniformity was a powerful unifying force, but such agreement overlooked the question of which state was to be unified. A major reason for the territorial settlement of 1815 had been to construct a political barrier to the forces of liberalism and nationalism in central Europe. The stronger the states of the German Confederation were, the poorer the chances of national unification on a liberal basis appeared. State codifications did not complement national codifications: the two were antithetical in terms of their political implications. As was to become obvious to most liberals after about 1840, policies which strengthened the individual states hindered the national cause. From that point onwards, the principal questions concerning legal codification were really the same as those which surrounded the 'German question'—to whom was sovereignty to be allocated and on what terms? It was for that reason rather than as a result of any serious doubts about the desirability of codification in principle, that the matter could not be resolved until after 1867.

Nationalism was not, of course, reducible to state formation even if the two were clearly related in the 1860s and 1870s. At the heart of the nationalist cause lay a commitment to the unity of the people, in which emphasis was placed on ethnic and cultural aspects of 'Germanness' rather than on bureaucratic policies of state formation. As one scholar has noted, 1870 saw a marked shift towards ethnic conceptions of the *Volk* and the *Volksgeist* in the arguments of many liberal nationalists.[11] But the relationship between this conception of nationality and the foundation of the Bismarckian state was tense and ambiguous. How could that state be seen as the expression of the German people when it included within its borders three major non-German national minorities, while excluding Austrian Germans? This difficulty tended to be glossed over in the polemics of the 1870s, but returned with a vengeance a decade and a half later. The liberals' tendency to ignore the difficulties in the relationship between ethnic nationalism and state formation left them vulnerable to attack as their constituency began to fragment in the 1880s. As early as 1837, Georg Gottfried Gervinus had presciently commented on what he saw as the political immaturity of the Germans:

---

[11] U. Tal, *Christians and Jews in Germany. Religion, Politics and Ideology in the Second Reich, 1870-1914* (Ithaca/London, 1975), 54 f.

'We have a confused *jus*, but no politics: all can be lost because of the damned habit of overplaying these areas of politics into the area of legal experts.'[12] For reasons which will become clear, those words could have been written about the preparation of the Civil Code. Here, as with other political issues in the 1880s and 1890s, the mobilization of sectional interests against established modes of politics was accompanied by constant challenges to the nationalist doctrines of the period of unification. As Geoff Eley has rightly pointed out, 'the central paradox of the post-unification period [was] the indisputable suffusion of national values in a society where the exact content of the national tradition and its future direction were a matter of bitter dispute.'[13] It is scarcely surprising that this basic feature of Wilhelmine politics should have emerged so clearly in the debates about the Civil Code, a piece of legislation which to many political observers had come to stand for the nation.

An important feature of the recent debates concerning the 'peculiarities' of German development has been the scholarly disagreement over the extent to which the Bismarckian and Wilhelmine system was characterized by the successful manipulation of public opinion from above—a view whose strongest formulation is to be found in Hans-Ulrich Wehler's provocative textbook. In contrast, historians such as Blackbourn and Eley see the 1890s as the time when the transition to mass politics produced extreme disruptions of the established political order, which could not be adequately contained by manipulative strategies on the part of the ruling élites. In this view, the emergence of radical nationalism and the mobilization of lower middle-class groups are considered to be part of a painful political restructuring which repeatedly threatened the ruling groups with loss of control. In a recent contribution, Blackbourn has attempted to show how these disruptive political developments were contained after 1900, but only through the adoption by the right-wing parties of the demagogic tactics of those who threatened them.[14]

---

[12] Gervinus to Georg Beseler, 2 Sept. 1837, quoted in C. E. McClelland, 'History in the Service of Politics: A Reassessment of G. G. Gervinus', *CEH* 4 (1971), pp. 385.

[13] G. Eley, 'State Formation, Nationalism and Political Culture in Nineteenth-Century Germany', in R. Samuel and G. Stedman Jones (eds.), *Culture, Ideology and Politics. Essays for Eric Hobsbawm* (London, 1983), 291.

[14] Wehler, German Empire, esp. pp. 90–136; G. Eley, *Reshaping the German Right. Radical Nationalism and Political Change After Bismarck* (New Haven/London, 1980) and his numerous essays, many of which have been reprinted in Eley, *From Unification to Nazism. Reinterpreting the German Past* (London, 1986); D. Blackbourn, *Class, Religion and Local Politics in Wilhelmine Germany. The Centre Party in Württemberg before 1914* (New Haven/London, 1980) and id., 'The Politics of Demagogy in Imperial Germany',

The history of the preparation of the Civil Code provides evidence enough of the extent to which the hold of the Establishment on politics could be challenged by movements from below. In this respect, the time-span within which the code was begun and completed (1874–96) is important in that these were precisely the years in which the decisive damage was done to the political patterns of the 1860s and 1870s. The publication of the 'First Draft' of the Code in 1888 unleashed a full-scale debate about the ideological foundations of the nation's legal system. Behind the rhetoric of that debate lurked a battle between different social interests which was strong enough to force the government to reconsider its earlier views about how the Code might be prepared. The inclusion of previously unheard voices in the process suddenly became a political imperative.

On the other hand, the actual effect of these new influences on the final version of the Code was remarkably slight, and Chapters 6 and 7 attempt to provide an explanation for that. A consideration of the relationships between the Reich's formal political institutions—the national government, the Bundesrat, and the Reichstag—is necessary here, particularly as the systematic study of this subject has been relatively neglected in the historiography of the period. The response of the bureaucracy to pressures from outside was anything but monolithic. Different sections of the government clashed over fundamental legal issues in ways which tended to mirror the divisions in the political nation. But, above all, the failure to introduce major reforms into the Civil Code in the 1890s was the product of the skill of the legal bureaucracy[15] in exploiting traditional conceptions of nationalism and its mastery of the complexities of the law to head off pressure from other elements. A succession of skilled politicians in charge of the Reich justice office showed no hesitation whatsoever in employing a range of manipulative techniques in order to isolate and neutralize the most dangerous critics of the Code. In this they were successful, but that success would have been impossible without concessions in other areas. The preparation of the Code in the 1890s suggests that successful manipulation from above and mobilization from below were hardly

Past and Present, 113 (1986), 152–84. A useful overview of this debate is R. G. Moeller, 'The Kaiserreich Recast? Continuity and Change in Modern German Historiography', *Journal of Social History*, 17 (1984), 655–83.

15 By 'legal bureaucracy' is meant the officials of the Reich Justice Office and the states' ministries of justice, the most important of which was of course the Prussian ministry.

mutually exclusive alternatives in Wilhelmine politics.[16] On the other hand, the success of manipulation was conditional upon a range of concessions and could not be taken for granted. The political manœuvres of the mid-1890s took place in a changed atmosphere, in which older traditions of thought concerning the nature of the state and of nationalism had been challenged but not yet effectively supplanted. This study attempts to use the Civil Code as a means of grasping the complexities of this process of challenge and response on the levels of political practice and ideology. The starting-point is that neither of these levels is comprehensible without the other.

The scholarly literature on the Civil Code has hitherto tended to consider it from a much more specifically legalistic point of view than is adopted here. In part, this reflects the traditional preoccupations of German legal history, which has concentrated on tracing the origins and development of specific doctrines and institutions through the investigation of legal sources.[17] An additional reason is that much of this work has been produced by trained lawyers, whose principal interests lie in the origins and development of the modern German legal system. This emphasis is easily understandable, especially in view of the Code's durability in the face of the many challenges to its survival in the twentieth century. Although crucial parts of the law—for example, labour law and company law—have developed essentially since 1900, it is nevertheless true that the Code remains the corner-stone of the Federal Republic's civil law. For that reason, much of the scholarship on this subject has been motivated by the need to provide an historical basis for practical interpretation and implementation of the Code's provisions. This goal has tended to determine the direction of research even where, as has frequently been the case, that research has gone far beyond what is strictly necessary for practising lawyers.

The modern historiogaphy of the Civil Code may be divided very broadly into three main groups. In the first place there are those studies, exemplified by the work of Franz Wieacker, whose major preoccupation is with the relationship between social development and legal ideologies.

[16] For a similar argument with regard to radical nationalist agitation, see M. S. Coetzee, 'The Mobilization of the Right? The Deutscher Wehrverein and Political Activism in Württemberg, 1912–1914', *EHQ* 15 (1985), pp. 431–52.

[17] The level of sophistication which this type of research has reached may be gauged from two major scholarly journals—*Ius Commune* and *ZRG GA*. See also many of the contributions in H. Coing and W. Wilhelm (eds.), *Wissenschaft und Kodifikation des Privatrechts im 19. Jahrhundert* (6 vols. Frankfurt, 1974–82).

A characteristic of this work is its implicit functionalism, in the sense that it concentrates on the civil law's responses to the needs of an industrializing society in the nineteenth century. A related feature of this approach is its attempt to unmask the 'social model' implicit in the legal system through the discovery of links between certain legal doctrines and the ideologies dominant in particular stages of social development or specific social groups. Thus the concentration of much of nineteenth-century jurisprudence on individual freedoms of contract and disposition of property is seen to 'correspond to' the needs of an entrepreneurial society in the period of early and high capitalism. The Civil Code's acceptance of these freedoms is seen as evidence that its 'social model' was that of the individual entrepreneur rather than the large-scale economic enterprise.[18]

A second approach concentrates in great detail on the evolution of a specific legal institution or set of institutions in order to trace the origins and development of legislation. It seeks to present a picture of the 'legal culture' of the day through an extensive reading of the relevant juristic literature, in which important theoretical developments as well as 'typical' discussions of a given problem are highlighted. An exhaustive treatment of previous statutes on the subject and a detailed study of the various drafts of the Code tend to be added to this picture in order to show how the legislator arrived at the final version. The aim here is to build up as complete a picture as possible of the juristic world of the legislator, and to assess the weight of the various influences in the development of a limited part of the law.[19]

The third approach is very much an outgrowth of the second. In the 1970s, scholars began to be aware of the range of source material for this type of detailed work to be found in Germany's central and state archives. Not only do these archives contain a large number of details omitted from published sources, but they also open up the possibility for a nuanced treatment of the non-juristic influences on legal developments. Scholars had of course been well aware of such influences before, but it would be fair to say that they had normally been discussed fairly

[18] F. Wieacker, 'Das Sozialmodell der klassischen Privatrechtsgesetzbücher und die Entwicklung der modernen Gesellschaft' (1953), in id., *Industriegesellschaft und Privatrechtsordnung* (Frankfurt, 1974), 14 and *passim*; cf. Wieacker, *Privatrechtsgeschichte der Neuzeit unter besonderer Berücksichtigung der deutschen Entwicklung* (2nd edn.; Göttingen, 1967), e.g. 441 f., 480 ff.

[19] The first two studies of this type were Mertens, *Entstehung* and W. Schubert, *Die Entstehung der Vorschriften des BGB über Besitz und Eigentumsübertragung. Ein Beitrag zur Entstehungsgeschichte des BGB* (Berlin, 1966). There have since been numerous others.

rudimentarily as background factors. It was only in the 1970s that archival sources were used to develop a detailed appreciation of the political complexities of the process of legislation.[20]

The consequence of these developments has been that, in the last decade or so, a number of monographs have appeared which have attempted to blend the traditional concerns of German legal history with modern scholarship on the social and political history of the nineteenth century. A particularly important stimulus here has been the Max Planck Institute for European Legal History at Frankfurt, which has been responsible for a range of publications which attempt to connect legal developments with the broader movements of the nineteenth century. In addition, the Institute's multi-volume general textbook on the history of modern European private law provides the most accessible statement of the fruits of modern research on the subject.[21] As a result of these scholarly developments, the level of knowledge concerning the history of legislation in the nineteenth century has risen dramatically in recent years.

These attempts to link legal developments with social and political history are motivated by considerations similar to those which lie behind the present work. The law, especially the civil law, is seen as part of a broader political culture in which forces were at work which both shaped and limited the actions of the legislator. However much German jurists might have liked it to be otherwise, the pursuit of legislative perfection and jurisprudential purity was repeatedly hampered by

---

[20] Important milestones here were P. Kögler, *Arbeiterbewegung und Vereinsrecht. Ein Beitrag zur Entstehungsgeschichte des BGB* (Berlin, 1974); T. Vormbaum, *Die Rechtsfähigkeit der Vereine im 19. Jahrhundert* (Berlin/New York, 1976). Above all, this approach is exemplified by W. Schubert, whose many important works on the Civil Code and other important pieces of legislation are listed in the Bibliography. His as yet unfinished source edition, prepared in conjunction with H. H. Jakobs, *Die Beratung des Bürgerlichen Gesetzbuchs' in systematischer Darstellung der unveröffentlichen Quellen* (Berlin/New York, 1978–) is unlikely to be surpassed as a source of detailed knowledge of the development of each section of the Code. The introductory volume in the series, subtitled *Materialien zur Entstehungsgeschichte des BGB, Einführung, Biographien, Materialien* (Berlin/New York, 1978)—hereafter cited as Schubert, *Materialien*—contains the best short outline of the history of the preparation of the Code and a wide range of reprinted sources on political aspects of the process of codification. By comparison, Wieacker, *Privatrechtsgeschichte*, ch. 25 is superficial and at times factually inaccurate.

[21] Publications associated with the Institute include Coing and Wilhelm (eds.), *Wissenschaft und Kodifikation* and the journal *Ius Commune*. The multi-volume textbook is H. Coing (ed.), *Handbuch der Quellen und Literatur der neueren europäischen Privatrechtsgeschichte* (3 vols. Frankfurt, 1973–82). An outstanding example of this type of work is S. Buchholz, *Abstraktionsprinzip und Immobiliarrecht. Zur Geschichte der Auflassung und der Grundschuld* (Frankfurt, 1978).

considerations of what was politically possible. As new needs and demands were articulated, the state's legislators had to respond, however reluctantly. Indeed, the tensions between the demands expressed in the political sphere and the lawyers' concern with systematic perfection in the law grew towards the end of the nineteenth century. The important question of why it was that the Code assumed the form it did, given the strength of these demands, is implicit in most of the work discussed above and forms the backbone of this study. The legal historians' emphasis on the interactions between jurisprudential doctrine and the mechanics of political decision-making provides a fruitful starting-point for the analysis of this important question.

The following chapters are heavily (and I hope obviously) indebted to this scholarship. However, certain important differences of approach should be made explicit at the outset. The primary aim of the legal historians is to explain why the legal system developed in the way it did. However sensitive they are to political, socio-economic, and other developments, in the last resort these operate as boundary conditions in their work. The law is certainly related to and influenced by such developments, but attempts in this literature to analyse the relationship between legal culture and political culture systematically are few and far between. A significant contrast exists between the depth of primary research devoted to bodies such as legislative commissions and the ministries of justice, and the rather schematic way in which the actions of other political actors are presented. The very best examples of this work are characterized by minute attention to the actions of the legal bureaucracy and an almost total reliance on printed sources for groups such as the Reichstag parties.[22] Furthermore, the political press is almost completely neglected as a source in this literature. The result of this emphasis tends to be that the political sphere is relegated to the role of a context within which lawyers have to work. Moreover, the interplay between legal decisions and social or economic developments is frequently alluded to but rarely worked out in a systematic way.[23]

In contrast, the present work will attempt to develop a different set

[22] A good example is Schubert's neglect of Karl Bachem's important papers in HA Cologne, and the views of economic interest groups in *Materialien, passim*; cf. chs. 6–7 below.

[23] An exception here is T. Bark, *Vertragsfreiheit und Staat im Kapitalismus* (Berlin, 1978), a Marxist study of changes in the law relating to usury and interest rates between 1850 and 1900. The major problem with this interesting work is its failure to give the political arena sufficient consideration. Despite the title, the role of the state as a mediator between economic interests and legal change remains ultimately obscure.

of arguments. The points of contact with the work of the legal historians are frequent but the central focus is different. The legal system is considered here as a way of looking at the fundamental changes in the main components of Germany's political culture in the second half of the nineteenth century. At one level, this is a history of ideas, in which the shifting meanings attached to ideas of nationalism, liberalism, and the state are traced. At another, it attempts to consider the nature of the political changes, which were part cause and part consequence of the emergence of new ways of thinking about the state and its legal system. The aim is to provide a coherent account of the relationship between the two, using the preparation of the Civil Code as means of giving the argument substance. That relationship is perceived as a complex interaction, mediated through sets of formal and informal political institutions about whose development in the 1880s and 1890s surprisingly little is known. It is surely through understanding the relationships between structures of power, social change, and intellectual developments that Germany's 'peculiarities' will one day become clear; and it is hoped that this book will make a modest contribution to that understanding.

2.

The Theory and Practice of Codification, 1814–1867

THE campaign for a national legal system was a prominent feature of political debate in nineteenth-century Germany. In the second and third decades of the century, it occupied the attention of some of the most famous writers of the day such as Hegel, Savigny, and Anselm von Feuerbach. From the days of the Wars of Liberation of 1813–14 until the foundation of the North German Confederation in 1867, the call for legal unity was intimately connected with the liberal/nationalist movement and it shared the fortunes of that movement. Thus the nationalist enthusiasms of the last years of the Napoleonic Wars were followed by a period of relative quiescence in the 1820s and 1830s. Towards the end of the 1830s, the resurgence of liberal nationalism brought with it a renewed concern with the question of legal codification, especially in southern and western Germany. The revolution of 1848 and the Reich constitution of the following year saw the expression of demands for the establishment of a national legal system through the preparation of a code. The early 1850s then saw renewed interest in the question as the Confederation attempted to use legal unification to strengthen itself against the forces of nationalism and Prussian expansion. This movement resulted in the completion of the first great national code of the century—the Commercial Code (*Handelsgesetzbuch*) of 1861. Shortly afterwards, work on other codes—of criminal law, civil and criminal procedure, and the law of obligations—began, and was completed in the very different political atmosphere of the period after 1867. The Civil Code, on the other hand, was produced entirely under the auspices of the 1871 Reich.

Nevertheless, the Civil Code was essentially the product of developments in politics and jurisprudence before 1867. The politicians, bureaucrats, and lawyers who were principally responsible for the work had generally come to maturity before 1871, and the way in which they approached the task of codification would be incomprehensible without

a consideration of that period. The period of the French Revolution
had seen the completion of three great 'natural law' codes in Prussia,
France, and Austria. All three had an important influence on the debates
concerning codification in nineteenth-century Germany. In Baden, a
code (the *Badisches Landrecht*) was completed in 1809 in which the
dominant influence was the French system. Indeed, the French code
with its connotations of rational government and modernity was highly
influential in spurring states such as Hesse-Darmstadt and Bavaria to
attempt to produce their own codes after 1815. Nor was the influence
of the French legal system restricted to governments in the *Vormärz*
period, but extended deep into the local populations of western and
southern Germany. In the new Prussian territories on the left bank of
the Rhine, the popularity of French law was such that the government
never dared to impose the *Allgemeines Landrecht*. For similar reasons,
the Bavarian government allowed French law to remain the law of the
land in the newly acquired Palatinate, while the same was true in
the Rheinhessen region acquired in 1815 by the Grand Duchy of
Hesse-Darmstadt. In none of these cases did the states' bureaucracies
regard this as an adequate permanent solution, and there were repeated
attempts to remedy the situation by producing new codes before 1848.
Such policies generally met with failure, which was in large part due
to resistance from the populations of the areas concerned.[1]

The bureaucracies' drive towards codification was the product of
changes which had taken place during the French wars. The Restoration
of 1815 was, indeed, no restoration in the sense of reproducing
the *status quo ante*. In southern and western Germany, Napoleon's
'mediatization' and secularization of the smaller principalities had
completely redrawn the map of Germany, creating new states and new
problems of political integration. These problems tended to push the
local bureaucracies in the direction of modernizing the administrative

---

[1] See F. Wieacker, *Privatrechtsgeschichte der Neuzeit unter besonderer Berüksichtigung
der deutschen Entwicklung* (2nd edn., Göttingen, 1967), ch. 19; B. Dölemeyer, 'Einflüsse
von ALR, Code Civil und ABGB auf Kodifikationsdiskussionen und -projekte in
Deutschland', *Ius Commune*, 7 (1978), 179-225; K.-G. Faber, *Die Rheinlande zwischen
Restauration und Revolution* (Wiesbaden, 1966), 118-86; E. Fehrenbach, 'Zur sozialen
Problematik des rheinischen Rechts im Vormärz', in H. Berding *et al.* (eds.), *Vom Staat
des Ancien Regime zum modernen Parteistaat. Festschrift für Theodor Schieder zum 70.
Geburtstag* (Munich/Vienna, 1978), 197-212; W. K. Blessing, 'Staatsintegration als soziale
Integration: Zur Entstehung einer bayerischen Gesellschaft im frühen 19. Jahrhundert',
Zeitschrift für bayerische Landesgeschichte, 41 (1978), 688-98. A good outline of attempts
to produce codes in Prussia, Bavaria, and Hesse-Darmstadt is contained in H. Coing
(ed.), *Handbuch*, iii/2 (Munich, 1982), 1472-530.

and political structures of their states. Between 1803 and 1815, new bureaucratic reforming élites had arisen in these states, which tended to see themselves as the embodiment of the interests of a unitary state constructed according to 'rational', modern principles in contrast to the socially and politically fragmented order of the *ancien régime*. The élites took the lead in the development of modern political institutions, which saw the introduction of chambers of deputies and constitutions in Baden, Württemberg, Bavaria, and Hesse-Darmstadt in the half-decade after 1815. Moreover, by the 1820s the monopoly of bureaucratic positions by trained lawyers was more or less complete all over southern Germany. With their premium on rational, systematized government, their legal backgrounds, and their quest for integration, it is not surprising that these bureaucratic élites should have pursued the cause of codification. An explicit statement of the motives of these bureaucrats in their support of codification was contained in the decree of the Grand Duke of Hesse-Darmstadt of 4 November 1816, which ordered the preparation of a code of civil law and civil procedure so that 'the bond between our old and new subjects on both sides of the Rhine [will be] tightened through uniformity of legislation'. The sheer complexity and regional variety of the legal systems of these new states made some attempt at rationalization an understandable goal after 1815. Indeed, the failure of almost all these early attempts at state codifications was in large part the result of those complexities, which in the case of Bavaria assumed seemingly insuperable proportions.[2]

The emergence of this bureaucratic élite in the states of the Confederation of the Rhine was closely associated with the planned introduction of French law in almost all of these states. These plans pushed to the fore men like Anselm von Feuerbach and Nikolaus Thad äus von Gönner in Bavaria and Ludwig Harscher von Almendingen in Nassau, who despite all their differences tended to see the introduction of a version of the French code as linked to a form of limited

---

[2] In general, see H.-U. Wehler, *Deutsche Gesellschaftsgeschichte*, i (Munich, 1987), 362–96; cf. Blessing, 'Staatsintegration als soziale Integration', pp. 663 ff.; F.-L. Knemeyer, *Regierungs- und Verwaltungsreform in Deutschland zu Beginn des 19. Jahrhunderts* (Cologne/Berlin, 1970), 274 ff.; L. Krieger, *The German Idea of Freedom. History of a Political Tradition* (Chicago/London, 1957), 229–42; L. E. Lee, *The Politics of Harmony. Civil Service, Liberalism and Social Reform in Baden, 1800–1850* (Cranbury, 1980), 17–59; L. Gall, *Der Liberalismus als regierende Partei. Das Grossherzogtum Baden zwischen Restauration und Reichsgründung* (Wiesbaden, 1968), 2–23. The Grand Duke of Hesse-Darmstadt's decree is quoted in I. Spangenberg, *Hessen-Darmstadt und der Deutsche Bund 1815–1848* (Darmstadt, 1969), 13.

constitutionalism, based on the guarantee of personal freedoms and formal legal equality within the sphere of civil law. For all the limitations of this vision and its impracticality in the political conditions of the period after 1815, it seems justified to talk of 'at least the possibility of a synthesis of enlightened despotism and early liberalism'.[3] This was clear in the case of Württemberg, where the highly conservative minister of justice, Baron von Maucler, pursued enlightened despotic policies which attracted the support of moderate liberals and nationalists.[4]

One figure of great influence among the southern bureaucratic reformers was a law professor at Heidelberg, Anton Friedrich Justus Thibaut, who in 1814 published a famous work calling for the immediate establishment of national legal unity. This proved to be the opening salvo in the famous 'battle over codification' (*Kodifikationsstreit*) of the Restoration years. Thibaut called for a code which would be 'clear, unequivocal, and exhaustive'. Such a code would have evident commercial and legal advantages; it would also bind the nation together. On the other hand, existing German law was 'an endless desert of conflicting, contradictory, and disorganized rules, which are exactly suited to the division of Germans from one another and to the creation of a situation in which it is impossible for judges and lawyers to have a profound knowledge of the law'. The creation of legal security through codification would, in Thibaut's view, increase social cohesion and secure the princes' place in the minds of their subjects.[5]

Thibaut's work found a considerable resonance in the excitement of the Wars of Liberation, but would probably have been rapidly forgotten after 1815 had it not been for the polemical response written by Savigny, a law professor at the recently founded university of Berlin. Savigny's response acquired an importance which went beyond the immediate polemic and had an enormous influence on the development of German legal studies and on the theory of codification in the nineteenth century. Savigny was concerned above all to deny that the present time had the capacity to produce worthwhile legislation. Commenting on the recent Prussian, French, and Austrian codes, Savigny emphasized that all failed

[3] E. Fehrenbach, *Traditionale Gesellschaft und revolutionäres Recht. Die Einführung des Code Napoleon in den Rheinbundstaaten* (Göttingen, 1974), 29-36, 57-69 (quotation, p. 69).
[4] For the liberal response to Maucler, see R. v. Mohl, *Lebenserinnerungen 1799-1875*, i (Stuttgart/Leipzig, 1902), 173; J. Rückert, *August Ludwig Reyschers Leben und Rechtstheorie, 1802-1880* (Berlin, 1974), 261 f.
[5] A. F. J. Thibaut, 'Ueber die Nothwendigkeit eines allgemeinen bürgerlichen Rechts für Deutschland', reprinted in H. Hattenhauer (ed.), *Thibaut und Savigny. Ihre programmatischen Schriften* (Munich, 1973), 61-94 (quotations, pp. 67, 68).

because of their authors' inadequate theory of legislation. But the real influence of his work came not from his comments about existing codes, but from his development of a theory of the origins of law which came to dominate the next generation of German lawyers. To Savigny, law was linked to language and culture as indivisible expressions of a united people: 'what ties them together as a whole are the common convictions of the people, the same feeling of inner necessity, which excludes any thought of fortuitous or arbitrary origins.' There was a permanent 'organic link between law and the character and essence of a people,' as was the case with language.[6]

The juxtaposition of 'arbitrariness' (*Willkür*) and 'inner necessity' provides the key to Savigny's theory of the true origins of the law. According to Savigny, the mistake made by the eighteenth century and by those who called for a code in 1814-15 was to exaggerate the potential of legislation as a source of law. The great problem in contemporary jurisprudence, as far as Savigny was concerned, was its tendency to formal abstraction and its belief that it could 'dispense with all actual reality'. Moreover, Savigny made it quite clear that 'actual reality' did not only mean the recognition of differences between different peoples, a denial of the validity of abstract reason governing the affairs of all mankind: just as important for the future was his emphasis on the special peculiarities of different regions in a given country. In any organic whole there was a question of balance between the different parts, and a dangerous form of national weakness would derive from the 'destruction of individual relationships' through rash changes in the civil law. The only way to avoid these difficulties was to improve the quality of German jurisprudence through profound study of the historical sources of law. Only thus might the inner development of a people's character and its cultural traditions be discerned. In a later piece announcing the foundation of the *Zeitschrift für geschichtliche Rechtswissenschaft* in 1815, Savigny re-emphasized the necessity of historical study in order to attain 'true knowledge of our own condition'.[7]

In the political circumstances of the Restoration, it is scarcely surprising that Savigny's views should have been welcome to conservative statesmen. They were an ideal defence against the nationalist liberalism, which seemed to lie behind the campaign for a code. Moreover,

---

[6] F. C. v. Savigny, 'Vom Beruf unserer Zeit für Gesetzgebung und Rechtswissenschaft' (1814), in Hattenhauer (ed.), *Thibaut und Savigny*, pp. 95-192 (quotations, pp. 102, 103).
[7] Ibid. 114 f., 121 f., 263.

throughout the century Savigny's theories proved attractive to conservatives, who sought to attack liberal nationalists on the grounds of their support for codification. It is this political aspect that has led many historians to ascribe to Thibaut and Savigny roles as representatives of the broader movements of the age. To Franz Wieacker, Thibaut and his supporters represented the new democratic nationalism, while Savigny was the ally of the legitimist Metternich. Certain Marxist scholars have seen Savigny as the mouthpiece of the feudal classes, while Thibaut represented that part of the capitalist bourgeoisie for whom legal unity was becoming a pressing necessity.[8] Other scholars have, however, raised serious questions about the usefulness or even accuracy of such ascriptions. In the first place, the closeness of Savigny's views to those of the Prussian reforming minister and nationalist, Baron von Stein, make him appear an unlikely ally of legitimism, however much his ideas may have been partially appropriated by reactionary interests. Stein and Savigny shared a hatred of the French Revolution and a belief in the specific historical development of the German nation, which was very different from the views of many bureaucratic reformers in the south. But that scarcely overrides the fact that neither of these men can realistically be termed a reactionary. Further evidence for this line of argument is provided by the influence on both men of the Hanoverian 'Reform Conservative', August Wilhelm Rehberg, whose attack on the *Code Civil* had originally occasioned Thibaut's polemic and had prefigured many of Savigny's arguments about the nature of law and historical development.[9]

A second view points to the essential similarities between the work

[8] F. Wieacker, 'Aufstieg, Blüte und Krisis der Kodifikationsidee', in *Festschrift G. Boehmer* (Bonn, 1954), 44; K. Heuer, 'Wissenschaftliche Studentenzirkel an der juristischen Fakultät der Humboldt-Universität', *Staat und Recht*, 2 (1953), 509–15; H. Wrobel, 'Rechtsgeschichte, Wirtschaftsgeschichte, Sozialgeschichte: die Thibaut-Savigny Kontroverse', *Kritische Justiz*, 6 (1973), 149–57. A more satisfactory Marxist analysis is provided in J. Kuczynski, *Studien zu einer Geschichte der Gesellschaftswissenschaften*, vi (Berlin-GDR, 1977), 149 ff.

[9] See K. Epstein, *The Genesis of German Conservatism* (Princeton, 1966), ch. 11; cf. B. Vogel, 'Beamtenkonservatismus: sozial- und verfassungsgeschichtliche Voraussetzungen der Parteien in Pressen im frühen 19. Jahrhundert', in D. Stegmann et al. (eds.), *Deutscher Konservatismus im 19. Jahrhundert. Festschrift für Fritz Fischer zum 70. Geburtstag und zum 50. Doktorjubiläum* (Bonn, 1983), 27 ff. G. Rexius, 'Studien zur Staatslehre der historischen Schule', *Historische Zeitschrift*, 107 (1911), 513–33; H. Kantorowicz, 'Volksgeist und historische Rechtsschule', *Historische Zeitschrift*, 108 (1908), 302 ff.; cf. H.-U. Stühler, *Die Diskussion über die Erneuerung der Rechtswissenschaft von 1780–1815* (Berlin, 1978), 56–9, and C. Varrentrapp, 'Briefe von Savigny an Ranke und Perthes', *Historische Zeitschrift*, 100 (1908), 330 f., 340 f. for Savigny's political views.

of Thibaut and Savigny. Thibaut clearly shared Savigny's views about the need for legal security and peace, the desirability of recognizing the multiplicity of Germany's regional variations, and the dangers of both bureaucratic centralization and liberal parliamentarism. There was further agreement on the notions that codification should not presume to create new law and that it should be entrusted to the best available representatives of jurisprudence rather than to a political body. Like Savigny, but in contrast to Feuerbach, Thibaut believed in the essentially unpolitical nature of the civil law. Finally, neither favoured particularism and both stressed their commitment to the national cause. Where they differed was on points of emphasis, which nicely highlighted the differences between the Prussian and south German responses to the French Revolution. Thibaut stressed unity more and regional variations less than Savigny; Savigny demonstrated substantially greater levels of Francophobia than Thibaut. But these were essentially differences within a broad camp of moderates stretching from reforming conservatives to the 'organic liberals' of the *Vormärz* period.[10]

There is the further question of why it was that Savigny's ideas should later have been taken up by most of the supporters of the liberal-nationalist cause when they called for a codification. There are a number of reasons for this, not the least important of which was the rapidly established intellectual hegemony of Savigny's Historical School in the law faculties of the universities of northern Germany. The influence of that dominance will be examined below, but it is also worth noting that Savigny's theory of the origins of the law (later known as the *Volksgeistlehre*) did not necessarily involve the rejection of all attempts at codification. As Pio Caroni had shown, Savigny's *Beruf* may for analytical purposes be split into two parts. The first of these contained the criticisms of the natural law codes with their arbitrary disregard of the real character of the people. The second attempted to show the ways in which legislation might become a valid source of law. In this section, Savigny laid out a set of principles which might be used to construct a successful code. Such legislation would contain a complete set of systematically organized basic legal principles, while leaving

---

[10] The main sources for this paragraph are H.-P. Benöhr, 'Politik und Rechtstheorie: Die Kontroverse Thibaut-Savigny vor 160 Jahre', *JuS* 14 (1974), pp. 681-4; H. Kiefner, 'Thibaut und Savigny: Bemerkungen zum Kodifikationsstreit', in A. Buschmann *et al.* (eds.), *Festschrift für Rudolf Gmür zum 70. Geburtstag 28. Juli 1983* (Bielefeld, 1983), 53-85; J. Rückert, *Idealismus, Jurisprudenz und Politik bei Friedrich Carl von Savigny* (Edelsbach, 1984), pt. 2, ch. 2. For Feuerbach, see Fehrenbach, *Traditionale Gesellschaft*, p. 60.

adequate room for local variations. Rigorous historical study was the key to the discovery of these basic principles and it was precisely in that area that Savigny considered contemporary jurisprudence to be deficient.[11]

Looking back in 1867, Leopold von Ranke spoke of the struggle in the Restoration period between two schools of thought—the philosophical and the historical. This distinction corresponds closely to Savigny's own division of the legal world into historical and non-historical jurists.[12] In fact, this distinction may have been an appropriate description of the battle-lines in Savigny's quite separate struggle with the Hegelians such as Eduard Gans at the University of Berlin,[13] but it was scarcely adequate as an explanation of the controversy over codification. Among Savigny's principal opponents in 1814–16— Thibaut, Gönner, Feuerbach, and D. B. W. Pfeiffer—only Gönner[14] did not reject the charge of neglecting history. Indeed, in many respects Pfeiffer's work in particular came close to Savigny's own views, except with regard to the desirability of codification.[15] What these men did oppose was the complete exclusion of philosophical enquiry from jurisprudence and the concentration on what they termed antiquarianism. Thibaut had good reason for his subsequent bitter rejection of the idea that he despised legal history; he merely denied that history alone could provide the most important thing, 'certainty and security in the legal order'.[16]

In the following decades the divisions between the north and the south, between Savigny and Thibaut, if anything widened. Savigny's

---

[11] P. Caroni, 'Savigny und die Kodifikation: Versuch einer Neudeutung des "Berufes" ', *ZRG GA* 86 (1969), pp. 97–176.

[12] L. v. Ranke, 'Ansprache beim fünfzigjährigen Doktorjubiläum, 20. Februar 1867', in A. Dove and T. Wiedemann (eds.), *Leopold von Ranke's sämmtliche Werke*, li/lii (Leipzig, 1888), 588; Hattenhauer (ed.), *Thibaut und Savigny*, pp. 261 ff.

[13] On this, see M. Lenz, *Geschichte der königlichen Friedrich-Wilhelms-Universität zu Berlin*, ii/1 (Halle, 1910), 390–3; J. E. Toews, *Hegelianism. The Path Toward Dialectical Humanism, 1805–1841* (Cambridge, 1980), 110 ff.

[14] N. T. v. Gönner, *Ueber Gesetzgebung und Rechtswissenschaft in unsrer Zeit* (Erlangen, 1815), *passim*.

[15] See D. B. W. Pfeiffer, *Ideen zu einer neuen Civil-Gesetzgebung für Teutsche Staaten* (Göttingen, 1815), e.g. 81 f., 94 ff., on the origins of the law and the necessity of the study of legal history.

[16] A. v. Feuerbach, 'Einige Worte über historische Rechtsgelehrsamkeit und einheimische deutsche Gesetzgebung' (1816), in Hattenhauer (ed.), *Thibaut und Savigny*, pp. 223 ff.; Pfeiffer, *Ideen*, pp. 94 ff.; Thibaut, 'Ueber die sogenannte Historische und Nicht-Historische Rechtsschule' (1838), in Hattenhauer (ed.), *Thibaut und Savigny*, pp. 282 ff.

unrivalled prestige at the University of Berlin attracted a large number of followers who accepted his emphasis on the history of Roman law and his philological method of research. Thibaut, on the other hand, retained enormous influence at Heidelberg and emphasized logical derivation in his teaching of the sources of Roman law.[17] In the 1820s and 1830s, some writers on the subject in southern Germany echoed Thibaut's call for a simple, comprehensible, national law and rejected Savigny's warnings. The famous Badenese liberal, Carl Theodor von Welcker, expressed his support for Thibaut and called for the preparation of 'a simple, patriotic code'. Further north, however, there was a much greater tendency to see Thibaut's views as excessively simplistic in the light of the growing complexity of the legal system, and to accept Savigny's views about the priority of jurisprudence over legislation.[18] Yet, despite all such continuities, there are signs that new issues were emerging by the late 1830s. As one of Savigny's pupils—the academic lawyer and liberal Johann Caspar Bluntschli—put it in 1839, the battle between the historical and non-historical theories of law had been decided in favour of the former, and the future battle would be between the Romanist and Germanist wings of the Historical School. Moreover, he anticipated later scholarship in claiming that Savigny had never been opposed to codification in principle.[19]

The emergence of a separate Germanist branch of the Historical School of Law in the 1840s has long been regarded as a major event in the history of nineteenth-century German jurisprudence. It derived in large part from the often noticed paradox in the work of Savigny and his principal followers—their emphasis on the search for the true traditions of German law through the investigation of predominantly

[17] Lenz, *Geschichte*, ii/2 (Halle, 1918), 134; G. Weber, *Heidelberger Erinnerungen. Am Vorabend der fünften Säkularfeier der Universität* (Stuttgart, 1886), 134 ff.; Mohl, *Lebenserinnerungen*, i. 106.

[18] See L. Minnigerode, *Bemerkungen über den Stand der Gesetzgebung und Jurisprudenz in Deutschland* (Darmstadt, 1836); C. v. Welcker, 'Gesetz', in C. v. Rotteck and C. v. Welcker (eds.), *Staatslexikon*, vi (Altona, 1836), 748 ff.; C. L. Runde, 'Über die Ungewissheit des positiven bürgerlichen Rechts' (1827), in id., *Patriotische Phantasien eines Juristen* (Oldenburg, 1836), 255–69. Minnigerode had until his somewhat mysterious dismissal been president of the royal court in Darmstadt; see S. Büttner, *Die Anfänge des Parlamentarismus in Hessen-Darmstadt und das du Thilsche System* (Darmstadt, 1969), 118. Runde held an equivalent position in Oldenburg.

[19] J. C. Bluntschli, *Die neueren Rechtsschulen der deutschen Juristen* (Zurich/Frauenfeld, 1841), 7, 15 f., 28, 32. For Savigny's approval of Bluntschli's views, see Savigny to Bluntschli, 13 Jan. 1840, in W. Oechsli (ed.), *Briefwechsel Johann Kaspar Bluntschlis mit Savigny, Niebuhr, Leopold Ranke, Jakob Grimm und Ferdinand Meyer* (Frauenfeld, 1915), 73 f.

Roman law sources. In fact, Savigny had called for study of the German
as well as the Roman legal tradition in 1814, and the involvement of
Karl Friedrich Eichhorn, the eminent historian of German law, in the
Zeitschrift für geschichtliche Rechtswissenschaft suggested that this was
meant in earnest. Moreover, in response to Bluntschli's forecasts of a
battle between Romanists and Germanists, Savigny repeatedly asserted
that the two approaches were complementary rather than incompatible.[20]

As early as the 1820s, Germanists such as Karl Joseph Anton
Mittermaier had begun to call for a separate journal of German legal
history, but it was only with the founding of the *Zeitschrift für deutsches
Recht und deutsche Rechtswissenschaft* in 1839 that Germanism began as
a movement specifically opposed to Savigny and his followers. In part,
this reflected a generational and occupational divide. The new journal,
founded by the former *Burschenschaftler* August Ludwig Reyscher,
encouraged the participation of younger, practising lawyers rather than
academics of Eichhorn's and Mittermaier's generation. Reyscher himself
fully accepted Savigny's theory of the origins of law and agreed that
lengthy historical study of the legal sources was necessary. But as early
as 1828 he was calling for a 'political rejuvenation' and looked to the
link between law and life as a positive means of producing reforms. The
contrast in tone between his position and that of Savigny, who saw a
barrier against the 'arbitrariness' of liberal reforms in the connection
between law and reality, could scarcely have been greater.[21]

There can be little doubt about the connections between the growing
Germanist movement and the upsurge of nationalism in the early 1840s.
As Reyscher put it in 1842, 'scholarship has partly followed this
movement of the times and has partly quietly prepared it'. Moreover,
although this was not true in all cases, Germanists had a strong
propensity to belong to the liberal movement, while their opponents in
the Romanist camp—especially Savigny himself and Georg Friedrich
von Puchta—were clearly associated with political conservatism by the
1840s. In part, the difference between the Germanists and Romanists

[20] Hattenhauer (ed.), *Thibaut und Savigny*, pp. 166 f.; Savigny to J. Grimm, 12 Oct.
1814, in A. Stoll, *Friedrich Karl v. Savigny. Ein Bild seines Lebens mit einer Sammlung
seiner Briefe*, ii (Berlin 1929), 118; Savigny to Bluntschli, 7 Oct. 1839, 13 Jan. and 25 Nov.
1840, 23 Nov. 1841, in Oechsli (ed.), *Briefwechsel Johann Kaspar Bluntschlis*, pp. 67, 73 f.,
79 f., 89. On the Germanists in general, see O. Gierke, *Die historische Rechtsschule und die
Germanisten* (Berlin, 1903).
[21] A. L. Reyscher (ed.), *Vollständige, historisch und kritisch bearbeitete Sammlung der
württembergischen Gesetze*, i (Stuttgart/Tübingen, 1828), xii–xxxvii; cf. Rückert, *Reyscher*,
pp. 111, 150 ff., 194–200; Gierke, *Germanisten*, pp. 12 f.

lay in their attitude to political reform and the process of legislation.
In particular, the development by Puchta of the highly complicated
science of 'conceptual jurisprudence' was seen by the more radical
Germanists such as Reyscher as paving the way for reaction by distancing
the people from their legal system. Yet this sentiment could also be
shared by men of much more moderate political views than Reyscher.
In this respect, Georg Beseler's famous *Volksrecht und Juristenrecht*
marked another important stage in the development of Germanism. Like
Reyscher, the moderate liberal Beseler fully accepted the validity of the
Volksgeistlehre, but expressed great concern about the consequences to
freedom of the lawyers' dominance over the legal system.[22]

Despite Beseler's involvement, the south made most of the early
running in the campaign for legal codification in the early 1840s. That
was scarcely surprising, as the movement had always been strongest
there. The Badenese chamber of deputies had called for the unification
of the laws of the German states in 1819 and had asked Thibaut and
Rotteck to do preparatory work on the subject. Similar resolutions were
passed by the second chamber in Hesse-Darmstadt in 1820–1 and 1829–
30.[23] In 1842 Anton Christ—a former bureaucrat and liberal deputy in
the Badenese Chamber, who had been strongly influenced by Thibaut—
published an important work calling for a national code. His concern
for legal unity was rooted in his desire for national unity and the
strength of the nation in relation to other countries. Like the Germanists,
he accepted that the historical method was 'the only one which is
suitable and beneficial' in the preparation of legislation, but he went
on to argue that the primacy of historical law lay in its source—the
collective will of the people—rather than in the will of an individual
or single estate. Foreign (i.e. French or Roman) laws weakened patriotism
and were incompatible with a powerful state; written in a foreign tongue,
they also denied access to the law to most of the population and thus
made law the property of professional lawyers.[24]

---

[22] A. L. Reyscher, 'Für und wider das deutsche Recht', *Zeitschrift für deutsches Recht*,
7 (1842), 141; Rückert, *Reyscher*, pp. 136–41, 157 ff., 218 f., 25 f.; G. Dilcher and B.-R.
Kern, 'Die juristische Germanistik des 19. Jahrhunderts und die Fachtradition der
Deutschen Rechtsgeschichte', *ZRG GA* 101 (1984), pp. 13–17; Gierke, *Germanisten*,
pp. 19–27; G. Beseler, *Volksrecht und Juristenrecht* (Leipzig, 1843), 58–70; on Beseler
in general, see B.-R. Kern, *Georg Beseler. Leben und Werk* (Berlin, 1982).

[23] Coing (ed.), *Handbuch*, iii/2, p. 1423; Dölemeyer, 'Einflüsse', p. 205; R. Polley,
Anton Friedrich Justus Thibaut (AD 1772–1840) in seinen Selbstzeugnissen und Briefen, i
(Frankfurt, 1982), 42.

[24] A. Christ, *Ueber deutsche Nationalgesetzgebung. Ein Beitrag zur Erzielung gemeinsamer
für ganz Deutschland gültiger Gesetzbücher, und zur Abschaffung des römischen und des*

Christ was also one of many south German liberals who were becoming increasingly worried about the moves towards codification in the individual states in the 1840s.[25] The 1840s saw a number of states attempting with varying degrees of success to strengthen themselves by codifying their legal systems. In principle there was little reason for liberals to oppose this trend, which at least promised certain advances in terms of legal certainty. The great fear, however, was that by strengthening the individual states, these 'particular' codes would set back the movement towards national unity, a movement in which liberals believed codification of German law had a major part to play. There were occasional arguments to the effect that particular codes might promote national legal unity,[26] but that was very clearly a minority position.

The problem was especially acute in Hesse-Darmstadt, whose government had progressed further with its plans for codification than any other. However, similar plans existed for the Prussian Rhineland and the Bavarian Palatinate. In each case, proposed codifications threatened the continued application of French legal institutions. These developments produced powerful opposition movements originating in the areas in which French law was dominant, above all in the part of Hesse-Darmstadt on the left bank of the Rhine (Rheinhessen). As had earlier been the case in the Prussian Rhineland, a struggle which was ostensibly concerned with the retention of local institutions against the centralizing desires of the bureaucracy in fact sought to defend and extend the progressive provisions of the French heritage. Since 1814, the provisions of the French code—equality before the law, freedom of property and contract, public and oral court procedure, and civil marriage—had been closely linked to the constitutional ideals of south-western Germany.[27] The major development of the 1840s lay in the defence of French law in the name of German nationalism. As one Hessian liberal wrote in 1846, 'even now nobody wants the French, but

---

französischen Rechts insbesondere (Karlsruhe, 1842), 4, 20, 42, 51, 57-65, 108 f.; cf. H. Getz, *Die deutsche Rechtseinheit im 19. Jahrhundert als rechtspolitisches Problem* (Bonn, 1966), 59-63; for Christ, see Lee, *Politics of Harmony*, p. 203.

[25] Christ, *Gesetzgebung*, pp. 112 f..

[26] F. Purgold, 'Praktische Bemerkungen zu dem Entwurf eines bürgerlichen Gesetzbuchs für das Grossherzogtum Hessen. Theil 1, das Personenrecht enthaltend', *Zeitschrift für deutsches Recht*, 7 (1842), 347 f.; Getz, *Rechtseinheit*, pp. 50-9.

[27] As the *Mainzer Zeitung* put it in 1817, 'we ... expect nothing more than what we already possess from a constitution for the whole of Hesse'; quoted in Fehrenbach, 'Zur sozialen Problematik', p. 197.

their institutions are being demanded for the whole of Germany'.[28] And one writer went so far as to claim in 1848 that the crucial parts of the French system were in fact German in origin.[29] A leading role in this growing public debate was played by practising lawyers. As Gagern put it in 1845, practising lawyers had been the 'leaders of the people' in the Bavarian Palatinate in the 1830s, and he placed great emphasis on the importance to the liberal nationalist cause of what he called 'the public confirmation of the opinion of the lawyers'.[30] The principal issue here was not so much national legal unity as the demand for reform of procedural law in order to introduce jury courts and public, oral procedure on the French model. These liberal aspects of the French system were one of the principal reasons for the popularity of that system in southern and western Germany. A further attraction from the point of view of the practising lawyers was the increased fees that they could command if the French system was adopted.[31] Such liberal demands came to be closely associated with the broader question of national legal unity through the preparations for the planned congress of practising lawyers in Mainz in 1844. In fact, this congress was cancelled at short notice after problems arose with the conservative government of Hesse-Darmstadt. From that point on, however, practising lawyers were among the keenest proponents of liberal reform through national codification.[32]

As the nationalist movement gained momentum in the mid-1840s, the demand for a national code spread across northern Germany from its bases in the south. The years 1846–7 saw this process accelerate with

---

[28] J. Brunk to H. v. Gagern, quoted in W. Schubert, 'Der Code Civil und die Personenrechtsentwürfe des Grossherzogtums Hessen-Darmstadt von 1842 bis 1847', *ZRG GA* 88 (1971), p. 171; in general, see Dölemeyer, 'Einflüsse', pp. 199–207; Coing (ed.), *Handbuch*, iii/2, pp. 1518–30; Faber, *Rheinlande*, pp. 175–83; Getz, *Rechtseinheit*, pp. 42 ff.; Büttner, *Anfänge des Parlamentarismus*, pp. 207–20.

[29] L. W. Fischer, 'Ueber die Reformfrage', *AcP* 31 (1848), p. 57.

[30] Gagern to Hofmann, autumn 1845 (draft) and Gagern to R. Eigenbrodt, 18 Oct. 1843, in P. Wentzcke and W. Klötzer (eds.), *Deutscher Liberalismus im Vormärz. Heinrich von Gagerns Briefe und Reden 1815–1848* (Göttingen/Berlin/Frankfurt, 1959), 296, 267.

[31] O. Bähr, *Erinnerungen aus meinem Leben* (Kassel, 1898), 61.

[32] See, in general, Getz, *Rechtseinheit*, pp. 72–101; Rückert, *Reyscher*, pp. 248 f.; D. Blasius, 'Der Kampf um die Geschworenengerichte im Vormärz', in H.-U. Wehler (ed.), *Sozialgeschichte Heute. Festschrift für Hans Rosenberg zum 70. Geburtstag* (Göttingen, 1974), 148–61; cf. L. W. Fischer, *Das teutsche Justiz. Für die Freunde des Rechts und der nationalen Einheit, auch zur Verständigung über Zweck und Ziel der bevorstehenden Mainzer Advocatensammlung* (Stuttgart, 1844). On the cancellation of the Mainz lawyers' congress, see Büttner, *Anfänge des Parlamentarismus*, p. 200 and *Preussische Gerichts-Zeitung*, 3/20 (10 Feb. 1861), 77 f.

the growth of institutional links between liberals in different parts of Germany.[33] The foundation of the *Deutsche Zeitung* in July 1847 as the press organ of this movement was an event of great importance in the pre-history of 1848. Perhaps even more significant were the two so-called Germanists' Congresses held at Frankfurt in September 1846 and at Lübeck a year later. At the first of these, radical Germanists such as Reyscher and Christ clashed with moderates like Jakob Grimm and Mittermaier over such questions as whether Romanists ought to have been present and what role Roman law should play in a future German code. But what was clear was the breadth of support for a legal codification and the degree to which the *Volksgeistlehre* had been accepted.[34]

The acceptance of Savigny's theory of the origins of law had important implications for the way in which a codification might be attempted. In particular, it meant lengthy study of the legal sources and the collection of materials from the different parts of Germany so that justice might be done to regional variations. As Beseler put it at the Lübeck Germanists' Congress: 'one can say that German national legislation can only be properly prepared if particular laws are collected and thus made easily accessible.'[35] The strength of this feeling was very clear during 1848. Supporters of legal unification began to warn of the dangers of over-hasty legislation, which might recklessly destroy long-standing institutions and practices.[36] This was the authentic voice of the Historical School of Law, which found strong support from Mittermaier later in the year. Successful codification required, according to Mittermaier, two things: the satisfactory collection of preparatory materials, 'on whose existence the success of the legislation completely depends'; and the attempt to codify a particular part of the law first. These ideas looked forward to Mittermaier's report to the Frankfurt Parliament on the activities of that body's legislative commission. Here, Mittermaier reiterated his support for codification in principle, but also emphasized the necessity of long preparatory study and collection of materials, and

---

[33] For the following, see in general T. Nipperdey, *Deutsche Geschichte 1800-1866* (Munich, 1983), 387 f.; Krieger, *German Idea of Freedom*, p. 286; I. Cervelli, 'Deutscher Liberalismus im Vormärz: Profil einer politischen Elite (1833-1847)', in W. Schieder (ed.), *Liberalismus in der Gesellschaft des deutschen Vormärz* (Göttingen, 1983), 330, 337 f.

[34] *Verhandlungen der Germanisten zu Frankfurt am Main am 24., 25. und 26. September 1846* (Frankfurt, 1847), 16, 63-83, 109 f.

[35] *Verhandlungen der Germanisten zu Lübeck am 27., 28. und 30. September 1847* (Lübeck, 1848), 194.

[36] Fischer, 'Ueber die Reformfrage', p. 35.

the participation of practising lawyers from all parts of the Reich. Above all, he insisted that a civil code would concern 'local relationships . . . which the national assembly has neither the power nor the right to regulate in a uniform fashion'. This argument won the support of the Reich minister of justice, Robert von Mohl, and succeeded in overcoming more radical demands for the appointment of a commission to make an immediate start on a code. Closing the debate, Mittermaier declared that full legal unity would have to await the political unification of Germany.[37]

The years around 1848 marked a turning-point in the attitude of the legal community of Germany towards codification. As Beseler later pointed out, it was the events of that year that overcame many of the hostilities provoked by his *Volksrecht und Juristenrecht*, and there was subsequently little opposition to legal unification on grounds of principle.[38] Article 64 of the abortive constitution of 1849 contained a commitment to the production of a civil code but was silent on how such a code might be achieved. With hindsight, a new type of consensus appears to have been emerging. Most agreed that 'the real home of German jurisprudence lies in the historical school' and thought of Thibaut's call for a simple code, which was accessible to all, as 'nothing more than a beautiful dream'.[39] On the other hand, it was now quite common for these tenets of the historical school to find agreement without the implication that all legislation was the arbitrary work of an individual will, while inherited customary law was somehow on a higher plane. Men like Mittermaier, Geib, and Wydenbrugk were already developing what came to be the standard moderate liberal position in the period after 1848—i.e. that it was possible to accept Savigny's theories of the origins of law while rejecting his negative views about legislation. It was this development which made it possible for the link between historical jurisprudence and political conservatism to be broken.

---

[37] K. J. A. Mittermaier, 'Ueber die nothwendigen Vorarbeiten zur Verwirklichung einer allgemeinen deutschen Gesetzgebung mit besonderer Beziehung auf die Bearbeitung eines allgemeinen Gesetzes über eheliche Güterrechte', *AcP* 31 (1848), pp. 110–11; F. Wigard (ed.), *Stenographische Berichte über die Verhandlungen der deutschen constituirenden Nationalversammlung*, viii (Frankfurt/M., 1850), 5588–94; in general, see Getz, *Rechtseinheit*, ch. 4, and G. Wesenberg, 'Die Paulskirche und die Kodifikationsfrage', *ZRG RA* 72 (1955), pp. 359–65.

[38] G. Beseler, *Erlebtes und Erstrebtes 1809–1859* (Berlin, 1884), 52; Getz, *Rechtseinheit*, p. 135.

[39] G. Geib, *Die Reform des deutschen Rechtslebens* (Leipzig, 1848), 15; O. v. Wydenbrugk, *Briefe über deutsche Nationalgesetzgebung* (Jena, 1848), 33.

As Geib put it, 'what we claim with regard to law is claimed by liberalism with regard to politics'.[40]

Looking back on these events, Bluntschli believed that while the Romanists were academically superior to their Germanist counterparts, the controversy had liberated a new generation of Romanist lawyers from 'the scholastic doctrines of academic jurisprudence (*Legaljurisprudenz*)'. These men, as far as Bluntschli was concerned, gained a better view of 'the youthful growth of national law'.[41] A case in point was the Romanist, Carl Georg von Wächter, who in the early 1840s had warned against moving too quickly in producing codes and had favoured piecemeal reform first.[42] By 1847 he was expressing great concern about the dangers to the national cause of particular codifications, and was campaigning for joint codifying commissions in the southern states in order to create the legal equivalent of the *Zollverein*. For men like Wächter, the years between 1847 and 1853 seem to have been something of a watershed. In 1847, a ministerial conference of the Confederation had finally produced a unified law of bills of exchange (*Wechselordnung*) and the Württemberg government took the initiative in promoting (through Wächter himself) the eventual establishment of legal unity within the Confederation. At the Germanists' congress of the same year, Wächter came to some agreement with the Germanists about the desirability of a code. Six years later, the first draft of a civil code for Saxony was completed, and was greeted with widespread criticism from a number of directions. On the one hand, there was opposition to the principle of codification as such on the basis of Savigny's views on the damage done to jurisprudence.[43] On the other, the common view that the Saxon draft code was inadequate re-emphasized the dangers of particular codifications which were causing concern among liberals in the 1840s. Wächter, in particular, developed his criticism of the Saxon draft code into an argument for the possibility and necessity of a German code. Nine years later, he announced in an article in the third edition of the *Staatslexikon* that the battle over codification was effectively decided. A true code was not, he said, a break with the past, and should as far as possible incorporate existing law. At the same time Carl

---

[40] Geib, *Reform*, p. 24; cf. Wydenbrugk, *Briefe*, pp. 7–10.

[41] Bluntschli, *Denkwürdiges aus meinem Leben*, i (Nördlingen, 1884), 201.

[42] C. G. Wächter, 'Die neuesten Fortschritte der Civilgesetzgebung in Württemberg, mit legislativen Bemerkungen und vergleichende Rücksicht auf das gemeine Recht', *AcP* 23 (1840), pp. 33 ff.

[43] C. F. F. Sintenis, *Zur Frage von den Civilgesetzbüchern. Ein Votum in Veranlassung des Entwurfes eines bürgerlichen Gesetzbuchs für das Königreich Sachsen* (Leipzig, 1853).

Theodor von Welcker reiterated his earlier call for 'a simple, patriotic code', but emphasized that this should include the best parts of historical law.[44]

The 1840s thus saw a transformation of the political battle lines with regard to national legal unity. As before, attitudes to codification were indicative of political affiliation. Recent research has demonstrated the connection in the Frankfurt Parliament between natural-law jurisprudence and democratic republicanism on the one hand and historical jurisprudence and moderate constitutionalism on the other. The former camp was, however, relatively weakly represented at Frankfurt, and the debates on codification, as on the broader questions of the constitution and the 'basic rights' (*Grundrechte*), tended to be dominated by moderate constitutional liberals. The moderate, 'organic' liberalism of men like Friedrich Dahlmann and Beseler was closely related to the major preconceptions of Savigny's historical school—the concern with historical institutions, regional particularities, and inherited rights as opposed to abstract, theoretical principles. In the case of legal codification, this meant time-consuming work in collecting and collating the sources of existing law, and a procedure which calmed the fears of conservatives about the potentially radical effects of codification on social and political relationships.[45] For the next forty years this was to be the basis of the theory of codification in Germany.

The period of reaction in the 1850s was thus accompanied by the growing belief in the need for legal unity, although differences remained on how this was to be achieved, which parts of the law were most suitable for unification and so on. Conservative opposition to unification,

[44] C. G. Wächter, *Der Entwurf eines bürgerlichen Gesetzbuches für das Königreich Sachsen* (Leipzig, 1853); Welcker, 'Gesetz' and Wächter, 'Gesetzgebung', *Staatslexikon*, vi (3rd edn. Leipzig, 1862), 479 f., 482-517. See in general Gierke, *Die historische Rechtsschule und die Germanisten*, pp. 29 f., Dölemeyer, 'Einflüsse', pp. 217-23, and F. Elsener, 'Carl Georg von Wächter (1797-1880) und die Bemühungen Württembergs um eine Vereinheitlichung des Privat- und Prozessrechtes in der Zeit des Deutschen Bundes (1847/48)', in K. Ebert (ed.), *Festschrift Hermann Baltl* (Innsbruck, 1978), 193-209.

[45] The basic work here is W. Siemann, *Die Frankfurter Nationalversammlung 1848/49 zwischen demokratischem Liberalismus und konservativer Reform. Die Bedeutung der Juristendominanz in den Verfassungsverhandlungen des Paulskirchenparlaments* (Frankfurt, 1976), esp. pt. 2. Siemann's argument that the followers of the Historical School were 'conservatives' while their opponents were left-liberals and democrats, leaving no real centre in politics, is inadequate. Rather, Germanist members of the Historical School tended to be moderate liberal constitutionalists, while full-blown Romanists, who were almost completely absent from Frankfurt, were reactionaries; see Dilcher and Kern, 'Die juristische Germanistik', pp. 24-9.

subsided as new doctrines of codification, which broadly accepted Savigny's theory of the origins of the law, were developed. By 1853 the moderate conservative *Wochenblattpartei* in Prussia, led by Savigny's pupil Moritz August von Bethmann-Hollweg, was arguing that, while Savigny's notion of the *Volksgeist* should be accepted, his negative attitude to the value of legislation and the political fatalism inherent in the Historical School's work should not. This is, of course, not to suggest that the cause of legal unity had ceased to be associated with the more radical liberal nationalists.[46] As the fortunes of moderate liberal nationalism revived towards the end of the decade, so too did many of the demands of the 1840b. In 1859 the *Preussische Jahrbücher* repeated the traditional liberal claims about the national importance of codification and the dangers of legislation by the individual states. The journal claimed that Prussia was the state best placed to prepare codes which might subsequently form the basis of national legislation. Furthermore, the last years of the decade saw the first attempt to appropriate the cause of legal unity for conservatism. Codification would, it was claimed, strengthen the Confederation against the forces of revolutionary nationalism.[47]

This broadening of the political roots of the campaign for legal unity had two main causes. In the first place, there was the gradual decline of older, predominantly 'southern', traditions of thought, with their emphasis on popular, simple codes developed according to the laws of reason. These traditions had, or were perceived to have, strongly radical implications, which made them unattractive to conservative statesmen and thinkers. 1848 had seen their last real expression on the political stage and, given the political composition of the Frankfurt Parliament, they could never hope to obtain a majority. In their place, the selective appropriation of Savigny's theories—the *Volksgeist* without the hostility to legislation—had far less alarming implications, both for the states' governments and for moderate conservative thinkers. This helps to explain why so many publicists in this period were convinced that

---

[46] On the *Wochenblattpartei*, see M. Behmen, *Das Preussische Wochenblattpartei (1851–1861). Nationalkonservative Publizistik gegen Ständestaat und Polizeistaat* (Göttingen, 1971), 165–71; cf. Christ's renewed call in 1850 for an immediate start on the work of codification, *Die Verwirklichung der deutschen Nationalgesetzgebung* (Stuttgart/Tübingen, 1850), esp. 13 ff.

[47] 'Das preussische Recht und das Rechtsstudium', *Preussische Jahrbücher*, 3 (1859), 35 f., 57; F. Noellner, *Die deutschen Einheitsbestrebungen im Sinne nationaler Gesetzgebung und Rechtspflege. Mit Benutzung amtlicher Urkunden* (Leipzig, 1857), esp. v–vii, 13 f.

Savigny's denial of the 'vocation' of the age for legislation had no continuing relevance.[48] The second major reason for the broadening of support for codification lay in the activities of the Confederation. Before 1848, this organization had been notoriously reluctant to engage in anything which might be seen to promote the nationalist cause. Nor had the *Zollverein* been much more successful until 1847, when a unified law regulating bills of exchange was finally produced. But in many ways this success marked a turning-point. The King of Bavaria became resigned to the inevitability of codification, and the government of Württemberg began to call for the unification of commercial law and, in the longer term, the law of obligations. This idea was picked up after 1848, when the southern states in particular realized the relevance of legal reform to the strengthening of the Confederation. In 1851, Bavaria, Saxony, and Württemberg took the lead in persuading the Confederation's Conference of Ministers to accept the idea of a commercial code and other reforms, such as the unification of weights and measures.[49] The policies of these so-called middle states in the 1850s was geared towards the preservation of their independent position in relation to Prussia and Austria through the strengthening of the institutions of the Confederation. By this time one of the key elements of the liberal nationalism of the *Vormärz* had become widely accepted, however powerful reactionary movements were in the domestic politics of the German states. Legal codification was considered to be of great importance in securing the political integration of the Confederation against the forces of nationalism. As Friedrich Noellner put it when looking back on the debates of the second decade of the century:

There is no form of unity more conservative than that of the law and of legislation. It was only because the campaign for unity was mixed up with ideas of freedom, which were based on anti-monarchical and democratic sentiments, that legislative unity could never come about.[50]

[48] e.g. Wächter, 'Gesetzgebung', pp. 500 ff.; J. C. Bluntschli, 'Der bayerische und sächsische Entwurf eines bürgerlichen Gesetzbuchs', *Kritische Vierteljahresschrift für Gesetzgebung und Rechtswissenschaft*, 3 (1861), 421; L. Goldschmidt, 'Der Entwurf eines Handelsgesetzbuch für die Preussischen Staaten', *Kritische Zeitschrift für die gesammte Rechtswissenschaft*, 4 (1857), 105.
[49] Coing (ed.), *Handbuch*, iii/2, pp. 1476 f.; F. Laufke, 'Der Deutsche Bund und die Zivilgesetzgebung', in P. Mikat (ed.), *Festschrift der Rechts- und Staatswissenschaftlichen Fakultät der Julius-Maximilians-Universität Würzburg zum 75. Geburtstag von Hermann Nottarp* (Karlsruhe, 1963), 5 ff.
[50] Noellner, *Die deutschen Einheitsbestrebungen*, p. 42.

In the context of the middle states' attempts to head off the threat posed by Prussia and by liberal nationalism, conservatives like Noellner saw clearly the need to move beyond the reactionary politics of the *Vormärz* period. The cause of selective legal unification was increasingly thought capable of serving the wider interests of conservatism by heading off liberal demands for a 'revolutionary' transformation of the German state system. It was hardly fortuitous that the Confederation's attentions should have turned first to commercial law. The very existence of the *Zollverein* gave those who sought further measures to ease trade between the member states a powerful argument, and much was made of the commercial difficulties which arose out of the uneven interpretation of the 1847 law regulating bills of exchange in the different states.[51] To this may be added the widespread appeal of unification in the sphere of material interests in a period in which the prospects for liberal nationalism looked distinctly bleak. As Levin Goldschmidt put it in 1857:

The more the present generation loses hope in the final success of the movement for political unity of the recent past, the more urgent is the requirement to do justice at least to the need for material unity. The further the extent of the unified customs area, the greater the number of common economic interests. This also means, however, that the disparity of legal norms, which lessens the consistency and certainty of trading relationships, is all the more disruptive. The necessity of moving towards the desired legal unity in precisely this area is generally recognized.[52]

For Goldschmidt, who was later a National Liberal deputy in the Reichstag and one of the most influential proponents of a civil code, these sentiments were evidently determined by what he considered to be politically possible in Germany in 1856. As he wrote after the completion of the Commercial Code, to have called for an all-embracing civil code at that time 'would have amounted to a rejection of any common legislation in commercial law'.[53] On the other hand, the political potential in this appeal to 'material interests' was increasingly obvious

[51] e.g. K. J. A. Mittermaier, 'Die neuesten Gesetzgebungsarbeiten auf dem Gebiete der Civilgesetzgebung etc', *AcP* 36 (1853), pp. 96 f.; cf. Coing (ed.), *Handbuch*, iii/3 (Munich, 1986), 2945.
[52] Goldschmidt, 'Der Entwurf eines Handelsgesetzbuchs', p. 105.
[53] Quoted in P. Raisch, *Die Abgrenzung des Handelsrecht vom Bürgerlichen Recht als Kodifikationsproblem im 19. Jahrhundert* (Stuttgart, 1962), 132.

to those who, in contrast to Goldschmidt, desired to bolster the individual states against the forces of nationalism. In February 1856 Bavaria once more took the lead and called for the preparation of a commercial code. The aim of Bavarian policy, as defined by the chief minister, Ludwig von der Pfordten, was to use the Confederation as a wider arena for Bavarian political activity at the expense of the smaller states. The call for a commercial code was thus part of a policy of asserting Bavaria's independence from Prussia and Austria and expanding her influence. Within two months, however, Prussia was already calling for delay so that her own draft commercial code could be completed. Prussia's aim in adopting this position was fairly clear. The middle states' attempt to reform the Confederation posed an implicit threat to Prussia's hold over the *Zollverein*, an institution whose influence had grown with the entry of states such as Hanover and Oldenburg in the early 1850s. The great danger from the Prussian point of view was that leadership of economic policy in Germany would pass from Berlin to Frankfurt. Bismarck's policy as Prussian ambassador to the Confederation between 1851 and early 1859 was thus to reject any organizational strengthening of the Confederation. However, there were considerable political risks involved in opposition to a proposal which enjoyed considerable popular support and which was closely connected with the King of Bavaria. Thus Prussia sought to take the lead by producing her own draft commercial code, which would be a desirable reform of the Prussian legal system and provide the basis for future national legislation. When the Prussian draft code was finally completed in late 1856, the principal political obstacle to the start of work on a national commercial code was overcome, and the preparatory conferences of representatives of the different states began in Nuremberg in early 1857. Not for the last time, the cause of legal unity was seen as a way of furthering Prussia's hegemonial ambitions.[54]

A further stage in these developments was reached in 1859 in response to the evidence of the Confederation's military weakness provided by

[54] See Coing (ed.), *Handbuch*, iii/3, 2948–56; Laufke, 'Der Deutsche Bund und die Zivilgesetzgebung', pp. 5–11, 28–35; Getz, *Rechtseinheit*, pp. 136 ff.; E. Wadle, 'Der Zollverein und die deutsche Rechtseinheit', *ZRG GA* 102 (1985), pp. 99–129; on Prussian policy, see E. E. Kraehe, 'Practical Politics in the German Confederation: Bismarck and the Commercial Code', *JMH*, 25 (1953), pp. 13–24, and R. v. Delbrück, *Lebenserinnerungen 1817–1867*, ii (Leipzig, 1905), 90 ff. On von der Pfordten, see, W. D. Gruner, 'Die Würzburger Konferenzen der Mittelstaaten in den Jahren 1859–1861 und die Bestrebungen zur Reform des deutschen Bundes', *Zeitschrift für bayerische Landesgeschichte*, 36 (1973), 186–9.

the outbreak of war in Italy. There were good reasons for thinking that the Confederation's military response was weakened by the rivalry between Prussia and Austria, and the middle states saw this failure to respond effectively to nationalism as a threat to their internal and external security. This was all the more the case as events in Italy had given a new lease of life to the nationalist movement in Germany, which Prussia was widely suspected of encouraging. Such feelings of insecurity revived the cause of institutional reform of the Confederation with strong support from Austria. On 3 November 1859 the Confederation installed a committee on the question of the establishment of a supreme court, and this led directly to the famous Würzburg Conference of November 1859, involving Bavaria, Saxony, Württemberg, the Hessian states, Mecklenburg, and a number of smaller states from central Germany. For all their differences on other matters, these states had little difficulty in agreeing in principle to a supreme court for the Confederation and to common legislation in criminal and civil law.[55]

At this point, Prussia's opposition came out into the open. The middle states' policies were repeatedly derided as mere propaganda, designed to win public support because of the popularity of the cause of legal unity. Yet for that very reason the Prussian government felt unable to oppose the cause of legal unity openly and instead concentrated its attacks on formal questions, in particular relating to the Confederation's constitutional right to produce uniform laws. The early 1860s saw continuing battles between Prussia and the other large states over the question of legal unity, the main point at issue being whether or not Prussia would accede to majority votes in the Confederation. Eventually, in February 1862, commissions were set up in Hanover and Dresden to prepare codes of civil procedure and the law of obligations respectively. In contrast to its attitude to the Commercial Code in 1856, the Prussian government refused to take part in either of these commissions and went ahead with its plans to produce separate Prussian legislation.[56]

These political manœuvrings aside, it seems clear that there was general agreement by the end of the 1850s that legal unification was desirable and possible. The foundation of the German Lawyers' Congress

[55] Gruner, 'Die Würzburger Konferenzen', pp. 189–218; Laufke, 'Der Deutsche Bund', pp. 7, 28 ff., 42–7.

[56] Laufke, 'Der Deutsche Bund', pp. 14–17; Getz, *Rechtseinheit*, pp. 149–52; J. W. Hedemann, *Der Dresdner Entwurf von 1866. Ein Schritt auf dem Wege zur deutschen Rechtseinheit* (Berlin, 1935), 8–12. Examples of Prussia's response may be found in Schleinitz's circular note of 6 June 1860, BA Koblenz, Kl. Erw. 319-7, fos. 8 ff. and Delbrück, *Lebenserinnerungen*, ii, pp. 229 f.

(*Deutscher Juristentag*) in 1860 was very much an expression of this growing consensus within the German legal community. At a meeting of the Berlin Law Society on 10 March 1860, the main speaker, Holtzendorff, pointed to the deficiencies of current attempts at common legislation and claimed that much more attention was being given to 'the material interests of economic life' than those things that the German 'legal consciousness' had in common. Two months later, the formal announcement of the establishment of the Lawyers' Congress was published with the goal of promoting the national unification of civil, criminal, and procedural law.[57]

This new body was one of a number of organizations founded in the period which have been rightly accredited with considerable influence in the formation of a nationalist communications system within Germany's educated classes. Many of the Lawyers' Congress' members had close links with the National Association and, as was the case in the Congress of German Economists founded in 1858, explicit statements of the connections between the goal of legal unity and the broader concerns of nationalist politics were common. In both organizations there were demands for the establishment of a national legislature to prepare and introduce desired reforms.[58] But the Lawyers' Congress was never merely a front for *kleindeutsch* political activity. Indeed, in line with Savigny's views about the links between language and law as expressions of the national spirit, Austrian German lawyers were invited to participate, and in the opinion of at least one observer the debates quickly took on unacceptably *grossdeutsch* flavour.[59] The decision to hold the 1862 meeting of the Congress in Vienna aroused widespread fears that the Congress would support Austria's policies in the Confederation—a feeling which the common emphasis on not excluding any German region, retaining a 'universal German character', and standing 'above the partisan politics of the present' did little to alleviate.[60]

---

[57] See the reports in *Preussische Gerichts-Zeitung*, 2.13 (28 Mar. 1860), 52 and 2.20 (15 May 1860), 77.

[58] For these connections, see in general T. Offermann, *Arbeiterbewegung und liberales Bürgertum in Deutschland 1850-1863* (Bonn, 1979), 165-71; T. S. Hamerow, *The Social Foundations of German Unification, 1858-1871*, i (Princeton, 1969), ch. 8; cf. V. Böhmert, *Rückblicke und Ausblicke eines Siebzigers* (Dresden, 1900), 21-6; J. C. Bluntschli, *Denkwürdiges aus meinem Leben*, ii (Nördlingen, 1884), 294-5; ibid. iii (Nördlingen, 1884), 52.

[59] Bähr, Erinnerungen, p. 66; on the decision to include the Austrians, see Bluntschli, *Denkwürdiges*, ii. 285.

[60] Bluntschli, *Denkwürdiges*, iii. 46; *Deutsche Gerichts-Zeitung*, 3.47 (17 July 1861), 185 f.; 3.58 (25 Aug. 1861), 234 f.; 4.50 (10 Sept. 1862), 205 f.

Thus, for all that the Lawyers' Congress talked of the relationship between legal and national unity, its stance on the details of that relationship was anything but clear. In this respect, the Congress mirrored the political developments of the day, in which general agreement about the desirability of legal unification concealed strong disagreements about how that goal might be achieved. The Congress quickly moved on from the principal question of the *Vormärz* period— i.e. whether it was appropriate to think about codification—to detailed investigations of which parts of the law should be unified. Here, once again, the influence of the Historical School made itself felt. Holtzendorff's speech to the Berlin Law Society in March 1860 had insisted that one of the Congress's essential roles would be to avoid blind centralization and to ensure that areas of the law which related to purely local circumstances should be left to the individual states. This concern with regional diversity was a central feature of the legal theory which emanated from the Historical School, and was frequently debated in the Lawyers' Congress. Subsequent discussions in the Congress's periodical concerning the law of property in marriage emphasized the deep roots of this section of the law in the popular consciousness, and came to the conclusion that the imposition of a single system was inappropriate.[61] A memorandum prepared for the Bavarian government by von der Pfordten made a similar point with regard to the scope of national legislation. In line with his state's policy, he saw progress towards legal unity as inevitable and supported common legislation with regard to the law of obligations. Such legislation in the sphere of land law was, however, more difficult and in family and inheritance law 'absolutely impossible'. This was not a view that commanded the support of the Lawyers' Congress,[62] but it was to recur constantly in the debates concerning the preparation of a civil code in the 1860s and 1870s.

By the early 1860s, then, there was widespread agreement on both the possibility and the desirability of national legislation in the sphere of the civil law. This was a question in which political considerations

---

[61] *Preussische Gerichts-Zeitung*, 2.13 (28 Mar. 1860), 52; 2.54 (29 Dec. 1860), 214 f.; 3.9 (20 Feb. 1861), 33 f.

[62] L. v. d. Pfordten, 'Gutachten, gemeinschaftliche Civil- und Criminal-Gesetzgebung für die deutschen Bundesstaaten betr.', 12 June 1861, BHStA Munich, MA 76158; H. Conrad, 'Der Deutsche Juristentag 1860-1960', in E. v. Caemmerer *et al.* (eds.), *Hundert Jahre Deutsches Rechtslebens. Festschrift zum hundertjährigen Bestehen des Deutschen Juristentages 1860-1960*, i (Karlsruhe, 1960), 17.

had determined policy from the start of the German Confederation. Hostility to national codes was closely associated with political conservatism in the period before 1848. Conversely, a commitment to national codification was a touchstone of political liberalism. On the whole, the former position derived powerful support from Savigny's theories of the origins and nature of the law. In the aftermath of the French Revolution, hasty legislation prepared in accordance with 'universal principles' was seen as a dangerous solvent of traditional political and social relationships. To conservatives of the *Vormärz* period, Savigny's criticisms of the legislative practices of the late Enlightenment became the basis of a rejection of legislation as such.

By the 1840s this was beginning to change. The resurgent liberal nationalism of that decade began to cast aside Savigny's negative assessment of the potential value of legislation, while broadly accepting his theories about the nature of the law. This implied a further set of opinions about how legislation should proceed, involving lengthy historical study of the sources of law and close attention to specific historical institutions. This was the position adopted by the majority in the Frankfurt Parliament, and was decisive in heading off radical demands for an immediate start on the work of codification.

The 1840s and 1850s were crucial to these developments. There were still isolated voices in opposition to the views of the Historical School,[63] but they were clearly in a minority. If a belief in national legal unity was still broadly associated with the liberal cause, it had now begun to win converts among those who would have no truck with the *Nationalverein*'s goals, as the different examples of von der Pfordten and Wächter showed. In Hanover, Ludwig Windthorst, who was to lead the opposition to attempts to lay the foundations for a civil code after 1867, was a keen supporter of attempts to promote legal unity within the German Confederation.[64] Only Prussia sought to hinder the progress towards national legal unity. As we have seen, that policy scarcely reflected an opposition to legal unity as such, but was rather a reflection of Prussia's determination to prevent any diminution of its influence in the solution of the German question. A principal motivation of those who called for the reform of the German Confederation was to achieve precisely what Prussia feared.

There can be little doubt that the selective appropriation of Savigny's

[63] e.g. C. J. Seitz, *Das praktische Bedürfniss der Rechtsreform gegenüber der historischen Schule* (*Erlangen, 1865*).
[64] M. L. Anderson, *Windthorst. A Political Biography* (Oxford, 1981), 53 f., 69.

theories by the supporters of legal unification had considerable influence here. As will be seen in subsequent chapters, the emphasis on study of the sources of law and on respect for local conditions provided a powerful guarantee that codification would not mean radical change or 'blind' centralization. This guarantee was essential if the resistance of conservative elements was to be broken down in the 1870s. It was, however, by no means the only factor which broke down the barriers to legal unification which were characteristic of the *Vormärz* period, nor arguably was it the most important. In the first place, the growth in the scale of economic activity within the German Confederation undoubtedly highlighted the problems which arose out of legal differences between the German states. Attempts to resolve those problems through the codification of the law of bills of exchange and the commercial code probably did more than anything else to undermine Savigny's denial of the capacity of jurisprudence to produce successful codes. They also threw the spotlight onto those parts of the law of direct interest to merchants and industrialists, which had not yet been unified. In that light, the Confederation's decision of 1862 to proceed with codes of the law of obligations and civil procedure—both of which were directly relevant to the interests of commerce—was hardly surprising.

Even more important than this economic motivation, however, were the political pressures which emanated from the state governments. As we have seen, the new states created in 1815 had seen the integrative power of 'particular' law codes early on, but little had come of their attempts to produce such codes apart from in Hesse-Darmstadt. The 1850s saw much greater attention being paid to this question, particularly in the Kingdom of Saxony and in Bavaria, the two most significant middle states which led the campaign for reform of the Confederation in the 1850s and early 1860s. Saxony was the one middle state which actually managed to introduce a civil code before 1866. A significant consequence of these attempts at legislation in the early 1860s was to revive the fears of the 1840s that such moves would delay a unified German legal system. Others, however, denied this point, and emphasized that codifiers operated under constraints which prevented the emergence of significant variations between different legal systems.[65]

Above all, the changed political situation in the German Confederation

---

[65] For contrasting views on this, see Gottlieb Planck's article 'Der Hannoversche Entwurf einer Hypothekenordnung', *Preussische Gerichts-Zeitung*, 3.19 (17 June 1861), 75 f., and F. Purgold, *Das nationale Element in der Gesetzgebung. Ein Wort zur deutschen Rechtseinheit* (Darmstadt, 1860), 3 f.

in the 1850s meant that codification in the middle states was no longer seen as an alternative to a national code. Instead, it was seen as part of the consolidation of the position of the middle states, in which a future national code of limited areas of the civil law would also play a role. The concentration of statesmen such as von der Pfordten on the appeal to 'material interests' showed how far conservative statesmen had come in perceiving the strength of the link between legal unity and political strength. In no case did the government of a significant German state dare to oppose the aims of the Lawyers' Congress, despite the ambiguous attitude of that body to the fundamental questions concerning Germany's future.[66] Support for legal unity was now part of the common currency of political debate with opponents very much in the minority. Disagreement now revolved around questions of detail: how legal unification should be achieved; who should be responsible for the proposed codification; and which parts of the law should be left to the individual states. Considerable differences on these important, essentially political questions existed throughout the 1860s and early 1870s, and were only partially concealed by the powerful consensus in favour of national legislation in the field of civil law. Accordingly, it was in these terms that the debate was principally conducted after Prussia's victory in 1866 overturned the institutional framework of the German Confederation.

[66] See the public statements of support for the Lawyers' Congress from the Ministers of Justice of Prussia, Austria, Bavaria, Württemberg, and Saxony, in *Preussische Gerichts-Zeitung*, 2.25, 2.28, 2.29 (20 May, 4 and 11 July 1860), 98, 112, 116.

3.
The Politics of Legal Unity, 1867-1873

THE campaign for a unified legal system thus enjoyed widespread support in Germany by 1867. The foundation of the North German Confederation in that year and the establishment of the Reichstag as a national forum for debate entirely changed the context of the discussions. Although the Lawyers' Congress continued to be important and its views widely reported, it ceased to be the main proponent of the cause of national legal unification.[1] The issue was now considered in a context in which the major question in party politics was the validity of Bismarckian politics. Attitudes developed in connection with conflicting notions of how a federal state should be constructed. The principal issue was not the merits or otherwise of national legislation, but the constitutional question of how far the arrangements made in 1867 and especially in 1871 were to be regarded as provisional. Bitter divisions opened up on this issue in the Reichstag and the press, calling forth reciprocal accusations of particularism and 'unitarism'. Before 1866, it had been Prussia which had resisted moves to unify German law on constitutional grounds. After that date, and particularly after 1871, the situation was reversed, with Prussia pressing ahead and Bavaria, Württemberg, and Saxony on the defensive. Although it was the National Liberals and their parliamentary allies who clearly made the running, the important decisions were made within the Bundesrat and were the result of a complex series of calculations on the part of the middle states. That fact was to be of great importance for the future of the Civil Code.

In the period covered by this chapter, the National Liberals were the dominant party in the Reichstag, although they never secured an absolute majority. The ideal of legal unity was deeply embedded in that party's approach to politics, which from the start emphasized the

---

[1] J. C. Bluntschli, *Denkwürdiges aus meinem Leben*, iii, (Nördlingen, 1884), 178.

strengthening and extension of the constitution to deal with all matters of national concern.[2] This expressed a powerful strand in the country's liberal tradition, which saw the state's actions as a powerful, potentially progressive force in German society. At the core of the party's policies in this period lay the belief in the link between national unification and the achievement of liberal goals, encapsulated in the famous slogan 'From unity to freedom—that is our party's way'.[3] Legal unification was an obvious area in which the twin demands of national unity and personal freedom could be reconciled without great difficulty. Like almost everybody else in the 1860s, the National Liberals believed that legal unity would contribute greatly to the strength of the nation-state. The fact that this belief amounted to a truism in this period did nothing to lessen the frequency with which it appeared in liberal polemics. On the other hand, a national code necessarily implied the introduction of positive laws, which lessened the scope for arbitrary intrusions on the freedom of the individual. Written codes meant formal acceptance by the state of the rights of the individual and of procedures to protect those rights against abuse, either by other members of society or by the state itself. Codification would thus contribute both to the new nation's strength and to the achievement of the *Rechtsstaat*. For liberals, no contradiction between these goals existed; they saw them as necessarily complementary. As one Bavarian commentator wrote with reference to the attempts to extend the constitution to cover the whole of the civil law, 'I do not believe that a liberal can oppose [this proposal].'[4] It was thus no surprise when the National Liberal professor Rudolf von Gneist asserted the link between the establishment of the *Rechtsstaat* and the demand for legal unity at the 1871 Lawyers' Congress and declared: 'famous victories and dazzling external successes will not turn us away from the unchanging demands for a secure legal system and for political participation in the reconstruction of the law.'[5] In fact, while the first of these demands may have been achieved, the second was not and was, moreover, not really pursued with any degree of seriousness by the liberals. The reason for this lay in the balance of political forces in the early years of Bismarck's Reich and the constraints those forces imposed on the political parties.

---

[2] See the relevant clause of the party's founding programme of 12 June 1867, reprinted in W. Treue, *Deutsche Parteiprogramme 1861–1954* (Göttingen, 1954), 50.

[3] Quoted in H. A. Winkler, *Preussischer Liberalismus und deutscher Nationalstaat* (Tübingen, 1964), 78.

[4] Völderndorff to Hohenlohe, 1 Nov. 1871, BA Koblenz, Hohenlohe-Schillingsfürst Papers 572, fo. 116.

[5] *Verhandlungen des Neunten Deutschen Juristentages*, iii (Berlin, 1871), 8 f.

Those who wished to see the creation of a national system of civil law had first to contend with the restrictions on the legislative competence of the new state enshrined in Art. 4, No. 13 of the 1867 and 1871 constitutions. This clause restricted the new state's legislative competence to 'the law of obligations, criminal law, commercial law, the law of bills of exchange and court procedure'. In 1867, the National Liberal politician Johannes Miquel proposed that this clause should be amended so that the whole of the civil law and the organization of the courts were included in the legislative competence of the North German Confederation. This motion became known as the Lasker–Miquel motion and reappeared in 1869, 1871, and (in amended form) in 1872 and 1873, when it finally secured the agreement of the Bundesrat.[6] The debates on the Lasker–Miquel motion are the major source for the following account.

The Lasker–Miquel motion gained growing majorities in the Reichstag, although the absence of division lists makes it impossible to gauge their precise size accurately. By 1873, probably only one deputy outside the Catholic Centre party still opposed the motion.[7] These impressive cross-party majorities did not, however, reflect anything approaching unanimity on important questions of detail among the motion's supporters. One such question involved the aims of legal unification. Another concerned the means by which unification might be achieved and, in particular, whether codification was the best way of tackling the problem. The answers to these questions were to have important consequences for the future of the legal system.

As was shown in the previous chapter, the period after about 1840 saw a growing acceptance of Savigny's historical theory of law by the supporters of national legal unification. In the 1860s and 1870s, supporters of the Lasker–Miquel motions tended to deny the validity of Savigny's hostility to codification, but on the whole they did so from within the historical camp. Gottlieb Planck, a Hanoverian National Liberal who was to be one of the most influential figures in the preparation of the Code, argued that after a common language, a national legal system was the clearest sign of national unity in which the 'creative strength of the nation' found expression. This connection between

---

[6] In general, see A. Laufs, 'Die Begründung der Reichskompetenz für das gesamte bürgerliche Recht', *JuS* 12 (1973), pp. 740–4.

[7] K. A. Maass, *Fünfundzwanzig Jahre Reichs-Gesetzgebung* (Leipzig, 1892), 458 n. 1; the deputy was a Hanoverian particularist, Heinrich Ewald; see *Schulthess' Europäischer Geschichtskalender*, 14 (Nördlingen, 1874), 107.

language and law as expressions of a nation's culture was, of course, a major part of Savigny's intellectual heritage. That connection was also often emphasized by other National Liberals such as Eduard Lasker.[8]

There can be little doubt that supporters of the Lasker–Miquel motions were sensitive to the possibility of opposition on the basis of Savigny's theories and were keen to head off such objections. Such opposition did, on occasion, arise, notably from Conservatives, who pointed to the deep roots of certain parts of the law in local conditions.[9] This was, however, a secondary argument as far as the motion's opponents in the Reichstag were concerned, and was almost never advanced with any seriousness by the Centre party's spokesmen.[10] Far more important for most of the opposition was the question of the rights of the individual states under the constitution, and the extent to which the motion was motivated by the liberals' desire to tear down the last remaining barriers to the 'unitary state'. Time and again, Windthorst and his cohorts attacked the National Liberals for seeking to destroy the liberties of the individual states and the rights of their chambers of deputies. While agreeing that 'the greatest possible legal unity in Germany [was] desirable', the Centre maintained its opposition to the centralizing implications of the motion to the end.[11]

The National Liberals were aware of the power of this appeal to particularist sentiment, especially in the south, and were careful to deny that they had any desire to destroy the independent rights of the individual states. As Miquel and Lasker repeatedly pointed out, the individual states would be free to legislate on any part of the civil law if the motion was accepted. The priority was not the construction of a 'unitary state', but the Reich's ability to legislate on matters where common needs arose without constantly being hampered by the charge of unconstitutional action. In this connection, the party's spokesmen made much of the indivisibility of the civil law. It was asserted, for example, that German land law was thoroughly imbued with principles

[8] *SBRT*, 28 Apr. 1869, p. 650 (Planck); ibid., 19 Apr. 1869, pp. 467 f. (Lasker).

[9] i.e. in family, land and inheritance law; see *SBRT*, 19 Apr. 1869, pp. 453 f. (Zehmen) and 28 Apr. 1869, p. 648 (Bassewitz); ibid., 9 Nov. 1871, p. 214 (Helldorf); ibid., 31 May 1872, pp. 631 f. (Rittberg).

[10] The one major exception to this was August Reichensperger, *SBRT*, 9 Nov. 1871, pp. 209 ff.

[11] The best examples are Windthorst's speeches, *SBRT*, 15 Nov. 1871, p. 280; ibid., 31 May 1872, pp. 617-20, ibid., 2 Apr. 1873, pp. 170 ff. (quotation). For Windthorst's belief in federalism as the best defence of constitutional liberties, see M. L. Anderson, *Windthorst. A Political Biography* (Oxford, 1981), 110 ff., 237.

derived from the law of obligations. The argument was then used to counter Conservative objections to unification of this area of the law, which emphasized the local variations in Germany's legal development. In view of these technical difficulties in separating one part of the civil law from another, the formulation of Art. 4, No. 13 of the constitution was, it was claimed, likely to lead to constant problems in the preparation of legislation.[12]

This technical argument was frequently buttressed by statements to the effect that Savigny's objections to codification were no longer valid, that it was precisely as a result of his work that German jurisprudence was now capable of successful legislation, and even that he was a covert supporter of a national code. These were favourite themes of Miquel in particular, but gained their credibility from the re-evaluation of Savigny's work, which was noted in the previous chapter. The 1870s saw a large number of publications, by no means all of which emanated from the National Liberal camp, which argued that the founder of the Historical School had been correct in his theory of the origins of the law, but had underestimated 'subjective factors'—i.e. the role of the legislator. This claim gained the support of prominent pupils of Savigny, such as Bernhard von Windscheid, who argued that the change in attitude to legislation merely reflected, 'differences with regard to the value given to different factors in historical development; we leave the principle of historical development inviolate.' Another of Savigny's pupils, M. A. von Bethmann-Hollweg, was arguing by 1876 that Savigny's opposition to Thibaut did not reflect hostility to the ideal of legal unity and that codification was 'unavoidable'. It would be correct to say that this view of Savigny's heritage dominated the German legal community by this time. Its importance in depriving the opponents of the Lasker-Miquel motions of a powerful argument against legal unification would be difficult to overestimate.[13]

---

[12] See in particular, *SBRT*, 9 Nov. 1871, pp. 207 ff. (Miquel); ibid., 15 Nov. 1871, pp. 284-8 (Lasker); ibid., 29 May 1872, pp. 607 ff. (Römer); cf. *Wochenschrift der Fortschrittspartei in Bayern*, 12 Nov. 1871, BA Koblenz, Hohenlohe-Schillingsfürst Papers 1330, fos. 28 f.

[13] *SBRT*, 20 Mar. 1867, pp. 285 ff. and 9 Nov. 1871, p. 208 (Miquel); B. Windscheid, 'Die geschichtliche Schule der Rechtswissenschaft' (1878), in id., *Gesammelte Reden und Abhandlungen*, ed. P. Oertmann (Leipzig, 1904), 73; M. A. v. Bethmann-Hollweg, *Ueber Gesetzgebung und Rechtswissenschaft als Aufgabe unserer Zeit* (Bonn, 1876), 2, 4; other representative examples of these views are C. G. Bruns, *Zur Erinnerung an Friedrich Carl von Savigny* (Berlin, 1879), 15 ff.; H. Brunner, 'Die Rechtseinheit' (1877), in K. Rauch (ed.), *Abhandlungen zur Rechtsgeschichte. Gesammelte Aufsätze von Heinrich Brunner*, ii (Weimar, 1931), 372 ff.; L. Enneccerus, *Friedrich Carl von Savigny und die Richtung der*

The National Liberals and their allies were right in sensing that, if the charge of 'unitarism' was dangerous to their cause, the counter-charge of particularism could equally be levelled at their opponents. Lasker muttered darkly about the 'political' motives of his opponents, and another supporter considered it 'no accident that the irreconcilable enemies of the German Reich are to be found among the opponents of national legislation'.[14] The opposition's difficulties with this accusation were increased by the fact that Savigny's emphasis on the *Volk* as the source of law could be used to argue against particularist claims. In any plausible reading, the concepts of *Volk* and *Volksgeist* referred to Germans rather than to, say, Bavarians, and it was not surprising that nationalist writers made much of this point. As Levin Goldschmidt put it in 1872: 'the words of the great jurist [Savigny] are misused if applied to the present situation, especially if they are used in defence of the codes of individual states against a common German code.'

Another National Liberal, Ludwig Enneccerus, went even further in claiming Savigny for the cause of national legal unity against the particularist designs of the states. In 1814–15, Savigny's views had apparently been determined by tactical considerations:

> it was above all particularism which opposed the idea of a civil code. Savigny opposed that [i.e. particularism] on theoretical and nationalist grounds. Well aware that Prussia and Austria would never give up their newly completed codes, he opposed the divisions which the supporters of a [national] code unwittingly threatened to introduce.[15]

With that the re-evaluation of Savigny's heritage was, in a sense, completed on the centenary of his birth. He was now considered the forerunner of a national code, rather than its enemy. Above all, the possibility that his theories might provide a fertile source of arguments for the particularist 'enemies of the Reich' in the 1870s was effectively excluded. As Eduard Hölder was to put it shortly afterwards, Savigny's opposition had been motivated 'solely by the desire to unite the legislative impulse of our time with Savigny's authority'.[16]

---

neueren Rechtswissenschaft nebst einer Auswahl ungedruckter Briefe (Marburg, 1879), 23 ff., 28 f., 34 f., 40–3; A. Brinz, 'Die Savigny-Feier am 21. Februar 1879', *Kritische Vierteljahresschrift für Gesetzgebung und Rechtswissenschaft, Neue Folge*, 2 (1879), 471–90.

[14] *SBRT*, 29 May 1872, pp. 596 f. (Lasker); L. Goldschmidt, *Die Nothwendigkeit eines deutschen Civilgesetzbuches* (Berlin, 1872), 18.

[15] Goldschmidt, *Nothwendigkeit*, p. 16; Enneccerus, *Savigny*, p. 43.

[16] E. Hölder, *Savigny und Feuerbach, die Koryphäen der deutschen Rechtswissenschaft. Vortrag gehalten in Erlangen* (Berlin, 1881), 29.

Enneccerus' evaluation of Savigny was, however, symptomatic of National Liberal attitudes in a further important respect. He accepted the *Volksgeistlehre*, but also stressed that law was rooted in a nation's will rather than in its consciousness (*Bewusstsein*), as Savigny had believed. A reforming legislator might well, he said, be ahead of the development of his nation's consciousness. Another commentator, Rudolf Sohm, went even further in this direction and denied the possibility of achieving the necessary reforms through customary law and judicial interpretation, on which Savigny had placed so much emphasis:

Will is the sole creative force in law and access to the administration of the law is denied to the nation's will by the judge's mode of thought. Thus our times rely above all on the will of the legislator for the creation of the law.[17]

These conceptions of the potentially innovative role of legislation and of the will of the legislator coexisted uneasily with the *Volksgeistlehre* and with Savigny's views on an ideal code.

Once again, these developments were important in relation to the political battles of the period. As we have seen, much of the controversy about the Lasker–Miquel motions concerned the constitutional question of the division of sovereign rights between the Reich and the individual states. The liberals' opponents argued that the constitutions of 1867 and 1871 had the nature of a contractual agreement between the participating states. Any change to those constitutions would thus legally require a renegotiation of the 'contract' and would have to secure the consent of the states' chambers of deputies. This position had been developed in the late 1860s and found expression in Windthorst's comparison of the Confederation to a joint-stock company. In Mecklenburg and in the Prussian Upper House, Conservatives attempted to make changes in the constitution of the North German Confederation dependent on the agreement of the local chambers of deputies. Acceptance of this argument would have meant that the post-1867 political arrangements were analogous to those that had existed before the battle of Königgrätz. Instead of being a federal state (*Bundesstaat*), the North German Confederation would have been a federation of states (*Staatenbund*), in which the individual states would have had the power to veto unwelcome changes.

That was something that the National Liberals and their allies could

<hr/>

[17] Enneccerus, *Savigny*, pp. 37 f.; R. Sohm, 'Die deutsche Rechtsentwicklung und die Codificationsfrage', in C. S. Grünhut (ed.), *Zeitschrift für das Privat- und öffentliche Recht der Gegenwart*, i (1874), 265.

never accept. Their response was to introduce a modified version of the Lasker–Miquel motion into the Prussian Lower House in November 1869, where it gained the support of the government and a majority of the deputies. Miquel's speech on 24 November stated his party's position unequivocally. Procedures for constitutional change, he argued, had been accepted in 1867 and the North German Confederation was a state whose powers in federal matters were completely independent of the individual states.[18] This line of argument became the standard National Liberal response to their opponents.

The question was revived in the south after 1871. In both Saxony and Bavaria, particularist forces were strong in the chambers of deputies, and the governments had to tread carefully on any issue which could be presented as a further restriction of their sovereign rights. Both governments felt it necessary to submit their policies with regard to the Lasker–Miquel motion to the approval of the chambers. Bismarck was more prepared to accommodate such sentiments after 1871 than he had been before and was, as we shall see, highly sensitive to the problems caused by particularism in the southern monarchies. But for National Liberals, this was an issue of principle. If the Reich was an independent state, any willingness to involve the local chambers of deputies in national matters smacked of particularism.[19] As far as they were concerned, the new state was an independent body, which through the exercise of its rights gave expression to the will of the people. The point was made quite clearly by Heinrich Brunner, who argued in 1877 that the political changes had created the means to realize the age-old cause of legal unity, which was demanded by 'the will and needs of the nation' and was 'the constant and immediate expression of unity of the national will'.[20]

The importance to liberals of the battle against particularism provided the context for such arguments. Controversies about the extent of the constitutional rights of the state reflected fundamental disagreements about the location of political power. As has often been noted, the National Liberals prided themselves on representing the people. But

[18] *SBRT*, 19 Apr. 1869, p. 458 (Windthorst); for events in Prussia, see H. v. Poschinger, *Fürst Bismarck und die Parlamentarier*, ii (Breslau, 1895), 68 ff.; Miquel's speech is reprinted in W. Schultze and F. Thimme (eds.), *Johannes von Miquels Reden*, i (Halle, 1911), 371–82; cf. H. Herzfeld, *Johannes von Miquel. Sein Anteil am Ausbau des Deutschen Reiches bis zur Jahrhundertwende*, i (Detmold, 1938), 122 ff.

[19] See esp. R. v. Friesen, *Erinnerungen aus meinem Leben*, iii (Dresden, 1910), 267–81; see also the materials relating to this matter in BHStA Munich, MA 76158.

[20] Brunner, 'Die Rechtseinheit' (quotations, pp. 365, 375).

their lasting contribution to Germany's political system lay in the sphere of the consolidation of the central powers of the Bismarckian state. Time and again, National Liberals made no distinction between the strength and unity of the nation and the rights of the state. As Enneccerus put it, in a striking example of this mode of thought:

constitutional change has ensured the influence of the people's convictions about the law; but above all it is the new German Empire and its powerful central authority that is the guarantee of a code, which is truly common to the whole of Germany.

Lasker made much the same point when he wrote that 'the essential thing is the unity of the German nation as a nation, through its embodiment in the Reich'.[21] This type of argument amounted to considering the constitutional rights of the new state as equivalent to the desire of the German people for national self-expression. This is what Uriel Tal has aptly termed the liberals' 'identification' view of the state, which posited a 'unified state will' with which citizens made an voluntary decision to identify.[22]

The supporters of the Lasker-Miquel motions tended to concentrate on the formal aspects of legal unification for several reasons. In the first place, the wide variety of opinions among the supporters of the Lasker-Miquel motions had considerable influence on the way in which the case for legal unity was presented. The National Liberals' main aim was to maximize the size of the Reichstag majorities in favour of the Lasker-Miquel motions. This strategy was a response to the constitutional framework of the Reich, in which fourteen votes in the Bundesrat sufficed to block constitutional change. In the face of opposition from the Bundesrat, the National Liberals concentrated on creating the largest possible majorities in the Reichstag, a policy which had the additional advantage of bolstering their frequent claims to be the true representatives of 'public opinion'. Windthorst's complaint that the debates in the Reichstag were a foregone conclusion and therefore a waste of time testified to the National Liberals' success in constructing these broad coalitions.[23]

There was, however, a price to be paid. The need to construct such

[21] Enneccerus, *Savigny*, p. 45; E. Lasker, *Die Zukunft des Deutschen Reiches* (5th edn., Leipzig, 1884), 11.
[22] U. Tal, *Christians and Jews in Germany. Religion, Politics and Ideology in the Second Reich, 1870-1914* (Ithaca/London, 1975), 38, 78 ff.
[23] *SBRT*, 15 Nov. 1871, p. 280.

coalitions meant that the National Liberals tended to look for allies on the right, particularly in the Free Conservative party. Lasker's posthumously published account of the politics of the period was quite specific on this point. He recorded that, because of the nature of the Centre and Conservative parties, the National Liberals had to look to the Progressives and Free Conservatives as allies. In each of these parties, the National Liberals had enough contacts to make *ad hoc* agreements without endangering their basic principles. Indeed, had Bismarck so desired he could easily have created a permanent governing majority out of these groups in the 1870s:

There was then as never before in Germany or Prussia a recognizable public feeling of a decidedly nationalist and moderately liberal complexion, represented more or less ... by the three parties—the National Liberals, the Free Conservatives and the Progressives—so that the government could justifiably consider the views which those parties held in common as truly representative of public opinion.[24]

The implication was that the representation of 'public opinion' depended on the successful construction of liberal/conservative alliances around policies of national integration. In the early 1870s, the central issue in national politics was the validity of the 1871 settlement, expressed in the battle against particularism. The construction of 'national' coalitions in a multi-party system reflected that priority.

Moreover, the distribution of Reichstag seats between the different parties and the escalating *Kulturkampf* tended to promote coalitions of the nationalist parties against the forces of particularism. That was not only a result of tactical calculations by the party leaders, but also reflected the local configuration of liberal nationalism in many regions of Germany. In states such as Bavaria and Württemberg, the local liberal parties were united against particularism at home, but their members often scattered into different parties—ranging from the Free Conservatives to the Progressives—when they entered the Reichstag. As one Bavarian liberal put it in 1869, 'they [the liberals] are united only in opposition to clerical representatives; otherwise they lack any unity.'[25] In the province of Hanover, which had been annexed by

[24] E. Lasker, *Fünfzehn Jahre parlamentarischer Geschichte (1866–1880)*, ed. F. Hertnech (Berlin, 1901), 91.

[25] Dr Buttenwieser to Heinrich v. Marquardsen, 25 May 1869; ZStA Potsdam, Marquardsen Papers 30, fo. 182. See in general F. Frhr. v. Rummel, *Das Ministerium Lutz und seine Gegner 1871–1882* (Munich, 1935), 36; D. Langewiesche (ed.), *Das Tagebuch Julius Hölders 1877–1880* (Stuttgart, 1977), 16 f.

Prussia amid much bitterness in 1866, the local governor was confident that:

among [the Hanoverian National Liberals], there is a large number of men, who under normal circumstances would be described as moderate conservatives rather than as liberals. At the moment, all those who are in agreement with the present situation are National Liberals.

The liberal–conservative alliance was thus not merely a tactical matter or an example of the susceptibility of liberalism to give in to conservatism; it was rooted in the nature of German political life in the 1870s.[26]

   The connection beteen national unification, the strengthening of the state and the advancement of liberty lay at the core of German liberalism even if the precise relationship between these elements was the subject of dispute. It was perhaps because that connection was taken for granted in the liberal/nationalist camp that supporters of the Lasker–Miquel motions did not trouble themselves unduly about the relationship between the increase of the powers of the state and the interests of the German people. But there was a further side to this matter, for the construction of cross-party coalitions necessarily meant compromises. In view of the nature of Reichstag politics outlined above, it was predictable that compromises would be concluded on the basis of agreement about issues concerning national integration above all else. It was on precisely those issues that the National Liberals, Progressives, and Free Conservatives found it simplest to reach agreement.

   The propensity of the National Liberals to conclude compromises with Bismarck has had a bad press from historians, who have tended to concentrate on those compromises, such as the Indemnity Bill of 1867 and the seven-year military budget of 1874, which are thought to have involved the party's neglect of its 'true' constitutional principles.[27] Such compromises were anything but unproblematic, and the history of German liberalism in the 1870s could perhaps be written in terms of the increasing restiveness of the left with this propensity to compromise, leading to the rift with the Progressives over the codes of court procedure and organization in 1876–7 and the secession of the National Liberal

   [26] This argument is put in detail in M. John, 'Liberalism and Society in Germany, 1850–1880: The case of Hanover', *English Historical Review*, 102 (1987), 579–98. The quotation comes from Stolberg, report of 6 Dec. 1867, HStA Hanover, Hann. 122a 1 no. 5, fo. 4.
   [27] The classic statement of this view is F. C. Sell, *Die Tragödie des deutschen Liberalismus* (Stuttgart, 1953).

left wing in 1880.[28] Yet it has been persuasively argued that compromise was essential to the strategy by which the National Liberals hoped to make themselves indispensable to the government. The aim of this strategy was to cement the party's occupation of the political middle ground, thereby increasing the pressure on Bismarck to accept such reforms as the gradual parliamentarization of government.[29] As part of this strategy, the National Liberals sought to produce the greatest possible unity of those parties which broadly favoured the 1871 settlement.

The supporters of the Lasker–Miquel motions were always divided over whether a code was desirable or practicable. While Miquel consistently argued that the civil law was an organic whole and hence indivisible, other National Liberals disagreed. In 1867, Lasker denied that an extension of competence to cover the whole of the civil law was necessary and, although he had changed his mind by 1869, he remained lukewarm about an immediate codification. Other members of the party, such as Gottlieb Planck and Karl Braun, agreed in opposing codification for the moment, with Braun arguing that the National Liberals merely wished 'to be free of the fetters that bind us in the preparation of certain laws'. An even sharper critic of the idea of codification within the National Liberal party was Otto Bähr, who emphasized that the main question at issue was not codification but the removal of constitutional constraints on the government's ability to respond to common needs as they arose. Comprehensive codes were, he said, 'always dubious'.[30]

If the National Liberals were divided about the merits of codification, some of their allies in other parties were even more sceptical. In 1867, the proposed extension of legislative competence had received strong support from Wächter and Carl Friedrich von Gerber, both of whom were keen to preserve the sovereignty of the individual states and opposed the National Liberals on most other issues. One National

[28] J. J. Sheehan, *German Liberalism in the Nineteenth Century* (Chicago/London, 1978), 137–40, 191–5.
[29] J. F. Harris, 'Eduard Lasker and Compromise Liberalism', *JMH* 42 (1970), pp. 342–60; G. Schmidt, 'Die Nationalliberalen—eine regierungsfähige Partei? Zur Problematik der inneren Reichsgründung 1870–1878', in G. A. Ritter (ed.), *Die deutschen Parteien vor 1918* (Cologne, 1973), 208–23.
[30] *SBRT*, 20 Mar. 1867, pp. 285 f. (Miquel); ibid., 28 Apr. 1869, pp. 652 f. and 31 May 1872, p. 623 (Lasker); ibid., 28 Apr. 1869, p. 650 (Planck); ibid., 19 Apr. 1869, p. 462 (Braun); ibid., 28 Apr. 1869, p. 647 (Bähr); cf. O. Bähr, *Der Rechtsstaat. Eine publicistische Skizze* (Kassel/Göttingen, 1864), 9.

Liberal commentator went so far as to describe Wächter as 'a fundamental enemy of the German state'.[31] Both men regarded a code as impossible in the foreseeable future; indeed, it was Gerber's disagreement with Miquel's views which had induced him to speak on the motion. Despite these disagreements, however, both men were willing to support the motion.[32]

The growth of active support for the Lasker-Miquel motions in groups to the right of the National Liberals accentuated such differences. In 1869, the Free Conservative Rudolf Friedenthal supported the motion but opposed a code which, he said, must in any case come from the government rather than the Reichstag. Dr Friedrich Schwarze, a Saxon who later joined the party, opposed the motion in 1869 on the grounds that he was 'against uniformity in those parts of the law which are not suitable because of their historical significance and historical development'. In 1871, he changed his mind and supported the motion in the belief that unified legislation would perform a valuable integrative role in the new empire. Once again, however, he emphasized his hostility to codification. Echoing the arguments of some of the National Liberals, he believed that the Lasker-Miquel motion was merely a way of 'giving us the constitutional power to legislate in those areas where a common need is evident'.[33]

The support of these men had to be won through careful wording and argument. One of the major objections to the motion concerned the inclusion of the organization of the courts in the legislative competence of the Reich. Windthorst reflected a view which went well beyond the Centre party when he claimed in 1871 that this part of the motion, more than any other, was an unjustifiable interference in the internal affairs of the states. He concluded that this was merely the most obvious sign that the supporters of the motion desired the annihilation of the states' sovereignty.[34] When the motion was next proposed in May 1872, the words 'including the organization of the courts' had been omitted.

---

[31] Hans Blum, *Auf dem Wege zur deutschen Einheit. Erinnerungen und Aufzeichnungen eines Mitkämpfers aus den Jahren 1867 bis 1870*, i (Jena, 1893), 16 f.; cf. *Carl Georg von Wächter. Leben eines deutschen Juristen dargestellt von O. v. Wächter* (Leipzig, 1881), 160 f.; 'Aus den Briefen Carl von Gerbers vom konstituierenden Reichstag des Norddeutschen Bundes', *Neues Archiv für Sächsische Geschichte*, 60 (1939), 224-79.

[32] *SBRT*, 20 Mar. 1867, p. 288 (Wächter); ibid., 20 Mar. 1867, pp. 290 f. (Gerber); 'Aus den Briefen Carl von Gerbers', p. 257.

[33] *SBRT*, 19 Apr. 1869, p. 452 (Friedenthal); ibid., 19 Apr. 1869, p. 469 and 9 Nov. 1871, p. 218 (Schwarze). Schwarze was at this time a member of the particularist *Bundes-Konstitutionelle Vereinigung* and joined the Liberal Imperial party in 1871.

[34] *SBRT*, 15 Nov. 1871, p. 280.

That change undoubtedly marked a turning-point in the attitude of the states and did much to assuage fears about the centralizing implications of the motion. As the Bavarian minister of justice, Johannes von Fäustle, said:

I cannot hide the fact that the connection between legal unity and the organization of the courts, which would have led in the last resort to the removal of the states' powers in judicial matters was the most dubious part of the former motion.[35]

However, the change had not been motivated by a desire to compromise with the Bundesrat[36] but rather by the concern to preserve the united front of members of the various 'middle parties' in support of the motion. Although Lasker did not divulge which of his allies had forced the change, it was in fact the Liberal Imperial party (*Liberale Reichspartei*). This small party, which was composed mainly of southern moderate liberals with a sprinkling of Saxons, had formed in March 1871 in an attempt to steer a middle course between the centralizing impulses of the National Liberals and the particularism so prevalent in the south.[37] The party's leader, Prince Chlodwig zu Hohenlohe-Schillingsfürst, stressed the necessity of maintaining the federal character of the constitution and opposed any constitutional change for the time being. Despite his hostility to constitutional change, however, he was prepared to support the extension of the competence of the Reich against what he called 'unjustified particularism'.

In November 1871 Hohenlohe's name was included in the list of proposers of the Lasker-Miquel motion, along with that of his party colleague, August von Bernuth. A party meeting on 29 October had, after much debate, agreed that Hohenlohe should take that course. In May 1872, however, the story was very different. There had evidently been some communication with the Bavarian government, for Hohenlohe made his continued support dependent on the omission of the clause

---

[35] *SBRT*, 29 May 1872, p. 601.

[36] As is suggested in W. Schubert, 'Franz von Kübel und Württembergs Stellung zur Erweiterung der Reichskompetenz für das gesamte bürgerliche Recht', *Zeitschrift für württembergische Landesgeschichte*, 36 (1977), 169 and H. Getz, *Die deutsche Rechtseinheit im 19. Jahrhundert als rechtspolitisches Problem* (Bonn, 1966), 160 f.

[37] On this party, see G. Fesse, 'Liberale Reichspartei', in D. Fricke *et al.*, *Die bürgerlichen Parteien in Deutschland*, ii (Berlin-GDR, 1970), 320 f.; G. Stoltenberg, *Der Deutsche Reichstag 1871-1873* (Düsseldorf, 1955), 31; and, above all, *Memoirs of Prince Chlodwig of Hohenlohe Schillingsfuerst*, ed. F. Curtius, ii (London, 1906), 38 ff.

relating to the organization of the courts. To his astonishment, Lasker agreed to modify the motion in line with these demands.[38] The support of the Liberal Imperial party was clearly important to Lasker, and it is not difficult to see why. Despite its weakness in numbers, the party was composed of extremely influential men. As a contemporary joke put it, it was 'the party of men who had been ministers and men who wanted to be'.[39] Its predominantly south German complexion and its support for a federal empire were useful counters to those critics who sought to associate legal unity with Prussian centralization. As Hohenlohe repeatedly stated, he was no friend of the 'unitary state'.[40] The National Liberals naturally made light of their concession, and claimed that the competence to legislate on judicial procedure covered the organization of the courts. In fact, the main battle on that issue still lay in the future.[41] The amendment to the motion at least separated the question of the states' control over the administration of justice from the broader question of the unification of the civil law. Although the National Liberals denied this, the amendment involved a real concession which contradicted the party's belief in the supremacy of the Reich in all spheres of the law. That Lasker was willing to give in so easily to a small, if influential, party when the majority for his motion was not in danger, provides clear evidence of the importance he attached to gaining the broadest possible support.

The arguments advanced by the supporters of the Lasker-Miquel motion thus revealed considerable disagreement about details. It was quite possible for contributors to the debate to accept the central National Liberal arguments—that the competence to legislate was inherent in the new state and that it would enhance national unity—while remaining divided on how legal unity might be achieved. As Miquel admitted in the Reichstag, there was little agreement about whether codification or special legislation was the best means of proceeding. Indeed, an important academic controversy on that point developed in the early 1870s, and the matter was still being debated

---

[38] *Memoirs*, ii. 64, 72. Hohenlohe's objection was based on the Bavarian King's opposition to this aspect of the motion.

[39] J. Ziekursch, *Politische Geschichte des neuen deutschen Kaiserreiches*, ii (Frankfurt, 1927), 219.

[40] See the draft speeches on this question in BA Koblenz, Hohenlohe-Schillingsfürst Papers 1330, fos. 4-27.

[41] Lasker, *SBRT*, 29 May 1872, p. 596; on this question in general, see W. Schubert, *Die deutsche Gerichtsverfassung (1869-1877)* (Frankfurt, 1980), 59-86, 406-22, 511-18, 616-741.

when events in Berlin settled the issue.[42] The wording of the motion, which, in contrast to the 1849 constitution, omitted any explicit commitment to codification, maximized the possibility of large majorities. By concentrating on the central powers of the new state and avoiding the divisive question of whether immediate codification was desirable, the National Liberals made possible a sustained alliance with the more conservative elements in the nationalist camp. Similar differences of opinion emerged on the question of which parts of the law, if any, were not suitable for national legislation. Some National Liberals, such as Planck, were willing to accept a long list of sections of the law which should be regulated locally. All the party's spokesmen emphasized that they had no intention of using the motion to level all local and regional peculiarities.[43] Once again, the motions' emphasis on the rights of the state, rather than the uses to which those rights would be put, prevented the emergence of serious divisions. It was the absence of such divisions which maintained the pressure on the Bundesrat.

This is not to suggest that individual supporters of the motion did not hint at the possibility of radical changes in the law. One speaker claimed that the motion was designed to permit the introduction of obligatory civil marriage, a point which Lasker rather half-heartedly denied. Lasker himself repeatedly stated his desire to extend the labour protection provisions of the Industrial Code (*Gewerbeordnung*) to disadvantaged rural workers.[44] Moreover, he had a stronger conception than most of his colleagues of the need to ensure popular participation in the framing of legislation. In terms reminiscent of Beseler in the 1840s, he declared that he was 'by no means a supporter of the method, which entrusts the preparation of a great code to a few theoreticians; I hold that procedure responsible for the fact that our codes contain so little popular law (*Volksrecht*).' That sort of language had lost none of the radical implications of the 1840s. To Lasker, special legislation was the best means of developing the capacity to produce a truly German code. Another National Liberal linked to the Germanist school, Karl Braun, agreed that special legislation was the best way of ensuring that

[42] *SBRT*, 29 May 1872, p. 606 (Miquel); H. Fitting, 'Ueber die Mittel zur Erzielung der Einheit des Privatrechtes im deutschen Reich', *AcP* 54 (1871), pp. 263–79; H. Bürkel, 'Ueber die Erzielung der Einheit des Privatrechts', *AcP* 55 (1872), pp. 145–66; P. von Roth, 'Unifikation und Codifikation', *Hauser's Zeitschrift für Reichs- und Landesrecht*, 1 (1873), 1–27.

[43] *SBRT*, 28 Apr. 1869, p. 650 (Planck); cf. ibid., 9 Nov. 1871, p. 208 (Miquel).

[44] *SBRT*, 9 Nov. 1871, p. 215 (Herz); ibid., 15 Nov. 1871, p. 285; ibid., 29 May 1872, p. 598; ibid., 31 May 1872, p. 622 (Lasker).

a future code corresponded to 'the real needs of the nation and not to the requirements of theoretical systems'.[45]

Such views were, however, isolated, and played a secondary role in the debates. National Liberals argued that social change had created an 'objective' need for reform of the law but they did not generally argue that legal unification should be used as an instrument of social reform. There could be little doubt that a majority of German jurists were cautious about radical legal change, and accepted Savigny's contention that successful legislation must be based on lengthy historical study. Supporters of the extension of competence tended to take this aspect of legislation for granted, and concentrated on the central issue of the rights of the new state. It was here that the liberal–conservative coalition found its real expression. The motion avoided any clear statement about how legal unity should be achieved and what the content of the new national legislation should be. Its supporters emphasized the constitutional powers of the new state and the historical development of the law. More radical figures like Lasker, who were still calling for popular participation in the preparation of the code in 1874,[46] were isolated as control passed to the Bundesrat—a development which was to have major consequences for the future.

The success of the National Liberals in mobilizing cross-party support for the Lasker–Miquel motion was the crucial factor in overcoming the opposition of the Bundesrat. By December 1872 the Bavarian minister of justice was reporting that he could see no end to the clamour for legal unity, which was constantly fuelled by 'the present political organism that is Germany with its close unity of the German race'. By the following February, he believed that:

there is very little more to be gained on the subject of the Lasker motion; on the other hand a great deal of political reputation and credit may be lost, which

[45] SBRT, 31 May 1872, p. 623 (Lasker); ibid., 31 May 1872, p. 630 f. (Braun); on Lasker's and Braun's links with the Germanist school, see G. Dilcher and B.-R. Kern, 'Die juristische Germanistik des 19. Jahrhunderts und die Fachtradition der deutschen Rechtsgeschichte', *ZRG GA* 101 (1984), pp. 28–9, and B.-R. Kern, 'Studien zur politischen Entwicklung des nassauischen Liberalen Karl Braun', *Nassauische Annalen*, 94 (1983), 185–201.

[46] See Lasker's speech to the Law Society of Berlin on 14 Feb. 1874, 'Einheitliches bürgerliches Recht: Eine Festrede Eduard Lasker's und eine Preisaufgabe', in G. Hirth (ed.), *Annalen des Deutschen Reichs*, 7 (1874), 743–8.

will be important in future activities in national affairs. I therefore agree that the issue should be solved as soon as possible in a nationalist direction.[47]

The Bavarian government and its counterparts in Württemberg and Saxony had hitherto formed the major obstacle to the passage of the motion. Together these states controlled fourteen votes in the Bundesrat, which under Article 78 of the constitution sufficed to block constitutional change. For the Lasker–Miquel motion to succeed, it was necessary at the very least to break this unity of the three largest middle states. The evidence suggests that late 1872 was the point at which southern politicians realized that they could not go on blocking the motion for ever. It is very doubtful that that change of view would have been accomplished so quickly without sustained pressure from the Reichstag.

The political manœuvres of late 1872 took place against a background of general agreement among the southern governments about the desirability of legal unity. In 1869, Saxony had instigated the establishment of a supreme commercial court for the North German Confederation. The Saxon government's view was that the great danger lay in the replacement of the Saxon Civil Code of 1863 by an inferior national code, 'which would probably be prepared in great haste'. Such fears had been heightened by the experience of the national penal code (*Strafgesetzbuch*) of 1870, which had aroused considerable opposition by reintroducing the death penalty in Saxony. The Prime Minister, Richard von Friesen, came to support the motion, however, when the value of a properly prepared code—i.e. one which was not dominated by Prussian bureaucrats—became clear.[48] At the 1871 Lawyers' Congress, Württemberg's leading statesman, Hermann von Mittnacht, declared his support for legal unity, although he carefully avoided prejudicing his government's position on the constitutional issue. As early as October 1870, Mittnacht had been reported as being favourably inclined to the extension of legislative competence, but not to the inclusion of the organization of the courts.[49] The Bavarian government was also widely believed to favour legal unity. Leading figures in Bavarian politics, such

[47] Fäustle to the King of Bavaria, 7 Dec. 1872, BHStA Munich, MA 76158; Fäustle to Mittnacht, 2 Feb. 1873, HStA Stuttgart, E 130a no. 819 (41).
[48] Paumgarten, report of 7 Nov. 1871, BHStA Munich, MA III 2844; Friesen, *Erinnerungen*, iii. 98, 266 ff.; cf. W. Schubert, 'Der Ausbau der Rechtseinheit unter dem Norddeutschen Bund: Zur Entstehung des Strafgesetzbuchs von 1870 unter besonderer Berücksichtigung des Strafensystems', in A. Buschmann et al. (eds.), *Festschrift für Rudolf Gmür zum 70. Geburtstag 28. Juli 1983* (Bielefeld, 1983), 157 ff.
[49] *Verhandlungen des Neunten Deutschen Juristentages*, iii (Berlin, 1871), 4 f.; Lasker to Forckenbeck, 6 Oct. 1870 (copy), ZStA Potsdam, Bennigsen Papers 98, fos. 18 ff.

as Fäustle and Baron von Lutz, were in frequent contact with liberal leaders, and Lasker evidently attempted to strike a bargain with the Bavarian government in late 1871. The negative stance of the Bavarians in December of that year therefore surprised many observers.[50]

Throughout the negotiations of 1871–72, Mittnacht and Fäustle continued to agree on the desirability of legal unity and on the inadequacy of the formulation of Article 4, No. 13 of the constitution. These men were anything other than particularists, as the Bavarian ambassador in Berlin discovered when he was reprimanded by his government for expressing negative opinions concerning the Reich.[51] Mittnacht's opposition to the Lasker–Miquel motion in December 1871 was related to the fear that a premature unification of the law would boost particularism in Württemberg and he was regarded with extreme suspicion by particularist elements in Stuttgart.[52] Despite National Liberal accusations that men like Mittnacht were particularists, the opposition of the southern monarchies was clearly not motivated by hostility to Berlin or to the 1871 settlement.

Opposition was in fact largely concerned with two related problems— the strength of particularist feeling in the south and the extent of the influence of the southern monarchies in Berlin. The governments of all three monarchies were placed in an awkward position, for the strength of particularist feeling made it necessary for them to distance themselves from Berlin despite their general support of the 1871 settlement. Conversely, Bismarck's policy towards these states (particularly Bavaria) was designed to minimize the impression of Prussian domination. This policy found expression both in the 1871 constitution with its famous special privileges (*Reservatrechte*) for Bavaria and in Prussia's policy in the Bundesrat. Both Mittnacht and the long-serving Bavarian ambassador in Berlin, Count Lerchenfeld, recorded their satisfaction with Bismarck's sensitivity to their states' wishes in the Bundesrat.[53] As Bismarck rightly saw, his best interests lay in maintaining men like Mittnacht and Lutz

---

[50] See *National-Zeitung*, 22 Aug. 1871; Spitzemberg, report of 24 Nov. 1871, HStA Stuttgart, E 73 no. 61, fos. 115 f.; Liebe, report of 19 Dec. 1871, NStA Wolfenbüttel 19 B Neu 464; Otto Elben to Lasker, 11 Dec. 1871, ZStA Potsdam, Lasker Papers 69, fo. 4.

[51] Ministry of State to Perglas, 18 Dec. 1871, BHStA Munich, MA III 2651.

[52] Rosenberg, report of 13 Dec. 1871, ZStA Merseburg, Rep. 81 Stuttgart I no. 71, fo. 99; Koenneritz, report of 11 Mar. 1872, StA Dresden, Gesandtschaft Stuttgart 14.

[53] H. v. Mittnacht, *Erinnerungen an Bismarck* (6th edn.; Stuttgart and Berlin, 1904), 20 ff.; Hugo Graf Lerchenfeld-Koefering, *Erinnerungen und Denkwürdigkeiten 1843 bis 1925* (Berlin, 1935), 192 f.

in power in the south, and the political longevity of these men was largely the result of Bismarck's support.[54] What that support entailed, however, was the necessity of avoiding policies which would make the domestic position of the southern governments untenable.

The southern governments' response to the Lasker–Miquel motion was closely connected with their domestic position. The Bavarian government faced particular difficulties, as the liberals had lost their majority in the chamber of deputies in May 1869 to the vociferously anti-Prussian Patriotic party. One observer reported that the Bavarian government's surprising opposition to the motion in December 1871 was the product of a new feeling in the state, which was 'anxious' and 'distrustful'.[55] The issue was complicated further by the start of the *Kulturkampf.* In October 1871, Lutz had inaugurated a new phase in the struggle with the Catholic Church in Bavaria by calling on the government in Berlin to introduce penal legislation against the priests, who constituted the backbone of the Patriotic organization. This move was understandable in view of the government's fears that it would be unable to push through legislation in the chamber in Munich against a Patriotic party, to which the *Kulturkampf* was giving new life.[56] It did however mean that the Lasker–Miquel motion was linked to a chain of events initiated by the struggle with the Roman Catholic Church.

To many Bavarians, the issue of the extension of legislative competence was above all connected with the central liberal demand for obligatory civil marriage. As the Bavarian minister of the interior, Sigmund von Pfeuffer, said, it was essential that the Lasker–Miquel motion was separated from this issue. The Bavarian prime minister Hegnenberg remarked that if Bavaria did not oppose the motion in Berlin, the suspicion would immediately spread that the government was attempting to use national legislation to attack the Catholic Church. The government was, he said, convinced of the inevitability of the motion's eventual acceptance. If Lutz opposed it in Berlin, it would be because of 'the peculiarity of our internal circumstances'. Brunswick's representative in Berlin, Friedrich August von Liebe, concurred in seeing the negative

---

[54] H.-O. Binder, *Reich und Einzelstaaten während der Kanzlerschaft Bismarcks 1871–1890. Eine Untersuchung zum Problem der bundesstaatlichen Organisation* (Tübingen, 1971), 173 ff.

[55] Liebe, report of 19 Dec. 1871, NStA Wolfenbüttel, 19 B Neu 464; on the Patriotic party, see F. Hartmannsgruber, *Die Bayerische Patriotenpartei 1868–1887* (Munich, 1986).

[56] On the Bavarian *Kulturkampf*, see D. Albrecht, 'Von der Reichsgründung bis zum Ende des ersten Weltkrieges (1871–1918)', in M. Spindler (ed.), *Handbuch der bayerischen Geschichte*, iv/1 (Munich, 1974), 321 ff.; Hartmannsgruber, *Patriotenpartei*, pp. 193 ff.

vote in December 1871 as being rooted in the particularism prevalent in the south. In June of the following year, Fäustle was in no doubt that 'in Bavaria, the chamber of deputies, public opinion, and the King were strongly opposed to any extension of competence'. Behind this public feeling lay a powerful combination of religious and particularist sentiments.[57]

The scale of the problems facing the Bavarian government at home was certainly not matched in any of the other southern states. The severity the Church-state conflict and the level of mobilization of opinion against the liberal ministerial oligarchy produced far more serious problems than in the other southern monarchies. Nevertheless, the freedom of manœuvre enjoyed by the ministry in Stuttgart was seriously limited by particularist opposition both within the chamber and at court. Mittnacht's position was, however, far stronger than that of his Bavarian counterpart, not least because of the strength of support for him in the chamber (based on the so-called Hölder group in the local National Liberal party) and because of the absence of a domestic Kulturkampf. The result of this situation was that while there were attempts to agitate against the 1871 settlement, the government never had to face a popular mobilization on the Bavarian scale. The absence of confessional strife meant that the Lasker-Miquel motion could be treated purely in terms of the constitutional rights of the state of Württemberg, without the religious overtones that it assumed in the Bavarian context.[58]

These local political conditions framed the responses of the southern governments to initiatives from the centre. As has been seen, men like Lutz and Mittnacht were dependent to a considerable extent on the support of Bismarck. The relationship was not, however, purely one-sided, for Bismarck could hope to derive considerable benefits from a productive alliance with men like Mittnacht in the Bundesrat. In the

[57] Pfeuffer to Marquardsen, 25 Oct. 1871, in J. Heyderhoff and P. Wentzscke, Deutscher Liberalismus im Zeitalter Bismarcks. Eine politische Briefsammlung, ii (Bonn, 1926), 30 f.; Koenneritz, report of 3 Nov. 1871, StA Dresden, Gesandtschaft München 79; Liebe, reports of 19 Dec. 1871 and 12 June 1872, NStA Wolfenbüttel, 19 B Neu 464; cf. Hartmannsgruber, Patriotenpartei, p. 373, and Rummel, Ministerium Lutz, pp. 38 ff.

[58] On particularism in Württemberg, see Krüger to the Bremen Senate, 11 Dec. 1871, StA Bremen, 2-M.6.b.3; G. H. Kleine, Der Württembergische Ministerpräsident Freiherr Herrmann von Mittnacht (1825-1909) (Stuttgart, 1969), 13. On the consolidation of pro-governmental forces in the Chamber, see Kleine, Mittnacht, pp. 30 ff. and Langewiesche (ed.), Tagebuch Julius Hölders, pp. 12-29. On the lack of a home-grown Kulturkampf, see D. Blackbourn, Class, Religion and Local Politics in Wilhelmine Germany. The Centre Party in Württenberg before 1914 (New Haven/London, 1980), 62, 75.

context of the confrontation between liberal policies of state-building and particularism, a good working relationship with the southern monarchies in the Bundesrat was Bismarck's best hope of combating particularism without becoming completely dependent on the liberal parties in the Reichstag. To this should be added Bismarck's increasingly close personal relationship with Mittnacht, despite occasional lapses when Mittnacht went too far in 'beating the particularist drum'.[59]

The southern governments spent much of 1871–2 groping towards a coherent policy *vis-à-vis* Berlin. They quickly realized that their position in Berlin was strong only to the extent that they were united. By September 1871, Friesen was placing considerable emphasis on diplomatic links between the three monarchies, and in December of that year the Württemberg ambassador in Berlin was ordered to cultivate good relations with Bavaria and Saxony.[60] The main problem lay with the understandable propensity of some members of the Bavarian government to seek solutions to their domestic problems through unilateral contacts with Bismarck, and in December 1871 the Saxon ambassador in Munich called for further pressure on the Bavarian prime minister to prevent 'the gravitation of individual Bavarian ministers towards Berlin'.[61] But this approach to politics made sense only in defensive terms. The southern monarchies' fourteen votes could and did block constitutional change, and a competent observer in the Bundesrat considered that the opposition to the Lasker–Miquel motion in December 1871 was based on the monarchies' need to stick together 'as only in that way did Article 78 of the constitution have any meaning for [them]'.[62] That was, however, hardly an adequate basis for positive participation in national politics. That desire for a greater degree of real influence on events in Berlin came to be the cornerstone of Mittnacht's and Fäustle's policy towards the Lasker–Miquel motion in 1872.

It was also important that the debates concerning the Reich's legislative competence came at a time when current procedures for the

[59] See Lerchenfeld, *Erinnerungen*, p. 203; the quotation is taken fom a comment by Fäustle in Mar. 1873, cited in Binder, *Reich und Einzelstaaten während der Kanzlerschaft Bismarcks, 1871–1890. Eine Untersuchung zum Problem der bundesstaatlichen Organisation* (Tübingen, 1971), 61 f. For Government inspired press attacks on Mittnacht, see Spitzemberg, report of 4 June 1872, HStA Stuttgart, E 74 I no. 26 A II, 5.

[60] Paumgarten, report of 2 Sept. 1871, BHStA Munich, MA III 2844; H. Fenske, 'Reich, Bundesrat und Einzelstaaten 1867 bis 1914. Ein Literaturbericht', *Der Staat*, 13 (1974), 269.

[61] Koenneritz, report of 2 Dec. 1871, StA Dresden, Gesandtschaft München 79; cf. Binder, *Reich und Einzelstaaten*, pp. 39 f.

[62] Krüger to the Bremen Senate, 11 Dec. 1871, StA Bremen, 2-M.6.b.3.

preparation of laws were already the subject of close scrutiny as a result of the codes of civil and criminal procedure and of court organization. By early 1872, Mittnacht was complaining that the Prussian minister of justice, Adolf Leonhardt, had failed to give Württemberg a great enough role in the preparation of legislation,[63] and in April and May, Fäustle and he developed a full-scale attack on current legislative practices. First in the Bundesrat and then in the Reichstag, Mittnacht and Fäustle set out the position which was to determine much of the future of the Civil Code. The Lasker–Miquel motion correctly pointed to the impracticability of the constitution in the long term, but its formulation contained great dangers even if the question of the organization of the courts were excluded. The central point was the failure to distinguish between codification and special legislation. Both ministers emphasized that *ad hoc* legislation, as proposed by several of the motion's supporters in the Reichstag, would merely increase the confusion in the present legal system. Mittnacht, on the other hand, concentrated on the danger that one state (obviously Prussia) would impose its own code on the nation without the effective participation of the other states. A complicated piece of legislation such as a civil code, which would have a profound effect on the individual states, required the participation of those states from the start.[64]

These complaints were the product of the legislative procedures adopted by the Reich's government. Even the liberal *National-Zeitung* admitted that Mittnacht's views had a certain justice, although it went on to attack him for being hostile to the Reich. Bavarian opposition was predictably put down to 'ultramontanism'.[65] Such attacks missed the point (perhaps deliberately), for Mittnacht was attempting to defuse particularist opposition in Stuttgart by defending Württemberg's 'justified' interests in Berlin. The normal method of preparing national legislation was that draft laws were prepared in the Chancellor's office, which normally relied on the relevant Prussian ministries to do the work. In 1872, the Prussian ministry of justice was in the process of preparing drafts of the procedural and organizational codes. The Criminal Code of 1870 was prepared in much the same way, as was the

[63] Rosenberg, report of 19 Jan. 1872, ZStA Merseburg, Rep. 81 Stuttgart 1 no. 74, fos. 11 ff.

[64] See the Bundesrat protocol for 9 Apr. 1872, reprinted in Schubert, *Materialien*, pp. 136 ff.; *SBRT*, 29 May 1872, pp. 601 ff. (Fäustle) and 610 ff. (Mittnacht).

[65] *National-Zeitung*, 1 June 1872, cited in H. v. Poschinger, *Fürst Bismarck und der Bundesrat*, ii (Stuttgart, 1898), 149 n. 1; Perglas, report of 1 June 1872, BHStA Munich, MA III 2652.

codification of the law of bankruptcy, where few essential changes were made to the Prussian law of 1855.[66] Work on all these codes had begun in the late 1860s, when Prussia had been powerful enough to overcome opposition to its legislative practices within the North German Confederation. A standard codification practice had thus emerged, which the southern states became determined to resist. This was all the more the case with a civil code, whose necessary complexity would mean that participation from the start was the only type of participation worth having. Mittnacht was well aware that the Bundesrat would have little effective power of amendment if presented with a completed code prepared by Prussia. That awareness explains his statement to Lasker that the south required 'guarantees of real, *not just apparent* participation in [the preparation of] national legislation'.[67]

There was in fact a very real danger that the Prussian government might go ahead on its own. In late 1871, a leading official in the Prussian ministry of justice, Franz Förster, called for a Prussian civil code, both to deal with the legal uncertainties introduced by the expansion of Prussia after 1866 and, more importantly, to prepare the way for an eventual German code. As he wrote: 'A Prussian civil code would undoubtedly soon be extended to the whole of Germany and the work can thus be started without prejudicing future Reich legislation and without leading to the isolation of Prussia in Germany.'[68] This memorandum was prepared without any communication with the other states, and was completed before the introduction of the Lasker-Miquel motion in November 1871. It seems very likely that the Prussian minister of justice was attempting to force the southern monarchies to accept the Lasker-Miquel motion,[69] and certainly other elements in the Prussian bureaucracy were keen to press ahead. That keenness may well explain Rudolf Delbrück's unexpected insistence that the relevant committee of the Bundesrat discuss the matter before Christmas, and the strong support for the motion from Prussia in the discussions.[70]

---

[66] See P. Landau, 'Die Reichsjustizgesetze und die deutsche Rechtseinheit', *Vom Reichsjustizamt zum Bundesministerium der Justiz. Festschrift zum 100 jährigen Gründungstag des Reichsjustizamts am 1. Januar 1877* (Cologne, 1977), 168 ff.; Schubert, 'Der Ausbau der Rechtseinheit unter dem Norddeutschen Bund', pp. 149-89; J. Thieme, 'Zur Entstehung der Konkursordnung', in *Einhundert Jahre Konkursordnung* (Cologne, 1977), 51 ff.; Schubert, *Gerichtsverfassung*, pp. 65-83.

[67] Mittnacht to Lasker, 19 May 1872, HStA Stuttgart, E 130a no. 819, fo. 16.

[68] GStA Dahlem, Rep. 84a 11772, fos. 13-26 (quotation, fo. 24). The archival material is partially reprinted in W. Schubert, 'Preussens Pläne zur Vereinheitlichung des Zivilrechts nach der Reichsgründung', *ZRG GA* 96 (1979), pp. 243-56.

[69] Schubert, 'Preussens Pläne', p. 245.

[70] Krüger, report of 9 Dec. 1871, AH Lübeck, 13 w I vol. A, fasc. 6.

It was this centralizing impulse on the part of certain elements in the Prussian bureaucracy that the southern governments really feared. In May 1870, Leonhardt had spoken ominously in the Prussian Crown Council of the role that legal unity would play in 'the expansion of Prussia's sphere of power'. As Richard von Friesen later wrote:

in many circles and especially among many senior Prussian bureaucrats there was great hostility to the admittedly difficult and time-consuming work involved [in codification], and it almost seemed as if the campaign for constitutional change was for some people linked more to the desire to withdraw some of those rights which were left to the individual states than to the intention of creating legal unity for the whole German people.[71]

However, the centralizers in the Prussian bureaucracy discovered that they had a formidable opponent in Berlin—the Chancellor himself. Direct evidence about Bismarck's attitude to legal unity is difficult to obtain. Adalbert Falk claimed that the Chancellor was sceptical about the contribution it would make to the national cause and thought the organization of the army and the attitude of the sovereign princes much more important.[72] There is no evidence that Bismarck sought to divert the Reichstag away from the Lasker–Miquel motion, a course of action which would in any case inevitably have failed. There is evidence, however, that from early 1872 he was keen to encourage the more powerful states in the Bundesrat to oppose National Liberal attempts to introduce further centralizing measures. In February 1872 he told Württemberg's ambassador in Berlin that

his [Bismarck's] position made it difficult to combat the unitarist tendencies and the liberal parties on which he had to rely on the German question. The main task of the federal states was to strengthen the monarchical principle in the individual states. Thus resistance to the unitarists must come from that quarter, as must the strengthening of the imperial constitution, whose most powerful bulwark was the Bundesrat.

At the same time, Bismarck was placing articles in the press extolling the contributions of men like Lutz and Mittnacht to the national cause.[73]

---

[71] Leonhardt, cited in Schubert, 'Der Ausbau der Rechtseinheit unter dem Norddeutschen Bund', p. 182; Friesen, *Erinnerungen*, iii. 267.

[72] ZStA Potsdam, Rep. 92 Falk no. 92 vol. x, fo. 3145; but see Bismarck's apparently more favourable remarks in H. v. Poschinger, *Fürst Bismarck und die Parlamentarier*, i (Breslau, 1894), 50.

[73] Spitzemberg to Wächter, 25 Feb. 1872, reprinted in Binder, *Reich und Einzelstaaten*, p. 193; M. Busch, *Bismarck. Some Secret Pages of His History*, ii (London, 1898), 148 f.

Although direct evidence for this is lacking, it is probable that Bismarck's concern for the preservation of good relations with the larger southern states was the reason for the failure of the centralizing officials in the Prussian government. Fäustle reported in April 1873 that Bismarck agreed with his complaints about the secrecy surrounding the drafting of legislation, which made active participation by the Bundesrat impossible. At the same time, Rudolf Delbrück deliberately avoided overriding Bavaria's views when the Lasker–Miquel motion finally gained the required majority in the Bundesrat in April 1873.[74] In adopting this line, Bismarck's goal was twofold: to defend the position of relatively friendly southern governments against local particularists; and to counterbalance his parliamentary dependence on the National Liberals with a separate power-base in the Bundesrat. Both ends were admirably served by the careful encouragement of the policies developed by Bavaria and Württemberg in 1872. As Bismarck was well aware, federalism was the best defence against parliamentarization. In the case of the unification of the civil law, the National Liberal motion was eventually carried but the parliamentary parties were effectively excluded from the vital first stages of the preparation of the Code.

In the Reichstag debate of 29–31 May 1872, both Fäustle and Mittnacht had indicated that they favoured codification as a means of unifying the legal system and that they were very hostile to special legislation. This argument had two strengths. On the one hand, it held out an olive branch to the Reichstag majority, which was divided about how best to unify the legal system. On the other, it gave the southern governments a strong argument against local particularists. This was above all true in Bavaria, a state which had spent much of the nineteenth century unsuccessfully attempting to produce a civil code. Men like Fäustle were well aware of the possibility that central legislation might introduce badly needed reforms in the Bavarian legal system. As he told the King in December 1872, it seemed quite possible that legal unity might, if anything strengthen, Bavaria. But that happy conclusion would only be possible if the acceptance of the Lasker–Miquel motion led to a carefully prepared code.[75]

Above all else, a commitment to codification implied that the establishment of legal unity would be a lengthy process, by the end of which the liberals' dominance of the Reichstag might have ended. The

---

[74] Fäustle to the King of Bavaria, 2 Apr. 1873, BHStA Munich, MA 76158.
[75] Fäustle to the King, 7 Dec. 1872, BHStA Munich, MA 76158.

problem with special legislation was that it could be completed much
more quickly, thus opening up the possibility that the extension
of competence might be used to effect radical reforms in the civil
law. This possibility was quite obvious to the opponents of the
motion, who saw in Lasker's ambivalence about codification a desire to
introduce 'modern ideas' into the legal system. The Catholic politician Bishop Ketteler went so far as to say that the introduction of
National Liberal policies into the civil law would be tantamount to a
revolution.[76]

Moreover, developments in Prussian legislation provided cause for
concern. The Prussian legislation of 5 May 1872 relating to the
acquisition of landed property, the establishment of a land register, and
the formulation of mortgage laws meant that the land law of Germany's
largest state had progressed considerably further in a liberal direction
than was the case in the south. In addition, liberal publicists were
openly applauding Prussia as the source of 'organic laws', and tended
to emphasize that Prussian legislation was an important step towards
legal unity.[77] To that extent, the choice between codification and special
legislation was not merely a question of legislative technique or even of
the states' right to participate, although the debates tended to be framed
in those terms. Special legislation meant the possibility of liberal reform
through the imposition of Prussian institutions with the support of the
Reichstag majority. To that extent, the fear of 'Prussianization' and of
'modern ideas' were two sides of the same coin. These dangers were
best averted by the preparation of a code in which the historical
development of the legal systems of the south was given its full weight.
Decisions about procedure thus implicitly involved choices about the
content of the future code.[78]

In Württemberg, Mittnacht and his advisers had come to similar
conclusions, and by 24 January 1873 Mittnacht was ready to support
the motion. Following the suggestion of one of his advisers and after
securing an agreement with the local National Liberals, he called upon
the state governments to take the initiative—a move which enabled him

---

[76] W. E. Frhr. v. Ketteler, *Die Centrums-Fraction auf dem ersten Deutschen Reichstag*
(2nd edn., Mainz, 1872), 104; cf. Windthorst's comments on 'modern ideas' in *SBRT*,
15 Nov. 1871, pp. 282 f.

[77] *National-Zeitung*, 1 June 1872; W. Endemann, 'Uebersicht der Thätigkeit der
Justizgesetzgebung im Norddeutschen Bunde während des Jahres 1869', in Hirth (ed.),
Annalen, 3 (1870), p. 18.

[78] On the connection between special legislation and liberal reforms, see Schubert,
'Franz von Kübel', pp. 179 ff.

to force Bavaria's hand on the issue.[79] With that, the deadlock in the Bundesrat was effectively broken, and by April Delbrück was able to announce the imminent acceptance of the Lasker-Miquel motion.[80]

The breakthrough in the Bundesrat was predictably regarded as a great triumph by the National Liberals and their allies. Nevertheless, the way in which this National Liberal success was achieved reveals the limitations on the party's power to force the hand of the Bundesrat in the early 1870s. It was the size of the repeated Reichstag majorities that persuaded the southern states that there was little to be gained and much to be lost by continuing to oppose the measure. In fact there was probably a majority within the German political nation in favour of legal unification, and the main difficulty concerned two obviously connected questions: how to maintain the rights of the individual states; and how to prevent the process of legal unification becoming a means of introducing radical, liberal reforms ('modern ideas') into the legal system. The political developments of 1872-3, which ensured the dominance of the Bundesrat in the preparation of the future code on the basis of an historically determined conception of legislation derived from Savigny, neatly produced the solution to both aspects of the problem.

In a more general context, these debates revealed much about the politics of the 1870s. The *Kulturkampf* was very much part of the battles over the legitimacy of the 1871 settlement and, in particular, the struggle against particularism. This aspect explains Bismarck's willingness to pursue anti-Catholic policies, which had the potential danger of leaving him dependent on the National Liberals and their parliamentary allies. Policies such as the *Kulturkampf* and the reform of Prussian local government in the early 1870s have rightly been linked to the National Liberals' desire for gradual parliamentarization in that

---

[79] See Schubert, *Materialien*, pp. 146 f.; Gasser, report of 1 Feb. 1873, BHStA Munich, MA III 3033; cf. Binder, *Reich und Einzelstaaten*, p. 61. While agreeing in principle, Fäustle had wished to defer a formal decision until the question of the organization of the courts was settled. Mittnacht had agreed to this in Oct. 1872, though he did not really regard the issue as central, since Württemberg did not possess its own supreme court whereas Bavaria did—see Schubert, *Materialien*, p. 142. It is true that Mittnacht had consulted Fäustle before making his declaration in Jan.; see Rosenberg, report of 25 Jan. 1873, ZStA Merseburg, Rep. 81 Stuttgart no. 75, fo. 79. Nevertheless, it seems clear that the declaration marked the end of Mittnacht's willingness to hold back in the interests of his Bavarian colleague.

[80] *SBRT*, 2 Apr. 1873, p. 169. The Bundesrat finally accepted the motion on 12 Dec. 1873; the delay was caused by the Bavarian government's desire to submit the motion to a vote in the chamber of deputies in Munich in the autumn.

they consolidated the party's status as a government party.[81] In a local and regional context, modern research tends to suggest that the *Kulturkampf* was a defensive response by National Liberal élites to the threat of popular mobilization from below.[82] Bismarck's policies from 1872 make quite clear his awareness that a continued centralization of sovereignty in Berlin would deliver him into the hands of the National Liberals. Conversely, the promotion of a moderate, non-particularist federalism was his best chance of avoiding the possibility of a gradual parliamentarization of the political system. That explains his encouragement of the southern states' resistance in the spring of 1872, his hostility to the establishment of independent Reich ministries in the mid-70s, his desire to slow down the *Kulturkampf* after the 1874 election, and his acceptance of a distinctly federalist solution to the Reich's financial problems through the so-called Franckenstein clause in 1879. A central element of Bismarck's system in the 1870s was thus the connection between federalism and anti-parliamentarism.[83]

The seeming harmony of aims between Bismarck and the southern statesmen should not, however, divert attention from basic differences in attitude. Bismarck's approach to the question of federalism was fundamentally instrumentalist: it was useful as a counterweight to the claims of the Reichstag in defence of what Bismarck termed 'the monarchical principle'. Men like Mittnacht were, in contrast, motivated by the desire to secure for the larger states an influence in national affairs commensurate with their size. That priority lies behind Mittnacht's preference for a parliamentary upper chamber in place of the Bundesrat, and the tendency of states such as Bavaria to turn away from activity in the Bundesrat and secure their interests through direct diplomatic contacts with the Prussian government. The consequence of this approach was the devaluation of the Bundesrat as a separate organ of government and the limitation of a meaningful federalism to Prussia and the larger states.[84]

[81] See especially Schmidt, 'Die Nationalliberalen—eine regierungsfähige Partei?', pp. 213 f.

[82] See above all L. Gall, 'Die partei- und sozialgeschichtliche Problematik des Kulturkampfes', *Zeitschrift für die Geschichte des Oberrheins*, 113 (1966), 151–96; M. L. Anderson, 'The Kulturkampf and the Course of German History', *CEH*, 19 (1986), pp. 82–115.

[83] See above all M. Rauh, *Föderalismus und Parlamentarismus im Wilhelminischen Reich* (Düsseldorf, 1973), 48 f., 65 f., and the important, extremely subtle argument of G. G. Windell, 'The Bismarckian Empire as a Federal State, 1866–1880: A Chronicle of Failure', *CEH* 2 (1969), pp. 291–311, esp. 299–306.

[84] On Mittnacht's preference for an upper house, see J. Jolly to H. Baumgarten,

As will be seen below, these political developments had important consequences for the future codification of law in imperial Germany. The Lasker–Miquel motion was accepted, but in a form which led to the exclusion of the Reichstag parties from the process of preparation, at least in the important early stages. Württemberg's seizure of the initiative ensured that the codification would proceed along the lines suggested by Savigny—i.e. that the Code would aim to be a systematic compilation of the existing legal systems of the German states. In this way, Conservative and Centre party fears that codification would mean the revolutionizing of the legal system through the introduction of 'modern ideas' proved to be groundless. By 1884, even Windthorst was prepared to praise the work of the codifiers and admit that his earlier fears had been unfounded.[85]

The fact that the National Liberals were willing to accept this type of codification—and indeed to regard it as a triumph—seems to say a great deal about the nature of German liberalism in the 1870s. In part it was a consequence of the widespread liberal acceptance of Savigny's theory of the origins of law (the *Volksgeistlehre*), even if, as we have seen, that acceptance coexisted somewhat uneasily with other doctrines which emphasized the will of the state. Moreover, many liberals tended to argue that a successful code must reflect the recent rapid changes in the social and economic structure of Germany. That idea lay behind Lasker's unsuccessful demand in February 1874 for the participation of commercial interests and the representatives of the people in the preparation of the code. As Lasker and others made clear during these debates, acceptance of the historical theory of law was not necessarily equivalent to a desire to maintain the legal status quo.

On the other hand, the parliamentary coalition in support of the Lasker–Miquel motion was a liberal/conservative alliance, which concentrated on the assertion of the rights of the new state against the forces of particularism. In many areas of the Reich, especially outside pre-1866 Prussia, that parliamentary coalition corresponded very closely to the alliance of political groups which made up the National Liberal power-base. The proponents of legal unity deliberately sought to play down differences within the coalition, for example over whether codification was really the best way forward. The National Liberals'

23 Feb. 1872, reprinted in W. P. Fuchs (ed.), *Grossherzog Friedrich I. von Baden und die Reichspolitik 1871–1907*, i (Stuttgart 1968), 79 f.; Rauh, *Föderalismus und Parlamentarismus*, pp. 52–5, 91 ff.; cf. Binder, *Reich und Einzelstaaten*, pp. 63 f., 188.

[85] *SBRT*, 12 Dec. 1884, p. 329.

greatest fear was that they might be supplanted by a Conservative/Centre party alliance on a particularist basis.[86] This possibility, which was almost certainly exaggerated in the early years of the Reich, dictated an approach to legal unification which emphasized its state-forming aspects over concrete proposals for liberal reform.

National Liberal reticence about pressing for concrete reforms was not, however, merely the product of its heterogeneous political composition or its acceptance of certain features of conservative legal ideology. As has been seen, the political situation in the south, especially in Bavaria, was extremely delicate. In the winter of 1871–2, there was a distinct possibility that moves to extend the constitution would lead to further clerical and particularist attacks on the essentially pro-Berlin, moderately liberal, southern governments.[87] For all their attacks on the 'particularism' of these Governments, the National Liberals were well aware of the problem. The great danger was that, by pursuing the desired extension of sovereignty, the party might well make the position of its allies in Munich untenable, leading to the fall of the ministry. As Lasker had recognized in 1870, while the population in Württemberg was largely 'secure', in Bavaria the liberal cause depended far more on the government.[88] These broader considerations, which were more a reflection of the liberal movement's vulnerability to hostile popular mobilizations than of weakness in commitment to the 'true' cause of liberalism, dictated prudence in the campaign for legal unity. But it was that arguably necessary prudence which opened the way for the preparation of a Code with conservative implications—a code which, in its emphasis on state formation and legal systematization, bore the unmistakable imprint of the early 1870s.

[86] On this fear, see M. Stürmer, *Regierung und Reichstag im Bismarckstaat* (Düsseldorf, 1974), 52.

[87] See *Allgemeine Zeitung*, 22 Dec. 1871.

[88] Lasker to Bennigsen, 24 Oct. 1870, ZStA Potsdam, Bennigsen Papers 98, fos. 21 f.

4.

The Approach to Codification, 1874–1888

THE Bundesrat's final acceptance of the Lasker-Miquel motion in December 1873 began a new period in the history of the Civil Code. It had been agreed that work on a code should be started immediately, but beyond that there had been remarkably little discussion about how the task should be approached. Proposals did exist within the Prussian government—connected with the ideas of men like Förster—but they aroused the southern states' fears of the twin dangers of 'modern ideas' and 'Prussianization'. The policies of the southern states in the decisive early months of 1874 were dictated by their determination to avoid such dangers. An important feature of these discussions was once again the realization that the method by which a code was prepared would be vital in determining what sort of code was prepared.

At the end of December 1873, the liberal *National-Zeitung* published an anonymous article which argued that a code would fail unless it was entrusted to a single individual. Any commission appointed to do the job would inevitably be a surrender to particularism, and would merely cover up the fact that the work was being delayed for as long as possible. The southern states predictably suspected that the article was officially inspired. Such a plan would work in Prussia's interests, as it was inconceivable that a single editor would not be a Prussian. Furthermore, the article concluded with favourable comments on the successes of the Prussian ministry of justice in the preparation of other pieces of legislation. To make matters worse, Under-Secretary Heinrich Friedberg of the Prussian ministry of justice suggested to the Bavarian ambassador that such ideas had certain merits, and something of a press campaign on their behalf seems to have taken place in early January.[1] From the very start, then, the southern states were forced to fight for the representation of their interests in the preparation of the Code—the

---

[1] *National-Zeitung*, 31 Dec. 1873; Perglas to Pfretzschner, 31 Dec. 1873 and 10 Jan. 1874, BHStA Munich, MA 76158 and MJu 16107.

issue which more than anything else had motivated their earlier opposition to the Lasker-Miquel motion.

The solution to this problem was eventually found in the appointment of a five-man Vorkommission in February 1874, whose task was to lay down guide-lines for a future codifying commission.[2] The appointment of a Vorkommission had originally been opposed by Württemberg and Saxony, both of which possessed their own civil codes.[3] Württemberg in particular also feared that such a body would too easily be dominated by Prussia, and that no larger commission would subsequently be appointed. Bavaria, on the other hand, was well pleased with the proposal, which ensured that the three southern monarchies held a numerical majority.[4]

The body which produced the plan for the codification was thus determined by the political relationships between Prussia and the larger southern states. As Mecklenburg's ambassador in Berlin reported, it was hoped that the Bavarian and Saxon representatives would hold the markedly 'unitarist' tendencies of the chairman, Levin Goldschmidt, in check, and oppose any attempt to entrust Goldschmidt with the sole responsibility for the preparation of the work.[5] In fact, despite Goldschmidt's claims that the particularist cause espoused by the representatives of Bavaria and Württemberg had achieved very little,[6] it appears that the southern monarchies had a considerable influence on the proceedings. In particular, Franz von Kübel (Württemberg's representative)[7] successfully pushed through a proposal that the preparation of the Code be divided between a number of different editors, against the wishes of Goldschmidt and the Prussian representative. On the question of the size of the proposed commission, Kübel and the Bavarian representative wished to restrict the membership to seven or

---

[2] See H.-P. Benöhr, 'Die Grundlage des BGB: Das Gutachten der Vorkommission von 1874', *JuS* 17 (1977), pp. 79-82; Schubert, *Materialien*, pp. 33 ff.

[3] M. Behn, 'Das Generalbericht der Badischen Kommission zur Begutachtung des Entwurfs eines Bürgerlichen Gesetzbuches für das Deutsche Reich: Ein Beitrag zur Mitwirkung der Bundesländer bei der Ausarbeitung des Bürgerlichen Gesetzbuches', *ZRG GA* 99 (1982), pp. 122 f.

[4] Krüger, report of 8 Feb. 1874, AH Lübeck, Senatsakten VIII 3a/1; Fäustle to the King, 8 Feb. 1874, BHStA Munich, MA 76 707/1. The Vorkommission included one representative each of the Reich, Prussia, Bavaria, Württemberg, and Saxony.

[5] Bülow, report of 8 Feb. 1874, StA Schwerin, Ministerium der Justiz 282, fo. 48.

[6] Goldschmidt to Jolly, 9 Apr. 1874, cited in Schubert, *Materialien*, p. 35 n. 42.

[7] On Kübel, see W. Schubert, 'Franz von Kübel und Württembergs Stellung zur Erweiterung der Reichskompetenz für das gesamte bürgerliche Recht', *Zeitschrift für württembergische Landesgeschichte*, 36 (1977). 167-98.

even five in order to minimize Prussia's influence. Here they lost the support of Saxony, and a figure of nine was agreed upon after Kübel changed sides on the question. Finally, Kübel scored a crucial success on the question of whether the code should stick close to existing law. According to Kübel, Goldschmidt wanted to see everything completely reformed, a claim which is difficult to evaluate given the fact that there are no surviving minutes of the meetings of the Vorkommission.[8]

The report of the Vorkommission was a document of the utmost importance in determining the way in which the task of codification was approached. In line with the precepts of the Historical School, the report proposed that

the future code will only correspond to the justified wishes of the German nation, the interests of all the individual states, the requirements of jurisprudence and legal practice, if it sticks to the proven common law institutions and axioms of the existing civil-law systems in Germany.

In cases of divergences between such systems, decisions were to be taken in the first place on the basis of what was deemed necessary and in the second place in line with jurisprudential logic. The report then went on to emphasize that the preparation of a code, which met the needs of the present, must be linked to a careful consideration of both existing law and 'particular local circumstances'.[9]

The final phrase relating to local circumstances had been added (probably on Kübel's insistence) to Goldschmidt's draft report, and was obviously intended to ensure that the process of producing a systematic compilation of existing law should not become a means of overriding the special interests of the southern states. This was especially true of such areas of the law as the law of property in marriage, where the extent of regional diversity led the Vorkommission to suggest the inclusion of two or three different systems. The Vorkommission insisted that the Code should cover the whole of the civil law, but nevertheless advised that certain exceptions should be made. Commercial and mining law should be unified on a national basis, but their special nature made

[8] Kübel to Mittnacht, 28 Mar. and 18 Apr. 1874, HStA Stuttgart, E 130a no. 819 (62) and (65); Neumaier to Fäustle, 14 Apr. 1874, BHStA Munich, MJu 16107. A comparison of Goldschmidt's draft report and the final version of the Vorkommission's report suggests that Kübel's changes were both editorial and substantive. The report is reprinted with footnotes indicating divergences from Goldschmidt's draft in Schubert, *Materialien*, pp. 170–85. This does not, however, inform us about victories Kübel may have won during the preceding debates.

[9] Schubert, *Materialien*, p. 170.

them unsuitable for inclusion in the Civil Code. Those parts of the law which dealt with the antiquated relics of feudalism—for example, hereditary tenures and ground rents (*Erbpacht* and *Erbzins*) or the family entail (*Fideikommiss*)—should be left to the individual states. Finally, the Vorkommission recognized that certain areas of the law transcended the boundary between public and private law and thus might not be suitable for codification.[10] The Vorkommission's report thus had a number of significant features. The first was the concentration on existing law and on the respect for local interests, neither of which was particularly surprising given the political and intellectual background in the 1870s. Kübel was surely stating a near-truism when he wrote: 'A codification should not seek to create new law, but rather to bring together in a manner corresponding to the current state of jurisprudence existing law as it has developed in Germany.'[11] Moreover, the debates on the Lasker-Miquel motion had been dominated by Württemberg's determination to secure a greater influence for herself; the commitment to respect local circumstances was part of that strategy, and found its justification in the widely accepted historical theory of law. But a striking feature of the report was the way in which it studiously avoided binding the hands of the future codifiers and, in particular, omitted any consideration of the material content of the Code. The process of codification was seen primarily in formal and technical terms, and the main problem seemed to be that of reconciling the regional diversity of German legal development and the need for systematic unity. As Leonhardt put it, the Vorkommission had 'principally to consider the formal side of the codification'.[12] And, perhaps most important of all, there was a clear assumption that the German common law would form the basis of the commission's work. Any other mode of procedure—such as following Heinrich von Dernburg's suggestion that the Prussian *Allgemeines Landrecht* should be made the basis of the Code[13]—would, for obvious reasons, have been unacceptable to the southern states. But this set of decisions, which emphasized the formal and technical aspects of the unification of German legal system, was to have extremely important consequences for the future. Dernburg's pessimistic prediction that the work of the

---

[10] Here the Vorkommission was thinking of such matters as the law relating to hunting, forests, the use of rivers, building, and domestic servants.

[11] Quoted in Schubert, 'Franz von Kübel', p. 186.

[12] Quoted in Benöhr, 'Die Grundlage des BGB', p. 80.

[13] F. Frensdorff, *Gottlieb Planck, deutscher Jurist und Politiker* (Berlin, 1914), 311 f.

codifiers was unlikely to be acceptable because 'something which affected the social conditions of the nation most profoundly [could] not be dealt with in purely formal terms'[14] was to find considerable support in the 1890s. This concentration on formal questions has often been considered to be responsible for the subsequent failure of the codifiers to address the question of social reform.[15] That view is, in some ways, correct; as will be seen, the demand for systematic coherence and precision did frustrate many of the reformist demands which were aired in the 1880s and 1890s. But the reluctance of the Vorkommission to lay down strict guide-lines on questions of detail also gave the codifiers considerable freedom of manœuvre. On some matters they even felt able to overturn specific recommendations by the Vorkommission. However, the lack of parliamentary influence on the selection of the codifying commission and on the way it approached its work was probably far more important in this regard. The formation of the commission and its approach to its work will be the subject of the rest of this chapter.

The Vorkommission's report was submitted to the Bundesrat on 19 April 1874 and was the subject of rather tortuous negotiations in June, during which the significance of the horse-trading between Prussia and the southern monarchies, to the detriment of the smaller states, became clear. The Bundesrat's justice committee produced a report which essentially welcomed the work of the Vorkommission while suggesting certain changes. The author of the Committee's report, Friedrich August von Liebe, attempted to water down the Vorkommission's emphasis on compilation, arguing that the Code should be 'a theoretical, systematic, and even artistic work,' and he rejected a 'purely empirical procedure'.[16] More immediately important, however, was the increase in the proposed size of the commission from nine to eleven. Attention was henceforth focused on the distribution of places in the commission, and, as Liebe reported, political considerations played a very large role.[17]

---

[14] See the 'Vorrede' to the 1874 edition of Dernburg's *Lehrbuch des Preussischen Rechts und der Privatrechtsnormen des Reichs*, i (3rd edn. Berlin, 1881), viii.

[15] See, above all, Schubert, *Die Entstehung der Vorschriften des BGB über Besitz und Eigentumsübertragung. Ein Beitrag zur Entstehungsgeschichte des BGB* (Berlin, 1966), ch. 2; H. Thieme, 'Aus der Vorgeschichte des Bürgerlichen Gesetzbuchs: Zur Gesetzgebung des Positivismus', *DJZ* 39 (1934), pp. 968–71.

[16] Liebe's report is reprinted in H. Rassow, 'Die Verhandlungen der Kommission zur Ausarbeitung eines bürgerlichen Gesetzbuchs für Deutschland', *Gruchots Beiträge zur Erläuterung des Deutschen Rechts*, 21 (1877), 195–214 (quotations, pp. 207 f.).

[17] Liebe, report of 2 July 1874, NStA Wolfenbüttel, 19 B Neu 464.

The way in which this matter was resolved is instructive about the way in which the federal system worked in the 1870s. If, as National Liberals and others insisted, the Reich was preparing legislation in its own right as an independent state, the composition of legislative commissions should have been determined by the need to take into acount different legal systems rather than the individual states. Prussia had tended to take this view before 1870, when the emphasis had been on the representation of persons rather than states in the commission to produce the penal code.[18] But the difficulty with that type of argument was that it led in practice to Prussian domination and an inevitable clash with the interests of the southern monarchies. As the tactics of the Reich government had for some time been to avoid such a clash and to work in collaboration with Bavaria and Württemberg, it is scarcely surprising that the interests of these states were given considerable weight in the summer of 1874.

Moreover, the limits of the federal system were revealed by the fact that the real losers in this process were the smaller states of northern and central Germany. A request for representation in the commission from Mecklenburg went unheeded. Liebe was unable to secure a place in the commission for a representative of the Thuringian states.[19] The greatest problem arose out of Hamburg's desire for representation, which fell foul of Leonhardt's belief that the representation of French law was essential. The tactical reason for Leonhardt's position was perfectly clear. His candidate, Gustav Derscheid, was a Rhinelander from Trier, who was employed as a councillor at the appellate court in Colmar. Leonhardt's desire to use the commission to wean Alsace-Lorraine and the Rhineland away from French law was quite explicit, and all arguments about the need to represent the smaller states and the over-representation of the south went unheeded. This revealed much about the way in which Prussia approached the politics of the Bundesrat. Hamburg's case for representation had considerable merit, and attracted the support of Saxony and all the smaller states in the Bundesrat. The Bavarian ambassador admitted that his sympathies lay with Hamburg, but he felt compelled to support the Prussian position on 2 July because of the fine treatment which Bavarian demands had received from men

[18] J. Thieme, 'Zur Enstehung der Konkursordnung', in *Einhundert Jahre Konkursordnung* (Cologne, 1977), 64 f.; Krüger to the Mayor of Hamburg, 30 June 1869, StA Hamburg, Archiv des Bevollmächtigten zum Bundesrat XI, 1.

[19] StA Schwerin, Ministerium der Justiz 282, fos. 59, 69; GStA Berlin-Dahlem, Rep. 84a 11772, fos. 73 f.; Liebe, report of 30 June 1874, NStA Wolfenbüttel, 19 B Neu 464.

like Friedberg.[20] The larger southern states may have felt that Prussia refrained from using the Bundesrat's committee system to override their interests. But in this case Prussia was quite willing to overturn a Bundesrat committee's decision when the interests of smaller fry were at stake. This seems to support the view that Mittnacht's campaign for greater participation in legislation was 'federalist' in only a very limited sense. In reality, that campaign was concerned principally with the entry of the southern monarchies into the charmed circle of decision-makers in the early Bismarckian empire.

During the Bundesrat's debates in 1874, Leonhardt had repeatedly stressed that the commission should represent all aspects of existing law adequately if its work was to be successful. This concern led to what one scholar has termed an 'institutionalization' of the legal systems of the individual states in the personnel of the commission,[21] in that those systems were made the starting-point of the commission's work. Thus the composition and initial work of the commission were in many ways the outcome of Kübel's work in the Vorkommission. That body had followed Kübel in suggesting that the preparation of the Code should be divided between perhaps five principal editors. When the chairman of the commission appointed these editors in September 1874, Prussian representatives took two of the posts and one each was allocated to Bavaria, Württemberg, and Baden.

This organization of the commission's work had far-reaching consequences for the future. Before 1881, the commission rarely met and the editors concentrated on the collection of legal materials from the different areas of Germany. For most of this time, these editors lacked any real contact with the other members except in the autumn of each year, when general sessions of the commission took place. The purpose of these general sessions was to lay down fundamental principles, solve conflicts of jurisdiction between different editors, and so on. Otherwise, the editors were given a very free hand with regard to the contents of their parts of the draft code (*Teilentwürfe*).[22]

---

[20] On these developments, see the reports of Krüger, 30 June, 1 July and 2 July, 1874, StA Hamburg, Senatskomm. für die Justizverwaltung 1 A a 1 vol. 1, nos. 17, 18, and 20; Perglas, reports of 30 June and 2 July 1874, BHStA Munich, MA 76 707/1; Turckheim reports of 30 June and 2 July 1874, GLA Karlsruhe, Abt. 233/13989.

[21] Behn, 'Generalbericht', p. 133

[22] See Schubert, *Materialien*, pp. 40 ff.; Schubert, *Entstehung*, ch. 3. The editors were Albert Gebhard (Baden)—general section; Franz von Kübel (Württemberg)—law of obligations; Reinhold Johow (Prussia)—law of property; Gottlieb Planck (Prussia)—family law; Gottfried von Schmitt (Bavaria)—law of inheritance. Leonhardt's original suggestion

The debates of the full commission on the editors' work began in October 1881, although Kübel's draft law of obligations was still incomplete. At this point, other members of the commission—in particular the famous academic lawyer, Bernhard von Windscheid—began to play an important role. Windscheid was principally concerned with the systematic rigour and formal precision of the work, and his influence continued after his resignation from the commission in September 1883.[23] He was later to be held largely responsible by critics for the tendency to extremely abstract and often near-incomprehensible formulations which were seen as characteristic of the commission's work. On the other hand, the increasingly obvious intellectual superiority of the Prussian representatives over their south German counterparts was at least as important as the technical refinement of Windscheid's jurisprudence. The chairman of the commission, Heinrich von Pape, was both a highly skilled and experienced bureaucratic negotiator and a lawyer of sufficient calibre to win the praise of Windscheid and Planck. If anything, his influence increased after Windscheid's resignation, as the reduction of the size of the commission to ten gave him a casting vote and placed the southerners in a minority. The five Prussians, supported from the outside by Windscheid, came to play the dominant role in the commission's deliberations.[24]

Pape was in many ways an interesting figure. He had studied law at the universities of Bonn and Berlin in the mid-1830s, a period in which the influence of Savigny at the latter university was at its height. He was a Roman Catholic from Westphalia, who had found his niche in the Prussian bureaucracy and had been closely involved in the codification of other parts of the law in the 1860s and 1870s. Above all, perhaps, he is to be considered as representative of the group of bureaucratic lawyers who created legal unity, whose main concerns were lengthy empirical research, conceptual precision, and exactitude in formulation, sometimes at the expense of fluency of expression. At the

that the Hanoverian Planck should be made editor for the law of property was reportedly ignored because it was thought that this vital post should go to an 'Old Prussian'—see Frensdorff, *Planck*, p. 310.

[23] See W. Schubert, 'Windscheids Briefe an Planck und seine für Planck bestimmten Stellungnahmen zum Schuldrechtssystem und zum Besitzrecht der 1. BGB-Kommission', *ZRG RA* 95 (1978), pp. 283–326; cf. G. Planck, 'Windscheid als Mitarbeiter am Bürgerlichen Gesetzbuche', *DJZ*, 14 (1909), pp. 951–4.

[24] See Schubert, *Materialien*, pp. 47 ff.; for Windscheid's support of the Prussians, see Windscheid to Planck, 21 Dec. 1886, reprinted in Schubert, 'Windscheids Briefe an Planck', p. 306.

very least, he reinforced the tendency of men like Windscheid and Planck to see such goals as the main concern of the legislator. In the opinion of one scholar at least, he was more influential than either of them in determining the outcome of the commission's work.[25]

One of Pape's major contributions to the work of the commission lay in his allocation of the five editorial posts within the commission. His starting-point was that the major legal systems of the Reich should be balanced, but he interpreted this in a way which was designed to secure the acceptance of the southern states. Thus, while he accepted that the Romanized common law provided some basis for unity, he argued that the fact that it had been constantly amended and reworked by legislation in the different states meant that it was necessary to appoint editors who were experts on the laws of Württemberg and Bavaria. As far as Prussia was concerned, he regarded it as essential to have an expert on Prussian law proper and on the legal systems of the new provinces which Prussia had acquired since 1866. Finally, the appointment of Baden's representative, Albert Gebhard, was considered a satisfactory means of giving French law a voice. It sems fairly obvious that this approach, with its emphasis on the particular interests of the larger states, undercut any possibility of opposition from the likes of Kübel. At any rate, Pape's selection of editors appears to have been accepted without any opposition in the commission.[26]

As the work progressed, however, it became more and more clear that Pape's selection of editors produced a distinct slant towards a particular type of code, which diverged in important ways from the wishes of the southern states. This was true above all with regard to land law. The Prussian legislation of 1872, which had sought to liberalize the terms on which land might be mortgaged and acquired, was particularly important here. Pape's decision to assign the task of drafting that section of the Code to the Prussian, Johow, was motivated by his belief that Prussian land law should form the basis of that part of the Code. As he explained to Bismarck:

It seemed to me appropriate to hand over the law of property to Johow, because Prussian law has become the foundation of modern German land law; in this area Prussian legislation has after comprehensive preparations carried out

---

[25] See H.-G. Mertens, 'Heinrich Eduard Pape (1816-1888)', in R. Stupperich (ed.), *Westfälische Lebensbilder*, xi (Münster, 1975), 153-71.

[26] Pape to Bismarck, 2 Oct. 1874, reprinted in Schubert, *Materialien*, pp. 274 f.

reforms which are of the greatest value for the German Civil Code, and which merit the most serious consideration.[27]

As we have seen, there was a widespread feeling in the 1860s and 1870s that certain sections of the civil law were more suitable than others for regulation in a civil code. In particular, parts of land law (especially those relating to mortgages), family law and inheritance law were often seen as unsuitable for national legislation because of regional variations in their development. In particular, the divergences between northern and southern systems in these parts of the law had caused concern before 1874, and that concern continued after the establishment of the commission. In 1881 the Bavarian minister of justice set up a commission in Munich with the specific task of checking whether the codifiers were introducing clauses (in inheritance and family law in particular), which contradicted the 'legal consciousness' (*Rechts-bewusstsein*) of the Bavarian people.[28] As the preparation of the Code progressed, it soon became clear that, for all the Vorkommission's insistence on respect for regional peculiarities, the extent of legal disunity in Germany made a purely compilatory code impossible.[29] At times the commission overrode the Vorkommission's suggestions. A good example concerned the law of property in marriage, where the second Bavarian representative, Paul von Roth, eventually voted with those who favoured a unified over the suggested two or three regional systems.[30] In other cases, such as mortgage law, four different systems were eventually allowed by the commission in order to accommodate different regional interests.

The important issue at stake here was the relationship between formal systematization and the preservation of the historical peculiarities of the different regions of Germany. That relationship was implicitly a difficult one despite the roots of both elements in Savigny's work. The 'legal certainty' which was so highly prized by the dominant legal positivism of the day stood in a somewhat ambiguous relationship to the historical theory of the origins of the law.[31] This was in fact a parallel problem

---

[27] Ibid. 275 f.

[28] As Fäustle explained to the Minister of Justice of Württemberg in a letter of 28 Mar. 1884, BHStA Munich, MJu 16110.

[29] See, in general, H. Coing's introduction to *J. von Staudingers Kommentar zum Bürgerlichen Gesetzbuch*, i (12th edn. Berlin, 1980), 17 ff.

[30] See P. v. Roth, 'Ueber den Stand der Bearbeitung des deutschen Civilgesetzbuchs, Sommer 1876', in G. Hirth (ed.), *Annalen des Deutschen Reichs*, 9 (1876), 932 f.

[31] One scholar has gone so far as to claim that the two approaches to the law—the

to that noted in the last chapter—the implicit contradiction between the people's 'legal consciousness' and the legislator's will as the source of true law. Planck argued, in a rather anxious passage on this question, that innovations might be introduced by the legislator in order to overcome regional variations, in so far as it might reasonably be expected that 'a unified legal consciousness will develop out of unified legislation'.

The constructive role of the legislator in leading the *Volk* towards unity was made quite clear, and was justified in terms of 'the demand of the German people for the unification of its civil law, which arises out of its national political needs'. Pape seems to have accepted this argument, with its implied limitation on respect for local tradition, in the interests of systematic clarity. As he wrote to Bismarck in 1884:

If the codification of civil law is not merely to consist of a systematic compilation of existing legal norms, a substantial number of changes in the law are unavoidable if only because of the influence of the new organization of the material. A further cause of changes is the necessity of ironing out contradictions in existing legislation, of deciding on matters of controversy and of filling gaps. Finally, the emergence of new needs and the development of legal practice cannot be ignored.

That is not to say that Pape was insensitive to the historical development of the law; as Windscheid once wryly noted, 'Pape is no friend of innovations'.[32] Nevertheless, Pape's conception of how a national codification should be approached reinforced the tendencies of men like Windscheid and Planck towards using the often highly abstruse techniques of 'conceptual jurisprudence' (*Begriffsjurisprudenz*) to create legal certainty through the logical derivation of the details of the system from a limited number of basic norms.[33]

The dominance of the conceptual jurisprudence of the common lawyers was a product of the way in which the Vorkommission and the Bundesrat had planned the process of codification. By insisting that the

historical and the 'conceptual'—were incompatible; see W. Wilhelm, *Zur juristischen Methodenlehre des 19. Jahrhunderts* (Frankfurt, 1958), 79.

[32] For Planck's arguments, which referred to the law of property in marriage, see W. Schubert, *Die Vorlagen der Redaktoren für die erste Kommission zur Ausarbeitung des Entwurfs eines Bürgerlichen Gesetzbuches. Familienrecht*, i (Berlin/New York, 1983), 440 f.; Pape to Bismarck, 5 July 1884, ZStA Potsdam, RJM 3810, fo. 122; Windscheid to Planck, 13 Jan. 1886, reprinted in Schubert, 'Windscheids Briefe an Planck', p. 305.

[33] The Code's system is treated in K. Zweigert and H. Kötz *An Introduction to Comparative Law*, i (2nd edn. Oxford, 1987), ch. 12; cf. H. G. Isele, 'Ein halbes Jahrhundert deutsches bürgerliches Gesetzbuch', *AcP* 150 (1949), pp. 3–7; F. Schmidt, 'The German Abstract Approach to Law: Comments on the System of the Bürgerliches Gesetzbuch', *Scandinavian Studies in Law*, 9 (1965), 131–58.

commission should attempt to bring the bewildering variety of statute and customary laws operating in Germany into harmony, the Bundesrat had placed a premium on the use of sophisticated legislative techniques. The rejection for political reasons of any idea of using an existing code—for example, the Prussian *Allgemeines Landrecht* or the Saxon Civil Code—as the basis of the commission's work was a further factor tending in the same direction. The dominant position of the common law in the university system and its superior conceptual possibilities made it more or less inevitable that it would be the basis of the Code's system. In addition, the old battle between 'Romanists' and 'Germanists' had largely disappeared in the quarter century after 1848, although it was to revive in very different political circumstances in the late 1880s.[34] By 1870 at the latest, conceptual jurisprudence—the basic technique of legal positivism—more or less had the field to itself as far as the technical approach to legislation was concerned.

In view of the importance of this approach to legislation, it is necessary to undertake a relatively detailed analysis of what it entailed. Legal positivism had developed as a system of jurisprudential techniques, not as a guide to the content of the legal system. Far from involving a rejection of the historical theory of the origins of law, it was really part of the reassessment of Savigny's theories in the middle of the century, which was discussed in a previous chapter. Windscheid believed that the common law provided the basis for responsible legislative progress within a historical framework. Planck, in his famous response to the critics of the common-law bias of the commission's work, agreed with the Historical School that a code should essentially deal with existing law, and that 'innovation was only justified if the trend of developments was unmistakable and if conditions and opinions were already so clear that even the type and form of regulation was not in serious doubt'. But he went on to stress the major contribution that the techniques of the common law made to the solution of the great problems facing the legislator in the rapidly changing society of late nineteenth-century Germany.[35] And twenty years later, while discussing Windscheid's

---

[34] See O. Gierke, *Die historische Rechtsschule und die Germanisten* (Berlin, 1903), 31 f.; K. Kroeschell, 'Zielsetzung und Arbeitsweise der Wissenschaft vom gemeinen deutschen Privatrecht', in H. Coing and W. Wilhelm (eds.), *Wissenschaft und Kodifikation des Privatrechts im 19. Jahrhundert*, i (Frankfurt, 1974), 260 ff.

[35] G. Planck, 'Zur Kritik des Entwurfes eines bürgerlichen Gesetzbuches für das deutsche Reich', *AcP* 75 (1889), 331 ff. (quotation, p. 332). In view of Planck's views on acceptable innovations noted above, it seems that he used historical arguments against codification when there was any question of the inclusion of progressive social reforms;

contribution to the commission's work, Planck reiterated the point that Windscheid's application of conceptual jurisprudence was a question of technique alone: '[i]t did not occur to him to wish to derive the contents of legal clauses exclusively or, even predominantly, from Roman law.'[36] This view of conceptual jurisprudence as determining legislative form and technique rather than the content of laws was both correct and misleading. Its mid-century founders—academic lawyers such as Puchta and Gerber—had effectively abandoned Savigny's notion of the organic relationship between law and society, putting in its place an emphasis on the productive development of new law out of concepts derived from study of the sources. The tasks of jurisprudence were narrowly defined, in the sense that the aims of the discipline were not to effect social reform or achieve an ethically desirable social order. Instead, following the work of the late Savigny (the Savigny of the *System des heutigen römischen Rechts*, rather than the Savigny of the *Beruf*), jurisprudence should seek to develop a system of rationally interrelated concepts, which were socially 'neutral' and without political relevance. It is this emphasis on political and social neutrality which has led one historian to assert in a striking phrase that legal positivism produced 'a mechanical and morally emasculated system of law'.[37]

To Windscheid, however, this apolitical jurisprudence did not imply a lack of concern for political and social issues, but merely that jurisprudence was not the same thing as legislation. Indeed, he specifically emphasized the limited role of jurisprudence in the preparation of laws. Legislation, he argued, 'in many cases depended on ethical, political or economic considerations or on a combination of those considerations, which are not the concern of the jurist as such'. The true contribution of jurisprudence was to provide scientifically based knowledge of existing law as a basis for successful legislation.[38] In this way, Planck's insistence on the basic distinction between technique and content was a faithful reflection of the

he was much more prepared to contemplate innovation where it would be used to advance the cause of unity over regional diversity.

[36] Planck, 'Windscheid als Mitarbeiter am Bürgerlichen Gesetzbuche', p. 952.

[37] J. Caplan, 'The Civil Servant in the Third Reich', D.Phil. thesis (Oxford, 1973), 36. On the development of legal positivism in general, see Wilhelm, *Methodenlehre*, pp. 70–87; F. Wieacker, *Privatrechtsgeschichte der Neuzeit unter besonderer Berücksichtigung der deutschen Entwicklung* (2nd edn., Göttingen, 1967), ch. 23, and, above all, G. Dilcher, 'Der rechtswissenschaftliche Positivismus: Wissenschaftliche Methode, Sozialphilosophie, Gesellschaftspolitik', *Archiv für Rechts- und Sozialphilosophie*, 61 (1975), 497–528.

[38] Windscheid, 'Die Aufgabe der Rechtswissenschaft', in *Gesammelte Reden und Abhandlungen*, ed. P. Oertmann (Leipzig, 1904), 112 ff. (quotation, p. 112).

views of the most influential common lawyer of late nineteenth-century Germany.

At the same time, this view of the distinction between technique and content was misleading. This was partly because any complete distinction between form and content was unconvincing. The history of the Civil Code was to be littered with cases where desirable reforms were rejected because their introduction would destroy the internal coherence of the Code's system. Equally important, perhaps, was the fact that the project was from the start considered to be a narrowly juristic exercise by a commission which consisted solely of legal bureaucrats, judges, and academic lawyers without any representatives of the political parties and economic interest groups. This left the preparation of the draft code in the hands of men who operated without much serious consideration of the political and social developments of the 1880s, and who interpreted their task very much in terms of constructing a national legal system from materials inherited from the period before 1874.

Above all, however, the fundamental norms from which conceptual jurisprudence attempted to deduce the details of the legal system involved value judgements with an obvious social and political relevance. To Savigny and his followers, the private legal order was composed of individual legal subjects whose wills operated within spheres of private autonomy. The role of the civil or private law was to regulate the arena within which collisions took place between the wills of different legal subjects. In Windscheid's words:

The law creates for every will an arena within which it is dominant and from which alien wills recoil. Law is, in the first place, not a restriction but a recognition of human freedom. The restrictive element is merely the other side of freedom thus guaranteed.[39]

As has frequently been pointed out, conceptual jurisprudence welded together these ideas (derived ultimately from Kant) with a reliance on Roman law, which was seen as being the purest legal expression of such private freedom. The value judgement involved in this selection of intellectual sources was then converted into the first principle from which the basic tenets of German civil law were deduced. Thus, in the spheres of contract and property law, personal freedoms were justified through a legal philosophy which emphasized the unimpeded exercise

[39] Windscheid, op cit., pp. 101 f.

of personal choice by autonomous legal subjects.[40] The nineteenth century saw the development of the concept of property as the total domination of a person over a thing, whereby the rights of the property-owner were conceived as absolute. The alternative method of enumerating the rights which went with property-ownership was steadily pushed back by Savigny and his followers, above all Windscheid.[41] By the 1860s at the latest, this 'absolute' conception of property with its emphasis on the property-owner's freedom of disposition had come to dominate German jurisprudence. Indeed, the Saxon Civil Code reflected this by including the strongest nineteenth-century statement of the property-owner's limitless freedom.[42] In fact, the legislators of the 1870s and 1880s retreated from that high point of liberal individualism by introducing a number of limitations on the freedoms of property-owners. But such limitations were conceived as exceptions to general principles rather than as part of any shift from those principles. Johow fully accepted the notion of property as the domination of a person over a thing; as the explanatory notes (*Motive*) to the relevant clause stated:

The draft code seeks to establish the essential content of the property-owner's rights, rather than provide a definition [of property]. . . . The positive side of this statement is less important than the negative side—that is, that the exclusive rights of disposition enjoyed by the property-owner are only limited by specific restrictions.[43]

In general, the same things could be said about inheritance law. The editor of this section of the Code, Gottfried von Schmitt, rejected the idea that the state was allowed to create a new inheritance law, and refused to consider the question of social amelioration through reform

---

[40] Dilcher, 'Der rechtswissenschaftliche Positivismus', p. 518; H. Coing, 'Bemerkungen zum überkommenen Zivilrechtssystem', in E. v. Caemmerer *et al.* (eds.), *Vom deutschen zum europäischen Recht. Festschrift für Hans Dölle*, i (Tübingen, 1963), 25-40; H. Kiefner, 'Der Einfluss Kants auf Theorie und Praxis des Zivilrechts im 19. Jahrhundert', in J. Blühdorn and J. Ritter (eds.), *Philosophie und Rechtswissenschaft. Zum Problem ihrer Beziehung im 19. Jahrhundert* (Frankfurt, 1969), 3-25.

[41] See D. Schwab, 'Eigentum', in O. Brunner *et al.* (eds.), *Geschichtliche Grundbegriffe*, ii (Stuttgart, 1975), 65-115; W. Wilhelm, 'Private Freiheit und gesellschaftliche Grenzen des Eigentums in der Theorie der Pandektenwissenschaft', in Coing and Wilhelm (eds.), *Wissenschaft und Kodifikation*, iv (Frankfurt, 1979), 19-26.

[42] J. W. Hedemann, *Die Fortschritte des Zivilrechts im XIX. Jahrhundert*, ii/1 (Berlin, 1930), 124.

[43] B. Mugdan (ed.), *Die gesammten Materialien zum Bürgerlichen Gesetzbuch*, iii (Berlin, 1899), 145. Para. 848 of the draft code stated: 'The owner of an object has the right to dispose of it as he pleases (*nach Willkür*) to the exclusion of others in so far as limitations of this right are not to be found in the law or in the rights of third parties.'

of that part of the law. Schmitt's starting-point was that inheritance law was to be based on the 'independence of the human will', which led him to see testamentary freedom as the basis of the law. This led to a certain amount of disagreement in the commission where some members attempted to overturn Schmitt's notion of the priority of testamentary over intestate succession. In the end, however, Schmitt's work was accepted by the commission with very few changes, and the principle of testamentary freedom was incorporated into the draft code.[44]

The third important principle which the codifiers derived from the doctrine of private autonomy was that of freedom of contract. In fact, this principle was hedged around with numerous qualifications and restrictions in order to prevent abuses. Contract law was the area in which the social dangers of unrestricted personal freedom were most clear and, by the late nineteenth century, legislators all over Europe were beginning to recognize that certain types of free contractual transaction might contradict the interests of the common good. But, as in the case of property law, the key point was that personal freedom of contract was absolute unless *specifically* restricted by the law. Once again, the codifiers built on previous developments in the legal system, leading one scholar to describe their work in this field as 'merely a copy of earlier legislation'.[45]

The commission's work thus accepted previous legal developments in the sphere of private autonomy and personal freedoms. In two other basic respects the draft code represented the culmination of the nineteenth-century jurisprudential world-view. In the first place, it accepted the sharp distinction between public and private spheres in the law which was so important a part of the emergence of a modern 'civil society' (*bürgerliche Gesellschaft*) out of the remnants of feudalism and absolutism during the first half of the century.[46] Broadly speaking, public law regulated transactions between individuals (or corporations) and the state, whereas private law concerned transactions between

---

[44] H.-G. Mertens, *Die Entstehung der Vorshcriften des BGB über die gesetzliche Erbfolge und das Pflichtteilsrecht* (Berlin, 1970) , ch. 2 (quotation, p. 25); cf. W. Schubert, *Vorlagen. Erbrecht*, i (Berlin/New York, 1984), xii–xv; R. Schröder, *Abschaffung oder Reform des Erbrechts* (Ebelsbach, 1981), 17-30.

[45] Hedemann, *Fortschritte*, i (Berlin, 1910), 123.

[46] See M. Riedel, 'Bürger, Staatsbürger, Bürgertum' and 'Gesellschaft, bürgerliche', in Brunner *et al.* (eds.), *Geschichtliche Grundbegriffe*, i (Stuttgart, 1972), 672-725 and ii, 719-800; cf. Jürgen Habermas's classic *Strukturwandel der Öffentlichkeit. Untersuchungen zu einer Kategorie der bürgerlichen Gesellschaft* (11th edn. Darmstadt/Neuwied, 1980), esp. ch. 3.

individuals. By the third quarter of the nineteenth century, civil law
and private law were generally regarded as being synonymous expressions
for that part of the legal system in which the state was permitted only
to establish the framework within which the autonomy of the individual
will might be exercised.

As has often been noted,[47] this distinction between the public and
the private sections of the law was a core component of German liberal
theories of the rule of law (*Rechtsstaat*). By the 1860s, the dominant
strand of liberal thought in Germany tended to argue that the state
existed in order to guarantee the unimpeded exercise of individual rights
within a legal order that was 'certain' and 'secure'. The principal
function of a constitution was to provide forms of legal control of the
executive in the search for guarantees that the state bureaucracy would
not encroach on the private autonomy of individuals. Much attention
was devoted in liberal circles to the question of how the bureaucracy
might best be subjected to legal control in the 1860s and 1870s.[48] To
most liberals in this period, then, the function of the constitutional
Rechtsstaat was essentially negative—i.e. to prevent the administration
overstepping the mark in its relations with the individual—rather than
positive in the sense of providing a basis for the actual takeover of
power in the state. The maintenance of the strict separation of public
and private law corresponded to this conception of the constitutional
Rechtsstaat as the guarantor of the freedom of action of the private
individual.[49]

Historians have not been slow to identify this negative doctrine of
the *Rechtsstaat* as a key failing of German liberalism in the third quarter
of the nineteenth century. The emphasis on the private, 'unpolitical'
sphere of property rights and the concern with formal certainty of the
law at the expense of ideal and moral issues is considered to have
signified the liberals' shift to a concern for order and social peace in
the interests of a bourgeoisie which was content to renounce further
emancipatory aspirations. This in turn has been seen as a 'depoliticization'
of liberal politics in the 1860s, in which legal positivism played a key

---

[47] For the following, see esp. L. Krieger, *The German Idea of Freedom. History of a
Political Tradition* (Chicago/London, 1957), 252-61, 430 ff.; H. Boldt, *Rechtsstaat und
Ausnahmezustand. Eine Studie über den Belagerungszustand als Ausnahmezustand des
bürgerlichen Rechtsstaates im 19. Jahrhundert* (Berlin, 1967), ch. 5.
[48] See the contrasting views of O. Bähr, *Der Rechtsstaat. Eine publicistische Skizze*
(Kassel/Göttingen, 1864) and R. Gneist, *Der Rechtsstaat* (Berlin, 1872).
[49] For the equation of the distinctions between state and society and public and private
law, see Boldt, *Rechtsstaat und Ausnahmezustand*, p. 184.

role. For Boldt, left-liberalism was 'governmentalized' in the 1860s by its acceptance of the protection of private property as the core of individual liberty. Legal positivism and *Rechtsstaat* theory, which articulated the distinction between public and private law and the primacy of the autonomy of the individual will in the latter sphere, are thus seen to have represented the neutralization of liberalism's threat to the prevailing political order. In socio-political terms, they served to integrate the liberal bourgeoisie into the Bismarckian state.[50]

As we have seen, it was certainly the case that the National Liberals were more concerned in the 1870s with the formal aspects of legal unification than with the content of the law. Similarly, the Bundesrat saw a historically based, systematic codification as a means of heading off further liberal reforms ('modern ideas'). But there are good reasons for scepticism about the 'depoliticization' thesis. In the first place, the previous chapter has shown just how far the whole question of legal unification reflected divisions in the decade of national unification. The fact that particularist resistance was so tenacious despite the absence of alternative positive suggestions about the future of the nation's legal system imposed real constraints on the supporters of legal unity. Secondly, it is far from clear that liberalism had in fact retreated from its emancipatory traditions into a purely conservative defence of the propertied order in the 1860s. To be sure, liberals emphasized that property was the foundation of the existing order, but that article of faith certainly did not preclude the enunciation of progressive policies, which tended to lead to the emergence of divisions over the exact definition of the interests of property.

A major example of such divisions arose in connection with the complex of Prussian land law reforms, which were prepared in the 1860s and finally became law in 1872.[51] This legislation aroused considerable hostility among groups of conservative landowners, not least because the proposals were perceived as a threat to the existing social order through the opportunities they offered for further penetration of the countryside by capitalist influences. This was, however, a battle which the conservatives could not win in the 1860s. The pressing need among the landowning classes for large-scale capital-borrowing facilities at a

---

[50] Boldt, *Rechtsstaat und Ausnahmezustand*, pp. 172-80 (quotation, p. 178). The most powerful recent statement of this thesis is to be found in M. Gugel, *Industrieller Aufstieg und bürgerliche Herrschaft* (Cologne, 1975), 81-91, 188-202.

[51] On this legislation, see Buchholz, *Abstraktionsprinzip und Immobiliarrecht. Zur Geschichte der Auflassung und der Grundschuld* (Frankfurt, 1978), ch. 5.

time of high land prices and buoyant prices for agricultural produce (which enabled landowners to contemplate increased indebtedness) combined to undermine the opposition's case. The argument that it was necessary to give the landowners equality of access to the capital market with urban groups was unassailable,[52] although the issue was to reappear in the very different circumstances of the 1880s and 1890s. The central point here, however, was that the Prussian reforms were rooted in the insistence on the equal treatment in law of land and other forms of property. That notion—developed by conceptual jurisprudence—contrasted strongly with the powerful German tradition of giving landownership a special place in the legal system. The political significance of these jurisprudential developments seems obvious. Landowners could only plausibly claim special treatment if landownership was considered as the exclusive basis of social and political power. The liberals' rejection of that postulate had as its logical consequence the refusal to accept conservative claims to a special place for land in the legal system.[53]

The denial of the special status of landownership came about essentially through the adoption of the so-called 'principle of abstraction' (*Abstraktionsprinzip*). This was the principle by which certain legal trasactions (e.g. the issue of promissory notes or land transfers through conveyance) were valid without reference to the circumstances within which the parties entered into them.[54] Like so many other key developments in nineteenth-century German law, this principle had its roots in the work of Savigny, and it was the key element in the law of obligations and land law in the last decades of the century. A theoretical breakthrough came in 1855 with the publication of Otto Bähr's famous book on the subject, in which it was argued that if the modern law of obligations was based on the unimpeded operation of the will, the will must have the right to dissolve the link between a promise and its legal

[52] See e.g. E. I. Bekker, *Die Reform des Hypothekenwesens als Aufgabe des norddeutschen Bundes* (Berlin, 1867); cf. Buchholz, *Abstraktionsprinzip*, pp. 359–65; M. Weyermann, *Zur Geschichte des Immobiliarkreditwesens in Preussen mit besonderer Nutzanwendung auf die Theorie der Bodenverschuldung* (Karlsruhe, 1907), 193–208; H. Kleine, *Die historische Bedingtheit der Abstraktion von der causa* (Berlin-GDR, 1953), 40 ff.

[53] K. Kroeschell, 'Zur Lehre vom 'Germanischen' Eigentumsbegriff', in *Rechtshistorische Studien. Hans Thieme zum 70. Geburtstag zugeeignet von seinen Schülern* (Cologne/Vienna, 1977), 45 f.

[54] Thus, for example, a person who signs an acknowledgement of a debt would be bound by it, even if he did not in fact receive the loan in anticipation of which he gave the acknowledgement. The transaction is, in legal terms, 'abstract', not 'causal'.

'cause'.[55] Thus, like the other elements of that individual autonomy which lay at the heart of conceptual jurisprudence, the principle of abstraction found its justification in the unrestrained action of the subjective will within its private sphere.

When applied to shares and other financial instruments, the principle of abstraction was not particularly problematic, in that the mobility of capital was fundamental to the development of the German capitalist economy. Its incorporation in the Prussian land law reforms as the foundation of the system of land transfers and indebtedness was, however, different. The reform had the twofold purpose of 'removing those attributes of land debts which render them less valuable to the capitalist than other similar investments, and [of] making such debts negotiable on the capital markets, where larger amounts of capital are available for investment'.[56] Prussian legislation built on earlier developments in this direction in the Hanseatic towns and in Mecklenburg with the explicit aim of creating an expanding market in negotiable credit instruments for the landowning sector.[57] This was one area of the law where a strong north/south divide had developed in the nineteenth century, and the prominent role ascribed by Johow to Prussian developments explains the bitterness of the southern representatives in the commission. As Schmitt reported to Munich in 1886, 'northern and southern legislation speak different languages'.[58] The best that the southern representatives could do to protect their interests was to secure the inclusion of four different types of mortgage system, as opposed to Johow's original suggestion of two. In this way, the techniques developed by conceptual jurisprudence created the framework within which the full entry of landownership into a market determined by the financial institutions of modern capitalism could take place. The equal treatment of land and other forms of capital within a unitary, private law of property was the jurisprudential reflection of the liberals' urge to remove the advantages that the existing political system gave to the landowning nobility. The 'principle of abstraction' ensured that the equal treatment

---

[55] O. Bähr, *Die Anerkennung als Verpflichtungsgrund* (Kassel, 1855).

[56] Bekker, *Reform des Hypothekenwesens*, p. 13.

[57] See, above all, Buchholz, *Abstraktionsprinzip*, pp. 321 ff. The basic principle of the land charge (*Grundschuld*) was that it dissolved the personal liability of the debtor and constituted a charge on the land alone.

[58] Schmitt to Fäustle, 29 Dec. 1886, BHStA Munich, MJu 16110. On the roots of Johow's work in Prussian law, see Schubert, *Entstehung*, p. 27 and Buchholz, *Abstraktionsprinzip*, ch. 8.

of land would take place on terms laid down in the 'modern', capitalist sectors of the economy.

We have considered land law at some length because of its connection with the liberals' broader concerns in the period of unification. It seems apparent that those analyses which emphasize the ability of the mid nineteenth-century state to pursue liberal social policies without the establishment of forms of liberal constitutional government are very plausible. One has only to compare the leading role played by ultra-conservative Mecklenburg in the liberalization of nineteenth-century mortgage law[59] with the relative conservatism on this matter of the more politically liberal southern states to see the force of this point. In the context of the recent historiography of Bismarckian Germany, however, that does not say very much. There is widespread agreement that Prussian-led unification offered the liberal bourgeoisie a wide range of socio-economic gains in return for their surrender of the substance of political power. Furthermore, most historians would agree about the essentially capitalist nature of Junker agriculture,[60] which is seen as a basic component of the class alliance of 'feudal' aristocracy and 'bourgeois' liberalism on which the Bismarckian state is believed to have rested. A somewhat extreme recent analysis sees the common subjection of both groups to capitalist methods of production and marketing as the basis for an 'elementary coherence of interests'.[61] Analyses which stress the political failings of German liberalism would have few difficulties in accommodating obvious 'bourgeois' successes such as the development of a liberal land law. The adoption of capitalist or bourgeois credit instruments might be seen as part of a necessary expansion of the capital available to landowners at a time of favourable agricultural prices and high purchase prices for land. The liberalization of mortgage law might thus be seen as a product of a period of unprecedented Junker economic power and dominance.[62]

It is of course true that the economic well-being of the Junkers in

---

[59] See Buchholz, *Abstraktionsprinzip*, ch. 3; Hedemann, *Fortschritte des Zivilrechts.* ii/2. 249 ff.

[60] The classic text here is H. Rosenberg, 'Die Pseudodemokratisierung der Rittergutsbesitzerklasse', translated in G. G. Iggers (ed.), *The Social History of Politics* (Leamington Spa, 1985), 81-112, esp. 92-107.

[61] L. Machtan and D. Milles, *Die Klassensymbiose von Junkertum und Bourgeoisie* (Frankfurt/Berlin/Vienna, 1980), 30.

[62] This is very much the tone of H.-U. Wehler's general comments in *The German Empire 1871-1918* (Leamington Spa, 1985), 9-31, esp. 12 f.

the 1860s was politically conducive and perhaps even indispensable to the acceptance of mortgage law reform. But that is not an argument for the primacy of Junker interests in the construction of the legal system: it could just as easily be interpreted in terms of a fortuitous and (as it turned out) transient identity of interests between urban and rural property-owners, with the former very much in the vanguard. It was after all liberal lawyers[63] who had developed the 'principle of abstraction', as part of the legal superstructure of a post-feudal, industrializing society in which urban interests could not be ignored. The landowners, induced by the carrot of market profits and the stick of escalating land prices and credit shortages, followed a trend that was set neither by them nor for them. And when agricultural prices fell from the mid-1870s, it was these same landowners who led the campaign for a reversal of the legal reforms which, it was felt, were largely responsible for the intolerable levels of landed indebtedness in East Elbia and elsewhere. As we shall see, that campaign was successfully, though not without some difficulty, countered by the lawyers in the 1890s.

There are thus grounds for thinking that the extent of the de-politicization of liberal conceptual jurisprudence in the 1860s has been exaggerated. It is perhaps the case that the social and political neutrality of legal positivism has been taken too much at face value. This analysis of legal thought has attempted to show that behind the ostensibly logical construction of the system of jurisprudence lay a distinct set of social and political postulates, involving the equality of citizens before the law, the freedom of the individual in relation to his property, and his right to conclude contracts. It is this set of postulates which has led scholars such as Wieacker to see the Civil Code as the 'late-born child of classical liberalism'.[64]

The connections between mid-century liberalism and legal positivism were hardly fortuitous. German liberal ideology made a strong claim to universality, to the representation of a united public opinion in a classless society, and many of its electoral problems after 1880 were linked to its problems with the rise of clamorous sectional interest groups within its constituency.[65] Conceptual jurisprudence neatly mirrored this

---

[63] For the leading role played by liberal bureaucrats like Franz Förster in the preparation of the Prussian legislation, see Buchholz, *Abstraktionsprinzip*, pp. 365 ff.

[64] F. Wieacker, *Industriegesellschaft und Privatrechtsordnung* (Frankfurt, 1974), 22.

[65] See especially L. Gall, 'Liberalismus und "bürgerliche Gesellschaft": Zur Charakter und Entwicklung der liberalen Bewegung in Deutschland', *HZ* 220 (1975), pp. 324–56; J. J. Sheehan, *German Liberalism in the Nineteenth Century* (Chicago/London, 1978), pt. v.

aspect of liberalism with its emphasis on social-neutrality, its hostility to interest group conflicts, and its difficulties in dealing with such conflicts when they arose as a result of economic development.[66] In both cases, ideologies of universality and social neutrality both veiled and legitimated attempts to recast society along middle-class lines.

This fairly positive view of the liberal foundations of legal positivism should not, however, divert attention from the shortcomings of conceptual jurisprudence as a vehicle for sustained progressive reform. Previous historians of German civil law have with good reason tended to emphasize the weaknesses of this form of jurisprudence when confronting the question of social inequalities.[67] The response of legal positivism to social problems had two distinct aspects which were to have important consequences for the future of the Civil Code. On the one hand, the method of legal positivism emphasized the generation of new law out of the systematic study of existing law—a view which strongly implied that the law developed independently of social changes. This did not mean that legislators ought simply to ignore social and political developments, as Windscheid's views on the distinction between jurisprudence and legislation make clear. The commission's work was in fact full of references to socio-economic and political considerations.[68] But on the whole the codifiers' views on such matters were not based— at least in any formal sense—on the work of contemporary national economists and social reformers. It was in these circles that the fundamental criticisms of the tenets of conceptual jurisprudence from the standpoint of the social question were first developed. With a few exceptions, such as Rudolph Jhering (1818–92), the community of lawyers more or less ignored the social question before 1890. As the commission contained no representatives of political parties or economic interest groups, there was no counterweight to the propensity of the professional lawyers to ignore developments in the non-juristic literature of the period.[69]

A second and perhaps more important aspect of conceptual juris-prudence in this context was the strict separation of public and private

[66] Wieacker, *Privatrechtsgeschichte*, pp. 439 ff.

[67] Apart from the works of Wieacker, see G. Dilcher, 'Das Gesellschaftsbild der Rechtswissenschaft und die soziale Frage', in K. Vondung (ed.), *Das wilhelminische Bildungsbürgertum. Zur Sozialgeschichte seiner Ideen* (Göttingen, 1976), 53–66.

[68] Wieacker, *Industriegesellschaft und Privatrechtsordnung*, pp. 62 f.

[69] See Schubert, *Entstehung*, p. 29; Wilhelm, 'Private Freiheit und gesellschaftliche Grenzen', pp. 27 ff.; cf. the discussions of the Verein für Sozialpolitik about inheritance law and the preservation of the peasantry in *Schriften des Vereins für Sozialpolitik*, xxi (Leipzig, 1882) and xxviii (Leipzig, 1884).

law. Following the Vorkommission's suggestions, Johow used this argument to exclude from the draft code those institutions, such as the remnants of feudal law, which had a primarily public character. This justification tended to be buttressed with assertions of the unsuitability for inclusion in the national Code of sections of the law which, had a purely local significance or which were in any case dying out.[70] Such areas of the law were to be left to legislation by the individual states, thus limiting the range of application of the Code's liberal principles. It was this survival of the remnants of feudalism through their exclusion from the Code that led Wieacker to see the Code as a blend of liberal legal positivism and conservative authoritarianism.[71]

It might be argued, however, that the failure to complete the collapse of feudalism in the Civil Code was of limited importance, given the dominance of capitalist relations in late nineteenth-century Germany. On the other hand, the separation of public and private law and the exclusion of sections of the law which had a purely local application did mean that the codifiers could avoid certain questions which were politically contentious or problematic. Thus, the commission accepted the Bundesrat's suggestion that the law relating to domestic servants (*Gesinderecht*) should be left to the individual states, on the grounds of the vast differences in the relevant law in the different regions of Germany. This was a matter of considerable social importance in view of the often scandalous situation of those classed as domestic servants, especially in the Prussian east where the category generally meant farm workers. The period of national unification saw a steady worsening of the legal position of this group, during which time they were denied the limited right of coalition granted to other groups of workers in the Industrial Code of 1869. Nor were domestic servants given an equal position *vis-à-vis* other workers in the social insurance legislation of the 1880s. Attempts at reform of this situation were constantly blocked by conservative groups in alliance with the Bundesrat and the Reich government, where there was much support for the survival of a situation which kept urban class conflicts out of the countryside. By leaving the matter to the individual states, the Civil Code commission was effectively cementing the authoritarian character of a section of employment law which retained many elements of a pre-modern, *ständisch* system within

[70] Mugdan (ed.), *Materialien*, iii. 2 f.
[71] Wieacker, *Privatrechtsgeschichte*, pp. 471 f., 479 f.; id., *Industriegesellschaft und Privatrechtsordnung*, p. 22.

a framework governed in theory by the liberal institution of contract.[72] The regulation of the law relating to domestic servants demonstrated the limitations of conceptual jurisprudence as an instrument of liberal reform. The failure to achieve legal unity in this area constituted a failure of social modernization through the law.

In other areas, too, the distinction between public and private law had negative consequences for the cause of liberal reform. Of these, the most important was undoubtedly the regulation of the law of associations. This part of the law had both public and private law aspects. The former dealt with the right to form associations of citizens for the pursuit of common goals and the conditions under which they had to operate with regard to the public authorities. Thus, for example, after 1848 many states introduced legislation to place restrictions on so-called 'political' associations with regard to the participation of women, children, and apprentices, and on contacts with other associations. This legislation empowered the police to dissolve any association which broke these rules, a situation which continued until the turn of the century.[73] The private law of associations, on the other hand, covered the question of the conditions under which associations might acquire (and lose) the capacity to act at law (*Rechtsfähigkeit*).[74]

The difficulty facing the codifiers lay in the fact that the distinction between the public and private spheres of the law was a guarantee of individual freedom in areas of life with no explicit political significance. But it was widely believed that, in the case of associations, the acquisition of private legal rights had a direct public or political significance. The granting of the right to own land or contract debts was commonly seen as important in the struggle between the state and the forces of subversion. Under the so-called concessionary system (*Konzessionssystem*), which allowed the state to grant or deny these rights at will, the private law of association was frequently used as a political

[72] See T. Vormbaum, *Politik und Gesinderecht im 19. Jahrhundert (vornehmlich in Preussen 1810-1918)* (Berlin, 1980), chs. 6-7, 9-10. The discussions in the Civil Code Commission are discussed on pp. 271-81.

[73] An overview of nineteenth-century developments is provided by A. Hueber, 'Das Vereinsrecht im Deutschland des 19. Jahrhunderts', in O. Dann (ed.), *Vereinswesen und bürgerliche Gesellschaft* [*HZ*, Beiheft 9 Neue Folge] (Munich, 1984), 115-32. For the Prussian and Bavarian laws of 1850, see W. Albrecht, *Fachverein—Berufsgewerkschaft—Zentralverband. Organisationsprobleme der deutschen Gewerkschaften 1870-1890* (Bonn, 1982), 34-7.

[74] This meant (among other things) the right of the association to own property in its own right and to contract debts without the members of the association assuming personal liability.

tool against opponents of the regime. Thus the Westphalian Peasants' Association was denied the right to act at law from its foundation in 1862 until 1891 as a result of the government's suspicion about the political reliability of the association's overwhelmingly Roman Catholic membership.[75] As late as 1908, this political motivation was clear; those associations on the register in Berlin, in so far as they had any political interests at all, were exclusively conservative in orientation.[76]

This political practice was rooted in the surviving hostility of the bureaucratic state to forms of autonomous political activity on the part of its citizens. This helps to explain why the state of Baden, with its long tradition of bureaucratic liberalism, was so hostile to national legislation on the matter, particularly if it involved any watering-down of the concessionary system.[77] As the example of the Westphalian Peasants' Association shows, a restrictive law of associations could be used against groups outside the socialist camp, however much the latter may have come to bear the brunt of the state's hostility after the 1870s. On the other hand, the enormous growth in the scale and range of associational life in the third quarter of the nineteenth century—a phenomenon rooted in social and economic change[78]—made some kind of legal regulation urgently necessary. Because of the perceived political relevance of the private law of associations, attention was focused on two areas in particular: the jurisprudential system used to define associations in law and the separate treatment of different categories of association according to their professed aims.

Nineteenth-century German jurisprudence developed two opposing views of the legal nature of associations. On the one hand there was the Roman law-based theory of the 'fictitious person', whereby the association was considered to be the bearer of the rights of its individual members for the purposes of the civil law. This view sought to adapt

---

[75] M. Erdmann, *Die verfassungspolitische Funktion der Wirtschaftsverbände in Deutschland 1815–1871* (Berlin, 1968), 70 ff.

[76] They included branches of the Farmers' League, the Kyffhäuser League of Veterans, and some industrialists' associations; see A. Thorndike, *Zur Rechtsfähigkeit der deutschen Arbeiterberufsvereine. Die Lage dieses Problems aus seiner Geschichte entwickelt* (Tübingen, 1908), 81 n. 1.

[77] T. Vormbaum, *Die Rechtsfähigkeit der Vereine im 19. Jahrhundert. Ein Beitrag zur Entstehungsgeschichte des BGB* (Berlin/New York, 1976), 192.

[78] See in general K. Tenfelde, 'Die Entfaltung des Vereinswesens während der Industriellen Revolution in Deutschland (1850–1873)', in Dann (ed.), *Vereinswesen*, pp. 51–114; cf. David Blackbourn's comments in D. Blackbourn and G. Eley, *The Peculiarities of German History. Bourgeois Society and Politics in Nineteenth-Century Germany* (Oxford, 1984), 195 ff.

the postulates of the essentially individualist Roman law to a society increasingly characterized by collective action. This argument, which was developed in Savigny's work, was often adopted by supporters of the restrictive concessionary system. The position of the common law in the first half of the nineteenth century was that the creation of a 'fictitious person' was dependent on the performance of a specific action by the state. On the other hand there was the theory of Germanists such as Otto von Gierke that an association was a 'real collective person' (*realer Gesamtperson*) with rights distinct from those of its individual members. This theory was often connected with the theory of the 'free creation of corporations' (*freie Körperschaftsbildung*)—i.e. the notion that an association gained the ability to act at law simply by existing. In addition to these categories, the system of so-called normative conditions (*Normativbestimmungen*), by which the association had to fulfil certain conditions such as the submission of statutes or membership lists in order to gain the right to act at law, had developed as a compromise position by the middle of the century.[79]

By the 1860s, the system of normative conditions was the chosen system for most of the attempts to regulate the rights of associations at law. The Saxon Civil Code had, it is true, retained the concessionary system, but five years later normative conditions were introduced for associations pursuing economic or 'ideal' goals, the latter category comprising those associations which were not involved in public affairs. In 1869, Bavaria introduced a set of laws for non-political associations based on the system of normative conditions. In the same year, the Prussian left-wing liberal, Hermann Schulze-Delitzsch, began a lengthy campaign in the Reichstag to reform the whole of the private law of associations on a similar basis. He was, however, unable to convince a majority in the Reichstag of the political wisdom of extending this system to political and religious associations, and to trade unions.[80] In this way, discussions of the private law of associations took over the distinction between political and non-political organizations which was already the basis of the public law.

In 1874, the Vorkommission and the justice committee of the Bundesrat had suggested that the commission should include the law of associations

[79] On this legal background, see Vormbaum, *Rechtsfähigkeit*, chs. 1-2 and P. Kögler, *Arbeiterbewegung und Vereinsrecht. Ein Beitrag zur Entstehungsgeschichte des BGB* (Berlin, 1974), pts. 1-2.

[80] Kögler, *Arbeiterbewegung*, pp. 23 f., 49 f.; Vormbaum, *Rechtsfähigkeit*, pp. 79-89, 109-14.

in the draft code. Nevertheless, in November 1879 the commission accepted Gebhard's suggestion that the matter should be left to the individual states, a position which was confirmed without debate in 1884. Gebhard's suggestion was apparently motivated by political doubts about introducing a national law based on normative conditions and on his desire to represent the interests of his own state (Baden). His legal justification for ignoring the stated wishes of the Bundesrat emphasized the problems in distinguishing the public and private law aspects of this part of the legal system.[81]

It has been argued, though without direct evidence, that the commission's decision reflected contemporary feelings about the growth in strength of the Social Democrats and the trade union movement.[82] It is certainly true that legislators in the 1870s were moving towards a much more restrictive position with regard to the legal rights of worker organizations than in the 1860s. Both this shift and the increasing use of police powers against the trade union movement have been plausibly viewed as a response to experiences of worker radicalism in the strike wave of the early 1870s, as well as to international events such as the Paris Commune.[83] Against this background, it was most unlikely that the commission would introduce a system of normative conditions which might strengthen socialist organizations, especially as special legislation and judicial practice tended to satisfy the demands of middle-class associations—both economic and 'ideal'—for legal recognition.[84] As in the case of the law of domestic servants, then, the failure to include a matter of socio-political importance in the Code demonstrated the limitations of the codifiers' desire for legal unity on a liberal, progressive basis. In both cases, the strict separation of public and private law was used to justify the maintenance of the existing, generally conservative laws of the individual states. The cases differed, however, in that the decision on the law relating to domestic servants represented a failure to remove a major bulwark of a conservative social order. The decision on the law of associations, on the other hand, reflected an unwillingness

---

[81] Kögler, *Arbeiterbewegung*, pp. 58 ff., 68 ff.; Vormbaum, *Rechtsfähigkeit*, pp. 130 ff.; for Gebhard's reasoning, see W. Schubert, *Vorlagen. Allgemeiner Teil*, i (Berlin/New York, 1981), 552-64.

[82] Kögler, *Arbeiterbewegung*, pp. 70-5.

[83] See Albrecht, *Fachverein*, pp. 196-205; the major legal weapons used against the labour movement were the broadening of the definition of a 'political' association and the part of the law which forbade links between associations.

[84] Vormbaum, *Rechtsfähigkeit*, pp. 71 ff., 116 ff., 127.

to extend the legislative achievements of liberalism to social and political groups which were perceived to be hostile.

As will be seen, the commission's treatment of the law of association was to be the subject of much criticism and amendment after 1888. Nor was it by any means the only area of the law in which the commission was widely felt to have failed to come to terms with Germany's needs. The adoption of the Roman-law rule that the sale of a property rendered pre-existing tenancy agreements and leases void (*Kauf bricht Miete*) and the rules on hire purchase agreements[85] were felt to bias the legal system against the socially disadvantaged. In the field of agrarian law, the draft code came under attack over its decision to reserve the question of a special inheritance law to prevent the splitting up of peasant holdings to the individual states. Once again, this decision was justified by the variety of peasant inheritance laws and customs operating in Germany.[86]

In these and many other parts of the law, the commission could produce impeccable arguments for the decisions it had taken, based on the use of the techniques of legal positivism to construct a secure, certain legal order. The problem was that this conception of the task of the legislator was fast losing legitimacy in the 1880s, as new ideas about the positive role of the state in relation to social policy began to gain ground. Opinions were now being aired which cut the ground from beneath the cherished shibboleths of conceptual jurisprudence: the primacy of individual autonomy; the distinction between public and private law; the idea of codification as a systematic presentation of existing law, and so on.

The commission could not help but notice the emergence of this new tone and Planck, in particular, felt the need to answer the charge that the commission had neglected its proper duties. Pointing to the poorly developed nature of many of the proposals for radical legal reform, he insisted that '[i]nterference [in existing law] is particularly to be rejected where things are still developing or in a state of flux and where opinions about legislation are not sufficiently clear'. In such cases the legislator must opt for existing law.[87] That view of the duties of responsible legislation, which implied a time-lag between social development and legal response, clashed with increasingly strident demands that the civil

---

[85] Broadly, these stated that the goods sold remained the property of the vendor until the final instalment was paid. In case of default by the purchaser, the vendor could reclaim his property in full without reimbursing the purchaser for money already paid.

[86] Mugdan (ed.), *Materialien*, i. 53 ff.

[87] Planck, 'Zur Kritik', p. 407.

law play a positive role in the shaping of the future social order. The publication of the draft code in 1888 was a vital catalyst in the emergence of such demands, which amounted to a rejection of the entire 'social model' which had guided the commission's work and in many ways pointed forward to twentieth-century legal developments.[88]

The dominance of the conceptual jurisprudence of the common lawyers in the commission was the result of a number of different factors. As a system, it stood alone in presenting the possibility of creating certainty in the law, given the great divergences between the laws of the different regions of Germany in 1870. It had no real competition in offering the chance of that unity in diversity—the construction of a modern, *national* legal system without destroying the special interests of the southern states—which had so preoccupied the politicians of the 1870s. The composition of the commission, its mode of working, and the dominant role of men like Pape, Windscheid, and Planck all helped to strengthen the role of conceptual jurisprudence in the preparation of the draft code. The relatively minor role played by Paul von Roth—the token Germanist—in the commission's deliberations merely accentuated this dominance.

The 1888 draft code thus reflected the main political and juris-prudential concerns of the third quarter of the nineteenth century. The work began at the height of the *Kulturkampf*, when the National Liberals were the largest party in the Reichstag. Much emphasis was placed on the integrative, nation-building aspects of a codification, which would both form a major institutional underpinning of the new state and give expression to the powerful drive of the German people towards unity. As was suggested above, the liberal supporters of codification collapsed two quite separate concepts—the expression of the German people's national identity and the power and the authority of the state—into one.

The National Liberals' emphasis on the formal aspects of unification was a response to the particular political circumstances of the early 1870s. This helps to explain why the political decisions of 1873–4 should have been acceptable to the National Liberals despite the clearly conservative implications of those decisions. But, in view of the strong parallels that can be discerned between legal positivism and liberal politics, it is possible to go further and state that, in most areas of the law,

---

[88] Wieacker, 'Sozialmodell', in *Industriegesellschaft und Privatrechtsordnung*, pp. 9–35.

German jurisprudence and modern legislation had already introduced the essential liberal demands. Legal positivism, with its strong emphasis on the public/private law distinction and on the private autonomy of equal individuals, was in many ways an ideology which mirrored the liberals' demand for the *Rechtsstaat*. Against the background of the political changes of 1866–71, the liberal programme in the sphere of the civil law could legitimately focus on the creation of legal certainty through the systematic ordering and reconciliation of existing legal systems, according to the principles of conceptual jurisprudence. This was the point that Friedrich Engels saw when he wrote of the procedural and organizational codes of 1877:

The removal of the motley array of formal and material legal norms emanating from the individual states was in itself an urgent necessity for bourgeois development and the main significance of the new laws lies in that removal— far more than in their content.[89]

The period between 1874 and 1884 saw the end of the National Liberals' electoral hegemony over those sections of society which broadly accepted the 1871 settlement, and the beginnings of disquieting anti-liberal mobilizations from below. This reflected a decline in the National Liberals' ability to speak for the nation and the loss of their monopoly of the national idea.[90] With their socially and regionally heterogeneous electorate, they were the major victims of an age in which the demand for state action to alleviate the suffering of individuals at the hands of capitalist individualism became almost universal.[91] Essentially, the problem was that measures to aid one section of the National Liberal electorate were always likely to alienate others.

In many respects, conceptual jurisprudence faced the same difficulties. It attempted to weigh up various social interests in the interests of balance and harmony but was increasingly threatened by groups demanding radical legal reform to protect their endangered position. The pursuit of legal certainty on the basis of individual freedoms came to seem a defence of the class ,interests of a narrow band of property-owners at the expense of the broader interests of the nation

[89] F. Engels, 'Die Rolle der Gewalt in der Geschichte', in *Marx–Engels Werke*, 31 (Berlin-GDR, 1962), 458.

[90] See Eley's comments in his 'State Formation, Nationalism and Political Culture in Nineteenth-Century Germany', in R. Samuel and G. Stedman Jones (eds.), *Culture, Ideology and Politics. Essays for Eric Hobsbawm* (London, 1983), 289 ff.

[91] H. Rosenberg, *Grosse Depression und Bismarckzeit. Wirtschaftsablauf, Gesellschaft und Politik in Mitteleuropa* (paperback edn. Frankfurt, 1976), 78 ff.

as a whole. The commission's failure to carry out social reform—indeed its rejection of the idea that a Civil Code had 'a particular social duty in that sense'[92]—left it vulnerable to attack from both the left and the right. Once the draft code was published in 1888 and subjected to public criticism, the social and political neutrality of conceptual jurisprudence could no longer be sustained. It was the scale of that public criticism which was responsible, above all else, for the lengthy revisions of the first commission's work in the 1890s.

[92] Planck, 'Zur Kritik', p. 406.

5.

The Public Response and the Campaign
for Legal Reform,
1888–1896

THE published draft code invited comments not only from professional lawyers and academics, but also from representatives of the various economic interests.[1] The opportunity was not missed and, according to one estimate, almost 400 individuals and eighty associations had produced their comments by 1896.[2] An enormous amount of newspaper space was devoted to the subject as well. In Britain, an impressed Maitland commented:

it shows that a nation can become profoundly interested in its legal system. A tornado broke loose. It rained, it poured books and pamphlets. At that time, I made a habit of looking through a weekly list of books published in Germany; and it struck me that no German could find anything else to write about except this embryonic code ... the whole nation seemed to convert itself into a large debating club, in which, however, everybody spoke at once.[3]

Even taking Maitland's evident hyperbole into account, it is clear that the volume and range of public comment were in stark contrast to the lack of attention paid to the deliberations of the commission before 1888. These debates reveal much about the nature of changes in the German political system in the late 1880s and early 1890s.

Opinions about the value of the draft code covered the whole spectrum from support for its introduction as soon as possible to complete denial of its value. The former view was especially strong among the chambers

---

[1] *Der erste Entwurf eines bürgerlichen Gesetzbuches für das Deutsche Reich. Amtliche Ausgabe* (Berlin/Leipzig, 1888), vii.

[2] L. Enneccerus, 'Die parlamentarischen Aussichten des Bürgerlichen Gesetzbuches', *DJZ* 1 (1896), p. 6.

[3] F. W. Maitland, 'The Making of the German Civil Code', *Independent Review* (1906), reprinted in H. A. L. Fisher (ed.), *The Collected Papers of Frederic William Maitland*, iii (Cambridge, 1911), 480.

of commerce,[4] though it was by no means unanimously shared. Thus the Cologne, Solingen, and Lübeck chambers argued that although the draft code undoubtedly contained errors, it was essential that the prospect of legal unity was not endangered by destructive revisions. As the Solingen chamber put it: 'Even if the Code were actually as bad as is claimed in certain circles, we would still rather see it accepted in spite of its faults than have the introduction of legal unity delayed for the foreseeable future.' The Schweidenitz chamber, on the other hand, denied that the present legal order was so unacceptable that any conceivable code would be preferable. It did, however, agree that the commission had generally satisfied the interests of trade and industry.[5]

It was predictable that National Liberal circles should lead the campaign to complete the unification of the legal system quickly—a policy which meant at most minor revisions of the work of the commission. In a brave attempt to revive the rhetoric of the 1870s, the *National-Zeitung* expressed the hope that 'the moral pressure created by the *existence* of a draft of this sort' would overcome any possible federalist or particularist opposition. Another prominent National Liberal organ claimed that earlier attempts to produce civil codes in Hessen and Bavaria had failed because of 'irresponsible criticism'.[6] The Bavarian lawyer and National Liberal, Melchior Stenglein, agreed, and criticized those who would have no code at all than accept the 1888 draft. Those who lived in Bavaria, he claimed, knew what problems were caused by the lack of legal unity, and the situation in Prussia was not much better. Voices began to be heard demanding 'resignation'—i.e. the acceptance of perhaps unwelcome details—in order not to endanger the greater cause of legal unity.[7] An extreme example of that sentiment was the famous criminal lawyer Franz von Liszt, who professed great disappointment with the draft code and agreed in general with the radical criticisms developed by Otto von Gierke. But he then went on to restrict his suggestions to matters which might be revised without upsetting the structure of the commission's work:

[4] The comments of the chambers of commerce are to be found in ZStA Potsdam, RJM 3838. For reasons of space, they will be cited as Cologne chamber, p.—, etc.

[5] Cologne chamber, p. 4; Solingen chamber, p. 2, Lübeck chamber, n.p.; Schweidenitz chamber, p. 3.

[6] *National-Zeitung*, 6 Jan. 1888; *Schlesische Zeitung*, 6 Apr. 1888.

[7] Stenglein to Marquardsen, 23 Apr. 1889, ZStA Potsdam, Marquardsen Papers 23, fo. 63; G. Planck, 'Zur Kritik des Entwurfes eines bürgerlichen Gesetzbuches für das deutsche Reich', *AcP* 75 (1889), p. 329; Windscheid, speech of 22 Sept. 1889, cited in G. Planck, 'Windscheid als Mitarbeiter am bürgerlichen Gesetzbuche', *DJZ* 14 (1909), p. 955.

Where it is a question of the legal unity of our German people, juristic doubts can play no role. I would vote for any draft of a unified civil code, however little it corresponded to my opinion of the requirements of a German code.[8]

General agreement existed in National Liberal circles that while some revisions might be called for, they should not be such as might endanger the rapid completion of national legal unity.[9] A wide range of arguments developed in the course of the debates concerning the draft code. There was, for example, a common feeling that the language and presentation of the draft code left a great deal to be desired. This was an important element in the more radical attacks on the work of the commission, but a similar view was also held by many of the code's supporters. The draft code was felt by many to be incomprehensible to the layman, unnecessarily formalized and abstract, and too dependent on an elaborate system of cross-references. Others, however, pointed out that these characteristics were inevitable in view of the complexity of modern German law.[10]

On the whole, there was a general feeling among lawyers that the draft code was at least suitable as the basis of a future code. As the President of the Lawyers' Congress wrote in 1890:

As far as I can see, practising lawyers are in general very favourable towards the draft code and keen that it should become law. The same view is more or less dominant in the judiciary, although there are notable exceptions. The centre of opposition lies with the university professors . . .

A senior official in the Reich Justice Office agreed, writing that 'apart from Gierke, the criticisms are on the whole overwhelmingly favourable, especially on the main questions'. When the practising lawyers were called upon to comment, the committee of their representative body (the Deutscher Anwaltsverein) expressed the wish that the draft code's virtues be extolled:[11]

---

[8] F. v. Liszt, *Die Grenzgebiete zwischen Privat- und Strafrecht* (Berlin/Leipzig, 1889), 4 f.

[9] e.g. *National-Zeitung*, 25 Mar. 1888; *Kölnische Zeitung*, 30 July 1888. One exception to this consensus was Otto Bähr, whose opposition to codes had not changed since the 1860s; see Bähr, *Das bürgerliche Gesetzbuch und die Zukunft der deutschen Rechtssprechung* (Leipzig, 1888).

[10] E. I. Bekker, *System und Sprache des Entwurfs eines Bürgerlichen Gesetzbuchs* (Berlin/Leipzig, 1888); P. Hinschius, *Suarez, der Schöpfer des preussischen Landrechts und der Entwurf eines bürgerlichen Gesetzbuchs für das deutsche Reich* (Berlin, 1889); Schweidenitz chamber, pp. 3 f.

[11] Gneist to Oehlschläger, 23 Feb. 1890, ZStA Potsdam, RJM no. 3812, fo. 84.; Struckmann to Planck, 22 Apr. 1890, NSUUB Göttingen, Planck Papers VIII, fo. 62. M. Hachenburg, *Lebenserinnerungen eines Rechtsanwalts* (Düsseldorf, 1927), 161.

This happy picture was misleading, however, in that it merely pointed to the majority view within the community of lawyers. The publication of the draft code came after Bismarck's first attempts at social reform, and aroused considerable protest from those who wished to see the new spirit reflected in the nation's civil code. A man of the academic stature of Heinrich von Dernburg rejected the fundamental postulate of conceptual jurisprudence and asked at the meeting of the Lawyers' Congress in 1889:

What is private law except the organization of society? Social considerations are the most relevant ones even for legislators. The jurist who produces a law should merely put what is socially useful into the necessary form. If therefore the social policy aspects are the most important ones in questions of legislation, it is precisely private law which regulates the relationship between the different classes, estates, and corporations that exist in society. The social element is what matters.[12]

Dernburg was not alone in believing this. At the same meeting of the Lawyers' Congress, Dr Ludwig Fuld began a long campaign to bring more consideration for the socially disadvantaged, and particularly for the peasantry, into the Code. In Fuld's opinion, the legislators had the duty of 'soaking' the Civil Code with the social demands of the time; Bismarck's famous 'drop of social oil' should, he argued, be extended to the vital area of the civil law.[13] These sentiments were by no means associated with opposition to a code in principle. An enthusiastic supporter of a national code such as Heinrich Brunner was deeply disappointed with the 1888 draft. Its allegedly excessive reliance on Roman rather than German law and its neglect of 'social' aspects of the private law made it, as far as Brunner was concerned, inferior to the Prussian *Allgemeines Landrecht*. In this respect, his position was close to that of his colleagues at the University of Berlin, Dernburg and Paul Hinschius.[14]

Of all the writers associated with this type of criticism of the 1888 draft code, Otto von Gierke was by far the most famous. His achievement was to place the widespread criticisms of the social consequences of the commission's emphasis on Roman law within a systematic social and political theory. Gierke was keen to influence the national and Prussian

[12] *Verhandlungen des Zwanzigsten Deutschen Juristentages*, iv (Berlin, 1889), 176 f.
[13] Ibid. 170 ff.
[14] Brunner to F. Althoff, 21 Sept. 1888, ZStA Merseburg, Rep. 92 Althoff no. 18 vol. 3, fos. 103-7. cf. Hinschius, *Suarez, passim* for the superiority of the *Allgemeines Landrecht* from the 'social' point of view.

governments through his work.[15] He also went to some trouble to win support elsewhere, for example in the Lawyers' Congress and the main representative body of Prussian agriculture, the Landes-Oekonomie-Kollegium. The government and the Code's supporters took Gierke's criticisms very seriously indeed. Planck's famous defence of the draft code was seen rightly as 'an anti-Gierke',[16] and Hermann Struckmann of the Reich Justice Office was dispatched to the meeting of the Landes-Oekonomie-Kollegium in November 1889 in order to ward off Gierke's attacks on the Code. As Planck recognized, Gierke's views were dangerous because they harmonized so well with the increasing demands by sectional interest groups for special treatment, and because his suggestions could not possibly be reconciled with the work of the commission.[17]

A favourite accusation against Gierke was that his demand for a truly 'German' code, which largely excluded Roman law elements, ignored the fact that Roman law had become part of the German legal tradition in the period since the Middle Ages. Gierke's work could thus be dismissed as a hopelessly nostalgic, conservative fantasy, with no bearing on modern needs. As one left-liberal newspaper put it, Gierke's views constituted 'the translation of Neo-Gothic from architecture to politics'.[18] Subsequent scholarship, too, has been concerned with the extent to which Gierke was merely a reactionary trying to put the clock back in the interests of East Elbian landowners and other endangered social groups.[19] If that were the case, however, how was Gierke able to gain the support not only of the ultra-conservative *Kreuzzeitung* but also, with reservations, of the socialist *Vorwärts?*[20]

Like the other 'social' critics of the draft code, Gierke was by no means an opponent of codification in principle. Indeed, he believed that the campaign against the draft code was a battle for a truly 'German' code.[21] According to Gierke, the commission had neglected the essential duties of the legislator. Its work was 'neither German, nor simple

---

[15] Gierke to Bismarck, 3 July 1889, ZStA Potsdam, Rkz 726, fo. 22; Gierke to Friedberg, 3 July 1889, GStA Berlin-Dahlem, Rep. 84a 11773, fo. 353.

[16] Johow to Planck, 29 Sept. 1889, NSUUB Göttingen, Planck Papers v, fo. 104.

[17] Planck, 'Zur Kritik', pp. 405 f., 415 f.

[18] *Vossische Zeitung,* 12 Aug. 1889; cf. *National-Zeitung,* 29 Aug. 1890.

[19] See the excellent discussion of this question in G. Dilcher, 'Genossenschaftstheorie und Sozialrecht: Ein "Juristensozialismus" Otto v. Gierkes?', *Quad. fior.* 3/4, t. 1 (1974–5), pp. 319–65.

[20] *Kreuzzeitung,* 29 Aug. 1888; *Vorwärts,* 2 Apr. 1891 and 1 June 1895.

[21] O. Gierke, *Der Entwurf eines bürgerlichen Gesetzbuchs und das Deutsche Recht* (Leipzig, 1889), vi.

(*volkstümlich*), nor creative—and the moral and social demands made upon a new system of private law do not seem to have entered [the draft code's] horizons at all.' Pouring scorn on the code's claims to social and political neutrality, he declared that if it had a hidden social tendency,

> it would be the individualistic and one-sidedly capitalistic tendency of the pure Manchester doctrine, that truly anti-social tendency—which is hostile to the community and aims at the strengthening of the strong against the weak—with which our recent German legislation has otherwise so decisively broken.

The development of German society demanded, he said, a break with the Roman law distinction between public and private law. Indeed, the connection of these two areas of the law through the development of an intermediate 'social' law was seen by Gierke as 'a matter of life and death' for the contemporary social order.[22]

Gierke and other 'Germanist' critics of the Code did, however, deny that legal unity was in itself such a pressing necessity for the state that all worries about the code's contents could be forgotten. What was required was not just a code but a good code, and such a piece of legislation was to be judged primarily in terms of its social content.[23] From that basis, which was diametrically opposed to the ideology which had guided the commission, Gierke developed his attack on the Code's Romanist character. Principles such as freedom of contract were, in fact, means of enslaving the weaker party to the stronger. The entire law of obligations proceeded from the assumption that only autonomous individuals were involved. With some justification, Gierke argued that this took no account of the fact that associations rather than individuals were the main source of economic activity in modern society. As a result of this 'individualism', the sections of the draft code on interest rates, usury, penalty clauses and tenancy law were biased in favour of the creditor, who was likely to be the stronger of the two contracting partners. Concealed behind contractual freedom was the great threat of exploitation of the socially disadvantaged. That exploitation was, in Gierke's opinion, a major source of modern social problems and urgently

---

[22] Gierke, *Entwurf*, pp. 2, 3 f.; Gierke, 'Die soziale Aufgabe des Privatrechts' (1889), reprinted in E. Wolf (ed.), *Quellenbuch zur Geschichte der deutschen Rechtswissenschaft* (Frankfurt, 1949), 485.

[23] Gierke, *Entwurf*, pp. 4 f.; a similar view on this question was taken by another Germanist, Felix Dahn, in the *Schlesische Zeitung*, 27 Nov. 1888.

demanded the attention of the legislator: 'Nowadays, more than ever before, private law must protect the weak against the strong and the interests of the community against the selfishness of individuals.'[24]

Gierke's reputation as 'the champion of the Germanist-Junker-reactionary opposition to the Civil Code'[25] rests mainly on the second major part of his attack on the draft code—his insistence on the need for a differential treatment of land and movable property. He accepted that landownership was the bulwark of the social order, and believed that to equate it with the ownership of movable property was the height of irresponsibility. The notion that property was the total domination of a person over a thing was pure anathema to Gierke, who denied that property was merely part of the private sphere of the individual, subject only to minimal external constraints. Prefacing his attack with the slogan 'No rights without duties', he declared: 'In cases of necessity the legal order should be willing not only to forbid the abuse of property, but also to make the duty of correct use of property in the context of what is socially desirable a legal obligation.'[26] According to Gierke, a measure of the superiority of the German (as opposed to Roman) legal tradition was that it insisted that landownership be tied to a set of social duties and political functions not associated with the ownership of other types of capital. Was it not ridiculous, he asked, to give the owner of land the same rights as the owner of an umbrella or a banknote?[27] Any legal order which sought to give the land the same velocity of circulation as that enjoyed by other goods posed an essential threat to society, in which landownership was supposed to play a conservative function: 'In this way [the draft code] arrives at a formulation of landownership which will be most welcome to those parties who see future salvation in the abolition of private property in land.'[28]

Gierke then developed a series of suggested reforms designed to bolster the position of the landowning classes in the legal system. In mortgage law, he supported the inclusion of annuity charges (*Rentenschulden*) by which repayments were calculated according to the productive value of the land rather than its capital value. In inheritance law, he joined the increasingly vociferous campaign for the inclusion in

---

[24] Gierke, *Entwurf*, pp. 192–244; 'Aufgabe', p. 499.

[25] U.-J. Heuer, *Allgemeines Landrecht und Klassenkampf* (Berlin-GDR, 1960), 15.

[26] Gierke, 'Aufgabe', pp. 490 f.

[27] Ibid. 492.

[28] Gierke, *Entwurf*, p. 280; on the conservative social role that landownership ought to play, see 'Aufgabe', p. 494.

the code of legal provisions to counteract the splitting-up of peasant holdings between several heirs by securing an undivided succession (*Anerbenrecht*). With regard to aristocratic landholdings, he sought to achieve the same result through a modified retention of the family entail.[29]

Gierke's work thus linked the assertion of 'German' legal traditions to the important social and political significance of landownership. In this respect, Gierke was very much a man of his time rather than an innovator. For some time before the publication of the draft code, agrarian groups had been aware of the political capital to be gained from the notion that they were defenders of society against socialism. By the early 1880s, that view was winning increasing support in academic circles as well. The discussions of the Verein für Sozialpolitik in 1882 and 1884 gave such ideas a powerful platform, and the work of August von Miaskowski in particular had done much to promote the connection between the survival of the peasantry and the reform of inheritance law in line with 'German' legal traditions.[30] Having outlined the dangers inherent in Roman law and the existence of alternative 'German' traditions, Miaskowski commented:

Thus, if landed property were to be subjected to a different system of law from capital, in so far as that is justified by its specific nature, that would not mean creating something entirely new; rather, it would bring out once more the idea at the root of the old law that differences in the economic nature of pieces of property must also determine the formulation of legislation.[31]

Partly as a result of Miaskowski's research, the matter was taken up by the German Agricultural Council (Deutscher Landwirtschaftsrat) in 1886, and a petition was sent to Bismarck requesting that the Code introduce undivided inheritance in cases of intestate succession to landed properties.[32]

The work of Miaskowski and others laid the intellectual foundations for the Germanist attack on the agrarian law of the Code, and in many

---

[29] Gierke, *Entwurf*, pp. 369 f., 570 f.; 'Aufgabe', p. 495; cf. Gierke, 'Die Stellung des künftigen bürgerlichen Gesetzbuchs zum Erbrecht in ländlichen Grundbesitz', in G. Schmoller (ed.), *Jahrbuch für Gesetzgebung, Verwaltung und Volkswirtschaft*, 12 (1888), 401-36.

[30] *Schriften des Vereins für Sozialpolitik*, xxi, xxviii (Leipzig, 1882, 1884); A. v. Miaskowski, *Das Erbrecht und die Grundeigenthumsverteilung im Deutschen Reich* (2 vols. Leipzig, 1882, 1884).

[31] Miaskowski, *Erbrecht*, ii. 260.

[32] 'Eingabe des Deutschen Landwirtschaftsrats', 1 July 1887, StA Hamburg, Senatskomm. für die Justizverwaltung 1 A a 1 vol. 1, fo. 45.

ways their ideas prefigured those of Gierke. Miaskowski believed that stable landownership was an important bulwark against socialism.[33] Like Gierke, he saw the essence of a truly 'German' law of landed inheritance as being anti-individualist, with the preservation of the family unit the major concern. The preservation of the family—conceived by Gierke as an 'organic unity'—was a matter which Miaskowski and the other Germanists considered to be of 'the most far-reaching socio-economic importance'.[34] Germanism linked an emphasis on the family unit, special treatment for the needs of the agrarian sector, and a priority for the needs of society over the rights of the individual in an all-embracing attack on the 'Romanist' individualism on which the draft code was based.

These ideas were to be taken up after 1888 by agrarian groups, which saw in Germanism a much-needed justification for their claims to special treatment at the hands of the state. It is this connection with agrarian conservatism which is principally responsible for the association of Gierke and the other Germanists with reactionary interests. The Germanists thus played an important role in the rapid radicalization of agrarian politics in anti-liberal directions in the 1880s and 1890s. Their emphasis on community, hostility to individualism and commitment to allegedly 'German' over 'foreign' (i.e. Roman) traditions were central features of the conservative backlash against the liberalism of the 1860s and 1870s.[35]

These issues will be considered at greater length later in this chapter. It must be remembered, however, that the Germanism of 1888 was by no means simply the tool of reactionary interests. Miaskowski's major concern was with the survival of a healthy peasantry, which he believed to be threatened not only by 'mobile' capital but also by worrying tendencies in the direction of the consolidation of larger estates. His work differed from Gierke's about the value of the aristocratic family entail (*Fideikommiss*), which he believed strengthened the strong against the weak and led to the absorption of peasant holdings into larger estates.[36] With regard to mortgage law, Gierke stressed the value of the Prussian legislation of the 1870s, a view which distinguished him from

[33] Miaskowski, *Erbrecht*, ii. 274.

[34] Gierke, *Entwurf*, p. 394; Miaskowski, *Erbrecht*, i. 241 ff. (quotation, p. 252); cf. Gierke, 'Aufgabe', pp. 504 f.; *Entwurf*, pp. 535 f.

[35] On these developments see S. Buchholz, *Abstraktionsprinzip und Immobiliarrecht. Zur Geschichte der Auflassung und der Grundschuld* (Frankfurt, 1978), 381–8.

[36] Miaskowski, *Erbrecht*, ii. 5–90. For Gierke's disagreement on this, see his 'Erbrecht in ländlichen Grundbesitz', pp. 427 ff.

the radical agrarians in the 1890s, for whom that legislation symbolized the supremacy of capital over landownership.[37] Above all, none of the major Germanists actually considered the rejection of the principle of testamentary freedom as such. Miaskowski actually saw salvation in an extension of testamentary freedom for landowners, but argued that this needed to be buttressed with undivided inheritance in cases where the owner died intestate. Gierke agreed that a modern *Anerbenrecht* could not restrict the freedom of disposition of landowners, which would be tantamount to the restoration of unfree property tenures. Like Miaskowski, his proposed reforms only applied in cases of intestate succession.[38]

Gierke's break with conservatism was most clear, however, in his views on the law of associations. As has been seen, he was the principal Germanist proponent of the 'free creation of corporations' system, whereby the decision of a group to form an association sufficed to give it the right to act at law. The radicalism of this suggestion meant that warm support for it was forthcoming only from the Social Democrats. Nevertheless, Gierke found the support of large numbers of his fellow lawyers for his attack on the exclusion of the question of the acquisition and loss of 'juristic personality' from the draft code. The strength of feeling against the commission was demonstrated by the support for reform at the 1888 Lawyers' Congress.[39]

Gierke regarded this section of the draft code as perhaps the most unsatisfactory of all and in urgent need of revision.[40] This was related to a central element of his social and political philosophy, which sought to develop the rights and powers of human associations in order to prevent the dissolution of society into two competing spheres, dominated by an omnipotent state and atomized individuals. Human associations offered the possibility of a reconciliation of different groups within a nation-state, in which personal freedoms could enjoy a proper area of autonomy without succumbing to the exploitative tendencies of individualism. Gierke accepted the liberal notion of the emancipation of civil society from the control of the state, and only supported

[37] Gierke, *Entwurf*, pp. 367–82.

[38] Miaskowski, *Erbrecht*, ii. 201 ff.; *Schriften des Vereins für Sozialpolitik*, xxi. 20 ff.; Gierke, 'Erbrecht in ländlichen Grundbesitz', pp. 410–20.

[39] *Verhandlungen des Neunzehnten Deutschen Juristentages*, iii (Berlin, 1888), 220 ff., 321 ff.; cf. T. Vormbaum, *Die Rechtsfähigkeit der Vereine im 19. Jahrhundert. Ein Beitrag zur Entstehungsgeschichte des BGB* (Berlin/New York, 1976), 150 ff.

[40] Gierke, *Entwurf*, p. 144, and id., *Personengemeinschaften und Vermögensinbegriffe* (Berlin, 1889).

restrictions on individual freedom when he felt there to be an overriding social need.[41] This last point becomes clear in his discussion of the law of inheritance of landed property:

> in general, the principle of freedom of private property in land has sunk such deep roots in modern legal consciousness and is so closely connected with our cultural development that it may only be infringed upon when every other means of protecting society has shown itself to be insufficient.[42]

But he also believed that contemporary social developments, whose greatest evil was exploitation of the weak by the strong, provided irrefutable evidence of the need for restrictions on the destructive force of individual selfishness. In this context, the law of associations was the sphere within which an integrative 'social' law might develop precisely because associational life expressed the possibilities of collective, rather than selfishly individualistic, human action.

These considerations help to explain what otherwise appears to be a paradoxical mixture of reactionary and progressive elements in Gierke's work. Liberal accusations that the Germanists were merely attempting to set the clock back and reinstitute medieval German institutions missed a central point about Gierke's views. Although his preference for 'German' legal institutions developed out of his historical study of medieval German corporations (*Genossenschaften*), purely historical considerations played at most a secondary role in the evolution of his thought. His principal concern was with the solution of contemporary social problems, while his historical arguments were developed in order to support the cause of reform.[43]

It was clear that Gierke could not command the support of the majority of lawyers on these matters. Brunner and Dernburg constituted a powerful source of backing for Germanist ideas in general, but Brunner in particular was far too much the loyal, academic civil servant to agitate in public against the work of the commission. Dernburg had few such reservations, but his influence on its own was hardly sufficient to overcome the pressure to accept the draft code as the basis of future

---

[41] Dilcher, 'Genossenschaftstheorie und Sozialrecht', *passim*; S. Pfeiffer-Munz, *Soziales Recht ist deutsches Recht. Otto von Gierkes Theorie des sozialen Rechts untersucht anhand seiner Stellungnahmen zur deutschen und zur schweizerischen Privatrechtskodifikation* (Zürich, 1979), chs. 3–6.

[42] Gierke, 'Erbrecht im ländlichen Grundbesitz', p. 416.

[43] Dilcher, 'Genossenschaftstheorie und Sozialrecht', pp. 356 f.; Pfeiffer-Munz, *Soziales Recht*, pp. 40 f. The title of the latter work is intended to express these priorities in Gierke's thought.

legislation. A clear statement of support for Gierke's views on many central points did come from one writer, Ludwig Fuld, who wrote of the 'deep, perhaps unbridgeable [*unausfüllbare*] gap [which] separates the supporters of previous legal developments and those who wish to open new paths and set new goals to the civil law through a particular emphasis on social interests.'[44] Fuld was particularly concerned with tenancy law and the law of peasant landed inheritance, in both of which areas he considered the work of the commission to have failed in its duty to produce legislation which did justice to 'the needs of our time and of our national economy'. Like Gierke, he opposed a merely compilatory code and castigated the 'one-sidedly private law education of jurists' which prevented them from taking full account of social and economic differences in the population.[45] Like other critics, he argued for an extension rather than a restriction of testamentary freedom in order to overcome the danger of the subdivision of landed property. He particularly opposed the French system, which applied in his native Mainz. Another point of contact with Gierke was Fuld's hostility to the draft code's treatment of the law of associations, where he advocated the system of 'free creation of corporations'. The concessionary system was, he said, merely 'a ruin left over from the police state'.[46]

Perhaps the essential characteristic of these criticisms was the perceived connection between formal equality before the law and social and economic inequalities. As Fuld put it: 'The legislator ignores the countless differences in social and economic relationships and in the sphere of the civil law maintains the fiction that people are equal to each other, whereas the reverse is true.' The same perception also lay behind the only explicitly socialist critique of the commission's work — a new departure, which on certain points gained the support of anti-socialist reformers such as Gierke and Fuld.[47] The Viennese socialist Anton Menger has only recently become the subject of serious scholarly

[44] L. Fuld, 'Das bürgerliche Gesetzbuch und das Sozialpolitik', *Gruchots Beiträge zur Erläuterung des Deutschen Rechts*, 35 (1891), 636.

[45] L. Fuld, 'Der Entwurf eines bürgerlichen Gesetzbuchs für das deutsche Reich und das bäuerliche Erbrecht', *Zeitschrift für Agrarpolitik*, 1 (1888), 148 f.; 'Sozialpolitik', pp. 639, 647.

[46] L. Fuld, 'Das Erbrecht des code civil und das bäuerliche Grundbesitz', in Schmoller (ed.), *Jahrbuch für Gesetzgebung, Verwaltung und Volkswirthschaft*, xii (1888), 999–1027; Fuld, 'Die rechtliche Stellung der juristischen Personen', *Allgemeine Zeitung*, 25 Oct. 1891.

[47] Fuld, 'Sozialpolitik', pp. 639 ff.; Gierke, *Entwurf*, p. 25.

attention.[48] His claim to a place in the history of the debates concerning the Civil Code does not depend on his direct influence on the project, which was probably small, though difficult to measure.[49] But he is of interest in showing how it was possible to attack the conceptual jurisprudence from the left in ways which had many affinities with positions adopted by the Germanists.

Menger's starting-point was that fruitful criticism must be based on an acceptance of the draft code's basic position, and he renounced any intention of proceeding 'from socialist conceptions of the law'. On that basis, Menger sought to demonstrate the draft code's strong bias against the interests of the poor. His main interest lay in the law of contract, which he believed concealed the disadvantages of poverty by ignoring the vast differences in power accorded to different social groups:

On the whole, the disadvantages of the propertyless classes are produced by the fact that legislation proceeds from a purely formalistic viewpoint to create the same law for rich and poor, whereas the completely different social position of the two groups calls for different treatment in law.

To make matters even clearer, he declared that 'nowadays, it is obvious that no greater inequality exists than the equal treatment of unequals'.[50] The inadequacies of the draft code were firmly rooted in the faults of nineteenth-century jurisprudence and especially in the legacy of the Historical School of law. The Vorkommission's insistence on a compilatory codification was blamed by Menger for the backward-looking aspect of the commission's work at a time when the eye of the true legislator should be fixed firmly on the future. Jurisprudence was, as far as Menger was concerned, 'the most retarded of all disciplines and the latest to be affected by the movement of the times'.[51]

This concern with the 'creative', forward-looking duties of the legislator had obvious points in common with Gierke's Germanism. In contrast to Gierke, however, Menger rejected the notion of an 'organic'

[48] K.-H. Kästner, *Anton Menger (1841–1906). Leben und Werk* (Tübingen, 1974); E. Müller, *Anton Mengers Rechts- und Gesellschaftssystem* (Berlin, 1975); D. Wilrodt-Westernhagen, *Recht und soziale Frage* (Hamburg, 1975); H. Hörner, *Anton Menger. Recht und Sozialismus* (Frankfurt, 1977); and the contributions of Ramm, Reich, and Orrù in *Quad. fior.* 3/4, t. 1 (1974–5).

[49] For contrasting views on this, see Kästner, *Menger*, pp. 166 f.; Hörner, *Menger*, pp. 179 ff.; K.-P. Schroeder, 'Anton Menger: Jurist und Sozialphilosoph', *JuS* 15 (1975), p. 680; G. Orrù, ' "Idealismo" e "Realismo" nel socialismo di Menger', *Quad. fior.* 3/4, t. 1 (1974–5), pp. 230 f.

[50] A. Menger, *Das bürgerliche Recht und die besitzlosen Volksklassen* (5th edn., Tübingen, 1927), 2 f., 19, 30.

[51] Ibid. 15 f., 30.

concept of law; indeed one of his major targets was the conservatism implicit in the organic analogy: 'Whoever is convinced by the organic notion of law and the state is only too prone and too willing to forget that hurricanes and earthquakes are just as much parts of the natural process as the peaceful growth of animals and plants.'[52] Thus, while Menger and Gierke overlapped on many details and even on important points of principle, their positions were fundamentally different. Gierke sought reforms in line with a supposed national tradition which was in many ways deeply conservative; Menger was an unashamedly socialist proponent of reforms in the interests of the working classes.[53]

Menger believed that the draft code, in placing so much emphasis on the law of obligations, had shown itself 'as the product of a predominantly commercial era, in which concern for the trader actually outweighed the interests of property-owners'; the code constituted 'a victory of the commercial spirit over the propertied order, of the law of trade over the law of property'.[54] There was no doubt that the interests of property-owners were reflected in the notion of absolute property, but to Menger that was scarcely more than a fiction with limited validity even in bourgeois circles. Instead, the code was mainly concerned with the 'easier circulation of goods and improvements in juristic technique'. Nothing showed the detachment of the law from its economic base more clearly than those parts of the draft code which promoted the interests of trade over those of property. An example of this 'bias' was the principle of abstraction, about which Menger argued:

Few institutions have shaken the credibility of the private law among large parts of the community quite so much as those legal transactions in which a particular declaration of will in itself creates a legal obligation without any consideration of whether it is justified by the legal or economic facts of the case . . .

The explicit protection of the rights of a person who had acquired property in good faith, irrespective of how the seller had acquired the object, constituted 'a comprehensive and permanent confiscation of private property for the benefit of the security of trade'. Such considerations led Menger to conclude (in contrast to Gierke) that the

---

[52] Menger, *Das bürgerliche Recht*, p. 13.

[53] See the excellent discussions of Menger's relationship to other 'social' critics of the draft code in Hörner, *Menger*, pp. 135 ff. and Orrù, ' "Idealismo" e "Realismo" ', pp. 207 ff.

[54] *Das bürgerliche Recht*, pp. 39, 127.

draft code's conception of property was 'harsh in outward appearance, but weak and arbitrary underneath'. This weakness was but one of a number of signs which pointed to the inevitable decline of private property and the transfer of more and more of the legal order from private to public law.[55]

Predictably, Menger was particularly concerned with those parts of the law of obligations which seemed to work against the interests of the poor. He agreed with Gierke and others that the basic principle of freedom of contract was likely to lead to the dependence of the poor on the rich in such important areas as tenancy law and labour law. He was also concerned to point out the inadequacies of the draft code's treatment of working conditions. To Menger, the fundamental error of the proposed legislation was to see the labour or service contract as a contract of sale. As such, the draft code ignored the general trend in modern legislation, which seemed to point to a take-over of the regulation of the labour relationship by the state and eventually to 'a codification of the entire organization of labour'. He also claimed that the social legislation of the 1880s had probably increased the likelihood of accidents at work. As the worker's only assets were his 'personal attributes', the employer must be made exclusively liable in civil law for damages arising out of such accidents. A further weakness of the draft code was that it ignored the question of the employer's disciplinary powers. Like other critics such as Fuld, Menger demanded the inclusion of the law covering domestic servants in the code.[56]

However, Menger gave such widely shared views a new twist by arguing that, as with the absolute concept of property, the principle of freedom of contract was not systematically applied. Rather, it was subject to restrictions based on the interests of the property-owning classes. Menger believed freedom of contract to be a means of extracting income from the working classes. He found it significant that where the interests of the propertied and propertyless classes were not in conflict, as in land law, freedom of contract did not apply. The minimal regulation of usury, which concentrated on money loans and ignored developments such as hire purchase, was similarly tailored to the interests of the propertied classes.[57]

Menger's explicit support for the interests of the working classes set him apart from other critics of the social philosophy of the draft code.

[55] Ibid. 114, 120 (quotation), 125 ff., 132, 141.
[56] Ibid. 163–94 (quotation, p. 182); Fuld, 'Sozialpolitik', p. 651.
[57] *Das bürgerliche Recht*, pp. 151 ff., 157 ff.

While the Germanists saw revision of the law of inheritance as an effective and important tool of social reform, Menger was quite categorical about the fate of inheritance as a social institution in the near future: 'the law of inheritance is nothing but the extension of private property beyond the narrow limits of the life of a person. Consequently, the fates of both these social institutions cannot be separated.'[58] 'But in spite of this explicitly socialist schema, it is surely correct to see Menger as part of a general movement towards a more 'social' jurisprudence,[59] which derived much of its momentum from the publication of the draft code. A basic assumption of this movement was that the state had a duty to take care of the socially disadvantaged. The evidence is that this trend had a substantial amount of influence, and not merely within the conservative and socialist camps. National Liberal newspapers increasingly joined the cry for more protection for disadvantaged social groups, particularly within the agrarian sector. Even the right-wing National Liberal *Kölnische Zeitung* agreed with many of his criticisms, but tempered its approval with the standard declaration that the civil law must represent the interests of all social groups equally, concluding that 'the civil code must consider the demands of social policy in so far as they are compatible with the principles of private law'.[60]

The *Kölnische Zeitung*'s opinion contained the essence of the problem of legal reform in a 'social' direction. The central question for Gierke, Menger, and almost all the other contributors to the discussion was the extent to which the basic principles of the legal order might be limited in the interests of the common good. Thus, all the reformers rejected the sharp distinction between public and private law, but nobody of any consequence attacked the principle of basing the civil law on individual freedoms. Many writers sought to strengthen the propertied order by placing the social responsibilities of the property-owner at the heart of the legal system. That position required certain limitations on property-owners' freedoms, particularly with regard to landownership, but no attack was envisaged on the institution of private property as such. Nobody really disputed that certain limitations on freedom of contract and freedom of disposition of property should exist, but there were very great differences of opinion over how radical those limitations

---

[58] *Das bürgerliche Recht*, p. 229.

[59] See R. Köhne, *Nationalliberale und Koalitionsrecht. Struktur und Verhalten der nationalliberalen Reichstagsfraktion 1890–1914* (Frankfurt, 1977), 81 ff.

[60] e.g. *Magdeburger Zeitung*, 9 Sept. 1889; *Schlesische Zeitung*, 17 June 1891; *Kölnische Zeitung*, 19 July 1890.

should be. What was really at stake in these debates was the conception of the role of the state in creating a desirable social order. The question of whether the Code should be 'creative' or merely a systematic compilation of existing law reflected differences in social and political values. The latter approach meant the dominance of conceptual jurisprudence, with its spurious claims to socio-political neutrality. The arguments in favour of social reform through the civil law emphasized the positive function of state intervention in the private legal order, thereby abandoning the notion that the state should merely provide the framework within which the private transactions of autonomous individuals were conducted. The contention of men like Planck that the civil law had no specific social function 'in that sense' was anything other than unproblematic by the late 1880s.

The association of conceptual jurisprudence with Roman law had as its counterpart the connection between 'Germanism' and social reform. It was the Germanists who broke down the distinction between public and private law, thus extending the interventionist possibilities of legislation. But the juxtaposition of national (i.e. German) and 'foreign' (i.e. Roman) traditions gave the reformers a valuable weapon against the draft code. The assertion of this new nationalism in the law implied the reformulation of the social bases of the legal order; it involved a redefinition of the national interest with a very different basis from that of the liberal nationalism of the 1860s and 1870s. Under the banner of 'German' social reform, a variety of different interest groups could make their claims to special protection in the legal system. Moreover, the cause of social reform became closely associated with Germanism. Interestingly, this connection was taken for granted in an academic reference written by Heinrich Brunner for the young Max Weber in 1893, in which Brunner stated: 'In his excellent work on Roman agrarian history, he has shown his talents as a Romanist and legal historian; his book on the conditions of rural workers in East Elbian Germany legitimizes his claim to be considered a capable Germanist as well.'[61]

This is not to say that non-Germanist conceptions of social reform did not exist. The liberal social reformer Lujo Brentano, for example, launched an attack in the mid-1890s on Germanist proposals for special treatment for agriculture, and denied that such proposals were indeed part of any meaningful German tradition. The political core of Brentano's

---

[61] Brunner to Althoff, 18 Feb. 1893, ZStA Merseburg, Rep. 92 Althoff A I no. 62, fo. 116; for a discussion of the connection between Roman and 'unsocial' law, see Schröder, *Abschaffung oder Reform des Erbrechts*, pp. 37–51.

position was that agrarian proposals in fact clothed the interests of aristocratic landowners in policies which were supposedly directed at the peasantry—a view which earned him a storm of abuse from the agrarian lobby in the Verein für Sozialpolitik.[62] But Brentano, for all his attacks on the likes of Gierke, Adolf Wagner, and Max Sering, considered the agricultural sector to be relatively unimportant to the cause of social reform, and was far more concerned with such matters as trade union rights. His Bavarian background and interests in relation to the agrarian question also detached him from the north German school of social reformers who sought to deal with the problems of agriculture in the mid-1890s.[63] To men like Gierke, Wagner, and Sering, the connection of German traditions and social reform remained an article of faith. In the political context of the 1890s, it was hardly surprising that such views found a large audience.

The growing power of interest and pressure groups is widely recognized as one of the key features of the Bismarckian and Wilhelmine political systems. Such groups have been variously seen by historians as agencies of manipulation or as expressions of a disruptive mobilization of opinion. Either way, modern research has convincingly established the centrality of interest and pressure groups in the 'participation revolution' of the last two decades of the century.[64] In some accounts of the period, interest groups have been elevated to the status of quasi-political parties—agencies for the mobilization and channelling of opinion, whose power derived from the relative weakness of the Reichstag parties. It is mainly for this reason that far more attention has been devoted to the activities of such groups in the 1890s than to the formal political institutions of the Reich.[65]

[62] L. Brentano, *Ueber Anerbenrecht und Grundeigenthum. Separat-Abdruck aus der 'Zukunft'* (Berlin, 1895); id., *Mein Leben im Kampf um die soziale Entwicklung Deutschlands* (Jena, 1931), 172 ff.
    [63] D. Lindenlaub, *Richtungskämpfe im Verein für Sozialpolitik*, i (Wiesbaden, 1967), 154 f., 185 f.
    [64] This phrase comes from R. Chickering, *We Men Who Feel Most German. A Cultural Study of the Pan-German League 1886–1914* (London, 1984), 25.
    [65] Good general introductions to this field are H.-J. Puhle, 'Parlament, Parteien und Interessenverbände, 1890–1914', in M. Stürmer (ed.), *Das kaiserliche Deutschland. Politik und Gesellschaft 1870–1918* (Düsseldorf, 1970), 340–77, and W. Fischer, 'Staatsverwaltung und Interessenverbände im Deutschen Reich 1871–1914', in id., *Wirtschaft und Gesellschaft im Zeitalter der Industrialisierung* (Göttingen, 1972), 194–213. See the interesting comments on the relationship between interest groups and political parties in T. Nipperdey, 'Interessenverbände und Parteien in Deutschland vor dem ersten Weltkrieg', in id., *Gesellschaft, Kultur, Theorie* (Göttingen, 1976), 319–37.

From the point of view of this account, there were essentially two different types of interest group. In the first place, there were the semi-official organizations such as the Deutscher Landwirtschaftsrat (founded in 1872), the Prussian Landes-Oekonomie-Kollegium (1842), and the chambers of commerce. In Puhle's appropriate phrase, these associations had become in a sense 'partners of the state',[66] their role being to provide the government with expert advice on legislation affecting their sectors of the economy. This was the explicit intention of governments when they set up bodies like the Landes-Oekonomie-Kollegium or the chambers of commerce in the first half of the nineteenth century.[67] The literature tends to agree that this role as a partner of the state, and the attempt to represent all interests within a given sector of the economy, tended to weaken the tendencies towards criticism of the government in such bodies.[68]

On the other hand, the 1860s and 1870s saw the foundation of a new type of pressure group with an essentially different set of goals. Typical of this trend was the appearance of a large number of new farmers' organizations, beginning with the foundation of the Westphalian Peasants' Association in 1862. The principal aim of this type of group was to shift away from a purely advisory capacity and increase the influence of specific social groups on the development of legislation. This conception of the independent role of society *vis-à-vis* the state bureaucracy in policy-making was developed in the 1870s by the foundation of major new industrial and agrarian pressure groups, which soon led campaigns calling for changes in state policy with regard to such matters as tariffs.[69] This trend towards organization of social interests continued in the 1880s and 1890s and was, at least in part, the response of different social groups to the opportunities offered by universal manhood suffrage and to the threat of economic decline.

---

[66] Puhle, 'Parlament', p. 344.

[67] See M. Erdmann, *Die verfassungspolitische Funktion der Wirtschaftsverbände in Deutschland, 1815-1871* (Berlin, 1968), 47 ff. On the chambers of commerce, see the comments in H. Kaelble, 'Industrielle Interessenverbände vor 1914', in W. Ruegg and O. Neuloh (eds.), *Zur soziologischen Theorie und Analyse des 19. Jahrhunderts* (Göttingen, 1971), 182 ff.

[68] Puhle, 'Parlament', p. 344; Fischer, 'Staatsverwaltung und Interessenverbände', pp. 195-8.

[69] 1876 saw the foundation of the Central Association of German Industrialists (*Zentralverband deutscher Industrieller*) and the agrarian Union of Tax and Economic Reformers (*Vereinigung der Steuer- und Wirtschaftsreformer*); see I. N. Lambi, *Free Trade and Protection in Germany 1868-1879* (Wiesbaden, 1963), chs. 8-9.

A central role in this process was played by the battles over the shift to tariff protectionism in the late 1870s and 1880s.[70]

The issue of tariff reform provided the context for a far-reaching reappraisal of the relationship between state and society, and of the way in which national politics ought to operate. The shift away from *laissez-faire* policies began a broad attack on the different aspects of liberal individualism in social and economic policy, in which certain key terms—such as *Gewerbefreiheit*—took on new (and usually highly negative) meanings. This attack led to the emergence of a new collectivist social philosophy, involving a mixture of state interventionism and corporative institutional reforms.[71] Tariffs were difficult to reconcile with the liberal conception of the harmony of equally treated social interests because they involved favourable treatment of some social groups at the expense of others. Among other things, this meant that there was a strong premium on the invention of general arguments to justify the favourable treatment of certain allegedly endangered social groups. The founding statute of the Union of Tax and Economic Reformers stated that the organization's aim was to 'spread the ideas and principles of an economic system based on Christian principles and serving the common good; and to give such ideas expression in legislation'.[72] In like vein, the programme of the Farmers' League, which was founded in 1893 to fight Caprivi's liberalization of the agrarian tariff system, opened with the words:

German agriculture is the first and most important section of the economy, the firmest basis of the German Reich and the individual states. Our first and principal task is to protect and strengthen it, because the welfare of all other sectors of the economy is ensured by the flourishing state of agriculture.[73]

As pressure groups came to concentrate increasingly on the mobilization of public opinion in order to force the government into action, the tendency to identify sectional interests with the national interest grew. This helps to explain why the frequent statements about the uniqueness of the peasant farmer's, the landowner's, or the artisan's contribution

---

[70] Nipperdey, 'Interessenverbände', pp. 320 ff.

[71] H. Rosenberg, *Grosse Depression und Bismarckzeit. Wirschaftsablanf, Gesellschaft und Politik in Mitteleuropa* (pbk. edn., Frankfurt, 1976), ch. 3; S. Volkov, *The Rise of Popular Antimodernism in Germany* (Princeton, 1978), 174 ff.

[72] Cited in Puhle, 'Parlament', p. 345.

[73] The programme is reprinted in full in H.-J. Puhle, *Agrarische Interessenpolitik und preussischer Konservatismus im wilhelminischen Reich 1893-1914* (2nd edn., Bonn, 1975), 314.

to the stability of the nation's social structure should have assumed so much political significance by the 1890s.

The mobilization of broad sections of rural opinion and many members of the urban lower middle classes against established modes of political activity took on new populist dimensions in the 1890s. The foundation of the Farmers' League in 1893 was perhaps the most obvious symptom of this new climate, but the phenomenon was by no means restricted to agriculture. It lay at the heart of the frequent attempts in this period to construct a viable lower middle-class politics as a barrier against the seemingly endless rise of Social Democracy. The fact that these projects generally foundered on (among other things) the deep fissures between the different sections of the lower middle class provides an ironical reminder of the divisive force of interest group politics, when carried to its furthest conclusion. It was by no means true, as we shall see, that all sections of the lower middle classes were equally endangered by the social changes engendered by industrialization and urbanization.[74] But in the context of this mobilization, the 'social' jurisprudence of men like Gierke had an important role to play because of his challenge to the legal aspects of what might be called the liberal consensus of the 1870s. Where the economic interest groups increasingly protested against *laissez-faire* economic policies, the Germanists castigated the intrusion of the 'Manchester doctrine' into the civil law. And where sectional interests proclaimed their own national worth, Gierke and his followers were there to tell them that they were in line with truly 'German' modes of thought. The remainder of this chapter will seek to consider the participation of the economic interest groups in the debates about the code with reference to the key issues of agrarian law, the various aspects of freedom of contract, and the special legal difficulties of artisans in the building trades.

There were several important features of the interest groups' responses to the Civil Code. The power of such groups derived, at least in part, from their ability to claim a superior knowledge of technical matters relating to 'their' sector of the economy. The code, with its claims to comprehensive treatment of almost all the civil law, was especially

---

[74] See the many articles by David Blackbourn, especially his 'Between Resignation and Volatility: the German Petite Bourgeoisie in the Nineteenth Century', in G. Crossick and H.-G. Haupt (eds.), *Shopkeepers and Master Artisans in Nineteenth-Century Europe* (London, 1984), 35–61. On the populist aspects of politics in the 1890s, see G. Eley's suggestive remarks in *Reshaping the German Right. Radical Nationalism and Political Change after Bismarck* (New Haven/London, 1980), 195 ff.

unsuited to be the object of critical scrutiny by sectional groups. Thus, many of the groups insisted that it was no part of their task to produce a comprehensive critique of the draft code. Instead, they concentrated on the particular interests of the sections of the population that they represented. In introducing the debate on the draft code, for example, the president of the Prussian Landes-Oekonomie-Kollegium simply assumed that no general discussion of the code would be attempted.[75] This method of approaching the criticism of the code—i.e. from a sectional rather than general standpoint—naturally did not prevent the expression of extremely critical opinions. It did, however, militate against Gierke's chances of securing widespread support for his plans for reform of the legal system in accordance with German traditions, which required a general restructuring of the draft code. This emerged clearly in the critical responses of a number of chambers of commerce to the questionnaires sent out by the German Commercial Congress (Deutscher Handelstag). A common view was that the Congress had been led by 'irrelevant considerations'—for example, the battle between Romanists and Germanists—into questions which did not concern the trading community.[76]

Furthermore, it was almost universally agreed that any sensible consideration of the draft code's merits and defects required a specialist knowledge of the law. Judges and practising lawyers played a leading role in the debates in the Landes-Oekonomie-Kollegium and its national counterpart, the German Agricultural Council. Their predominance was even greater in smaller bodies, such as the Westphalian Peasants' Association, whose commission of four on the code included three lawyers.[77] The president of the Landes-Oekonomie-Kollegium took the lead in suggesting that that body should discuss the draft code, and emphasized that outside legal experts would have to be brought in. His subsequent plan involved the use of specialist lawyers to prepare the materials for the debates of the Kollegium's debates.[78] These lawyers, especially those involved in the more radical provincial associations,

[75] *Verhandlungen des Königlich Landes-Oekonomie-Kollegiums über den Entwurf eines bürgerlichen Gesetzbuches für das deutsche Reich und andere Gegenstände* (Berlin, 1890), 436.
[76] e.g. Breslau chamber, pp. 3 f.; Schweidnitz chamber, p. 4; Solingen chamber, p. 1.
[77] *Verhandlungen des Westfälischen Bauernvereins über den Entwurf eines bürgerlichen Gesetzbuchs für das Deutsche Reich* (Münster, 1890), 3.
[78] Marcard to Lucius, 15 Feb. and 17 Oct. 1888, ZStA Merseburg, Rep. 87B 8114, fos. 88 f. and 8115, fo. 3.

were by no means deaf to the demands of sectional interests, and their proposals often involved radical revisions of the draft code. Their dominance did, however, strengthen the commitment of most interest groups to legal unity in principle, and helped to foster existing tendencies towards a narrow interpretation of sectional interests. The most important effect of these factors was to head off Gierke's hopes that 'practical men' would reject the principles of the draft code as a whole. His influence on the formulation of specific demands and on the vocabulary in which such demands might be expressed could be very great. On issues of more general interest or of purely legalistic importance, however, a substantial amount of resistance to his proposals developed. Thus Gierke was able to secure substantial support in the Landes-Oekonomie-Kollegium on issues such as rural usury, where a specifically agricultural interest was thought to be involved. However, when the debate turned to the draft code's rejection of 'customary law' (*Gewohnheitsrecht*) as a source of law, the president agreed with a previous speaker that the question had no real place in the debates of an agricultural association.[79] This approach undoubtedly worked against Gierke's campaign for the rejection of the 1888 draft code, as the basis of the future national code and helps to explain Hermann Struckmann's belief that Gierke had made very little impact.[80]

The most significant campaign for radical reform came without doubt from the various agrarian interest groups. Reforms of mortgage and inheritance law and other measures to protect the agrarian interest had all been subjects of debate long before 1888. As early as 1876, the founding statute of the Union of Tax and Economic Reformers had stated: 'Rural landownership is to be freed from the clutches of Roman law. In particular, it is to be given a form of indebtedness which corresponds to its nature and an inheritance law in line with German traditions.'[81] By 1882, the Bavarian nobleman Karl von Thüngen-Rossbach was calling in the Congress of German Farmers for a whole package of defensive measures including tax reductions, a stock exchange law, undivided peasant inheritance (*Anerbenrecht*), perpetual annuity charges (*unkündbare Rentenschulden*), and homestead legislation to prevent the loss of the entirety of a farmer's property in the event of

---

[79] *Verhandlungen des Königlich Landes-Oekonomie-Kollegiums*, p. 453.
[80] Struckmann to Planck, 30 Dec. 1889, NSUUB Göttingen, Planck Papers VIII, fo. 61.
[81] *Bericht über die Verhandlungen der XIV. General-Versammlung der Vereinigung der Steuer- und Wirtschaftsreformer* (Berlin, 1889), 55.

foreclosure.[82] The movement swelled in the mid-1880s in the aftermath of the Verein für Sozialpolitik's discussions of 1882-4.

By 1885, the Hessen Peasants' Association was arguing that the peasantry needed no more easy credit, but rather 'the removal of certain principles which dominate mortgage law and which must lead to the ruin of the debtor, as they are concerned merely with the absolute security of the creditor.'[83] The general meeting of the Union of Tax and Economic Reformers in 1887 called for legislative action against landed indebtedness as an urgent necessity 'in the interests of the whole productive, industrious nation, and above all to support the state'. After this classic statement of the agrarians' belief that their special political function entitled them to be paid off by the state, the Union proposed a limitation of debts to 50 per cent of the net product of the land, undivided inheritance, the corporate organization of landed credit and, above all, the introduction of annuity charges.[84] The draft code of 1888 thus entered a public arena in which coherent proposals for radical reform had already emerged.

The effect of the publication of the draft code was to increase the scale of public concern about such matters. As a senior official in the Prussian Ministry of Agriculture explained in 1894:

An essential role in the growth of interest group activity concerning inheritance law was played by the progress of the preparation of the civil code, which led the agrarian interest groups to take up positions concerning the law of inheritance for landed property.[85]

The reasons for this agitation lay in the widely held belief that the future of agriculture was in mortal danger. Most agrarian spokesmen saw the roots of this crisis in two related phenomena: the falling prices of agricultural produce in Germany after 1875 and the phenomenon of over-indebtedness among landowners. The first of these phenomena provided the motive for the rapid shift of agrarian spokesmen away from *laissez-faire* tariff policies in the late 1870s. The second was related to the fall in prices, in that the purchase price of land remained high

[82] GStA Berlin-Dahlem, Rep. 84a 1915, fo. 17.
[83] *Der Hessische Bauer*, 5 July 1885, p. 167.
[84] See the Union's petition to the government, 10 May 1887, ZStA Potsdam, RJM no. 4017, fos. 14 f.
[85] Dr Hermes in *Schriften des Vereins für Sozialpolitik*, vol lxi (Leipzig, 1894), 46; cf. the Prussian ministry of justice's 'Denkschrift über die zur Forderung der Landwirthschaft in den letzten Jahren ergriffenen Massnahmen' (1896), GStA Berlin-Dahlem, Rep. 84a 1906, fos. 20 f. on the influence of the agrarian response to the Civil Code.

despite the fall in the market value of its produce, and capital inputs in order to introduce productivity improvements remained relatively expensive. In the eyes of historians such as Hans Rosenberg, the two phenomena were further related in that tariff protection—by raising the domestic price of agricultural produce above the world market price— made landownership much more desirable than it should have been in terms of the real state of the market. This desirability was then reflected in higher land prices, with obvious consequences for the level of indebtedness.[86]

There can be very little doubt about the existence of the phenomenon of rapidly increasing landed indebtedness, especially in the Prussian east. Johannes Conrad's investigations for the Verein für Sozialpolitik calculated that the total level of mortgage debts in Prussia rose rapidly to 2,416 million marks between 1886 and 1897, and that the annual rate of increase was accelerating substantially in the last few years of that period.[87] Other sources point in the same direction. Thus, a survey of 56 Prussian districts conducted in 1896 demonstrated the heavy indebtedness of the larger East Elbian landowners, who had been especially hard hit by rising costs and falling prices.[88] In the province of Hanover, a survey conducted in the mid-1880s warned of the danger of growing indebtedness among smaller farmers as a result of increases in local taxation, wages, and the amounts of capital required to compensate co-heirs during inheritance.[89] It has been calculated that between 1880 and 1900 there were 5,650 compulsory auctions of landholdings in Prussia as a result of failure to pay mortgage debts. The corresponding figure for Bavaria was 11,400, involving 89,000 hectares of farm land.[90]

It is easy to see why landowners should have been so concerned about their level of indebtedness. It has, however, been argued that the root cause of the increasing indebtedness of the landowners and of the much-reviled speculation in land was the intensification of cultivation through the increasing use of root crops such as sugar-beet. The ratio of indebtedness to land tax per hectare increased most in those areas

---

[86] Rosenberg, *Grosse Depression*, pp. 184 f.

[87] *Schriften des Vereins für Sozialpolitik*, xc (1900), 144 f.

[88] T. Frhr. v. d. Goltz, *Geschichte der Deutschen Landwirtschaft*, ii (Stuttgart/Berlin, 1903), 402 ff.

[89] L. Danger and C. Manz, *Der Grundbesitz in der Provinz Hannover* (Hanover, 1886), 16.

[90] E. Klein, *Geschichte der deutschen Landwirtschaft im Industriezeitalter* (Wiesbaden, 1973), 125.

of Germany, such as Prussian Saxony, where the intensity of cultivation was greatest. On the other hand, it is not clear that a substantial increase in the ratio of indebtedness to land prices took place, despite the contrary assertions of agrarian groups. Indebtedness correlated positively with intensity of cultivation, which was itself related (though decreasingly so) to the size of landholding. As a result of these agricultural improvements, substantial rises in yields for wheat and rye took place in the last two decades of the nineteenth century.[91] That being the case, the problems of landed indebtedness and rapid turnover in ownership were more the result of intensive capital investment in the agrarian sector than of the 'artificial' maintenance of prices through tariff protection. The landowners' protests about the structure of credit seem to reflect their desire to confuse the difficult position of individual agrarian entrepreneurs in a newly and harshly competitive world with the impression of a ghastly crisis facing German agriculture as a whole, and therefore the German economy.

Nevertheless, the fall in prices for agricultural goods was undoubtedly a large part of the reason for the short-term credit difficulties some landowners faced. Their response to these difficulties was to turn against the legislation of the early 1870s, which many of them had promoted at that time in response to the shortage of credit. Thus a central feature of the agrarian campaign was the revival of calls for the introduction of the annuity charge (*Rentenschuld*) as the basic form of landed debt. This idea had first been developed in the late 1860s by J. C. v. Rodbertus-Jagetzow, whose work enjoyed a new vogue in the 1890s. Rodbertus argued that the 'true' value of the land was determined by the value of its product (*Ertragswert*), rather than by its 'artificial' capital value. A mortgage form appropriate to the needs of landownership would be based on that 'true' value, and the law should exclude the right of the creditor to terminate the loan at will. To ensure a sufficient supply of capital, negotiable annuity bonds should be issued. In contrast to many of his later admirers, Rodbertus emphasized that his suggestions involved no restriction on the freedom of action of the property-owner, and expressly rejected a formal limit on the extent of permissible debt as a proportion of the value of the land's produce. On the other hand, his stated desire to reinstate landownership as 'an independent power in society' and his early linking of the restoration of the old German

---

[91] For this reassessment, see J. A. Perkins, 'The Agricultural Revolution in Germany 1850-1914', *Journal of European Economic History*, 10 (1981), 71-118.

mortgage law and the 'social' duties of legislation related him very obviously to Gierke and the Germanists. For all these reasons, Rodbertus' initiatives in the 1860s found a wide audience after 1880.[92]

Rodbertus' insistence on the difference between the capital value and value in terms of the product of the land highlighted what many landowners believed to be the essence of their difficulties in a period of falling product prices and buoyant capital values. As we have seen, the Prussian legislation of 1872 sought to make land a more attractive source of investment for capital, and the draft code followed this line. As the explanatory notes put it:

> If legislation undoubtedly has the duty of protecting and promoting the interests of landownership as the strongest foundation of the state, it must seek above all to provide opportunities for credit. In the sphere of private law, this task is essentially limited to an appropriate formulation of the mortgage and other forms of landed credit.[93]

As agrarian groups began to perceive the dangers of unrestricted credit in the next decade and a half, landowners came to see that type of argument as evidence that the legal system was geared to the interests of capitalist creditors rather than to those of agrarian debtors. As the president of the Union of Tax and Economic Reformers wrote to the Prussian minister of agriculture, it was necessary to replace 'capitalist law' with the annuity charge, but the draft code had merely made matters worse.[94] H. G. Opitz, the Union's main spokesman on the Code, considered the draft code to be representative of capitalist interests and went so far as to say that measures such as tariff protection or bimetallism were useless without some protection against landed indebtedness. Occupying a similarly prominent position in the Congress of German Farmers, Opitz insisted that indebtedness was rooted in legislative errors and, above all, in the introduction of Roman ideas into land law. In both cases, Opitz insisted that land was not in itself a form of capital and that Roman law doctrines, which treated land as comparable to other forms of capital, were therefore inappropriate and dangerous.[95]

---

[92] J. C. v. Rodbertus-Jagetzow, *Zur Erklärung und Abhülfe der heutigen Creditnothes des Grundbesitzes* (2nd edn., Berlin, 1893), 6 ff., 129 ff., 181–218. The first edition was published in 1868 in connection with the preparation of the Prussian land law reforms; see Buchholz, *Abstraktionsprinzip*, pp. 291–9.

[93] B. Mugdan (ed.), *Die gesammten Materialien zum Bürgerlichen Gesetzbuch*, iii (Berlin, 1899), 334.

[94] Mirbach-Sorquitten to Lucius, n.d., ZStA Merseburg Rep. 87B 8115, fos. 120 f.

[95] *Bericht über die Verhandlungen der XIV. General-Versammlung der Vereinigung der*

Support for the annuity charge was common among agrarian organizations. The commission appointed by the Landes-Oekonomie-Kollegium on the whole found the draft code's mortgage law satisfactory and saw no problem with the retention of the abstract land charge (*Grundschuld*). It was, however, thought desirable that the Code should include the annuity charge as well. Approximately the same position was adopted by the German Agricultural Council, although some doubts about the practical value of annuity charges were expressed.[96] Only the Rhenish Peasant Association joined the Union of Tax and Economic Reformers in calling for the introduction of the annuity charge as the sole mortage form. Of all the groups under discussion here, only the Westphalian Peasants' Association agreed with the draft code's exclusion of annuity charges on the grounds that such charges would probably destroy the system of landed credit.[97]

One feature of the debates about annuity charges was that the main proponents of reform along the lines suggested by Rodbertus often distanced themselves from many of the suggestions of the Germanists. Thus Opitz emphasized that the commission had been right to attempt to codify existing law, and he rejected the idea that the code as a whole was not 'German'. His major concern was to break the hold of capital over the formulation of legislation and to create an agrarian law which met the special needs of agriculture. His main target was those types of mortgage which created negotiable bonds, the most obvious symbol of the capitalist economy. His opposition was aroused by the fact that land could be bought and sold like any other goods. This argument was given a certain ethical content by Opitz's insistence that a man could not in all honesty separate his personal credit from charges on his land. He believed that much of the legislative encouragement of over-borrowing was rooted in this basic feature of the Prussian mortgage law, and he argued that the principle of the liability of the whole of a man's property for his debts was essential to the concept of 'good faith'.[98]

Rather closer to Gierke was Dr Hartmann, who in the debates in the

---

Steuer- und Wirtschaftsreformer (Berlin, 1889), 54 ff. *Bericht über die Verhandlungen der XX. Haupt-Versammlung des Congresses Deutscher Landwirte* (Berlin, 1889), 14 ff.

[96] *Verhandlungen des Königlich Landes-Oekonomie-Kollegiums*, pp. 318 f.; *Archiv des deutschen Landwirthschaftsraths*, 13 (1889), 196 f.; 14 (1890), 343 f., 370 f.

[97] *Der Entwurf eines Bürgerlichen Gesetzbuches für das Deutsche Reich und der Rheinische Bauern-Verein* (Cologne, 1890), 31, 103; *Verhandlungen des Westfälischen Bauernvereins*, pp. 44 ff.

[98] H. G. Opitz, *Gutachten über den Entwurf eines Bürgerlichen Gesetzbuchs für das Deutsche Reich. Erstattet für den Landeskulturrath des Königreichs Sachsen* (Leipzig, 1889),

Congress of German Farmers emphasized the differences in the German people's notions of landed and movable property. In contrast to Opitz, Hartmann opposed the draft code's 'absolute' conception of landed property, supported the legal protection of the weaker contracting party, and advocated regulation of interest rates, usury, and penalty clauses in the Code. Other speakers in this debate expressed their hatred of Roman law and the necessity of a legal distinction between landed and other forms of property.[99] It is possible that, as Baron von Hövel suggested in the Landes-Oekonomie-Kollegium,[1] Gierke's views aroused greater sympathy among the farmers who made up the rank and file of the deputies than among the speakers, many of whom were professional lawyers. One of the main thrusts of the agrarian attack was, in any case, directed against the Prussian mortgage law reforms, which Gierke had in part supported as a progressive step for many parts of the Reich.[2]

What did develop, however, was a more general association of the draft code's Roman-law origins with the interests of a form of urban capitalism, which was hostile to the justified claims of agriculture. As Opitz put it:

It was not the interests of the credit-seeking landowners which principally concerned the commission in its work on the law of landed credit, but the interests of the capitalist creditor . . . There can be no doubt that their reasoning in relation to landed credit was based more or less on the dubious attitude which tends to be called the 'Manchester' viewpoint—i.e. the view which makes the greatest possible concessions to the 'free play of forces' without any consideration of the practical consequences which may arise out of the inequality of those forces.[3]

The final phrase in particular showed the broad connection between these agrarian ideas and those of men like Gierke, for much of the tone of the agrarian response was dictated by the belief that agriculture was the weaker party in the 'battle for existence' with capitalism. Pro-agrarian policies thus came to be seen as a vital (if not the vital) part of social

33–44; *Archiv des Deutschen Landwirthschaftsraths*, 13 (1889), 255–66; *Bericht der Vereinigung der Steuer- und Wirthschaftsreformer*, pp. 54–71.

[99] *Bericht*, pp. 37 ff.

[1] *Verhandlungen des Königlich Landes-Oekonomie-Kollegiums*, p. 453.

[2] Gierke, *Entwurf*, p. 367; Gierke did however insist on the need for an identity of personal and real credit, ibid. 370.

[3] Opitz, *Gutachten*, p. 35.

policy.[4] Meanwhile other speakers such as Baron von Cetto-Reichertshausen complained sarcastically of the legislative bias in favour of the creditor,

as if capitalist interests were making a great patriotic sacrifice in lending money on the security of land for which they required particular encouragement and rewards and as if the economic interests of capital did not seek and find advantages in landed credit, in the same way as the interests of the landowners did.[5]

Gierke's Germanism should thus be placed in the context of a general association of Roman law and urban capitalist interests, which increasingly emphasized the disharmony of interests between agriculture and industry. Gierke's social philosophy in a sense 'codified' the wide variety of anti-liberal intellectual currents which concentrated on ethical questions such as 'good faith', the primacy of the family over individual egoism, the right of society as a higher unity to restrain individual freedoms, and so on. These matters were then linked to the specific interests of agriculture, which were believed to be particularly consonant with 'German' traditions and which derived their legitimacy from their special place in the social and political fabric of the nation.

One reform proposal which was often discussed in these years was the introduction of homesteads on the American model. The essence of this idea was that part of the homestead-owner's property was exempt from foreclosure in the event of his being unable to pay his mortgage debts. Homesteads attracted a certain amount of attention in the early 1880s as a means of protecting the smaller peasant, not least from Bismarck.[6] In the 1882 general meeting of the Union of Tax and Economic Reformers, a discussion of the matter produced many of the standard agrarian arguments in classic form. The main speaker called for the replacement of Roman law principles with German-Christian ones and proposed a resolution to the effect that Roman law was the prime cause of the social question. The main point, he argued, was 'to regain for landed property the independent place in the legal system, which is afforded by German law'. He concluded, however, that the real problem lay with the possibility that mortgages could be terminated

---

[4] See e.g. the comments of Hartmann and Thüngen in the debates of the Congress of German Farmers, *Bericht*, pp. 30 ff, 53.

[5] *Archiv des Deutschen Landwirthschaftsraths*, 13. 197.

[6] See Bismarck's 'Votum' of 13 Nov. 1881, GStA Berlin-Dahlem, Rep. 84a 5943, fos. 1 f.; *Norddeutsche Allgemeine Zeitung*, 8 Nov. 1881.

by the creditor. Thus the only solution to the problem lay in annuity charges rather than homestead legislation on the American model.[7]

Of the interest groups that responded immediately to the draft code, only the Westphalian Peasants' Association supported homestead legislation. The other groups, especially the semi-official organizations, came out against it, although the German Agricultural Council did recognize the 'healthy principle' which lay behind the idea.[8] To conclude from that near-unanimity that homestead legislation was irrelevant would, however, be incorrect. As with other areas of the law, the effect of the publication of the draft code was to breathe new life into an existing debate. This debate did not essentially concern the inclusion of homestead legislation in the code itself. Rather, it was the widespread perception of the inadequacy of the draft code's land law in general which led to various demands for a *special* Reich homestead law. As Baron von Riepenhausen-Crangen, the author of a draft Reich law on the subject in 1890, stated, his proposals had been motivated by agrarian dissatisfaction with the 1888 draft code.[9] Riepenhausen's campaign was characterized by extreme anti-socialism and the usual platitudes about the naturally conservative nature of a healthy peasantry. On that basis, it secured the support of the ultra-conservative *Kreuzzeitung*, which called for legislation to remove the unrestricted right of the landowner to divide and encumber his land.[10]

This marked a new stage in the campaign for reform of agrarian law, which had until this point generally sought to accommodate its demands to a legal order based on the freedom of action of the property-owner. Riepenhausen explicitly opposed such freedoms as 'dangerous to smallholders', whose survival he considered to be the most important social question of the time. As he emphasized in a letter to the *Kreuzzeitung*,

homesteads will counteract the process of social stratification which in the form of Social Democracy is finding expression in a strong movement to undermine the main elements of our culture—landownership, the family, the monarchy, and Christianity.[11]

[7] *Bericht über die VII. General-Versammlung der Vereinigung der Steuer- und Wirtschaftsreformer* (Berlin, 1882), 1-10.

[8] *Verhandlungen des Westfälischen Bauernvereins*, pp. 53 f., 90. See the Council's report to the Reich Justice Office, 9 Mar. 1893, ZStA Potsdam RJM 557, fo. 62.

[9] K. v. Riepenhausen-Crangen, *Gesicherte Familienheimstätten im Deutschen Reich* (Berlin, 1890), 11. Riepenhausen's draft law is to be found in *SBRT, Drucksachen* 1890, no. 99.

[10] *Kreuzzeitung*, 24 Apr. 1890.

This more radical agrarian position found the support of the German Peasants' League (Deutscher Bauernbund), whose chairman, Bernhard von Ploetz, began to bombard the government with statements of support for the 'German' institution of the homestead.[12] Furthermore, Riepenhausen also gained powerful support from Gierke, who wrote in an open letter that:

the restoration of harmony in our entire economy depends in the first place on not imposing the law of movable capital on landed property but rather on securing for it the law which it was born with. Above all, this poses the question of whether Roman or German law should prevail in Germany, which is a question of life or death for our people.

As far as Gierke was concerned, homesteads were archetypally German institutions.[13]

The debate about homestead legislation showed the way in which controversies stimulated by the publication of the draft code could broaden out into demands for separate reform legislation. In the case of the discussion about annuity charges, there had been some connection with the conception of German legal traditions, but it was rather remote and vague. Most supporters of the measure relied far more on the essentially economic arguments advanced by Rodbertus. The campaign for homesteads tended to involve much more radical, ideological statements, which gained the support of those groups which sought to mobilize the disaffected peasantry, whereas the campaign for annuity charges was led by organizations such as the Union of Tax and Economic Reformers and the Congress of German Farmers, in which the larger landowners were predominant. The two demands were not mutually exclusive, and both were included in the 1893 programme of the Farmers' League. Yet the contrast between that programme and the evidence of the hostility of most of the regional semi-official agricultural associations to Riepenhausen's homestead law in the same year makes the rift between agrarian radicals and moderates clear. The most common reason given by the semi-official associations for their opposition was the principle of freedom of disposition of the property-owner.[14]

---

[11] Riepenhausen to Bismarck, 21 Mar. 1890, ZStA Potsdam, Rkz 740, fo. 202; *Kreuzzeitung*, 29 Apr. 1891.

[12] Ploetz to Caprivi, ZStA Potsdam Rkz 740, fos. 260 f.

[13] Gierke to Riepenhausen, 30 Sept. 1890, published in *Deutsches Tageblatt*, 24 Oct. 1890, *Beilage*.

[14] Farmers' League programme, cl. 10, reprinted in Puhle, *Agrarische Interessenpolitik*, p. 314; the reactions of the regional agricultural associations are recorded in GStA Berlin-Dahlem, Rep. 84a 5943, fo. 64 (pp. 4 ff.).

The difference between radicals such as Riepenhausen and Ploetz and the more moderate agrarian critics of the draft code thus effectively concerned the extent to which the principle of the autonomy of the individual in the legal system was acceptable. In this context, Gierke's support for homestead legislation stood in an unclear relationship to the hostility towards unfree tenures which ran throughout his work. In fact, his motives were probably tactical. He regarded homesteads as being organically related to the principle of undivided inheritance of peasant holdings (*Anerbenrecht*) which was for him the really central point in agrarian reform. Furthermore, he saw in a Reich law on homesteads a means of forcing the codifiers to restructure the whole of the Code's land law in line with 'social' principles. In particular, the argument that regional variations imposed constraints on national legislation would be undermined:

If the Reich were to produce a law like the homestead law [before the completion of the Civil Code], the future code would have to bear it in mind and would be forced to adopt different approaches in dealing with land law. Such a law would also be an illuminating example of how it is possible to create a common law on matters where the economic and habitual differences between German districts prohibit uniform treatment, while leaving enough room for all justified variations.[15]

Gierke might, then, be said to stand somewhere near the centre of an agrarian spectrum, in which certain maxims were taken for granted by all but then infused with different contents, according to the degree of radicalism of the speaker. These maxims included: the belief in the central importance of agriculture to the social order; a consequent insistence that the legal order ought to treat landownership as a special case in accordance with its 'special' nature; the beliefs that Roman law was linked to the interests of urban capital, while German law was favourable to agriculture, and that these two sets of interests had little or nothing in common. Riepenhausen showed how deeply these ideas had taken root, when he asserted as a principle: 'the most important question to be decided in relation to agriculture is whether we will progress down the Romanist-capitalist road or the German-agrarian road.'[16]

The principle of undivided inheritance of peasant holdings (*Aner-benrecht*) was probably the issue which found the greatest support among

[15] As above, n. 13.
[16] Riepenhausen to Rottenburg, 24 May 1890, ZStA Potsdam, Rkz 740, fo. 244.

the proponents of the 'German-agrarian' road. Of the major agrarian organizations which commented on the Code, the Saxon Agricultural Council, the Agricultural Council for Alsace-Lorraine and the Westphalian Peasants' Association opposed the inclusion of *Anerbenrecht* in the revised Code. In the latter case, this was almost certainly because Westphalia was one of the regions to have received a form of undivided peasant inheritance through Prussian legislation earlier in the 1880s. The rejection of national legislation on the subject thus did not damage peasant interests in that region, while the inclusion of the matter in the Code might possibly worsen the situation.[17] The Landes-Oekonomie-Kollegium and the German Agricultural Council, on the other hand, came out strongly in favour of the inclusion of undivided inheritance in the revised Code. Such was the strength of feeling in the former organization that Gierke was able to win over its commission for the idea that undivided succession required 'positive encouragement from legislation'.[18] In the German Agricultural Council, the campaign for national legislation was led by Baron von Cetto-Reichertshausen, who pointed out that undivided succession might not survive if it was left to the individual states.[19]

Supporters of the measure were always keen to point out that the proposal did not involve any restriction on the testamentary freedom of the peasant and that the system would only apply in cases of intestate succession. Almost all agrarian representatives agreed that undivided succession was *in principle* a suitable means of protecting the peasantry. As Cetto pointed out in his report to the German Agricultural Council, 'the main question was whether, from the point of view of agriculture, undivided succession should be introduced by legislation at national or state level'.[20] Opinions on this matter varied widely and were largely related to the place of origin of the speaker. The Saxon landowner Opitz, for example, had little doubt that the matter should be reserved for state legislation. The low level of landed indebtedness in Saxony and the relatively favourable distribution of landed property there meant that no real need for national legislation on the matter could be

---

[17] *Verhandlungen des Westfälischen Bauernvereins*, pp. 75, 91 ff. U. Bähr, 'Die berufständischen Sonderinteressen und das BGB. Ein Beitrag zur Entstehungsgeschichte des BGB', Jur. Diss. (Heidelberg, 1973), 60 f.; H.-G. Mertens, *Die Entstehung der Vorschriften des BGB über gesetzliche Erbfolge und das Pflichtteilsrecht* (Berlin, 1970), 115, 124 ff.

[18] *Verhandlungen des Königlich Landes-Oekonomie-Kollegiums*, pp. 352 f.

[19] *Archiv des Deutschen Landwirthschaftsraths*, 14. 425.

[20] Ibid. 425.

demonstrated. This was also the view of the Westphalian Peasants' Association, which represented an area in which, according to Miaskowski, the peasantry was still 'healthy'.[21] Cetto's native Bavaria was also considered to have a generally healthy peasantry. However, as he made clear in a report on the subject for the German Agricultural Council in 1886, he believed the future survival of traditional peasant inheritance practices to be threatened if such practices were not given legislative encouragement.[22] He succeeded in persuading the Council that great danger would come from a Civil Code which was dominated by liberal conceptions of inheritance and which left the special needs of agriculture to the individual states. As the Council's submission to Bismarck in April 1886 stated:

the inner strength of a legal statute increases in relation to the size of the area to which it is applied. In the face of the pressure towards legal unity in such a large body, it will be impossible for local and particular statute and customary laws, let alone morality, to find fitting expression.[23]

This viewpoint reflected an extremely important aspect of the campaign for legal reform in the interests of agriculture. Many of the reformers tended to place great hopes on the 'educational' importance of legal change in bringing about a change of social practices. As Ludwig Fuld put it when arguing for the inclusion of undivided succession in the Civil Code, '[t]he educational effect . . . the pedagogical importance would be seriously restricted if it were not introduced at Reich level.'[24] The main question for Fuld, as for Gierke and Cetto, was not whether the new Civil Code would allow certain agrarian demands as special cases, as exceptions to general rules. Leaving these matters to the individual states would have accomplished this limited aim. Rather, these men concentrated on the recognition by the Code of agriculture's special needs as equal to those of other sections of society. Only national legislation could satisfy people like Gierke, because they accepted the superiority of the moral and political force of the nation over subordinate authorities.

This emphasis on the inclusion of agrarian demands in the national Civil Code, as opposed to other forms of legislation, reflected the

---

[21] Opitz, *Gutachten*, pp. 9 f.; *Schriften des Vereins für Sozialpolitik*, xxi. 9.

[22] *Archiv des Deutschen Landwirthschaftsraths*, 10 (1886), 89.

[23] German Agricultural Council to Bismarck, 27 Apr. 1886, StA Hamburg, Senatskomm. für die Justizverwaltung 1 A a 1 vol. 1 (45), fo. 6.

[24] Fuld, 'Erbrecht', p. 162.

development of new, competing forms of nationalism in early Wilhelmine Germany. As we have seen, codification in the 1870s was seen largely in terms of the systematic presentation of existing law in Germany. In so far as this reflected a precise social philosophy, it was the notion of balancing social interests in the common good within a national, 'certain' legal system. The Germanist attack on the Code implied a very different conception of the nation's needs and, as the case of Gierke made clear, opposed the growing calls for 'resignation' on the part of sectional interests for the greater national good. Gierke's message to the agrarians were that their interests very much *were* the national good. Why should they exercise 'resignation' in order to secure the passage of a major piece of legislation which was contrary to the interests of the nation?

All of the organizations studied here were convinced that the draft code was dominated by the views of the 'Manchester School', which discriminated against the agrarian debtor in favour of the capitalist creditor. Yet this was a unity of rhetoric rather than of substance, for none of these interest groups felt it necessary to follow Gierke in his denunciation of the Code as a whole. The related questions of mortgage law, homestead legislation, and undivided succession revealed important differences within the agrarian camp, which were related to regional variations in the socio-economic development of German agriculture. On the whole—and despite the extreme anti-Romanism of many of the pronouncements of these organizations—the agrarian interest groups were prepared to work within the framework established by the Code. There were even signs from agrarian interest groups of support for the commission's work as the basis for a future national Code.[25]

The demand for homestead legislation was essentially different. This was a measure which went well beyond the bounds of the Civil Code and attracted the support of the more radical agrarian organizations such as the German Peasants' League. It constituted something of a bridge between 'respectable' agrarian criticism of the Code and the radical attacks on the work from the Farmers' League in the mid-1890s. The Farmers' League did include a clause in its programme relating to agrarian law, but its main interests lay elsewhere, at least for the first eighteen months of its existence. By June 1895, however, with the preparation of the Code nearing completion, things began to change. A

---

[25] Bemberg-Flamesheim (President of the Agricultural Association of Rheinpreussen) to Lucius, 24 Feb. 1889, ZStA Merseburg, Rep. 87B 8115, fos. 94-109.

series of essays appeared in the following months under the names of Gustav Ruhland and Lorenz Kroidl in the Farmers' League newspaper.[26] The starting-point of the League's campaign was that a fundamental criticism of the work from an economic point of view was absolutely necessary. By insisting on such criticism, which by late 1895 necessarily meant prolonged debate by the Reichstag over several years, the League rejected in advance all arguments for 'resignation' in the face of over twenty years of preparatory work by legislative commissions. The League thus joined the growing opposition to the government's plan to 'whip' the code through the Reichstag in 1896.[27] That feeling was compounded by the view that the Reichstag had more important legislative tasks in 1896 than the civil code, such as the Stock Exchange Law and the law against 'unfair competition'. As one League newspaper wrote:

Or should two-thirds of the session be devoted to the Civil Code? That is surely not so urgent and a fundamental revision of the draft code is all the more necessary as it is based on foreign legal principles, which are unsuitable for German conditions.[28]

The criticisms advanced by Ruhland and Kroidl demonstrate the extent to which the Germanist critique of the Code could be twisted to suit the purposes of a radical pressure group. The connection between Roman law and liberal economic legislation was accepted. So too was Gierke's insistence on the differences between landed and movable property. Ruhland and Kroidl argued that landownership should be considered a 'quasi-public office' and demanded a special agrarian law to limit the sovereignty of the individual will in line with true German traditions.[29] The connection of these ideas with the radical Germanist critique of the 1888 draft code was obvious.

However, Ruhland and Kroidl also managed to link these ideas to the League's other major concerns. Pointing to the prominence of Eduard Lasker in the movement for legal unity in the 1870s, they made the connection between Roman law and Jewish interests, which lay in their common association with the representatives of mobile capital. It was therefore hardly surprising that it was in these sections of the

---

[26] Suchsland to Roesicke, 11 June 1895, ZStA Potsdam, Roesicke Papers no. 19, fo. 211. The essays were subsequently published together in *Stimmen aus dem agrarischen Lager*, i (Berlin, 1896), 16–36.

[27] G. Ruhland, 'Vorwort', *Stimmen aus dem agrarischen Lager*, i, p. ii; *Deutsche Tageszeitung*, 8 Dec. 1895, Ruhland and Kroidl—'Wem verdanken wir den Entwurf des Bürgerlichen Gesetzbuches?'

[28] *Korrespondenz des Bundes der Landwirthe*, 20 Oct. 1895.

[29] *Stimmen aus dem agrarischen Lager*, i. 21, 31 ff.

community that calls for the rapid completion of a Code based on 'foreign' principles was loudest. Pouring scorn on this 'hurrah patriotism' which placed the establishment of legal unity above the 'Germanness' of the contents of the Code, Ruhland and Kroidl established a strong connection between Germanism and anti-Semitic agrarianism of the most radical variety.[30]

The League also clearly saw the campaign against the Code as part of a larger movement against the influence of urban capital on legislation. The Civil Code was a fine example of such influence, but it was seen in relation to a much broader campaign on behalf of the threatened lower middle classes of Germany. The League differed from other agrarian groups in refusing to see the Code merely in terms of the immediate interests of agriculture. Instead, it followed Gierke in considering that the essential issue at stake was the general social philosophy of the Code. The Civil Code was merely an important and rather blatant example of the general legislative dominance of capitalist–Jewish interests, which had to be combated in all its manifestations. As Ruhland and Kroidl wrote: 'We need a rejection of capitalist interests in legislation as much as our daily bread. What are nowadays called the agrarian, Mittelstand, and worker questions demand legislation in a spirit diametrically opposed to Lasker's views'.[31] In terms of detailed policies, there was little or nothing in Ruhland's and Kroidl's work which added to what had already been said by others. But the radicalism of the League's overall position did distinguish it from earlier, more distinctly sectional, positions that had emerged in the course of the debates. This was no longer merely a campaign for the specific protection of agrarian interests within a legal system which accommodated capital as well. It was, rather, part of the broader debate about whether Germany should be an agrarian or an industrial state, which developed rapidly in the early 1890s.[32]

There are signs that influential men within the League saw the debates about the Civil Code in this exclusively 'ideological' light. Ruhland and Kroidl made much of the logical connection between grain tariff policy and the way in which agrarian law was formulated, but the

---

[30] *Deutsche Tageszeitung*, 8 Dec. 1895.

[31] *Stimmen aus dem agrarischen Lager*, i. 19.

[32] On this see K. Barkin, *The Debate over German Industrialization 1890–1902* (Chicago/London, 1970), ch. 4; H. Lebovics, ' "Agrarians" versus "Industrializers": Social Conservative Resistance to Industrialism and Capitalism in Late Nineteenth-Century Germany', *International Review of Social History*, 12 (1967), 31–65.

League's chairman, Gustav Roesicke, considered the former to be much more central to the problems facing landowners than the latter. As he told Ruhland in May 1894, low grain prices were much more important than over-indebtedness, and the first necessity was to secure a substantial increase in agricultural profits.[33] The evidence is that this view of the League's priorities had won the support of the organization's leaders in the period before the Reichstag's debates on the Code. A declaration issued by the League's committee in November 1895 made the point very clearly:

The complete solution of the agrarian problem can only occur if all agrarian demands including a systematic formulation of agrarian law are carried out: but an indispensable precondition for the effectiveness of all measures associated with agrarian law is the improvement of agricultural prices. The means to remove indebtedness from agriculture can only come from recreating profitability.[34]

This view found expression in the way in which Ruhland and Kroidl approached the task of formulating specific demands. Their work was strong in general denunciations of the Jewish nature of capitalist Roman law but weak in detailed policies. This approach often led the League into positions far removed from other agrarian voices, as was shown by its conception of undivided peasant inheritance as a restriction on the freedom of the individual will. The fact that no detailed consideration of the Code, similar to the attention given to the bill to create a state monopoly in the grain trade (the *Antrag Kanitz*) or the reform of the stock exchange,[35] took place is indicative of the League's belief in the secondary importance of the Civil Code in the desired agrarian reorientation of German politics. The code could provide useful ammunition for propaganda but little more.

Agriculture was not the only sector of the economy to feel that the Code paid inadequate attention to its interests. The question of the legal protection of artisans in the building trade was another issue which attracted considerable public concern in the 1890s. Once again, the issue raised the question of whether a pressing economic need could

[33] Ruhland, 'Vorwort', in *Stimmen aus dem agrarischen Lager*, i, p. i; Roesicke to Ruhland, 23 May 1894, ZStA Potsdam, Roesicke Papers no. 24, fos. 1–10 (quotation, fo. 8).
[34] *Deutsche Allgemeine Zeitung für Landwirtschaft*, 17 (Nov. 1895), 247.
[35] G. Roesicke, 'In letzter Stunde', *Deutsche Tageszeitung*, 25 June 1896; ibid., 23 July 1896; see Puhle, *Agrarische Interessenpolitik*, pp. 230 ff.

justify exceptional legislation, on behalf of a disadvantaged group, which broke with the system adopted by the codifiers. In this case, the matter was complicated by the fact that the draft code actually worsened the legal position of this category of artisans, at least in Prussia.[36] The background to this campaign was provided by structural changes in the building trades as a result of rapid urbanization in the late nineteenth century. The essence of the problem facing the builders did not lie in the difficulties created by technological change, as was the case with certain other categories of artisan. The building trades had undergone a lengthy period of growth from the 1850s, as a result of a massive increase in demand for urban building at a time when revolutionary technological innovations in this sector did not take place. Between 1882 and 1895, this led to a spectacular boom in the building trades in the larger cities, particularly Berlin, Cologne, and Leipzig, and a growth in the size of building concerns. There is, however, some statistical evidence that the 1890s saw increased difficulties for master builders with falling real incomes and turnovers recorded for the years 1892 and 1894–5.[37]

At first sight, it is slightly surprising that by the early 1890s representatives of this group should be arguing that 'things have never been worse for the building industry than now, especially in the large towns'. An extremely influential article in the *Westfälischer Merkur* went further, arguing in October 1891 that 'in Berlin, the complete ruination of the community of master builders is to be feared'.[38] The reasons for the builders' campaign against the draft code lay in their belief that it failed to respond to the problems caused by speculative building in the larger towns. Even before the publication of the draft code, interest groups had begun to demand protection in civil law for the building

[36] The *Allgemeines Landrecht* had allowed the artisan to enter a 'cautionary mortgage' (*Sicherungshypothek*), which was designed to secure future contractual claims. This right was removed by the draft Code, but reinstated during the process of revision.

[37] W. Fischer, 'Die Rolle des Kleingewerbes im wirtschaftlichen Wachstumsprozess in Deutschland 1850–1914', in id., *Wirtschaft und Gesellschaft im Zeitalter der Industrialisierung. Aufsätze—Studien—Vorträge* (Göttingen, 1972), 343 f.; Volkov, *Rise of Popular Antimodernism*, p. 42 n. 20; for the 1890s, see the tables in A. Noll, *Sozio-ökonomischer Strukturwandel des Handwerks in der zweiten Phase der Industrialisierung unter besonderer Berücksichtigung der Regierungsbezirke Arnsberg und Münster* (Göttingen, 1975), 240–378. On the continued dominance of the building trades by artisanal modes of production, see F. Naumann's comments in 'Neudeutsche Wirtschaftspolitik', in id., *Werke*, iii (Cologne/Opladen, 1964), 151 f.

[38] F. L. Haarmann's *Zeitschrift für Bauhandwerker. Organ der Herzoglichen Baugewerkschule Holzminden*, xxxv/14 (Halle, 1891), 105; *Westfälischer Merkur*, 13 Oct. 1891.

trades through petitions to the Reichstag. The source of this demand was the relatively disadvantaged position of a builder's claims against a building contractor who went bankrupt. The draft code's mortgage law laid down that claims on land should be met in the order in which they were placed in the land register. In the rash of speculative building in Berlin and other large towns, which was characterized by an array of unsound financing techniques, 'straw men', and so on, builders were placed in a risky position, because their claims were necessarily placed *after* those of creditors who had advanced the initial capital for the project. The risks were apparently greatest for those artisans—glaziers, joiners, locksmiths, and so on—who were employed in the later stages of building work. According to a Verein für Sozialpolitik investigation of the city of Leipzig, the average rate of losses to creditors in foreclosure proceedings was 27–36 per cent, although in the unusual year of 1891 such losses averaged almost 70 per cent. The bulk of such losses apparently fell on smaller concerns. Building speculation was thus rooted in developments in the financing of urban building, whereby the artisan was habitually a creditor and the building contractor a debtor. The policy of some urban councils in pushing up the price of building land was also thought to abet speculation, while maximizing the possibility of the contractor's bankruptcy by inducing him to borrow excessively. Corroboration on these points is also to be found in a report on the subject by Berlin's chief of police, who placed the blame for the frequency of such cases firmly at the door of the building speculation prevalent in the capital.[39]

In October 1888, the Association of German Builders' Guilds began a long campaign with a petition demanding that the claims of building artisans be given first place in the order of creditors in the land register.[40] This campaign derived much of its moral force in the early 1890s from the argument that speculation lay at the root of the problem. A break with the established principles of the legal system was much easier to justify if that system could be shown to be a means by which honest artisans were exploited and ruined by unscrupulous speculators. As the Christian Social preacher, Adolf Stoecker, put it in April 1893, the case of the builders was a prime example of the struggle between

---

[39] *Schriften des Vereins für Sozialpolitik*, lxx (Leipzig, 1897), 593 f.; cf. ibid., pp. 389 ff. for comparable conditions in Breslau and *Schriften*, lxiv (Leipzig, 1895), 71 ff. for the system of financing in Karlsruhe; Richthofen to Schelling, 10 Mar. 1892, GStA Berlin-Dahlem, Rep. 84a 11876, fos. 37–65.

[40] ZStA Potsdam, RJM 1335, fos. 12–21; cf. Bähr, 'Sonderinteressen', pp. 86 ff.

'honest work and swindling capital'.[41] The campaign contained a strongly anti-Semitic element from the start, as was shown by the inclusion of measures against building scandals in the 1890 programme of the anti-Semitic German-Social party and the frequent association of such scandals with 'Jewish swindlers'.[42] As in the case of agrarian reform, conservative interests quickly latched on to the prevailing mood, with the *Kreuzzeitung* repeatedly calling for changes in the system of registration of land debts in order to protect the 'economically weak'. The obvious anti-capitalist and anti-Semitic aspects of the matter also predictably brought the Farmers' League into the campaign.[43] In this sense, the issue of the building artisans became an important element of attempts to produce a coherent conservative *Mittelstandspolitik*.

A central role was played by the League for Reform of Landownership (Bund für Bodenbesitzreform), which managed to secure control of the campaign in early 1892 with a much-reported petition to the Reich Justice Office. The League's principal aim was to abolish private ownership of urban land, and its petition argued that the only true solution to the housing and building problems was to be found in the 'communalization' of the land. However, the League also claimed that the Civil Code could and should legislate against the 'undeserved losses' of the builders; the economic salvation of this group was 'a matter of life and death for the artisanal class'. The League claimed the support of the General Congress of Artisans (Allgemeine Handwerkertag) for this petition, a body which was said to represent two million artisans. Throughout the early 1890s, the League organized mass meetings to pressurize the Reich and Prussian governments and, as liberal newspapers complained, agitated in 'demagogic ways'[44] for legislation to defend the artisans in the building trades against the evils of capitalism.

The League was in many ways a typical phenomenon of the 1890s. Its demagogic style, pursuit of collective solutions to the social problems engendered by industrialization, and tendency to equate the problems

[41] *Kreuzzeitung*, 15 Apr. 1893.

[42] The German-Social programme is reprinted in Puhle, *Agrarische Interessenpolitik*, pp. 321 f. (art. 15); cf. the report of a speech to the *Deutscher Bürgerverein Blücher* by Dr Stein in *Das Volk*, 13 Feb. 1891.

[43] *Kreuzzeitung*, 8 July 1892, 30 June 1893, 22 Jan. 1896; for the Farmers' League, see *Deutsche Tageszeitung*, 8 Sept. 1894.

[44] The petition, which was drawn up on 11 Oct. 1891 and sent to the government on 8 Jan. 1892, is to be found in GStA Berlin-Dahlem, Rep. 84a 11876, fos. 97–119; *Frei-Land*, 7 Mar. 1892. *Magdeburgische Zeitung*, 22 June 1894; *Freisinnige Zeitung*, 30 June 1895.

of a sectional group with those of society as a whole displayed strong similarities with other political organizations of the period. There was also a powerful anti-Romanist tinge, in that the root of the problem was seen as lying in the failure of the legal system to apply the old German legal distinction between the land and its buildings.[45] The League was not, however, merely another group on the radical right, seeking to mobilize the lower middle classes against traditional liberalism. Its chairman, Heinrich Freese, who had been a keen left-liberal in his youth and was a friend of the social reformer Friedrich Naumann, is best known to historians as the promoter of the 'constitutional' factory system.[46] Another leading figure in the League, Adolf Damaschke, moved from support for left-wing liberalism of the Richterite variety towards land reform as a result of his disappointment at Richter's hostility to state-led social reform, and came to play an important role in Naumann's National-Social movement in the late 1890s. The cause of protection of the builders also found the support of Dr August Althaus, the left-liberal deputy for Potsdam-Oberbarnim in the Reichstag.[47]

There are grounds for thinking that this reflected the considerable complexity of social reformism in the early and mid-1890s. As the composition of such bodies as the Verein für Sozialpolitik and the Evangelical Social Congress showed, it was for a time possible for the cause of state action on behalf of the socially disadvantaged to unite radical conservative and left-liberal groups in the same organizations. Naumann's breach with Stoecker's Christian-Social movement in the period 1894–6, the battle with the Conservative party over the agrarian issue, and the formation of the National-Socials around a policy of gearing reform demands to the needs of the industrial working class clarified things greatly in the mid-1890s. In these developments, a growing rejection of anti-Semitism and issues such as the defence of

---

[45] For this formulation, see A. Damaschke, *Zeitenwende. Aus meinem Leben*, ii (Leipzig/Zürich, 1925), 210. On the League's campaign against the draft code, see Damaschke, *Leben*, i (Berlin, 1928), 287 ff.

[46] See, above all, H. J. Teuteberg, *Geschichte de industriellen Mitbestimmung in Deutschland* (Tübingen, 1961), 260–6. For Naumann's acceptance of the central ideas of the League's programme, see F. Naumann, 'Gedanken zum christlich-sozialen Programm' (1895), in *Werke*, v (Cologne/Opladen, 1964), pp. 67 f.

[47] Damaschke, *Leben*, i. 242 ff.; D. Düding, *Der Nationalsoziale Verein 1896–1903. Der gescheiterte Versuch einer parteipolitischen Synthese von Nationalismus, Sozialismus und Liberalismus* (Munich/Vienna, 1972), 167–173. *Eingabe des Handwerker-Vereins für den Westen und Südwesten Berlins an den Reichskanzler wegen Abänderung einiger den Handwerkerstand betreffenden Bestimmungen des Entwurfs des bürgerlichen Gesetzbuches für das deutsche Reich* (Berlin, 1892).

artisanal interests, which were seen to be related to anti-Semitism, played a fundamental role.[48] But it is important not to antedate such changes. As the left-liberal Freisinnige Vereinigung showed, many peoples' attitudes changed as a result of the social policy of the 'New Era' in the early 1890s. With this temporary acceptance by the government of the need to institute social reforms, a considerable number of liberals joined the right in rejecting the principles of absolute *laissez-faire*, whose defence was increasingly confined to an embittered minority around Eugen Richter.[49] In the formative period of the early 1890s, there were many crossing-points in terms of language and rhetoric between right- and left-wing reformers, which helped to conceal their basic differences in political aims. The very meaning of the words 'social', 'social reform' and 'social policy' was fluid in the early 1890s, and varied according to the political position of the speaker. Max Weber's sardonic comment about the conservatives' propensity to cloak their class rule with 'the whole sorry apparatus of "Christian", "monarchist", and "national" slogans' and his scepticism about a return to German law as a means of solving the social question reflected very clearly these deep political differences within the camp of social reformers.[50]

The success of this campaign in raising public awareness of the problems faced by the master builders is difficult to contest. By 1894 most observers were in agreement that a serious social problem did exist, and National Liberal newspapers began to come round to the view that something needed to be done, if only to calm the agitation against the Reich and Prussian governments.[51] Powerful voices within the government, such as that of Karl Boetticher of the Reich office of the interior, were raised in opposition to the contention of the codifiers that the builders' losses were due to their carelessness in the conclusion of contracts. In the increasingly common language of 'social' jurisprudence,

---

[48] See Düding, *Nationalsoziale Verein*, pp. 22 ff.; W. Struve, *Elites against Democracy. Leadership Ideals in Bourgeois Political Thought in Germany, 1890–1933* (Princeton, 1973), 80–5.

[49] On this, see especially K. Wegner, *Theodor Barth und die Freisinnige Vereinigung. Studien zur Geschichte des Linksliberalismus im wilhelminischen Deutschland (1893–1910)* (Tübingen, 1968), 16–27.

[50] Cited in D. Beetham, *Max Weber and the Theory of Modern Politics* (2nd edn., Oxford, 1985), 156. For Weber's view that Roman law was a 'social-political scapegoat', see A. Brand, 'Against Romanticism: Max Weber and the Historical School of Law', *Australian Journal of Law and Society*, 1 (1982), 94.

[51] *National-Zeitung*, 22 Aug. 1894; *Magdeburgische Zeitung*, 22 June 1894; *Kölnische Zeitung*, 10 Dec. 1895.

Boetticher insisted that this constituted an example of the major duty of the legal system—i.e. the protection of the economically disadvantaged.[52] Yet at this point it became clear that opposition to the builders' case was mobilizing around the argument that protection would damage the supply of landed credit by undermining the security offered to the investments of other creditors. The Central Committee of Berlin Commercial and Manufacturing Associations denounced such protection as creating exceptional privileges for one group of people at the expense of the many others who depended on a secure supply of credit.[53] The Central Union of German House and Landowners' Associations advanced similar views as, rather later, did several chambers of commerce and other organizations.[54]

The counter-attack by such groups is hardly difficult to explain. Neither houseowners nor mortgage-brokers could realistically be expected to promote the interests of master builders at their own expense. But an interesting feature of this campaign was the way in which it turned the artisans' arguments on their head. Protection, it was argued, was likely to be self-defeating in that it would strengthen the pressures towards concentration in the building trades and thus contradict the long-term interests of the artisans. A petition from the Association for the Protection of Berlin Building Interests, for example, emphasized that the proposal 'would widen the gap between capital and labour through the concentration of the building trade in the hands of large capitalists and therefore contradict the goals of the social legislation of the last decade'. Similar views had already been expressed by the Schöneberg House and Landowners' Association in early 1895, and this type of argument rapidly became part of the standard defence of existing law against the demands of the radical reformers.[55]

These developments are of obvious interest in that they signify the ways in which a straightforward defence of the needs of landed credit

---

[52] Boetticher to Nieberding, 21 Mar. 1894, ZStA Potsdam, RJM 1335, fos. 189 f.

[53] See the Committee's report of 23 Apr. 1895, ZStA Merseburg, Rep. 120 II b 1 no. 54 vol. 1, fos. 163 ff.

[54] *Das Grundeigentum. Zeitschrift für Hausbesitzer*, xiv/33 (18 Aug. 1895); Frankfurt chamber to minister of trade, 27 May 1898; Wiesbaden chamber, *Eingabe*, 16 July 1898; *Verein der Berliner Grundstücks- und Hypotheken-Makler* to minister of trade (May 1898), all in ZStA Merseburg, Rep. 120 II b 1 no. 54 vol. 4.

[55] Petition of the Schutzverein der Berliner Bau-Interessenten to Prussian minister of justice, 15 July 1895, GStA Berlin-Dahlem, Rep. 84a 11878, fos. 174 f.; 'Bittschrift des Haus- und Grundbesitzer-Vereins zu Schöneberg (Berlin) betr. die Bekämpfung bezw. Beseitigung des Bauschwindels', 9 Feb. 1895, GStA Berlin-Dahlem, Rep. 84a 11877, fo. 562.

at the apparent cost of the *Mittelstand* was increasingly felt to be politically inappropriate by the mid-1890s. It is important that groups such as houseowners' organizations began to feel the need to argue their case in terms of the 'true' interests of the artisan. On this issue at least, the moral high ground had clearly been won by those demanding protection for those disadvantaged by modern social developments, even if the immediate consequences in terms of legislation were hardly spectacular. As we shall see in the next chapter, the arguments of Freese and his fellow campaigners cut little ice with the codifiers. From the artisans' point of view, a modest legal improvement was introduced during the revision of the Civil Code, but comprehensive regulation of the legal position of the master builders had to await a special law passed in 1909. In terms both of the debate's rhetoric and of its outcome, the case of the master builders was highly indicative of the possibilities of and hindrances to legal reform in Wilhelmine Germany.

The responses of commercial and industrial interest groups to the draft code are rather more difficult to analyse because the scope of their criticisms was not precisely defined. In 1889, the German Commercial Congress circulated a questionnaire which excluded questions of a purely legalistic importance and areas of the draft code which did not affect the trading community *more* than other sections of society. As the interests of commerce mainly involved the law of movable property, the questionnaire concentrated on the draft code's law of obligations. General questions, such as the validity of the draft code's treatment of 'juristic personality', land law, and family law, were deliberately ignored, despite the importance of these areas of the law for commercial life in many areas of Germany.[56]

As we have seen, this limited conception of the critical function of the most important commercial interest groups generally led to praise for the draft code as a suitable basis for legal unity. The point was not lost on the National Liberal press. As the *National-Zeitung* wrote:

The questionnaire proceeded from the assumption that the legal unity sought by the draft code was far too important for the German people to allow the members of the Commercial Congress to reject the draft code and thus produce a delay . . . [57]

---

[56] *Mittheilungen des Deutschen Handelstages*, xxix/11 (1889), 1; a question was, however, included on the decision to leave the question of 'juristic personality' to the individual states.

[57] *National-Zeitung*, 22 May 1890.

This is not to say that the chambers of commerce were unanimous in praising all aspects of the draft code. Doubts about the abstraction and legalism of the language of the draft code were widespread, but on the whole the general feeling was that the draft code was acceptable, if linguistic improvements were introduced. On that basis, the chambers were willing to comment on such controversial areas as the law of associations and the various applications of the principle of freedom of contract.

The vast majority of chambers of commerce opposed the exclusion of the law of associations from the draft code. Only the Leipzig and Solingen chambers agreed with the codifiers on this question; all the others saw some sort of national regulation of the matter (generally according to the principle of 'normative conditions') as desirable.[58] The main objections to the draft code concerned the damage done to legal unity, and the problems which might arise out of contracts between trading corporations, which tended to possess 'juristic personality', and other associations, which frequently did not. The Munich chamber was representative of this feeling in arguing that '[i]f the draft code becomes law, legal disunity and legal uncertainty will be created instead of a common system'.[59] This could be taken to imply a liberal political standpoint in some cases; the Munich and Chemnitz chambers, for example, believed that the relatively progressive regulations operating in their own states (Bavaria and Saxony respectively) should be extended to the Reich. Conversely, the position adopted by the Leipzig chamber may well have been a reflection of its satisfaction with the state of affairs in Saxony. However, the main concern of other chambers of commerce was to secure the closely linked advantages of legal certainty and legal unity without incurring any of the political disadvantages which might arise out of a thoroughly liberal formulation of the law. Thus both the Cologne and the Brunswick chambers supported national regulation of the private law of associations, while suggesting that the principle of state approval of associations should be retained.[60] That position reflected the chambers' principal concern with legal unity and certainty at all costs; it did not, however, accord with the views of those who saw the 'concessionary system' as the remnant of an outdated form of political organization.

---

[58] See e.g. Leipzig chamber, p. 6; Halle chamber, p. 4; Kassel chamber, pp. 2 f.; Cologne chamber, p. 6.
[59] Munich chamber, p. 9.
[60] Cologne chamber, p. 6; Brunswick chamber, p. 19.

This attitude emerged most strongly in the views of the various interest groups associated with heavy industry, two of which commissioned a report from Dr Josef Esser in 1890. Among other things, the report supported a national regulation of the law of juristic personality.[61] Among the members of the committee which accepted Esser's report was Wilhelm Beumer, a National Liberal industrialist who was later to lead the Central Association of German Industrialists' attack on the more liberal formulation of the law of association introduced by the Reichstag in 1896. By that time Beumer was insisting on the authorities' right to dissolve associations which pursued anything other than 'ideal' goals, and he pointed to the dangers inherent in the system of normative conditions. His motion to petition the Reichstag to restore the earlier distinction between 'ideal' and other associations was accepted by the delegates' congress of the Central Association on 3 June 1896. Beumer's campaign was motivated by the fear that trade unions would be accorded juristic personality by the provisions of the new Civil Code. He rejected the suggestions of writers such as Rudolf Sohm that easier acquisition of the right to act at law would help to integrate worker organizations into the existing order.[62] The Central Association had itself been refused juristic personality in 1895, and and had decided not to press the issue in view of the increasing public interest in the relationship between workers and their employers. The Association had already attacked the 'socialist' notion of giving trade unions the right to act as corporations in law and was therefore extremely sensitive to any suggestion that the Civil Code might make life easier for the labour movement.[63] The direct influence of this campaign on the final version of the Civil Code was probably slight, the matter being decided by a compromise between the Reichstag parties. The Association's standpoint was, however, symptomatic of the hardening of attitudes among the heavy industrialists towards the labour movement which marked the end of the Kaiser's 'New Course' in 1894.

As has been seen, the principle of freedom of contract was a source of major controversy in the 1890s and seemed to many of the Code's critics to be the principal manifestation of the class bias of the legal system. As the Commercial Congress's questionnaire concentrated on

[61] A copy of Esser's report is to be found in ZStA Potsdam, RJM 3838, Bl. 134.
[62] H. A. Bueck, *Der Centralverband deutscher Industrieller 1876-1901*, iii (Berlin, 1905), 358-63; cf. R. Sohm, *Ueber den Entwurf eines bürgerlichen Gesetzbuchs für das Deutsche Reich in zweiter Lesung. Ein Vortrag* (Berlin, 1895), 14-17.
[63] Bueck, *Centralverband*, i (Berlin, 1902), 263 f.

the law of obligations, it naturally touched on several important issues connected with contractual freedom—interest rates, tenancy law, labour law and so on. The responses of the chambers of commerce on such matters are highly revealing with regard to the attitude of those organizations towards the legal system.

All of the chambers started from the notion that freedom of contract was a fundamental principle, which should only be modified in cases of the most pressing necessity. As the Lübeck chamber put it, '[a] restriction of contractual freedom, even with regard to the form of a contract, should only be introduced when there are pressing reasons for thinking that an abuse might take place.' Thus, the refusal of the draft code to restrict the freedom of contracting partners to agree on interest rates was generally welcomed, and the Halle chamber was very much on its own in seeing in these clauses 'a somewhat one-sidedly favourable treatment of the creditor'.[64] In general, the chambers agreed that it was not the duty of the civil law to prevent usury—a goal which was to be attained through special legislation in the field of criminal law. Gierke's views about the social duties of the legal system, which had motivated many of the points raised in the Commercial Congress's questionnaire, found little response here.

On other issues, such as tenancy law and the law governing the 'contract of service',[65] the chambers of commerce were divided. However, there was no systematic critique of these two areas of the draft code, which had major social implications in a period of rapid industrialization and urban growth. With regard to abstract obligations, there was unanimity that this part of the law, which had developed in response to the needs of commerce, should be included. Only the Brunswick chamber expressed any reservations, and these merely concerned matters of formulation.[66] Once again, the main representatives of trade and industry gave scant support to the 'social' critics of the draft code.

Commercial interests were distinguished from other interest groups by the extent of their commitment to the rapid establishment of legal unity on the basis of the draft code. By 1895, a powerful movement in favour of acceptance of the revised code *en bloc* had arisen within these groups. It was with great difficulty that a Commercial Congress resolution to that effect was toned down in December 1895—a move prompted by

---

[64] Lübeck chamber, p. 19; Halle chamber, p. 9.

[65] This included all kinds of service, making no distinction between different kinds of labour contract—e.g. contracts for artisans, doctors, and industrial workers.

[66] Brunswick chamber, pp. 29 f.

the fear that the Reichstag might take umbrage at an implied diminution of its right to discuss the Code.[67] The general mood was reflected by the Association for the Preservation of Rhine Shipping Interests which wrote to the Prussian minister of trade on 21 December 1895:

> it seems to us that in such an important national question, one must stress that a unified German law covers the civil law. The significance of that is too great for its completion to be threatened, even if only unconsciously, by too much concern to change material aspects of the Code to satisfy all interests.[68]

In January 1896 the Halle chamber demanded that the Reichstag accept the Code 'as soon as possible and with as few changes as possible'.[69] The call was echoed by other industrial representatives and very little criticism was heard from this section of society in 1896. The establishment of legal unity was far more important to Germany's industrial and trading communities than any quibbles about the content of the new legislation.

On balance, the influence of the various interest groups on the final version of the Code was disappointingly small in relation to the amount of attention they devoted to the matter. On certain issues—for example, the inclusion of the annuity charge as an *optional* form of landed indebtedness and the restoration of a certain level of protection for master builders—the 'improvements' of the revised Code may be directly linked to the campaigns of the interest groups. In the first case, success was due to the support of the 'respectable', semi-official organizations, such as the Landes-Oekonomie-Kollegium. Perhaps more important was the fact that optional annuity charges could be integrated into the Code's system, whereas the radicals' demand that such charges be made the sole form of landed debt could not.[70] In the second case, the builders' attempt to identify their interests with the common good gained considerable credibility from abuses linked to the process of rapid urbanization. In neither case, however, did the more radical demands for the restructuring of the legal system win the day. Reforms in a 'social' direction were constrained by the overriding necessity of preserving the systematic coherence of the legal system. The notion of

[67] ZStA Merseburg, Rep. 120A I 1 no. 1 vol. 4, fo. 266.
[68] Ibid. vol. 5, fo. 105.
[69] Halle chamber to Berlepsch, ZStA Merseburg, Rep. 120A I 1 no. 1 vol. 5, fos. 114 ff.
[70] Bähr, 'Sonderinteressen', pp. 177 ff.

the balance of different social interests precluded changes which favoured one group at the expense of others.

The reasons for this relative lack of influence will be the subject of the next two chapters. In part, it was because of the limited responsiveness of the government and political parties to the frequently dubious claims made by sectional interests. But it is also important to note that the very structure of interest-group activity militated against the successful application of pressure in relation to this type of legislation. For one thing, the vast majority of the groups concerned obeyed a self-denying ordinance with regard to the scope of their discussions. None of them seriously considered the Code as a whole, despite the frequency with which rhetorical links were made between Roman law and capitalist or creditor interests. Gierke's Germanist, 'social' jurisprudence provided the agrarians and others with a language and a justification. The language linked the special treatment of landownership to the broader concerns of social policy, which might very broadly be defined as the protection of the weak against exploitation by the strong. The justification lay in the assertion that these concerns were in line with 'true' German, as opposed to foreign (Roman), traditions. But when Gierke sought to convert these perceptions into a detailed attack on the system of the draft code, he was rebuffed.

A second, perhaps more important, feature of the debates is that they tended to reveal the disunity of opinions among the groups commenting on the draft code. The debates were full of the standard assertions of the importance of landowners or artisans to the future of the German social order, and to the battle against 'international' Social Democracy or Jewish capitalist interests. But it would be difficult to find cases where such assertions were translated into genuine common action to give substance to the rhetoric of conservative *Mittelstandspolitik*. The master builders were not at the forefront (or even in the rearguard) of the campaigns for undivided peasant inheritance or homestead legislation. The Farmers' League, it is true, did lend the builders some support, but that organization regarded the Civil Code more as a test case to show the level of its influence over national politics than as a piece of legislation on which the future of the German *Mittelstand* depended. There is nothing in the debates about the Civil Code to lead one to contradict the suggestion of David Blackbourn's recent research on the politics of the German lower middle classes—that behind the strident rhetoric of the unity of the *Mittelstand* lay conflicting interests whose divisions simply could not be bridged.[71] Moreover, the preceding discussion of agrarian demands provides clear evidence of the different, often contradictory, suggestions of the representatives of Germany's farmers. Such disunity and confusion gave credibility to defenders of the Code, who argued that demands for reform were insufficiently clear and that developments were still in a state of flux. And the fact that differences among the farmers were often rooted in regional variations in Germany's agrarian development only encouraged the legislators to exclude certain contentious issues, such as undivided peasant inheritance, from the Code altogether.

On the whole, these different characteristics of interest group activity meant that they tended to make a lot of noise to little effect. The codifiers' argument that all social interests had to be considered was compelling, and could hardly be challenged effectively by groups which refused to consider any interest other than the one they existed to represent. It was precisely because these organizations represented a small section in society that they tended to have the greatest effect when campaigning on issues which had a strictly limited impact. The 1890s saw a considerable number of special laws designed to benefit specific groups within the population, such as the artisans, shopkeepers, and peasants. These efforts included a stock exchange law, legislation against 'unfair competition', and a law which in 1897 reintroduced the guild system where certain conditions were met. Such legislation was an important part of shift in official attitudes towards social policy in the 1890s, and was generally buttressed by conventional conservative assumptions about the 'state-supporting' nature of the *Mittelstand*. It is this feature of Wilhelmine politics which has led historians to talk of a 'reinsured *Mittelstand*', although it is difficult to demonstrate that these initiatives had much more than a cosmetic effect.[72] The point about such laws, whether they were cosmetic or not, is that they were conceived as special responses to special needs, as exceptions to general trends in German legislation. But there were forces both inside and outside the government which wanted more than this exceptional legislation. Such an approach, which would have led to the systematic elevation

---

[71] See, above all, D. Blackbourn, 'The *Mittelstand* in German Society and Politics, 1871–1914', *Social History*, 4 (1977), 409–33.

[72] See the contrasting views of H. A. Winkler, 'Der rückversicherte Mittelstand. Die Interessenverbände von Handwerk und Kleinhandel im deutschen Kaiserreich', in Ruegg and Neuloh (eds.), *Zur soziologischen Theorie und Analyse*, pp. 163–79; and the various works of David Blackbourn, whose views on this point are neatly summarized in D. Blackbourn and G. Eley, *The Peculiarities of German History, Bourgeois Society and Politics in Nineteenth-Century Germany* (Oxford, 1984), 247 f.

of threatened sectional groups over the rest of society in the legal system, was never a practical proposition. That type of special treatment was what the radical reformers of the civil law actually wanted; it lay at the core of the debates over what type of state the future Germany should be and over whether Germany should sacrifice the *Mittelstand* in order to secure creditor interests. But, in the end, the countervailing interests were too strong, the proponents of radical reform too divided, and the response of the legislators too skilful for the radicals.

The question of the legislators' response will be considered in greater detail in the following chapters. At this point, however, it should be noted that the debate about the Civil Code reflected political developments of great importance in Wilhelmine Germany. The fact that the radicals were ultimately unsuccessful is what requires explanation, for it was their existence, and the popularity of many of their arguments, which highlighted the extent to which things had changed since the 1870s. As we have seen, when work on the codification began in 1874, the main issue was the constitutional question of the rights of the Reich in relation to the individual states. With very few exceptions, lawyers accepted the desirability of legal unity, and the matter became a subject of controversy only in relation to the central political question of the time—the validity of the 1871 settlement. Nor was there any storm of protest when the decision was taken to produce a systematic compilation of existing law—a decision which was likely to produce the sort of code whose contents were found so objectionable by those interested in the health of the German social fabric in the late 1880s. If, as Gierke postulated, the codifiers had neglected their duty, it was because the conception of the legislator's duty had changed in the intervening fourteen years. On all major issues, the commission fulfilled the expectations of the Bundesrat admirably.

It is possible to describe the dominant position of the 1870s as follows. Codification was conceived as an important aspect of state formation, the crowning achievement of national unification, and part of the package of measures which constituted the major successes of the period of National Liberal dominance. By the late 1880s, serious doubts were emerging in relation to the social philosophy which was believed to lie behind the National Liberals' emphasis on formal unification. Questions of justice (the protection of the disadvantaged) and fairness (Stoecker's juxtaposition of 'honest work and swindling capital') were involved. And, most important of all, Gierke and the Germanists provided a framework within which critics could legitimately question the Code's nationalist credentials. If the draft code did not proceed in line with national traditions, how could its completion be considered a 'great national achievement'?[73] And, on the party-political plane, if Gierke was right, how national were the National Liberals, who enthusiastically supported the work?

This brings us back to the point raised at the end of Chapter 4— the symmetry between National Liberalism and conceptual jurisprudence. The political equivalent of the attack on conceptual jurisprudence was that 'fragmentation of the middle strata,' which was the principal source of the National Liberals' electoral problems.[74] What made the attack of the reformers so serious from the point of view of the government and the National Liberals was that it involved a competing conception of the national interest, which threw the achievements of the 1870s into doubt. It is this that explains the evident desire of the government to head off public criticism. Equally significant was the influence that such attacks had on the language of National Liberal polemics. As the debate progressed, more and more National Liberal polemicists began to accept the justice of many of the criticisms of the existing legal order and to call for reform. It was quickly perceived that the rhetoric of the 1870s was insufficient in the changed political context. By the 1890s the pages of the *National-Zeitung* and the *Kölnische Zeitung* were filled with tortured attempts to link the enthusiasms of old to the demands of the new. By 1896 both National Liberals and Progressives had learned to read the signs correctly, and were arguing that the Code was the beginning, not the end, of a fruitful period of reform on behalf of the socially disadvantaged.[75] Even if, as was clearly the case, opinions diverged about the nature of desirable social and legal reforms, the speed with which the terrain of the argument had shifted was striking. Many contemporaries evidently believed that this shift had a great deal to do with the intensity of debate about the Civil Code—a piece of

[73] Paradoxically, this phrase was uttered by the radical agrarian Thüngen-Rossbach at the 1889 meeting of the Congress of German Farmers—a sign of the contradictory blandishments of older and newer conceptions of nationalism and the limited acceptance of Gierke's more extreme views, even among radicals—see *Bericht über die Verhandlungen der XX. Haupt-Versammlung des Congresses Deutscher Landwirte* (Berlin, 1889), 49.

[74] The phrase is taken from the title of ch. 16 of J. J. Sheehan, *German Liberalism in the Nineteenth Century* (Chicago/London 1978).

[75] Enneccerus, 'Die parlamentarischen Aussichten', pp. 7 f.; *Freisinnige Zeitung*, 3 July 1896.

legislation which derived its importance from its national significance rather than from its suitability as a tool of social reform. With these considerations in mind, it is time to look in detail at the responses of the Reich's political institutions to this heated public debate.

6.

The Wilhelmine State and the
Revision of the Code, 1888–1896

THE nature of the Wilhelmine state occupies a prominent position in the modern historiography of this period of German history. Many of the major studies written in the late 1960s and early 1970s sought to use an exhaustive research into the governmental archives to develop a set of arguments about the Wilhelmine state which originated in the writings of earlier historians such as Eckart Kehr.[1] There can be no doubt that Kehr's ideas about the way in which Wilhelmine politics worked have been extraordinarily fruitful in stimulating research into this period. This is accepted even by those who have begun to question Kehr's interpretations. There are nevertheless grounds for looking more closely at the model of the Wilhelmine state adopted by Kehr and those who have followed him.

In the first place, it is worth noting that Kehr's principal concern was not with the nature of the Wilhelmine state as such, but with the ways in which the state was related to the key social interests which underpinned the late nineteenth-century German polity—in particular, the Junkers and heavy industrialists. The reasons for this particular emphasis lay in Kehr's desire to analyse the 'weak' development of liberal-democratic values in Germany after 1871. Writing in conscious disagreement with the prevailing school of German historiography, Kehr sought to consider the state's actions against a background in which the dominant influence was the clash between the traditional élites' claims to exercise power and the problems associated with a period of rapid social and economic change. The work of Kehr and his followers may be seen as a sustained attempt to 'demystify' the claims of the

---

[1] Good examples are H.-U. Wehler, *Bismarck und der Imperialismus* (Cologne, 1969); P.-C. Witt, *Die Finanzpolitik des deutschen Reiches von 1903–1913* (Lübeck, 1970); D. Stegmann, *Die Erben Bismarcks* (Cologne, 1970); V. Berghahn, *Der Tirpitz-Plan* (Düsseldorf, 1970).

German bureaucratic tradition to social neutrality and non-democratic but benevolent social leadership. That laudable aim had certain important consequences. The first and perhaps most significant of these has been a strong tendency to assume things which really require demonstration, for example the role of the state as the executive of the interests of the dominant classes or élites. In the words of Hans-Ulrich Wehler, the bureaucracy 'co-operated closely with the ruling élites, particularly the aristocracy, and exerted influence as an obedient executive'.[2] This argument has frequently been buttressed with assertions about the heavily aristocratic social composition of the senior bureaucracy. This is a factor which looms large in both Kehr's and Wehler's analyses of the period, with particular emphasis being placed on the conservative personnel policies allegedly pursued by the Prussian minister of the interior, Robert von Puttkamer, in the 1880s.[3] An essential feature of this school of thought, then, is the assumption that the social composition of a bureaucracy offers important clues as to the policies that that bureaucracy will favour.

A second important consequence of Kehr's approach has been to guide research into certain (undoubtedly important) areas of policy-making. Kehr's starting-point was the central importance in Wilhelmine politics of the relationship between the decision to build a battle fleet and agrarian tariffs in the period 1897-1902.[4] These decisions were motivated by the desire to secure conservative political hegemony at home through the construction of bulwarks to the electoral advance of the Social Democrats. A central aspect of Kehr's assault on traditional German historiography was his assertion of 'the primacy of domestic politics' in foreign policy-making. The consequence of this emphasis has been that modern research in Germany has tended to focus on certain principal areas: the pursuit of various forms of *Weltpolitik* (e.g. naval expansion, the pursuit of colonies, and, after 1911, European expansionism); the negotiation of economic alliances between different sections of the dominant élites; and the prevalence of anti-socialism within the governing élites. A further important consequence of the assumptions lying behind this historiography is the relative neglect of

[2] H.-U. Wehler, *The German Empire 1871-1918* (Leamington Spa, 1985), 65.
[3] This argument is to be found in E. Kehr, 'Das soziale System der Reaktion in Preussen unter dem Ministerium Puttkamer', in id., *Der Primat der Innenpolitik. Gesammelte Aufsätze zur preussisch-deutschen Sozialgeschichte im 19. und 20. Jahrhundert*, ed. H.-U. Wehler (Frankfurt, 1965), 64-86.
[4] E. Kehr, *Schlachtflottenbau und Parteipolitik 1894-1901* (Berlin, 1930).

the Reichstag in favour of detailed studies of interest-group politics. Because the Wilhelmine Reich is seen as an authoritarian, quasi-constitutional system, its formal political institutions have not received anything like the attention devoted to their counterparts elsewhere.

In the last few years, serious doubts have begun to emerge about the validity of many of these propositions. The notion that the bureaucracy was the executive of dominant class interests has come under attack from a number of directions. Questions have been raised about the dominance of the bureaucracy by aristocrats and the nature of the Puttkamer purges in the 1880s, and it has been suggested that the nobility were fighting a rearguard action from shrinking enclaves of power.[5] Moreover, it is by no means self-evident that the social composition of a bureaucracy necessarily determines the policies it will adopt in any given situation. Indeed, recent empirical research suggests that the social background of bureaucrats provides little or no explanation of their attitudes to questions of vital importance to the economic interests of the Junkers.[6]

A third set of problems relates to the whole area of the autonomy of the state's actions from social interests, and the existence of major divisions within the state bureaucracy about important political questions. To assign the state a certain degree of autonomy is not to reinstate the Idealist conception of the bureaucracy as a 'universal class' transcending the divisions of civil society, however much this comfortable view may have accorded with the self-image of the bureaucrats concerned. In fact, it is striking that Kehr and his followers on occasion follow Max Weber in seeing the bureaucracy as operating according to rules of its own making. This leads to a curious, hybrid analysis in which the bureaucracy is presumed both to have serviced aristocratic class interests and to have developed a separate bureaucratic ethos of its own.[7] The difficult question of the autonomy of bureaucratic actions will be considered later in the light of the evidence presented in this chapter.

The 1890s was a period of political flux, not least in the balance of

---

[5] M. L. Anderson and K. Barkin, 'The Myth of the Puttkamer Purge and the Reality of the Kulturkampf: Some Reflections on the Historiography of Imperial Germany', *JMH*, 54 (1982), pp. 647-86; D. Blackbourn and G. Eley, *The Peculiarities of German History. Bourgeois Society and Politics in Nineteenth-Century Germany* (Oxford, 1984), 244 ff.

[6] G. Bonham, 'Bureaucratic Modernizers and Traditional Constraints: Higher Officials and the Landed Nobility in Wilhelmine Germany, 1890-1914', Ph.D. thesis (Berkeley, 1985), esp. 337 ff.

[7] See the comments in G. Bonham, 'Beyond Hegel and Marx: An Alternative Approach to the Political Role of the Wilhelmine State', *German Studies Review*, 7 (1984), 211-14.

power within the government, where the secretaries of the various Reich Offices increasingly showed themselves to be capable of distancing themselves from the powerful forces in the Prussian government. This was, at least in part, a consequence of the expansion of parliamentary business, which in turn led to the increasing circumvention of the Bundesrat through direct negotiations between the Reich offices and leading figures in the Reichstag. It is this development which has led one historian to speak (rather misleadingly) of the gradual 'parliamentarization' of the Reich in this period.[8] What is beyond doubt is that important divisions about policy-making did open up within the Reich and Prussian governments, and that the notion of a monolithic conservative administration is hard to sustain. As we shall see, the debates within the government about the Civil Code revealed substantial evidence of the existence of such divisions, which in many ways mirrored the arguments considered in the previous chapter.

There is finally the question of the type of policy-making issue considered by the historiography. This is of central importance because it is related to the difficult area of what conservatism actually means to different people and in different historical periods. A compelling line of argument in the more recent, 'revisionist' historiography has suggested that the undoubted hostility of powerful elements in German society to democratization and socialism cannot be taken as necessarily being indicative of 'backward', 'feudalized' attitudes to the problems of government. In the light of this research, it is difficult for example to see the phenomenon of radical nationalism in terms of the desire to preserve an antiquated socio-political structure.[9] Moreover, Bonham's study of the Wilhelmine bureaucracy suggests the existence of an important group of modernizing bureaucrats, who were distinguished from their more reactionary colleagues by their commitment to the expansion of manufacturing industry and the pacification of the working classes through lower food prices and industrial growth, even if these desirable results were to be achieved at the expense of the Junkers.[10]

---

[8] M. Rauh, *Föderalismus und Parlamentarismus in Wilhelminischen Reich* (Düsseldorf, 1973), sect. B1. It is far from obvious that increasing contact between government and Reichstag necessarily meant that the Reich was progressing towards a parliamentary constitutional system.

[9] The major works here are G. Eley, *Reshaping the German Right. Radical Nationalism and Political Change After Bismarck* (New Haven, Conn./London, 1980), and R. Chickering, *We Men Who Feel Most German. A Cultural Study of the Pan-German League 1886–1914* (London, 1984), e.g. 302 ff.

[10] Bonham, 'Bureaucratic Modernizers and Traditional Constraints', pp. 330 ff.

It seems very probable that, however successful the government was in purging bureaucrats with liberal opinions about the political system, a substantial number remained who were unwilling to toe the Junkers' line when it came to social and economic policies. A hostility to democratic forms of government simply cannot, then, be equated with a commitment to conservative social interests.

This line of argument finds confirmation when bureaucratic attitudes to a wide range of policy questions are considered. One such question concerned the future of the educational system, where the complex interactions between social conservatism and the needs of an in-dustrializing society, between the classical pursuit of self-cultivation (*Bildung*) and the demand for more 'practical' forms of training, split the German élites down the middle. Here, once again, the connection of the 'modernizing' reform movement, radical nationalist aspirations and debates within the bureaucracy is clear. A recent study of the responses of both government and élites to the disturbing developments in the visual arts associated with the rise of modernism suggests similarly that those responses were 'fragmented and contradictory'.[11] The point here is not that education and the arts were matters of secondary political importance. Indeed, influential figures in the government, not least the Kaiser himself, believed that both were vital to the smooth functioning of society. Rather, it is the evidence of uncertainty and disunity on the part of the government which deserves our attention.

Turning to the legal system, we have already seen the ways in which the publication of the draft civil code in 1888 divided the political nation. Those divisions cannot simply be described in terms of conservatism against liberalism; as the issue of social reform showed, the situation was much more complicated, with frequent points of contact between right and left. Among other things, the debates signified the declining legitimacy of mid-century political doctrines which were associated with liberal state formation. As was the case in other areas of politics, this involved a changing perception of the true role of the state in relation to the social order; in other words, it had consequences for the practice of government as well as for liberal politics. Furthermore, the sheer volume of criticism placed the government in something of a quandary. Most political leaders, including Bismarck,[12] agreed that the

---

[11] J. C. Albisetti, *Secondary School Reform in Imperial Germany* (Princeton, 1983), esp. chs. 3 and 5; P. Paret, *The Berlin Secession. Modernism and Its Enemies in Imperial Germany* (Cambridge, Mass./London, 1980), 90 f.

[12] Bismarck to Schelling, 25 Jan. 1888, ZStA Potsdam, RJM 3811, fo. 47.

Vorkommission's suggested procedure for revision—i.e. that the original commission should be entrusted with the task—was unacceptable because it offered little hope that the more justified criticisms of the work would receive adequate consideration. That meant, however, that the whole future of the Code was placed in doubt. In the years between 1888 and 1890, a range of solutions to this problem were suggested. Nor, as will be seen, were the discussions on the matter merely concerned with the formal techniques of government. In the 1870s, the southern monarchies had recognized that a close connection existed between the method of legislation adopted and the contents of laws produced. For all the political changes of the intervening period, that connection still existed and may even have become stronger. The fact that the public discussion about the draft code had brought doubts about the nature of the legal system into the open meant that a special premium was placed on the mode of legislative procedure. This question was to lead to serious disagreements within the Prussian and Reich governments, the resolution of which had a profound impact on the future of the legal system.

The first response of the Bundesrat to the completion of the commission's work was one of confusion. The initial assumption was that the state governments would be given time to prepare their responses, and that that preparation would take at least a year.[13] A major problem was posed by the fact that most of the states (with the exception of Bavaria) had ignored the development of the commission's work; Prussia, for example, was reportedly 'surprised' by the publication of the draft code and spent nearly two years catching up on time lost while the commission had been at work.[14] For some of the smaller states, such as the Hanseatic cities, the problems involved in responding to such a large piece of legislation were found to be almost insuperable. Among the larger states such as Prussia, such problems led to delays and complaints from the Reich justice office about the effect these had on the process of revision.[15] Most of the states consulted local judges and lawyers and some (for example, Baden) appointed special ministerial commissions because of the heavy workload on the courts. The government of Mecklenburg, which had a wealth of legal talent at its disposal and a

[13] Stieglitz, report of 24 Jan. 1888, HStA Stuttgart, E 130a no. 820.
[14] Marschall, report of 25 Oct. 1889, GLA Karlsruhe, Abt. 233/13994.
[15] On the Hanseatic states, see the material in AH Lübeck, Senatsakten VIII 3a/9; on Prussia, see Nieberding to Schelling, 12 Nov. 1894, GStA Berlin-Dahlem, Rep. 84a 11778, fos. 307 ff.

continuing sense of injustice at its exclusion from the commission in 1874, began a detailed criticism of the draft code.[16] All such responses were however time-consuming, and tended to generate uncertainty about the future of the Code.

That uncertainty had considerable dangers. In the winter of 1887–8, the government was still mainly concerned to prevent any shift away from the goals of the 1870s—i.e. the adherence of the code to existing law and the avoidance of the temptation to override the interests of the southern states, above all Bavaria. At this point, this position was represented above all by the secretary of the Reich justice office, Heinrich von Schelling, whose main aim was to secure maximum direct control over the process of revision for the Bundesrat. Schelling was a renowned conservative, who owed his position at the head of the Reich justice office to Bismarck's desire to give that notoriously liberal body a more conservative appearance.[17] In agreement with Heinrich von Friedberg, the Prussian minister of justice, Schelling proposed a ministerial conference with Bavaria in order to agree on the approach to the revision of the Code.[18] The proposed conferences, involving Schelling, Friedberg, and the Bavarian minister of justice, Leonrod, began on 27 January 1888.

As public criticism of the work developed, however, other ideas began to emerge. By October, Friedberg seems to have been toying with the idea of entrusting the revision to a single lawyer. Friedrich Althoff in the ministry of education was reported to have considered a similar plan, involving the appointment of Dernburg as sole editor with possible assistance from Gierke and Josef Kohler. Such a scheme would have placed the future of the Code firmly in the hands of the commission's 'social' critics and was turned down after opposition from Bismarck or perhaps Miquel.[19] By the late spring other influential voices were beginning to make themselves heard. In April 1888 Carl Hagens, a

---

[16] GLA Karlsruhe, Abt. 234/3548, fos. 38–40, 81–2; StA Schwerin, Neu-Strelitz 10/228; A. Langfeld, *Mein Leben. Erinnerungen* (Schwerin, 1930), 132 ff.

[17] R. Morsey, *Die oberste Reichsverwaltung unter Bismarck 1867–1890* (Münster, 1957), 267.

[18] Schelling to Leonrod, 6 Dec. 1887 and Schelling to Friedberg, 26 Jan. 1888, GStA Berlin-Dahlem, Rep. 84a 11773, fos. 147–58 and 181–4; Schelling to Friedberg, 26 Dec. 1887, ZStA Potsdam, RJM 3810, fo. 185.

[19] Krüger to the Lübeck Senate, 5 Oct. 1888, AH Lübeck, Senatsakten VIII 3a/7; on Althoff's role, see F. Frensdorff, *Gottlieb Planck, deutscher Jurist und Politiker* (Berlin, 1914), 349 ff.; A. Sachse, *Friedrich Althoff und sein Werk* (Berlin, 1928), 300. For Kohler's strong criticisms of the draft code, see J. Kohler, *Vom Lebenspfad. Gesammelte Essays* (Mannheim, 1902), 35 ff.

senior official in the Reich justice office, expressed the view that if substantial criticism emerged, a new commission would have to be formed. At the end of the next month, a widely reported speech by Miquel called for the appointment of a new commission containing representatives of the various spheres of economic activity, on the grounds that he believed 'the task of a future commission to be more a question of material legislation than of legal technique'.[20] This suggestion might well have been ignored had a change not occurred at the head of the Reich justice office in February 1889.

The appointment of Karl von Oehlschläger to replace Schelling (who in turn became Prussian minister of justice) had a powerful influence on the future of the Code. Oehlschläger, like his predecessor, was reportedly conservative in political views. Nevertheless, within a month rumours were circulating in Berlin that he was in touch with the National Liberal leaders, Bennigsen and Miquel, on the question of who might chair a future commission. This in itself suggests that Oehlschläger was already moving away from Schelling's plans, since the implication was that the matter would not be dealt with solely by the ministerial bureaucracy. This impression is confirmed by developments in June, when Hagens was entrusted with the preparation of a circular letter to the state governments, which contained sixty-eight points of political, social, and economic importance arising in the draft code. The governments were asked to concentrate on these points in their written comments.[21] This procedure clearly contradicted Schelling's plans, and the latter continued to emphasize prior verbal agreement between the larger states in the Bundesrat before a new commission began its work.[22]

By December 1889 at the latest, Oehlschläger had come round to Miquel's view that the future of the Code was best assured if the draft code was revised by a commission which included representatives of the various economic-interest groups. The Bundesrat's and Reichstag's eventual acceptance of the revised Code might be secured if adequate representation in the new commission was given to those institutions.[23]

---

[20] For Hagens' views, see Marschall, report of 27 Apr. 1888, GLA Karlsruhe, Abt. 233/13993; for Miquel's speech, see *Frankfurter Journal*, 29 May 1888.

[21] Bismarck to Wilhelm II, 19 Feb. 1889, ZStA Potsdam, Rkz 1616, fo. 40; Schubert, *Materialien*, pp. 53, 329–33.

[22] Schelling to Caprivi, 4 July 1890 and Schelling to Crailsheim, 18 July 1890, GStA Berlin-Dahlem, Rep. 84a 11775, fos. 11–18, 91 ff.

[23] Johow to Planck, 29 Dec. 1889 and Struckmann to Planck, 30 Dec. 1889, NSUUB Göttingen, Planck Papers v, fo. 105 and VIII, fo. 61. Both Struckmann and Frensdorff, *Planck*, p. 351, ascribed a leading role to Miquel in persuading Oehlschläger to take this line.

Oehlschläger's plans were accepted, with small concessions to Schelling, at a meeting chaired by Caprivi on 17 July, and they became the policy of the Prussian government nine days later.[24]

The acceptance of Oehlschläger's plan marked a new stage in the history of the Code. For the first time, groups outside the ministerial and judicial bureaucracies and the community of academic lawyers were to be given a formal hearing. Oehlschläger's main concern was, it would seem, to find some way of reconciling the desire for the rapid completion of the work with the common demand for substantial revisions. From 1888 onwards the rapid completion of the Code had been an important feature of the debate in ministerial circles, and it was on this basis that Caprivi recommended Oehlschläger's plan to the Prussian ministry of state on 26 July 1890. As everybody realized, the premium on speed meant taking the draft code as the basis of the final legislation. On the other hand, the Reich justice office was well aware of the problems created by certain aspects of the draft code, especially when dealing with controversial political, social, or economic questions. Oehlschläger's major concern was to minimize any future difficulties for the code, whether in the Reichstag or from the economic interest groups. His main contribution lay in his early recognition of the changes that were taking place in the political process, and in foreseeing that extra-parliamentary pressure groups might exercise considerable influence in the future. His answer to this danger was to broaden the basis of decision-making early, in the hope that this might be sufficient to neutralize potentially dangerous criticism later on.

These views were expressed in a memorandum written by Carl Hagens on 11 July 1890. This document stressed more than anything else the necessity of hearing the views of the various governments in order to cut short subsequent debates in the Bundesrat. The representation of the Reichstag parties and the interest groups was also considered important, though less so. Moreover, a wide range of legal opinion was to be heard, and radical opponents of the draft code, such as Gierke and Bähr, were even suggested as possible members of the commission. Above all, the commission's work was to be guided by preparatory discussions within the Reich justice office, which would seek to ensure that the views expressed by the States were given proper consideration.[25]

---

[24] ZStA Potsdam, RJM 3811, fo. 99, marginal note; minutes of the meeting of the Prussian ministry of state, 26 July 1890, GStA Berlin-Dahlem, Rep. 84a 11775, fos. 99 f.

[25] C. Hagens, 'Promemoria betr. die weitere Behandlung des Entwurfs eines Bürgerlichen Gesetzbuchs', reprinted in Schubert, *Materialien*, pp. 334–7.

This seemingly innocent suggestion was to give the Reich justice office a great deal of power to determine the outcome of the commission's debates.

The views adopted by the Reich justice office in 1889–90 were evidently a response to the surprising strength of the public reaction to the draft Code. In the wake of that reaction, Oehlschläger came to realize that the code stood little chance if its revision was confined to the Bundesrat, where the Prussian and Bavarian ministers would inevitably combine to push through their views. It was no coincidence that Miquel was closely associated with these developments in the Reich justice office. A previous chapter has suggested certain parallels between the fortunes of National Liberalism and those of 'conceptual jurisprudence'. Miquel was one of the first National Liberals to recognize that the changed political situation after 1879 required a change in the party's political profile, particularly with regard to social reform and the satisfaction of the growing demand for tariff protection. In the course of the 1880s he became closely associated not only with the movement to reform the law of landed inheritance but also, as mayor of Frankfurt, with the pressing question of working-class housing. Yet he was still too much of a traditional National Liberal in 1890 to pursue these ends at the expense of a rapid conclusion of the process of legal unification, and was responsible for the clause supporting the code in the party's election manifesto of that year.[26]

Oehlschläger's strategy of broadening the decision-making process while limiting the nature of the debate in order to ensure the rapid completion of the Code was in a sense a bureaucratic response to the same problems which exercised Miquel. The Reich justice office effectively admitted what the public debate about the draft code implied—that the supposedly 'neutral' civil law was, in fact, a legitimate arena for sectional disagreements. Oehlschläger's policy was to recognize the existence of such disagreements while minimizing their impact. In

[26] For the development of Miquel's views on the future of the National Liberals, see H. Herzfeld, *Johannes von Miquel. Sein Anteil am Ausbau des deutschen Reiches bis zum Jahrhundertwende* (2 vols., Detmold, 1938), ii. 65 ff.; D. White, *The Splintered Party. National Liberalism in Hessen and the Reich, 1867–1918* (Cambridge, Mass., 1976), ch. 4; Miquel to Bennigsen, 10 July and 29 Aug. 1880, 29 Apr. and 5 May 1884, all reprinted in H. v. Oncken, *Rudolf von Bennigsen. Ein deutscher liberaler Politiker*, ii (Stuttgart/Leipzig, 1910), 435, 438, 514, 516; N. Bullock and J. Read, *The Movement for Housing Reform in Germany and France 1840–1914* (Cambridge, 1985), 64–70; for the 1890 manifesto, see Herzfeld, *Miquel*, ii. 169.

adopting this policy, he may conceivably have salvaged the work of the first commission.[27]

A further consequence of this method of procedure was the loosening of the control of Prussia and the larger states over the work. It is true that the Reich justice office continued to be closely linked to Prussia, and never obtained the power to present legislative proposals without the prior agreement of the Prussian ministry of state in the 1890s.[28] Nevertheless, it would be wrong to conclude from this that the office merely acted as the agent of Prussian policy. The states' responses to the draft code were produced in a variety of ways. In Prussia, for example, Schelling called a special commission, and suggestions were circulated to other ministers for comment before they were published. In Bavaria, on the other hand, one official prepared his government's response, which was subsequently published under his own name.[29] The purpose of these responses was, however, always to comment on the draft code in relation to existing state and local law. The Reich justice office then produced a digest (*Zusammenstellung*) of the states' views to help the codifiers.[30] Naturally, the Reich justice office could not override the wishes of the more powerful states, and a tension certainly existed between the claims of the Bundesrat to exercise control and the Reich office's perception of political necessity. Nevertheless, the history of the codification of civil law seems to bear out the contention that a transition had taken place in the normal practice of government since the 1870s. That change involved a shift of effective power away from the Bundesrat to the Reich's agencies.

That shift of power was rooted in the changing nature of politics. As we have seen, the Bundesrat operated as an imperfect federal agency even in the 1870s. The checks and balances introduced by the 1871 constitution certainly acted as a hindrance to the development of a unitary state, but the cumbersome machinery of committees and ministerial conferences was ill-suited to decisiveness in policy-making.

---

[27] See H. Hattenhauer, 'Vom Reichsjustizamt zum Bundesministerium der Justiz', *Vom Reichsjustizamt zum Bundesministerium der Justiz. Festschrift zum 100-jährigen Gründungstag des Reichsjustizamt am 1. Januar 1877* (Cologne, 1977), 37 f.

[28] Ibid. 27 f.; Rauh, *Föderalismus und Parlamentarismus*, p. 97.

[29] The work of the Prussian commission is to be found in GStA Berlin-Dahlem, Rep. 84a 11845–11849; Bavaria's response was K. Jacubezky, *Bemerkungen zu dem Entwurfe eines bürgerlichen Gesetzbuches für das deutsche Reich* (Munich, 1892).

[30] *Zusammenstellung der Aeusserungen der Bundesregierungen zu dem Entwurf eines Bürgerlichen Gesetzbuchs, gefertigt im Reichsjustizamte. Als Manuskript gedruckt* (2 vols. Berlin, 1891).

In the 1870s, the question of legal unity was generally considered by governments to be a question of the location of sovereignty, and there are signs that such matters were uppermost in the minds of many ministers after 1888. A large proportion of the states' comments on the draft Code concentrated on the question of whether their particular legal system had received adequate recognition; calls for greater attention to local conditions and extensions to the list of parts of the law excluded from the code were frequently made. Only occasionally, as in the case of Schelling's demand for the restoration of the *Allgemeines Landrecht*'s provisions for the protection of master builders,[31] did the states' responses come close to the 'social' criticisms of the draft code.

The Reich justice office's concerns were very different. Its almost exclusive concern with the preparation of national legislation led it to assume an intermediary role between the Bundesrat and Prussian ministry of state on the one hand and the Reichstag on the other. In contrast to the politicians in the Bundesrat, the Reich justice office were thus forced to face the realities of the political mobilization of the 1890s head on. Apart from anything else, the state governments were partly shielded from those realities by the restricted suffrages which operated in many of the states. Above all, however, the Reich justice office's approach was guided by two complementary considerations: the need to create majorities within an expanding political nation, in which the state governments were only one of a number of elements and the recognition that this could not be achieved merely by ironing out disagreements between the legal systems of the different states in the Bundesrat. With these considerations in mind, Oehlschläger set about appointing a second codifying commission.

By July 1890, when Caprivi's intervention finally overcame Schelling's resistance to Oehlschläger's plans, preparations for the new commission were well under way. Miquel had for some time been considered the best available chairman, but that prospect was terminated when he was made Prussian minister of finance on 23 June. In view of the speed with which Miquel shifted to the right and began to champion conservative agrarian policies after his appointment, it seems likely that

---

[31] *Bemerkungen zum Entwurf eines Bürgerlichen Gesetzbuchs für das Deutsche Reich* (Berlin, 1891), 115 ff. This could of course also be interpreted as a defence of existing Prussian law.

the unrelated events which prevented him taking up the chairmanship of the commission had important consequences for the future of the code.[32] The question of the chairmanship of the commission was eventually resolved in early December, when Caprivi ordered Oehlschläger to take the chair himself.[33] Meanwhile the plan for a commission had been presented to the Bundesrat's justice committee on 16 October and precipitated the usual flurry of diplomatic activity as the states attempted to secure adequate representation for themselves. There was almost no discussion of the merits of Oehlschläger's plan; only Baden wanted a different type of commission, more tightly linked to the Bundesrat. This view failed to gain any support when the matter was discussed on 30 October.[34] The principal concern of the other states was with the personnel of the commission.

Oehlschläger's first aim was to offer places to men of political influence who were also capable of representing economic interests. He was surprisingly willing to consider strong critics of the draft code, despite his determination to use that work as the basis for discussion. Thus he initially suggested Baron von Cetto-Reichertshausen as a man who could represent both the Centre party and Bavarian agriculture—a proposal which was dropped after the Bavarian government expressed its opposition.[35] Oehlschläger also supported (though with some degree of reluctance) the inclusion of Gierke in the commission after the famous economist Gustav Schmoller had turned down the offer of membership. He insisted on the inclusion of a Germanist, and Gierke had the advantage of being capable of representing both the Germanist legal tradition and academic economics. Moreover, Oehlschläger seems to have believed that Gierke's inclusion would negate opposition to the Code in future, while the composition of the commission would prevent the introduction of Germanist ideas 'which no longer have a place in the legal life of the present'.[36] That proposal aroused the solid opposition of the southern states, with Bavaria in particular fearing that Gierke's appointment would lead to major disagreements within the commission. In the end, only Prussia and Saxony supported the inclusion of Gierke, and Johannes Conrad and Rudolf Sohm were chosen as the

[32] See J. C. G. Röhl, *Germany Without Bismarck. The Crisis of Government in the Second Reich, 1890–1900* (London, 1967), 60 ff.

[33] Reichskanzlei note, 5 Dec. 1890, ZStA Potsdam, RJM 4078, fo. 21.

[34] Brauer, report of 30 Oct. 1890, GLA Karlsruhe, Abt. 233/13994.

[35] Lerchenfeld to Pfistermeier, 22 Oct. 1890, BHStA Munich, MA 76 707/2; Stengel to Leonrod, 21 Oct. 1890, BHStA Munich, MJu 16112.

[36] Stieglitz, report of 26 Nov. 1890, HStA Stuttgart, E 130a no. 821, 95[b].

representatives of academic economics and Germanist jurisprudence respectively.[37]

Other appointments to the commission produced disagreements as well. The Centre party leader, Ludwig Windthorst, objected to the proposal that his party should be represented by the Bavarian Baron von Gagern and the Silesian Baron von Huene. As a Bavarian representative in Berlin explained, '[Windthorst] wanted two lawyers who belonged to the Centre party to be members of the commission, obviously in order to secure an adequate representation for Catholic views on the law of marriage.' Gagern's name had first been mentioned in late October as a possible substitute for Cetto, and his appointment had won the support of the Bavarian government, which evidently saw him principally as the representative of Bavarian agriculture rather than Catholic interests. Not surprisingly, Oehlschläger refused to accede to Windthorst's original demand, but he did agree to replace Huene with Peter Spahn, a judge and Centre party deputy in the Reichstag.[38] As both Gagern and Huene lost their influence in the Centre party after the 1893 election, Oehlschläger's willingness to compromise was perhaps crucial in undermining opposition from that quarter.

In attempting to select people who could represent several interests at once, Oehlschläger sought to create the impression that the commission represented the maximum number of social interests and political affiliations. One interest whose views did not find expression in the commission was the labour movement. Initially, Oehlschläger had suggested the inclusion of Karl Flesch, a subordinate of Miquel's in the municipal administration of Frankfurt, who had been closely associated with the movement to improve working-class living conditions and who was linked to the southern democrats.[39] This suggestion was quietly dropped when it became doubtful that Flesch's appointment would receive sufficient support, and there was no subsequent attempt to include representatives of the working classes or the labour movement in the commission. Nor was there any provision for the separate representation of peasants and artisans. Industry, on the other hand,

[37] Heller, reports of 30 Oct., 25 Nov., and 4 Dec. 1890, BHStA Munich, MA 707/2 and MJu 16112; Stieglitz, reports of 26 and 30 Nov., 3 and 4 Dec. 1890, HStA Stuttgart, E 130a no. 821, 95[b], 96[a], 96[c], 96[d]. Apparently, Conrad owed his inclusion to the behind-the-scenes influence of Friedrich Althoff; see J. Conrad, *Lebenserinnerungen* (Berlin, 1917), p. 187.

[38] Heller, report of 25 Nov. 1890, BHStA Munich, MJu 16112; Crailsheim to Gagern, 7 Nov. 1890, BHStA Munich, MA 76 707/2.

[39] Heller, report of 30 Oct. 1890, BHStA Munich, MA 76 707/2.

was represented by the mine director Ernst Leuschner and the brewery director Ludwig Goldschmidt, agriculture by Gagern and the director of the forestry academy at Eberswalde, Bernhard Danckelmann, and finance and commerce by Emil Russell, the chairman of the Diskonto-Gesellschaft and a leading figure in the German Commercial Congress.[40]

A combination of accident and design thus led to the formation of a commission which was unlikely to introduce major reforms into the draft code. The Germanist representative, Rudolf Sohm, was correctly regarded as much more moderate in his views than Gierke. The Free Conservative Wilhelm von Kardorff was initially considered but was thought dubious because of his extreme support for bimetallism, which tended to align him with the pro-agrarian wing of his party.[41] Conrad regarded himself as a National Liberal, and found himself in agreement with Russell on most questions and with Sohm on issues affecting the working classes. The two left-liberal representatives—Adolf Hoffmann and Goldschmidt—were attacked in the socialist press as two of the 'tamest' that the left-liberals could produce. Of the four Catholics on the commission, it is interesting to note that Conrad saw Danckelmann and Gagern as being very inflexible on issues connected with Church doctrine. The two professional lawyers, Spahn and Gustav Mandry (who represented Württemberg), were apparently much more accommodating.[42] On the whole, then, the composition of the commission was such as to justify hopes that the work would be completed relatively rapidly, while heading off public concern about the code's treatment of important social questions. Meanwhile, the much closer involvement of the larger states in the Bundesrat (except once again for Mecklenburg[43]) and of representatives of the Reichstag parties gave grounds for optimism about the eventual reception of the commission's work by the legislature. This optimism helps to explain why it was widely believed that the commission might complete its work within two years.[44]

[40] A full list can be found in Schubert, *Materialien*, pp. 350 f. Richard Wilke was added to the commission in Mar. 1891 as a representative of practising lawyers. Biographical details on all of these figures can be found in ibid. 69-124.

[41] Burchard, report of 4 Dec. 1890, StA Hamburg, Archiv des Bevollmächtigten zum Bundesrat xi, 5; Heller, report of 30 Oct. 1890, BHStA Munich, MA 76 707/2.

[42] Conrad, *Lebenserinnerungen*, pp. 191 ff.; *Vorwärts*, 6 (Jan. 1891), *Beilage*.

[43] As in 1874, Mecklenburg's demand for representation went unheeded because only those states which were members of the Bundesrat's justice committee had the right to have a member on the commission. This led Mecklenburg's government to produce a detailed critique of the draft code, which was published as *Bemerkungen der Grossherzoglich Mecklenburg-Schwerinischen Regierung zu den Entwürfen eines Bürgerlichen Gesetzbuchs . . .* (2 vols. Schwerin, 1891-2).

[44] Planck, for example, believed this; NSUUB Göttingen Planck Papers xvii, fo. 72.

The influence of the way in which the commission was appointed was to be very great in the years after 1891. Of equal significance was the way in which the Reich justice office proposed to approach the work of revision. Hagens's memorandum of July 1890 had envisaged an important role for the office in preparing materials and guiding the debates of the commission. In his opinion, this was the only way in which the views of the state governments could realistically find expression, given the nature and complexity of the material in question.[45] In fact, plans for a smaller sub-commission, the so-called Vorkommission of the Reich justice office,[46] were far advanced by July 1890. In June, Oehlschläger had invited Planck to come to Berlin to discuss the future of the Code with Miquel and officials of the Reich justice office, and Struckmann had been empowered to offer Planck the post of general reporter to the commission. In August, Struckmann gave details about plans for the sub-commission, on which Planck and four or five representatives of the Reich justice office were to sit.[47]

This sub-commission was unable to continue meeting after April 1893, presumably because of pressure of time. At that point, it had considered the whole of the first book of the Code (the so-called general section) and parts of books 2 and 3 (law of obligations and property). Its decisions were communicated to the commission in the form of official motions by one or other of the Reich bureaucrats involved. Despite the sub-commission's premature end, government motions were presented for the remaining two books (family law and inheritance law). In this way, the Reich justice office took the lead throughout the five years during which the second commission sat.[48]

A few examples will show the importance of these official motions. In the case of tenancy law, the first commission had adopted the Roman law principle of *Kauf bricht Miete*—i.e. that sale of a property dissolved the pre-existing contractual rights of the tenant. This ruling had attracted a great deal of public criticism on 'social' grounds, and by July 1890 Oehlschläger was convinced that it would need revision.[49] The commission was united on the need for this change, but differed on the question of formulation. In the end, it was Struckmann's 'official'

---

[45] Schubert, *Materialien*, pp. 335 f.
[46] On this, see ibid. 54.
[47] Frensdorff, *Planck*, p. 348; Struckmann to Planck, 10 June, 1 July, 11 and 25 Aug. 1890, NSUUB Göttingen, Planck papers VIII, fos. 63–6.
[48] The published protocols of the commission do not give details about who proposed the various motions. These are to be found in ZStA Potsdam, RJM 4104–11.
[49] Struckmann to Planck, 1 July 1890, NSUUB Göttingen, Planck Papers VIII, fo. 64.

motion which won the day.[50] In the case of the protection of master builders, the sub-commission decided to follow the suggestion of the Prussian minister of justice, which essentially involved the reinstatement of the relevant part of the *Allgemeines Landrecht*. This was then put to the full commission by Struckmann, who argued at length against the more radical proposals of groups such as the League for the Reform of Landownership. His motion was one of four which had the same basic goal, but it was his arguments which deprived the League of any chance of success.[51]

In the controversial area of agrarian law, things were rather different. In the general discussion of mortgage law, the lead was taken by professional lawyers—Isaac Wolffson, Wilke, and Sohm—rather than by the Reich's bureaucrats. A motion to make the annuity charge (*Rentenschuld*) the sole form of agrarian credit was proposed by Gagern, though this seems to have been an expression of belief which he did not think had any real chance of success. The commission quickly agreed that the annuity charge could not possibly be made the sole form of landed credit, and cited the reports of the German Agricultural Council and the Landes-Oekonomie-Kollegium, and the experiences of Mecklenburg and Prussia, to discredit agrarian attacks on the 'capitalist' land charge (*Grundschuld*).[52] The subsequent detailed debate on the annuity charge, however, produced a rather different result. There was general agreement that the wishes of some agrarian groups for the inclusion of the annuity charge in the Code were justified. The debate was then taken over by the lawyers, with Struckmann, Jacubezky, and the two assistants provided by the Reich justice office arguing over the best legal formulation. After much debate, the more 'capitalist' formulation favoured by Jacubezky was rejected in favour of a motion which emphasized the annuity charge as a new institution independent of the land charge. It is clear from the protocols that the issue was largely decided by those sympathetic to agriculture, for whom the main feature of the annuity charge was that it was perpetual and only terminable with the agreement of the debtor. That view was accepted against a minority of five, who sought to water down this aspect in the

---

[50] B. Mugdan, *Die gesammten Materialien zum Bürgerlichen Gesetzbuch*, ii (Berlin, 1899), 814 ff.

[51] H. H. Jakobs and W. Schubert, *Die Beratung des Bürgerlichen Gesetzbuches in systematischer Darstellung der unveröffentlichen Quellen. Schuldrecht*, ii (Berlin/New York, 1978-), ii. 878 f; Mugdan, *Materialien*, ii, 927 ff.

[52] Mugdan, *Materialien*, iii. 787 ff.

interests of the creditor. Those closely involved with agriculture managed to persuade the others that the principle would have major advantages for landed credit.[53]

These debates showed, then, that it was possible to gain limited successes for the agrarian cause. Such successes were, however, dependent on circumstances which were difficult to reproduce. In the first place, there was no serious attempt to introduce the more radical agrarian demand that the land charge be abolished. The support of 'respectable' organizations, such as the German Agricultural Council and the Landes-Oekonomie-Kollegium, for the annuity charge as an optional form of credit was probably of great importance in persuading the commission the demand was legitimate. Moreover, it was quite clear that the spokesmen for agriculture gained the support of a large number of the professional lawyers and bureaucrats on this issue. That was a comparatively rare achievement, and was almost certainly the result of the fact that the creation of this new, voluntary legal institution could not be said to harm the 'legitimate' interests of other social groups. The annuity charge could thus be accommodated without too much trouble into the existing structure of the civil law, and most of the discussion on 15 November 1893 was conducted between professional lawyers and bureaucrats on the question of how best to adapt this new type of mortgage to the rest of the Code.

When the question of the inheritance law of peasant farms arose, the result was very different. As has been seen, the proposal to allow the inheritance of peasant farms in single units (*Anerbenrecht*) had considerable popular support. It also gained powerful defenders within the Prussian government. In February 1895, five members of the commission proposed that the question should be included in the Code and that only the details should be left to the individual states. At this point, however, the professional lawyers and bureaucrats closed ranks, and the motion was defeated by fifteen votes to five after a debate in which Peter Spahn is reported to have taken a leading part.[54] The interesting point here, however, concerns the reasons for the rejection of this motion. As in the first commission, the problem seems to have been the difficulty of formulating a national (as opposed to local) law rather than any fundamental hostility to the peasants' cause. One speaker did deny

---

[53] Ibid. 904–11.
[54] Jacubezky to Leonrod, 28 Feb. 1895 and Gagern to Leonrod, 14 Mar. 1895, BHStA Munich, MJu 16115; the motion's 5 supporters were Conrad, Danckelmann, Gagern, and the two Conservatives, Helldorff and Manteuffel.

that a crisis of the peasantry actually existed, but there does seem to
have been a great deal of sympathy with the proposal in the commission.
As the special representative of the Prussian minister of agriculture
reported, 'the majority of the commission did not seem to oppose the
most far-reaching proposals for the introduction of *Anerbenrecht* by
legislation in the individual states'.[55] Furthermore, Wilke reported to
the Lawyers' Congress in September 1895 that the commission was not
hostile to the idea in principle but merely rejected national legislation
on the matter, and a large majority of those present at the congress
supported this argument.[56]

On the whole, the direct influence of the political and economic
representatives in the commission was small. Where 'social' criticisms of
the draft code were met, it tended to be in cases where the legal
profession itself was divided—as with tenancy law—or where the
proposed reforms were compatible with the structure of the draft code.
At no time was there any successful assault on the basic principles of
the legal system. The debate on the definition of property, for example,
involved only lawyers, took place in the absence of Conrad, Gagern,
Helldorff, and Sohm, and concerned the best formulation of the 'absolute'
concept of property, limited only by the rights of third parties and the
criminal law.[57] Little was heard of the Germanists' attack on this
'Romanist' view of property, and the commission's Germanist was not
even present.

Indeed, absenteeism was of some importance in explaining the
dominance of the profesional lawyers and the bureaucrats in the
commission. The tendency of members to be absent was encouraged by
Oehlschläger's division of the commission into groups of continual
(*ständige*) and occasional (*nichtständige*) members. The first group
comprised the representatives of the state governments and Planck; the
second consisted of the representatives of the political parties and
interest groups. One of the latter actually informed Oehlschläger at the
outset that he would often be absent. Other frequent absentees were
Conrad, Sohm, and the two Conservatives, Manteuffel and Helldorff—
i.e. precisely those members who were likely to be most sympathetic to
the main criticisms of the draft code. On the other hand, the absences

[55] Mugdan, *Materialien*, i. 195 ff; Hermes to Hammerstein, 28 Feb. 1895, ZStA
Merseburg, Rep. 87B 8123, fo. 356.
[56] *Verhandlungen des Dreiundzwanzigsten Deutschen Juristentages*, ii (Berlin, 1895), 101,
113.
[57] Mugdan, *Materialien*, iii. 577 ff.

of the professional lawyers—Spahn, Cuny, Hofmann, and Wilke—were comparatively rare.[58]

Furthermore, it was not necessarily the case that these absences tended to occur when the commission was debating matters of limited social or political importance. When the question of the legal protection of the builders was discussed on 31 May 1892, Conrad, Danckelmann, Gagern, Helldorff, Leuschner, Russell, and Sohm were absent. As a result, a controversial part of the draft code, which had been criticized above all for its dogmatic attention to theory at the expense of practical needs, was left almost completely in the hands of professional lawyers and bureaucrats. Similarly, when the details of property rights and their limitations—a central feature of Gierke's attack on the draft code— were debated in seven sessions between 13 and 27 February 1893, Sohm was absent on all seven occasions, Manteuffel on four, and Helldorff on three. Incredibly, Manteuffel was also absent from the general debate on the law of mortgages on 6 June of the same year.[59]

This absenteeism was scarcely surprising in view of the prominence of these men in other spheres of public life. Helldorff, for example, was beset by opposition to his leadership within the Conservative party and frequently insisted on his need to rest after his political labours. Illness also often caused absenteeism, particularly in the case of Sohm.[60] But this frequent non-participation may also have reflected an awareness of the effective impotence of those involved, particularly on issues where they were likely to come into conflict with the views of the professional lawyers and bureaucrats. There is comparatively little evidence concerning the attitudes of the political and economic representatives on the commission, but some idea of their sense of frustration may be gained from Conrad's description of the normal mode of procedure:

In general, the professional jurists stuck together too much for a fundamental revision [of the Code] from an economic standpoint to be possible, and they naturally found support from other members of the commission, who, on account of a lack of understanding, assured them of a majority.[61]

[58] Leuschner to Oehlschläger, 18 Nov. 1890, ZStA Potsdam, RJM 4078, fo. 32; E. Strohal (ed.), *Plancks Kommentar zum Bürgerlichen Gesetzbuch*, i (4th edn. Berlin, 1913), xxxiii.

[59] Information on absenteeism is drawn from the attendance lists in the duplicated minutes of the commission, ZStA Potsdam, RJM 4088–4102; this information is omitted from the published protocols.

[60] See the letters from members of the commission to Oehlschläger and his successors excusing their absences in ZStA Potsdam, RJM 4081.

[61] Conrad, *Lebenserinnerungen*, p. 195.

The commission's debates provide strong evidence for the survival of the jurisprudential considerations which had in large part determined the decisions taken in the first commission. Despite the very different composition of the second commission, the organization of the work left real power firmly in the hands of the representatives of the state governments, the professional lawyers and, above all, the Reich justice office. It is significant that neither Oehlschläger nor his successor, Robert Bosse, ever chose to reveal the intentions of the Bundesrat about the method to be adopted in revising the draft code to the commission.[62] Equally important was the fact that the Prussian government did not seek to profit from the link between the Secretaries of the Reich justice office and the Prussian ministry of state. It was this connection which had made Oehlschläger originally reluctant to take up the chairmanship of the commission. His fears of a conflict of loyalties did not, however, convince the Prussian ministry of state. As Boetticher pointed out, there was no reason why Oehlschläger should not speak and vote in the commission according 'to his personal conviction'.[63] Furthermore, this freedom of action was on occasion exploited, as when Bosse voted against the representatives of the Prussian government on the crucial political issue of the private law of associations. Bosse was a noted conservative but nevertheless supported a more liberal line on the law of associations. As he explained:

I found it embarrassing that as a subordinate of the Chancellor, who was also president of the Prussian ministry of state, I was forced to put myself in opposition to him. But I had no choice. I was convinced of the necessity of legislation on the matter by the Reich, which was expected and demanded by the entire legal community of Germany. As a member of the commission, I had to follow my own conscience and I had to put this consideration above the views of the Prussian government. Had I not dared to do this, I would have given up the best part of my position on the commission. My convictions would have been sacrificed to a binding instruction; I would then have been a mere delegate of the government, whose hands were tied by a prior instruction.

Only later, it seems, did Bosse learn that Miquel had supported the motion in the Prussian ministry of state in November 1891. At the time, he believed that he was going against the wishes of the Prussian government on perhaps the most politically sensitive issue in the

---

[62] Frensdorff, *Planck*, p. 353.
[63] Minutes of the ministry of state, 13 Oct. 1890, GStA Berlin-Dahlem, Rep. 84a 11775, fos. 283 f.

Code[64]—a move which is surely evidence of the considerable degree of independence enjoyed by the secretary of the Reich justice office. As will be seen, this independence, together with the office's control over the proceedings of the commission, meant that the Reich justice office could effectively take responsibility for the contents of the proposed legislation. As so often in the history of the Code, the answers to questions about the contents of the legal system were in many ways foreshadowed by decisions about the mode of procedure.

In contrast to the first commission, the debates of the second commission took place against a background of sustained interest on the part of the state governments. It is clear that those states which were represented in the commission took the opportunity to influence the work through those representatives. When Adolf Langfeld arrived in Berlin in the autumn of 1895 to propose a long list of amendments on behalf of the government of Mecklenburg, he discovered that there was little chance of success, as the larger states' views had already been heard on most issues.[65] The southern states appear to have been happy with the extent to which their views were represented, and the fact that the members of the commission were not given imperative mandates by their governments seems to have made little practical difference.

Of all the states involved, Prussia probably devoted the greatest attention to the task of revising the Code. Schelling felt that the draft code had paid insufficient attention to practical needs and he invited comments from both the law courts and from other ministries on individual points of controversy, particularly where social or economic questions were involved. On such matters as hire purchase agreements, usurious exploitation of contractual freedom, the protection of master builders, and agrarian law, debates began within the Prussian and Reich governments which showed how the public debates on social reform had penetrated sections of the bureaucracy.

Hire purchase agreements, which were generally seen as part of the wider problem of the exploitation of the weaker party through contractual obligations, were a case in point. The matter had aroused considerable

---

[64] See Bosse's diary for Dec. 1891, ZStA Merseburg, Rep. 92 Bosse 2, fos. 32 f.; cf. Röhl, *Germany Without Bismarck*, p. 68. For Bosse's conservatism, see Morsey, *Die oberste Reichsverwaltung*, p. 269. It is worth noting that Jacubezky reported that Planck had outlined Miquel's views to the commission during the debate report of 17 Dec. 1891, BHStA Munich, MJu 16113.

[65] Langfeld, *Mein Leben*, p. 137.

attention among artisans in the late 1880s, and both the Prussian minister of agriculture and the Secretary of the Reich office of the interior pressed for action against abuses through amendments to the civil law.[66] Oehlschläger's reply emphasized the technical difficulties which would follow from special treatment of hire purchase agreements within the Civil Code; it would for example be incompatible with the principle of contractual freedom in agreements concerning penalty clauses. A more appropriate way of dealing with the problem was through a revision of the Industrial Code (*Gewerbeordnung*). Schelling agreed with this view. He was sympathetic to the cause of reform, but saw the problems arising out of hire purchase as part of the wider question of usury. This led him to see amendments to the criminal law as much more suitable than changes in the civil law. In this way, abuses could be remedied without breaching the code's principle of contractual freedom. In the end, a special law on hire purchase agreements was accepted in May 1894.[67]

The Minister of Agriculture was moved to make a stand on this issue by an increase in public concern in the late 1880s, when both the Landes-Oekonomie-Kollegium and the Verein für Sozialpolitik had debated the matter. Of particular concern to Lucius and his successor, Heyden, was the suggestion that rural usury was responsible for the upsurge of peasant anti-Semitism in Prussia's western provinces.[68] As was seen in a previous chapter, the legal protection of master builders was another issue which attracted a considerable amount of public attention. Once again, it was that pressure from outside which pushed the bureaucracy into considering reforms in the civil law in order to solve an apparently pressing social problem.

A complicating factor in this case was the interest of the Kaiser. The

---

[66] See the 31 petitions from guilds and similar organizations in *SBRT, Drucksachen,* 1888–9, no. 122; Lucius, 'Votum', 23 May, GStA Berlin-Dahlem, Rep. 84a 11774, fos. 559–63; Boetticher to Oehlschläger, 25 Sept. 1890, ZStA Potsdam, RJM 1068, fos. 21–4.

[67] Oehlschläger to Boetticher, 22 Oct. 1890, ZStA Potsdam, RJM 1068, fos. 38–40; Schelling to Lucius, 5 June 1890, GStA Berlin-Dahlem, Rep. 84a 11774, fos. 565–8; cf. Schelling's arguments in *Bemerkungen zum Entwurf eines Bürgerlichen Gesetzbuchs für das Deutsche Reich. Bemerkungen des Königlich Preussischen Justizministers über die in dem Rundschreiben des Reichskanzlers vom 27. Juni 1889 hervorgehobenen Punkte. Als Manuskript gedruckt* (Berlin, 1891), 70–3; on the 1894 law, see H.-P. Benöhr, 'Konsumentenschutz vor 80 Jahren. Zur Entstehung des Abzahlungsgesetzes vom 16. Mai 1894', *Zeitschrift für das gesamte Handelsrecht und Wirtschaftsrecht*, 138 (1974), 492–503; and W. Schubert, 'Das Abzahlungsgesetz von 1894 als Beispiel für das Verhältnis von Sozialpolitik und Privatrecht in der Regierungszeit des Reichskanzlers von Caprivi', *ZRG GA* 102 (1985), pp. 130–67.

[68] See Lucius, 'Votum', 18 Jan. 1889, and Heyden's *Votum*, 9 Nov. 1891, GStA Berlin-Dahlem, Rep. 84a 5721, fos. 66–9 and 5722, fos. 1 f.

Westfälischer Merkur's revelations had attracted his attention in October 1891, and he demanded a report on the subject from the Prussian ministers of justice and the interior.[69] In March 1892, the Berlin police chief and the president of the Berlin state court both agreed that a serious situation existed and that legal cases arising out of the problem were very frequent. Both however felt that the proposed solution—i.e. the amendment of the 'principle of publicity' in order to give builders' claims a privileged position in the land register—would damage the supply of landed credit and was therefore not to be recommended.[70]

Robert Bosse was sympathetic to the builders' plight and, in February 1892, told a deputation which included Freese that he would try to achieve as much as possible. Bosse's principal interests lay in practical administration and social policy rather than in the technicalities of the law and, like Arnold Nieberding after him, he had come to the secretaryship from the Reich office of the interior.[71] He went on to recommend the League for the Reform of Landownership's petition to Schelling, in the belief that it attempted to satisfy the interests of other creditors as well as those of the master builders. Schelling was, however, distinctly unimpressed, and was still unwilling to go any further than the restoration of the *Allgemeines Landrecht*. He also tended to regard the gloomy reports of the builders' situation as 'exaggerated' and denied the need for stronger measures to protect them. As he put it: '[i]t is not the task of civil legislation to protect participants in contracts from losses which arise out of dangerous transactions.'[72]

That was not, however, the end of the matter. Agitation for reform continued, various private bills were introduced into the Reichstag and the Prussian chamber of deputies, and, after lengthy negotiations, a special Reich law was introduced in 1909. The main obstacle to such a law was the strong opposition of the legal bureaucracies of the Reich and Prussian governments. In 1897, when a commission to prepare a special law met, the representatives of the Reich justice office strongly opposed such a law on the grounds that the problem only existed in certain areas of certain states. Nieberding argued that the Reich should merely legislate to remove the restrictions on the individual states' freedom of action.[73]

---

[69] *Westfälischer Merkur*, 13 Oct. 1891; ZStA Merseburg, 2.2.1. 17542, fo. 273.

[70] GStA Berlin-Dahlem, Rep. 84a 11876, fos. 37–65, 247–92.

[71] *Frei-Land*, 7 Mar. 1892; ZStA Merseburg, Rep. 92 Bosse 2, fo. 2.

[72] Bosse to Schelling, 3 Mar. 1892, ZStA Potsdam, RJM 1335, fo. 117 f.; Schelling to Hanauer, 28 June 1892, GStA Berlin-Dahlem, Rep. 84a 11876, fos. 227–36; Schelling to the Kaiser, 16 Sept. 1892, ZStA Merseburg, 2.2.1. 17543, fos. 12–23 (quotation, fo. 18).

[73] GStA Berlin-Dahlem, Rep. 84a 11880, fo. 355; cf. Struckmann's comments in GStA

On most issues concerning the relationship between the Code and social reform, however, the legal bureaucracy was anything but unsympathetic to the views of the interest groups. In the sphere of agrarian law, the question of the law of inheritance for peasant landholdings shows how sensitive the Prussian ministry of agriculture was to the mobilization of popular opinion. In contrast to the problem of usury, however, there was in this case no alternative but to attempt to introduce reforms through the civil (as opposed to criminal) law—a plan which encountered powerful opposition from the legal bureaucracy. In June 1890 Lucius began to campaign for the introduction of undivided landed inheritance as a form equal in status to the inheritance law governing movable property. He emphasized that modern economists took the distinction between landed and movable property for granted, and suggested that the Civil Code should do the same.[74] The following year Lucius' successor went further and demanded a form of undivided inheritance by which the heir received land directly by law rather than through the other heirs. This procedural change marked an important breach with existing law, the justification for which shows how far Germanist criticisms had penetrated sections of the senior bureaucracy:

But this existing legislation is rooted in the equal treatment of movable and immovable property, which was taken over from Roman law; and if the German idea (which lies behind that of *Anerbenrecht*) that the inheritance of landed property should take place according to different principles from that of movable property is in any way justified, it is only logical to use it in the systematic formulation of the law of inheritance.[75]

Schelling's response to this demand revealed that he was willing to accept the standpoint of the minister of agriculture in principle, and the evidence concerning his views on other agrarian demands, such as homestead legislation,[76] suggests that he was sympathetic to the plight of agriculture. In any case, Schelling believed that this was primarily

Berlin-Dahlem, Rep. 84a 11879, fos. 525 f. On the background to the 1909 law, see P. Oertmann, 'Bauforderungen, Sicherung der', *Handwörterbuch der Staatswissenschaften*, ii (4th edn. Jena, 1924), 417–30; H.-P. Benöhr, 'Das Gesetz als Instrument zur Lösung sozialpolitischer Konflikte: das Beispiel des Bauforderungssicherungsgesetz von 1909', *ZRG GA*, 95 (1978), pp. 221–8.

[74] 'Votum', 6 June 1890, GStA Berlin-Dahlem, Rep. 84a 11775, fos. 473–81.

[75] Heyden to Schelling, 13 Mar. 1891, GStA Berlin-Dahlem, Rep. 84a 11776, fos. 309–34 (quotation, fos. 312 f.).

[76] For Schelling's support of homestead legislation, see Riepenhausen to Caprivi, 23 Apr. 1890, ZStA Potsdam, Rkz 740, fo. 207.

an economic question and his main concern was with the problems of formulating any national legislation on the subject:

> In considering this matter, I have restricted myself to the question of whether the regulation of *Anerbenrecht* in the Civil Code would be compatible with the interests of the administration of justice, and in particular whether the necessary clarity and consistency of the legal system can be maintained, if this legal institution is placed in the Code.

A major problem would be created by the relationship between Reich and state law; in Schelling's view, the only way to avoid that problem was to hand the matter over to the individual states.[77] Despite Schelling's continued support for the satisfaction of this fundamental agrarian demand,[78] the Prussian ministry of justice never wavered from its technical objections to the use of the Civil Code to achieve the desired reform. As we have seen, Schelling's views on this matter were close to those of many of the members of the commission; opposition to the agrarians' proposal was in general motivated, not by hostility to the agrarian cause, but by doubts arising from problems in formulating a national law with the required degree of systematic precision.

The minister of agriculture regarded Schelling's response as inadequate, and followed Gierke and many of the agrarian critics of the draft code in drawing attention to the educative value of national legislation on the subject: 'I am also of the opinion that, if *Anerbenrecht* is excluded from the law of the Reich and restricted to that of the individual states, it will lead not to a strengthening but to a further decline of that custom.'[79] The ministry of agriculture continued to press for the inclusion of undivided inheritance in the Code, and was in contact with those members of the commission who favoured the reform.[80] This view was supported by Miquel, a man who could never be called an enemy of the code. In late 1893 Miquel and Heyden began a major offensive in the Prussian ministry of state, which led to the calling of the famous 'Agrarian Conference' in the ministry of agriculture in April 1894. The purpose of this conference was to help overcome the breach between the conservative agrarians and the government, which was the product of Caprivi's tariff policies, and marked a further

---

[77] Schelling to Heyden, 21 Nov. 1890, ZStA Merseburg, Rep. 87B 8123, fos. 208-11 (quotation fo. 208).
[78] Schelling to Caprivi, 28 June 1891, ZStA Merseburg, Rep. 87B 8123, fos. 238-8.
[79] Heyden to Schelling, 13 Mar. 1891, GStA Berlin-Dahlem, Rep. 84a 11776, fo. 310.
[80] Conrad to Heyden, 16 Aug. 1893, ZStA Merseburg, Rep. 87B 8123, fos. 260 f.

stage in the developing rift between Caprivi and conservative elements in the Prussian ministry of state. The conference produced a resounding victory for the supporters of undivided peasant inheritance, and led even the left-liberal *Vossische Zeitung* to call for its inclusion in the Civil Code.[81]

In the spring of 1894, the issue of undivided peasant inheritance thus became linked to the growing crisis facing Caprivi's government. It has been argued with some justification that Caprivi's approach to politics was based on an attempt to rule through the Reichstag, and his policy of giving the secretaries of the Reich offices far greater leeway than they had enjoyed under Bismarck was a fundamental component of that approach.[82] It is likely that the necessity of developing good relations with the Reichstag imposed political constraints on the secretaries of the Reich offices. Given the political composition of the national parliament, the secretaries simply could not promote radical agrarian policies. This factor led them to promote more liberal social and economic policies than their counterparts in the Prussian ministry of state.[83]

The influence of such considerations on the policy of the Reich justice office with regard to the Civil Code was plain. That body was the principal supporter of the view that the major goal was to complete the Code as soon as possible, and this priority grew in importance with the appointment of Nieberding to the secretaryship in the summer of 1893.[84] Indeed, Nieberding's main concern was in some ways the logical extension of the policies pursued by Oehlschläger in the years between 1889 and 1891—i.e. the completion of a Code which would secure the agreement of the Bundesrat and Reichstag. The rise of radical agrarianism in the mid 1890s, the repeated governmental crises of 1892–4, and the role of the Centre party as an increasingly vital element in the construction of Reichstag majorities for the government after the 1890 and 1893 elections[85] all created problems for this policy.

[81] Herzfeld, *Miquel*, ii. 324 ff.; Röhl, *Germany Without Bismarck*, p. 112; J. A. Nichols, *Germany After Bismarck. The Caprivi Era, 1890–1894* Cambridge, Mass., 1958), ch. 8; *Vossische Zeitung*, 21 June 1894.

[82] Nichols, *Germany After Bismarck*, pp. 223, 370 f.; Röhl, *Germany Without Bismarck*, pp. 64–8; Rauh, *Föderalismus und Parlamentarismus*, pp. 123 ff.

[83] Röhl, *Germany Without Bismarck*, pp. 67 f.; Bonham, 'Bureaucratic Modernizers', pp. 361 ff., 376 f.

[84] Nieberding's principal task, according to Caprivi, was to accelerate the work of the commission; see R. Sohm, 'Die Entstehung des deutschen bürgerlichen Gesetzbuchs', *DJZ*, 5 (1900), p. 7; Frensdorff, *Planck*, p. 352.

[85] On the Centre's role as a pro-governmental party, see Blackbourn, *Class, Religion and Local Politics in Wilhelmine Germany. The Centre Party in Württemberg before 1914*

These features of the political system in the mid 1890s gave Nieberding considerable leverage in his battles with conservative, pro-agrarian elements in the Prussian bureaucracy. When, in January 1896, Miquel and Hammerstein (Heyden's successor as minister of agriculture) sought to commit the Prussian ministry of state to the inclusion of certain agrarian demands in the Code, they met solid opposition from the lawyers. Nieberding's central argument—that the proposal 'would introduce the whole problem of agrarian law into the debates on the Civil Code, which would pose grave problems for the completion of the work'—found the support of the new Prussian minister of justice, Karl von Schönstedt. The latter reiterated the standard view of his ministry— that the question was best left to the individual states.[86]

The political argument relating to the exclusion of areas of the law which might endanger the Reichstag's acceptance of the Code was used increasingly often in 1895-6. Furthermore, it tended to complement earlier arguments about the obstacles posed by the requirements of legal technique and systematic precision to the inclusion of popular reforms in the Code.[87] As attention began to focus on the responses of the Bundesrat and Reichstag to the Code, it seemed likely that problems would arise over two major sections of the Code—the private law of associations and the law of marriage. It was on the first of these questions that Bosse had felt obliged to vote against the wishes of the Prussian ministry of state in late 1891. The commission had then proceeded to override the wishes of the larger states in the Bundesrat, which were generally hostile to the inclusion of the matter in the Code.[88] There was no evidence in 1895 that the states' opposition to the commission's suggestions had substantially abated.[89] On the other hand, Nieberding was convinced that the Reichstag would cause great problems for the

(New Haven /London, 1980), 36 ff.; R. Morsey, 'Die deutsche Katholiken und der Nationalstaat zwischen Kulturkampf und dem ersten Weltkrieg', *Historisches Jahrbuch*, 90 (1970), 31-64; W. Loth, *Katholiken im Kaiserreich. Der politische Katholizismus in der Krise des wilhelminischen Deutschlands* (Düsseldorf, 1984), pp. 51-80.

[86] Ministry of state minutes, 7 Jan. 1896, GStA Berlin-Dahlem, Rep. 84a 11834, fos. 71-7.

[87] Thus Wilke used both arguments together in justifying the commission's decision on undivided peasant succession at the 1895 Lawyers' Congress; see *Verhandlungen des Dreiundzwanzigsten Deutschen Juristentages*, ii (Berlin, 1895), 101.

[88] For the commission's debates on this issue, see P. Kögler, *Arbeiterbewegung und Vereinsrecht. Ein Beitrag zur Entstehungsgeschichte des BGB* (Berlin, 1974), 97-107; T. Vormbaum, *Die Rechtsfähigkeit der Vereine im 19. Jarhundert. Ein Betrag zur Entstehungsgeschichte des BGB* (Berlin/New York, 1976), 154 ff.

[89] *Zusammenstellung der Aeusserungen der Bundesregierungen zu dem Entwurf eines Bürgerlichen Gesetzbuchs zweiter Lesung*, i (Berlin, 1895), 3-9.

government, if the law of associations was excluded at the insistence of the Bundesrat.

Nieberding's problems were increased by the fact that most of the Prussian ministers had expressed their opposition in the course of 1894. The increasingly conservative climate of opinion in the Prussian ministry of state in that year found expression in the views of Bosse and Miquel, both of whom seem to have shifted from their earlier views on the subject. In Bosse's case this seems to have been largely the result of his appointment as minister of education, which led him to fear the pernicious influence of educational associations.[90] Nieberding's response to this opposition was to turn first to Boetticher, who was successfully persuaded of the need to retain the commission's proposals and who secured the support of the new Chancellor, Hohenlohe. It seems clear that Nieberding's victory on this issue in the autumn of 1894 was the result of the fear that the Reichstag would not accept the exclusion of the law of associations.[91] By the end of November Nieberding had won an important new ally in Schönstedt, after which the Prussian ministry of state moved reluctantly into line. The ensuing conferences between different ministries on the matter showed without doubt the leading role of the legal bureaucracy in determining the course of the proceedings. The representatives of the Reich justice office and Prussian ministry of justice argued strongly against the proposals of other ministries that certain categories of association (e.g. political, social, religious, or educational associations) should be excluded from the Code's general provisions. Once again, Hohenlohe left no doubt about his belief that the line taken by the lawyers was essential to the successful completion of the Code.[92] Even then, the question of the law of associations was to cause serious difficulties for Nieberding in the Bundesrat and Reichstag, which were only finally overcome by a complicated compromise in June 1896.

[90] Bosse, 'Votum' of 10 July 1894 and Miquel, 'Votum' of 17 Sept. 1894, GStA Berlin-Dahlem, Rep. 84a 11778, fos. 149–62 and 291–5.

[91] Nieberding to Boetticher, 20 Oct. 1894, ZStA Potsdam, RJM 690, fos. 1–6; Boetticher to Hohenlohe, 5 Nov. and Hohenlohe to Boetticher, 22 Nov. 1894, ZStA Potsdam, Rkz 728, fos. 67 ff.; Kögler, *Arbeiterbewegung*, pp. 105 f.; Vormbaum, *Rechtsfähigkeit*, pp. 163, 173 f.

[92] Ministry of state minutes, 30 Nov. 1894, GStA Berlin-Dahlem, Rep. 84a 11778, fos. 341–65; ZStA Merseburg, Rep. 77 Tit. 114 no. 297 Beiakte 2, fos. 133–77; Rep. 87B 8118, fos. 202–8, 216–21.

Nieberding's attempts to find compromises which would secure the acceptance of the Code by the legislative institutions of the Reich were obviously related to the attempts of his predecessors to overcome public criticism of the draft code without rejecting that work altogether. In some respects that was an impossible task, and the secretary of the Reich justice office often had to fall back on the old argument that the achievement of national legal unity was so desirable from a national viewpoint that sectional interests might be legitimately asked to make concessions. On the other hand, he had certain advantages over those who wished to introduce major changes. In the first place, he knew that no state government or political party would dare to take responsibility for the failure of the Code after twenty-two years of work. One perceptive observer had predicted in October 1891 that if the second commission finished its work, the Reichstag would be faced with 'the fatal choice between rejecting the Code and thereby postponing the establishment of legal unity for the foreseeable future, or giving the German people a Code which was a curse rather than a blessing'.[93] Nieberding knew how to exploit this factor to the full. However, the success of the Code was by no means self-evident in the winter of 1895–6, when the Bundesrat and Reichstag debates began. The pages of the National Liberal press were full of pessimism about the Code's chances in the Reichstag, and several broadsides were directed at the left-liberal newspapers when they seemed to lack the required enthusiasm for the completion of the great national work. Knowledgeable observers such as Sohm and Planck regarded the fate of the Code as anything but certain in January 1896.[94]

Nieberding's response to these uncertainties concentrated on favourable publicity and skilful tactics. He encouraged expressions of support for the rapid completion of the Code from commercial and other interest groups. He also recommended that the government give financial support for a proposed series of lectures on the code sponsored by the Law Society of Berlin, on the grounds that such lectures would have considerable influence on the Reichstag's deliberations. Such efforts were complemented by frequent meetings arranged by local National Liberal parties with the aim of mobilizing support for the revised

[93] G. Pfizer, 'Geflickte Schienen', *Allgemeine Zeitung*, 10 Oct. 1891, Beilage.
[94] *National-Zeitung*, 15 Sept. 1895; *Kölnische Zeitung*, 10 Sept. 1895; R. Sohm and A. Wach, 'Arnold Nieberding', *DJZ*, 14 (1909), p. 1345; NSUUB Göttingen, Planck Papers XVIII, fo. 95.

Code.[95] As we have seen, such efforts found considerable support from
the trading community's representative organizations.

The major problem facing the Code's supporters was that their
opponents had cast doubt on the Code's validity as an expression of
national values. The controversy over the draft code had sharpened
antagonisms between two alternative conceptions of nationalism: the
concern for German/Christian traditions, emphasized by Gierke and the
agrarians; and the older governmental/liberal nationalism, which stressed
the unity of the State and its law and the concern with systematic
precision and 'legal certainty'. As the Code's defenders marshalled their
arguments in the winter of 1895-6, the second of these conceptions
tended to come to the fore. Thus Ludwig Enneccerus, a National
Liberal Reichstag deputy, spoke of the sorry state of German law and
believed that 'the Code will give the law back to the people'. Other
commentators took the same line while also arguing that the second
commission had introduced many important improvements from the
'social' point of view. This was the approach adopted in an influential
lecture by the second commission's Germanist, Rudolf Sohm, and even
Gierke was forced to agree, though he continued to criticize the work.[96]
It is difficult to avoid the conclusion that in late 1895 the tide was
turning against the radical critics of the Code, and that the government's
and National Liberals' conception of the work as an instrument of state
formation rather than as the embodiment of allegedly 'German' values
was gaining the upper hand. It was a sign of the times that, in early
1896, a leading 'social' critic of the Code advocated 'resignation' in the
face of the Bundesrat's acceptance of the revised Code, and asked 'who
could ignore the magic of the words: one Kaiser, one Reich, one law?'[97]

One important reason for this change was Nieberding's success in
securing the public support of the Kaiser. There was a long history of
interest in the work within the royal family; the Kaiser's father, Friedrich
I, had been very keen that the Code should come into operation before
he died. Wilhelm II was quick to proclaim his support for the rapid

[95] Nieberding to Hohenlohe, 5 Dec. 1895, ZStA Potsdam, RJM 3865, fos. 30 f.;
Kölnische Zeitung, 5 Nov. 1895; *Magdeburgische Zeitung*, 6 Nov. 1895; *DJZ*, 1 (1896), 32;
Schwäbischer Merkur, 21 Jan. 1896; *Hannoverscher Courier*, 10 Feb. 1896.

[96] For Enneccerus, see *Hannoverscher Courier*, 10 Feb. 1896; cf. Max Rümelin's views,
reported in *Schwäbischer Merkur*, 21 Jan. 1896; Sohm, *Ueber den Entwurf eines Bürgerlichen
Gesetzbuches*; O. Gierke, *Das Bürgerliche Gesetzbuch und der Deutsche Reichstag* (Berlin,
1896), 6.

[97] H. v. Dernburg, *Persönliche Rechtsstellung nach dem Bürgerlichen Gesetzbuch* (Berlin,
1896), 5 f.

conclusion of the work when laying the foundation-stone of the Reich Supreme Court in Leipzig in October 1888.[98] With the exception of the case of the master builders, Wilhelm's direct involvement was minimal, but senior officials were quick to see the propaganda value of associating him with the work. Bosse had had the idea of inviting him to a session of the commission in 1891, but the proposed visit had been cancelled. In the autumn of 1895 the idea was revived by Nieberding, and the Kaiser attended the discussion of the inheritance of peasant landholdings on 13 November. Baden's ambassador in Berlin laid considerable emphasis on the importance of this move as 'a further encouragement' to the successful completion of the Code, and Planck thought likewise.[99]

The Kaiser's involvement was part of a broader set of policies designed to link the Code with symbols of national unity and progress. Hohenlohe was, for example, keen to submit the code to the Reichstag on the twenty-fifth anniversary of the proclamation of the Reich—a tactic which found considerable resonance in the press.[1] It was rumoured that the Kaiser had intervened to press for the Code's completion so that it could come into force on 1 January 1900. One commentator considered this to have been a good idea in that it created 'an anniversary . . . for this most important national achievement, which will stick in the minds of future generations'.[2]

By these means, the Code's supporters managed to outflank and neutralize the threat of radical reform, which would have delayed the completion of the work for the foreseeable future. In a largely successful attempt to mould public opinion, the Reich justice office took the lead in concentrating on the Code's national virtues. In April 1895, Nieberding informed the ambassador of Baden that the time had come for a press campaign to emphasize the Code's national virtues and interest the public in the completion of the work. As one commentator put it, the Code would be 'the completion of the foundation of the

[98] *Bismarck-Erinnerungen des Staatsministers Freiherrn Lucius von Ballhausen* (4th edn. Stuttgart/Berlin, 1921), 400; Frensdorff, *Planck*, p. 323; *Danziger Zeitung*, 10 Nov. 1890.
[99] ZStA Merseburg, Rep. 92 Bosse 2, fo. 46; Jagemann, report of 14 Nov. 1895, GLA Karlsruhe, Abt. 233/34801, fo. 224; NSUUB Göttingen, Planck Papers XVIII, fos. 92 f.
[1] See Spahn's lecture in *Kölnische Volkszeitung*, 7 Mar. 1903; P. Laband, 'Zum 18. Januar', *DJZ*, 1 (1896), p. 22.
[2] M. Hachenburg, *Lebenserinnerungen eines Rechtsanwalts* (Düsseldorf, 1927), 167; Dittmar to Planck, 31 Dec. 1899, NSUUB Göttingen, Planck papers no. IV/3, fo. 119. Once again, Bosse had earlier had the same idea, ZStA Merseburg, Rep. 92 Bosse 2, fos. 18 f.

Reich'.[3] The appropriation of the symbolism of national unity went hand in hand with the message that the Civil Code would strengthen the social order against the forces that were threatening to overturn it—i.e. Social Democracy. Such ideas were quite consciously deployed as an antidote to Germanist, 'social' criticisms of the revised Code.[4] By 1896 radical Germanist opposition to the Code was at most a marginal phenomenon, the approach adopted by a few agrarians, anti-Semites, and other elements on the extreme right. The anti-Semitic deputy for Marburg, Otto Böckel, dismissed the revised Code in August 1895 as an academic, theoretical 'product of the green table [i.e. the bureaucracy]'.[5] But this campaign was little more than an irritant to Nieberding and the Code's supporters. Their own attempts to shape public opinion in the winter of 1895–6 had been successful in isolating those who argued that the Civil Code had betrayed the national interest. By 1896, certain agrarian interest groups even praised the codifiers for their concern to help agriculture from the standpoint of German legal traditions![6]

The actions of the bureaucracy thus had a powerful influence on the outcome of the movement towards legal unity in the late nineteenth century. The history of the second commission shows quite conclusively how much of the state-forming ideology of codification of the 1870s lived on into the 1890s, when many of the fundamental presuppositions of that ideology were coming under attack. Certain reforms in line with the views of the 'social' critics of conceptual jurisprudence were introduced during the revision of the Code by the second commission. But the potential for such reform was always limited by what might be termed bureaucratic imperatives: the need to retain the unity of the overall system, the construction of 'legal certainty' through the derivation of legal rulings from a small number of fundamental norms and, not least, the increasing emphasis placed on the rapid completion of the Code. This last imperative tended to undermine further the attempts on the part of sectional-interest groups to secure special treatment for

---

[3] Jagemann, report of 7 Apr. 1895, GLA Karlsruhe Abt. 233/13995; Laband, 'Zum 18. Januar', p. 22.

[4] See, e.g. Enneccerus' speech reported in *Hannoverscher Courier*, 10 Feb. 1896; cf. Spahn's comments along the same lines in the Reichstag, *SBRT*, 5 Feb. 1896, p. 771A and H. v. Marquardsen, 'Die nationale Bedeutung des Reichscivilgesetzbuchs', *DJZ* 1 (1896), pp. 326 f.

[5] O. Böckel, 'Umwälzungen im Eherecht', *Deutsches Volks-Recht*, 13 Aug. 1895.

[6] 'Das neue bürgerliche Gesetzbuch und die Landwirtschaft', *Der Ost- und Westpreussische Bauer*, 14 (1896), 178–86.

themselves in the nation's legal system. The government justifiably feared that the inclusion of the more contentious reforms in the Code would lead to problems in the Reichstag. As time went on, the need to secure a majority in the Reichstag became an increasingly powerful feature of the calculations of the government. For all these reasons, the Civil Code appears to have been relatively unaffected by the wider political changes of the previous fifteen years or so.

Yet this is in many ways a misleading picture. The detailed evidence presented in this chapter shows the extent to which the bureaucracy was consciously responding to the dominant features of the new political age. This was not only true of the composition of the second commission. It was also clearly the case that conflicts between different agencies within the government developed in response to organized pressure from outside. The Prussian ministry of agriculture, with its close connections with local agricultural associations and with Conservative agrarian interests in general, was the best example of this. As we have seen, the new, 'social' ideas of the legal system's Germanist critics had penetrated important sections of the bureaucracy. This part of the story confirms the view that the bureaucracy was anything but a unitary agency, detached from the conflicts of civil society in the 1890s.[7]

The history of the Civil Code suggests that the legal bureaucracy succeeded in defeating calls for fundamental reform in parts of the law which had a bearing on social problems. This impression is in a sense true and was largely a product of the tendency of the professional lawyers in the commission to side with the government representatives on key questions. This balance of forces in the commission meant that the tangible effect of the inclusion of representatives of economic interests and political parties was very limited. Indeed, the principal function of such representatives seems to have been to legitimate the frequent claims of the Code's supporters that the work was the product of the 'whole nation'.[8]

On the other hand, the lawyers were well aware that they were living in a period of change. As one commentator put it in 1896, the 1870s had been dominated by the 'Manchester theory', whereas the 1890s

---

[7] J. Caplan, ' "The Imaginary Universality of Particular Interests": The "Tradition" of the Civil Service in German History', *Social History*, 4 (1979), 309 f.

[8] e.g. L. Enneccerus, 'Die parlamentarischen Aussichten des Bürgerlichen Gesetzbuchs', *DJZ* 1 (1896), p. 6; cf. F. Stoerk, 'Das Bürgerliche Gesetzbuch und der Gesetzgebungsapparat des deutschen Reiches', *Festgabe der Greifswalder Juristenfakultät für Ernst Immanuel Bekker zum 17. Februar 1899* (Greifswald, 1899), 102–14.

were principally concerned with social policy.[9] As we have seen, the lawyers in the bureaucracy and in the commission were often highly sympathetic to the reformers' demands, particularly those which were designed to improve the lot of the peasantry or the artisans. Their opposition to the inclusion of such matters in the Code seems to have arisen quite independently of their political views or opinions about social policy. The major objection to proposals for radical legal change was almost always formal rather than substantive. One typical argument was that special measures to deal with problems relating to specific groups or regions had no place in a Code which was designed to regulate the affairs of the whole nation. Another was that great dangers would arise if the basic principles of the legal system were continually breached in order to satisfy sectional interests. On the whole, it would probably be correct to say that the overwhelming majority of German lawyers agreed with this view. The 1895 Lawyers' Congress saw very little support for Gierke's continuing campaign against the Code, and it seems probable that the German legal community was overwhelmingly in favour of accepting the revised Code and introducing it as soon as possible. In this respect, the Reich justice office represented the views of that community very accurately.

An important feature of the government's standpoint was that codification was a special type of legislation, which was not equivalent to the whole of the legal order. The claims of previous codes, most notably the *Allgemeines Landrecht*, to cover the whole of the legal order were rejected by legislators in the late nineteenth century. By the 1890s it was standard procedure for bureaucrats to divert calls for major legal reforms into other types of legislation. On the one hand, there was the possibility of using legislation by the individual states to achieve reforms which were not considered suitable for the whole of Germany. This was deemed particularly appropriate where, as in the case of agriculture, conditions varied greatly from region to region. This approach led to the exclusion of extensive areas of the law from the code. On the other hand, the use of special national laws to deal with particular problems grew very rapidly after the start of social legislation in the 1880s. The 1890s saw a large number of such laws addressing such matters as the control of the stock exchange, the question of 'unfair competition', the partial reintroduction of the guilds, and amendments to the law relating to usury. The fact that such legislation was principally cosmetic

[9] F. André, 'Die zweite Lesung eines Bürgerlichen Gesetzbuches gegenüber der ersten. Ein Vergleich', *DJZ* 1 (1896), p. 102.

in nature and generally failed to achieve the desired goals of conservative social policy is relatively unimportant in this context. What mattered was that the state had a variety of legislative tools at its disposal and was capable of responding flexibly to demands for change.[10] The promise of special legislation, whether at local or national level, was of critical importance in the defeat of the radical opponents of the draft code.

The main effect of this was to dash the hopes of the radical reformers, whose major aim was to see the inclusion of their demands in the Code itself. We have already seen the extent to which the more radical critics of the draft code tended to talk in terms of the positive, 'educative' effect of the inclusion of their schemes in the Code itself. This was far more a reflection of their desire to 'capture' the Code for their schemes than a serious statement about the inherent superiority of the Civil Code as a tool of social policy. It was precisely the Code's status as a major national institution which motivated men like Gierke to criticize it so relentlessly from an alternative, nationalist perspective. The aim was to secure from the government a powerful rhetorical statement of intent of a kind which could never be obtained through mere special legislation. But the interest groups were too disunited and the codifying commission too carefully chosen for this strategy to have much chance of success.

The process of revision also illustrates the importance of bureaucratic control as a source of power. The debates in the second commission, though they disappointed many by their length, were conducted in such a way that alternative perspectives could only occasionally win the day. This was buttressed by the increasing ability of the secretaries of the Reich justice office to overcome opposition within the Prussian ministry of state. That independence was never anything like absolute. There is no doubt, however, that the secretaries' sometimes precarious position as the principal intermediary between the Prussian government and the Bundesrat and Reichstag gave them a powerful hold over proceedings. It was they who had to negotiate the various compromises to secure the Code's acceptance—a goal which was desired even by those like Miquel who were sharply critical of some of the Code's provisions. As Hans Herzfeld has rightly pointed out, 'the campaign for special consideration of landownership in the Civil Code foundered on the demand for formal legal unity and the rejection by the Reich offices of the conservative wishes of Prussia.'[11]

---

[10] See the important article of H.-P. Benöhr, 'Wirtschaftsliberalismus und Gesetzgebung am Ende des 19. Jahrhunderts', *Zeitschrift für Arbeitsrecht*, 8 (1977), 187–218.

[11] Herzfeld, *Miquel*, ii. 457, 488 (quotation).

The Civil Code was a very unusual piece of legislation, in terms both of its scope and of its complexity. For that reason, it would be wrong to infer too much about the operation of the Prussian and Reich governments in the 1890s from the Code's history. Bonham's work on bureaucratic divisions has suggested that 'modernizers' within the bureaucracy were likely to favour the exclusion of outside interests, while conservatives wished to include them when preparing important legislation. This is almost certainly related to the types of issue studied by Bonham, all of which were the focus of strong, well-organized opposition from Junker interests.[12] Oehlschläger's policies in 1889-90 do not correspond closely to this pattern, in that he saw the representation of groups outside the bureaucracy as an urgent political necessity, if opposition from conservative interests (among others) was to be headed off. However, it is worth remembering that the Reich justice office took care to counterbalance this representation with careful management of the commission's discussions.

Much of the recent work on the bureaucracy (including Bonham's) has tended to argue that conflicts within the government were importantly influenced by departmental considerations. Bosse's change of mind about the law of associations was a classic example of the influence of such considerations. The Reich justice office was in many ways an unusual department. Three of its secretaries in this period (Bosse, Hanauer, and Nieberding) had risen through the central Reich administration, with Bosse and Nieberding differing from Hanauer in that they had previously been employed by the Reich office of the interior.[13] Though trained in the law as all civil servants had been, their main experience had been outside the narrow world of the lawyers, in social policy and administration. In Bosse's case, this almost certainly led him to look more favourably on the builders than a dyed-in-the-wool legal bureaucrat would have done. Bosse's successor, Hanauer, was one such legal bureaucrat and seems to have been much closer to Schelling's negative views about the builders than Bosse had been.[14] Moreover, Bosse's memoirs make clear that he felt inadequately prepared for the post of chairman of the commission, and influence on most issues seems to have

---

[12] Bonham, 'Bureaucratic Modernizers', èsp. pp. 180 f., 216 f., 258 ff., 325, 332.

[13] These were the only three heads of department in the national bureaucracy to come up by this route in Wilhelmine Germany; see J. C. G. Röhl, 'Higher Civil Servants in Germany, 1890-1900', *Journal of Contemporary History*, 2 (1967), 120.

[14] Hanauer to Schelling, 7 July 1892, GStA Berlin-Dahlem Rep. 84a 11876, fo. 243.

passed to the legal specialists in the Reich justice office, particularly Hanauer and Struckmann.[15] Nieberding, on the other hand, was far more concerned with speeding up the completion of the work and the main focus of his efforts was outside the commission itself. All in all, these factors meant that the Reich justice office's supervision of the commission's work led to a strong emphasis on the technical concerns of the specialist lawyers.

The existence of a specific ideology of codification common to both the legal bureaucracy and most of the community of lawyers outside was probably the greatest of all obstacles to the proposals of the Code's more radical critics. The pursuit of legal unity and certainty through codification placed a tremendous premium on avoiding formulations which were at variance with the existing patterns of thought derived from conceptual jurisprudence. The point is not that the codifiers neglected practical considerations in the pursuit of jurisprudential perfection. The protocols of the commission show the constant concern with practical questions, in which the motivating spirit tended to be the ideal of balancing different interests.[16] The problem was that the more radical opponents did not want a law which balanced interests; they desired a law defined in terms of their own interests at the expense of others. Moreover, there were grave doubts in the minds of many of the codifiers about whether the true interests of the social groups in question were adequately represented by those who spoke in their name. Was it really true, for example, that farmers wanted restrictions on their right to borrow money and dispose of their property freely? Certainly, the negative reactions of many peasants to the Nazis' Entailed Farm Law of September 1933 suggest that one should be sceptical about some of the wilder claims of the agrarians.[17] The rhetoric of the Germanists had a strong anti-capitalist tinge, and in the context of the 1890s this often meant attacking creditor interests in the name of allegedly disadvantaged debtors. In both agrarian law and the section of mortgage law which concerned the master builders, the codifiers were strongly influenced by the fear that they would damage the supply of credit by over-hasty moves to satisfy demands which were often based on highly

---

[15] ZStA Merseburg Rep. 92 Bosse 2, fos. 3 f., 14 f.

[16] H.-P. Benöhr, 'Das Gesetz als Instrument zur Lösung sozial-politischer Konflikte: Das Beispiel des Bauforderungssicherungsgesetz von 1909'. *ZRG GA* 95 (1978), pp. 227 f.

[17] See I. Kershaw, *Popular Opinion and Political Dissent in the Third Reich: Bavaria 1933–1945* (Oxford, 1983), 42 ff.; J. E. Farquharson, 'The Agrarian Policy of National Socialist Germany', in R. G. Moeller (ed.), *Peasants and Lords in Modern German History. Recent Studies in Agricultural History* (London, 1985), 239 f.

dubious factual information.[18] They therefore proceeded carefully, and preferred to approach special problems outside the framework of the Code.

The Code's critics had made a powerful point when they focused attention on the social implications of the contents of the legal system. But they had not answered, and arguably could not answer, the question of how the interests of creditors could be accommodated in their schemes. Moreover, if such an accommodation was impossible, was it not likely that creditors would refuse to lend money to those who needed it? This is what Enneccerus had in mind when he warned 'whoever endangers the foundations of the Code out of an excessive enthusiasm for agrarian interests or social policy is the bitterest enemy of his own efforts'.[19] The growing use of this type of argument was of great importance in creating the possibility for the resurgence of older doctrines of codification in the mid-1890s. If the tendency of the draft code was 'one-sidedly capitalistic', as Gierke claimed, his own Germanist doctrines were not without problematic social implications of their own. Given the acute nature of political divisions and the high premium placed on the Code as a binding agent in society and as a symbol of national unity, the doctrine of balancing social interests had a considerable appeal. All of these elements entered the picture when Nieberding presented the Code to the Bundesrat in October 1895.

[18] e.g. Freese's assertion that, in 1893, 356 of the 388 new buildings in Berlin had been subjected to foreclosure: *National-Zeitung*, 12 Apr. 1894.

[19] Enneccerus, 'Die parlamentarischen Aussichten des Bürgerlichen Gesetzbuchs', p. 8.

7.

The Final Stage: The Civil Code in
the Bundesrat and Reichstag,
1895–1896

THE months between October 1895 and July 1896 gave the Reich's legislative institutions the chance to discuss the Code at length for the first time. This in turn generated considerable levels of public interest, with the press devoting far more attention to the Code than at any previous stage. The Code now became a pressing issue for politicians, forcing them to define their parties' attitude to a law which many considered to be an indicator of the strength of the German body politic. As a result, the volume of documentary evidence for this stage in the Code's history is substantially greater than for earlier periods. It is thus possible to consider the final discussions about the nation's legal system in much more depth than any of the preceding stages.

The justification for doing so does not, however, lie in the influence of the Bundesrat and Reichstag on the final content of the Code. In fact, that influence was relatively limited. No clause-by-clause discussion of the work took place, and it was debated and accepted in considerably less than a year. As was pointed out a few years later, a major reason for this speed was the fact that most of the possible debates had been pre-empted in the second commission, where both the major states and the larger political parties (the Social Democrats excepted) had had their say.[1] A speedy conclusion to the work thus relied on the willingness of the states and political parties to renounce their constitutional rights to subject the Code to a fundamental revision. This was indeed what happened, although the Reichstag rejected the view that the second commission's work should be accepted without alterations. As we shall see, this outcome was by no means inevitable, and the mode of procedure

---

[1] F. Stoerk, 'Das Bürgerliche Gesetzbuch und der Gesetzgebungsapparat des deutschen Reiches', in *Festgabe der Greifswalder Juristenfukultät für Ernst Immanuel Bekker zum 17. Februar 1899* (Greifswald, 1899), 102–7.

to be adopted by the legislature was the cause of important political debates. Once again, disagreements over such procedural questions concealed profound differences of opinion about the desired contents of the Code. Not surprisingly, those who were most satisfied with the Code as it stood (such as the National Liberals and Free Conservatives) were most willing to see the Reichstag renounce its right of debate. Those who were not satisfied tended to call for the Reichstag to exercise that right to the full.[2]

The completion of the Code held opportunities and dangers for the larger parties in the Reichstag. It gave the Social Democrats the chance to show that they were capable of responsible political participation, but it exposed the deepening divisions within the Conservative party. It revived, however temporarily, the ailing fortunes of the National Liberal party and and helped to cement the position of the Centre at the heart of the Wilhelmine party system. A fundamental feature of Wilhelmine politics in the following years—the conclusion of *ad hoc* National Liberal/Centre party alliances to carry most major pieces of legislation—may be said to have come into being with the debates concerning the Code.[3]

The parliamentary debates showed just how far politics had moved on from the concerns of the 1870s. The nervousness of the Code's supporters about its prospects was not produced by widespread hostility to the completion of legal unification as such. In fact, all the major political parties were willing to accept a national Code. The contention of one newspaper that 'little Savignys' were appearing, who sought to deny the present age's capacity to produce worthwhile legislation,[4] missed the point. The real questions concerned the extent to which the divisions over the content of the Code would find reflection in the attitudes of the parties. In the winter of 1895-6, the Code's fate at the hands of the Reichstag was anything but secure.

There was also the question of how the Bundesrat would deal with the Code. Nieberding's main goal was to secure the agreement of that body as quickly as possible, which meant the frustration of the desire of some states (especially Mecklenburg) for a detailed debate on the whole of the code. Nieberding's priorities thus determined his views on

---

[2] e.g. *Kölnische Zeitung*, 17 June 1895; O. v. Gierke, *Das Bürgerliche Gesetzbuch und der Deutsche Reichstag. Sonderabdruck aus der täglichen Rundschau* (Berlin, 1896), 1-5.

[3] G. Eley, *Reshaping the German Right. Radical Nationalism and Political Change After Bismarck* (New Haven/London, 1980) 239 ff.

[4] *Leipziger Tageblatt*, 29 Jan. 1896.

the role of the Bundesrat in the completion of the work. As he put it to the Bundesrat's justice committee on 7 October 1895:

The size of the task urgently requires resignation in the debates on the Code and confidence that the two commissions have created an acceptable work. Any other type of approach would have a disastrous influence on the debates in the Reichstag; the latter would consider itself equally justified in thoroughly revising the draft code. That would be the end of the whole great legislative project. The political consequences of the failure of this work would, however, be so far-reaching that the Bundesrat must do everything to prevent it. It must therefore consider the Code as if it had itself produced it and only correct any omissions, errors, and obscure passages which may have been included. Occasionally, perhaps, political considerations, which naturally did not receive adequate attention in the commission, might be brought up.[5]

The most important of such political considerations concerned the private law of associations. Württemberg proposed a series of amendments which amounted to the restoration of the old concessionary system. Even before the debate began, Baden's ambassador was convinced that such a proposal would founder on the opposition of Prussia, Bavaria, and Saxony. Hessen supported the total exclusion of the law of associations from the Code in principle, but was unwilling to create problems with the Reichstag on the matter. As always, Nieberding was quick to exploit such uncertainties, pointing out that the Reichstag might well introduce even less acceptable provisions into the Code. In that case, the Bundesrat would be left with the unhappy choice of accepting those provisions or rejecting the Code as a whole. Repeating his usual argument, Nieberding in effect blackmailed the Bundesrat into accepting his proposals: 'If [the governments] rejected the Code, they would take on a political responsibility of far-reaching importance.' In the event, all the states represented in the justice committee, with the exception of Württemberg, came round to Nieberding's point of view.[6]

Considerable disagreements also arose in relation to the details of the Code's land law, family law, and inheritance law. As we have seen, many earlier commentators had argued that national legislation was inappropriate in these areas of the law because of the degree of regional variations. In the Bundesrat, however, the major question was the extent

---

[5] Heller, report of 7 Oct. 1895, BHStA Munich, MA 76729.
[6] Ibid.; Sieveking, report of 7 Oct. 1895, StA Hamburg, Archiv des Bevollmächtigten zum Bundesrat XI, 5; Jagemann, telegram of 5 Oct. 1895, GLA Karlsruhe, Abt. 233/13995; cf. Langfeld, report of 8 Oct. 1895, StA Schwerin, Ministerium der Justiz 298, fos. 283–93, which reveals that Württemberg's proposals emanated from Mecklenburg.

to which south German legal developments were to be accommodated in the Code. This was potentially an issue of great importance in that it revived the old southern fears of the 1870s that codification meant the 'Prussianization' of the legal system. For all that political debate had moved on to other concerns by the mid-1890s, particularism and hostility to Prussia were by no means dead and may even have been on the increase, particularly in Bavaria.[7]

These problems emerged clearly when the questions of conveyancing and the law of mortgage were discussed. In both cases the codifiers had essentially followed Prussian law, and this aroused the resistance of the southern states. The problem of conveyancing was complicated by the fact that certain interest groups, in particular those representing the notaries, were pressurizing governments in the south to retain existing local legislation, which required the participation of a notary or the courts in land transfers. To Nieberding, this constituted 'an attack on the principle of conveyancing' which was totally incompatible with the Prussian legal system. In the case of mortgage law, the North German institution of the negotiable mortgage bond (*Briefhypothek*) aroused the opposition of the Bavarian government, which argued that it was an innovation likely to discriminate against the poorer debtor. On both issues Bavaria was unable to win through against Nieberding, who mercilessly exploited the divisions and uncertainties of the southern states. In effect, his policy was to force them into compliance by concentrating on the need to avoid any major changes in the Code which might endanger its acceptance either in the Bundesrat or in the Reichstag. In the last resort, he could rely on the widespread feeling among the governments of states such as Baden that 'the completion of the national work is more important to us than the way in which individual problems are resolved'. As a result, he could persuade the doubters that the proposed reforms were impractical or politically impossible. Meanwhile, Mecklenburg's extensive proposals for changes in the Code's mortgage law found almost no support.[8]

Bavaria's amendments concerning family and inheritance law were

[7] See I. Farr, 'Populism in the Countryside: The Peasant Leagues in Bavaria in the 1890s', in R. J. Evans (ed.), *Society and Politics in Wilhelmine Germany* (London, 1978), 144 f.

[8] Heller, reports of 9, 10, 15, and 16 Oct. and 10 Dec. 1895, BHStA Munich, MA 76729; cf. the materials relating to the campaign of the notaries' organizations in BHStA Munich, MJu 16119; Langfeld, report of 20 Oct. 1895, StA Schwerin, Ministerium der Justiz 298, fos. 332-40; Brauer to Jagemann (telegram), 5 Oct. 1895, GLA Karlsruhe, Abt. 233/13995.

equally unsuccessful. Attempts to introduce restrictive provisions in the law of divorce, to admit the Roman Catholic notion of separation as an alternative legal form, and to bolster the religious aspects of marriage all failed. Nieberding's principal argument here was that concessions to Catholic sentiment on marriage law were best left until the time came for bargaining with the Centre party in the Reichstag. The various attempts by the southern states to introduce their native institutions and customs into the law of inheritance generally failed as well, on the whole because Nieberding stressed the dangers of delaying matters further.[9]

Nieberding was thus able to dominate the proceedings of the Bundesrat and generally overrode the interests of the southern states, in so far as they differed from those of Prussia. At no time in the previous twenty-two years was the inability of the larger southern states to get their own way so complete. Nieberding exploited the political dangers facing the Code in the Reichstag concerning the key questions of the law of associations and marriage and divorce law. The Bundesrat was forced to give in by the threat that the Code would fail if the states maintained an intransigent attitude. Nobody really wished to take responsibility for such a failure. Nieberding's position was all the more powerful because he alone was responsible for the negotiations with the leaders of the Reichstag parties. Moreover, the southern states were disunited on points of detail and, as in the 1870s, unity was the only way to overcome Prussian opposition. Prussia's habit of dealing with the larger states independently and the growth of the Reich offices as relatively independent forces at the centre of government had tended to undermine the overall importance of the Bundesrat and the *esprit de corps* of the southern states within it. Finally, many of the politicians involved were prepared to accept the Code, despite the defeat of their amendments, because it nevertheless offered them an improvement of their existing laws. Such was certainly the feeling of the Bavarian government about the law of divorce,[10] and it put yet another trump card into Nieberding's hand.

By Christmas 1895 there was considerable speculation about the fate of the Code in the Reichstag. The government's intention to push the

[9] Langfeld, report of 6 Nov. 1895, StA Schwerin, Ministerium der Justiz 298, fos. 372–89; Heller, report of 11 Dec. 1895, BHStA, Munich MA 76729; Krüger, reports of 11 and 19 Dec. 1895, StA Hamburg, Archiv des Bevollmächtigten zum Bundesrat XI, 5.
[10] Leonrod to Prince Luitpold, 6 Jan. 1896, BHStA Munich, MA 76729.

Code through before the summer recess was well known, but it was by no means clear that that would be possible. Too many doubts surrounded the attitude of the Centre party. The Social Democrats were generally felt to be hostile, and commentators could not ignore the hostility of radical agrarian and anti-Semitic groups. The National Liberal press seems to have been curiously optimistic about the Centre given that negotiations with that party were still in their infancy.[11] There was certainly no guarantee at the beginning of 1896 that the Reichstag would accept the Code as it stood.

In the end the National Liberals' confidence in the Centre party was justified, and the Code was accepted by a majority of two hundred and thirty-two votes to forty-eight on 1 July 1896. The majority comprised eighty members of the Centre party, thirty-eight National Liberals, thirty Conservatives, twenty-eight left-liberals, fourteen Free Conservatives, and a number of members from other parties. The minority included forty-two Social Democrats, three Conservatives, and three representatives of the Bavarian Peasants' League. The predicted opposition of the anti-Semites failed to materialize, and one of their number—Heinrich Lieber—actually voted in favour of the Code. The majority also included several noted National Liberal agrarians, such as Baron Cornelius Heyl zu Herrnsheim and Diederich Hahn.[12]

The size of the eventual majority in favour of the Code would have surprised many commentators at the beginning of the year, and was the result of lengthy and often tortuous negotiations between and within the parties. Once again, the question of procedure became important. Hohenlohe and Nieberding desperately wanted a legislative success in the year of the twenty-fifth anniversary of the Reich, but a piece of legislation of this size and complexity clearly could not be completed in six months if the Reichstag adopted its normal method of debate. The question of how the Reichstag should proceed was already being discussed in the press in late 1895 after the *Kölnische Zeitung* had called

---

[11] *National-Zeitung*, 27 Sept. 1895; *Kölnische Zeitung*, 29 Dec. 1895.

[12] See the division list in *SBRT* (1895–7), pp. 3104D–3106C; for a breakdown of the voting by party, see D. Brandt, 'Die politischen Parteien und die Vorlage des Bürgerlichen Gesetzbuches im Reichstag', Jur. Diss. (Heidelberg, 1975), 165 ff.; for the anti-Semites, see R. S. Levy, *The Downfall of the Anti-Semitic Parties in Imperial Germany* (New Haven/London, 1975), 169 f. Puhle's calculation that there were 48 agrarian opponents of the Code in the Reichstag is clearly incorrect: *Agrarische Interessenpolitik und preussicher Konservatismus im Wilhelminischen Reich (1893–1914). Ein Beitrag zur Analyse des Nationalismus in Deutschland am Beispiel des Bundes der Landwirte und der Deutsch-Konservation Partei* (2nd ed., Bonn/Bad Godesberg, 1975) 243 n. 126.

for the acceptance of the Code more or less as it stood in June.[13] The matter was taken up in left-liberal circles and especially by Eugen Richter, who called for the establishment of a standing Reichstag commission to consider the Code in detail, as had happened with the procedural and organizational Codes in the 1870s. Richter was particularly concerned to ensure that a full debate took place on the most important social and political issues, such as the law of association, the exclusion of the remnants of 'feudal' law from the Code and the law of divorce. In the following months the anti-Semites and radical agrarians joined in the battle against what came to be known as the 'hurrah-patriotism' of those who wished to 'whip through' the Code. The Social Democrats adopted a similar line, arguing that most of the German population had had no say in the preparation of a Code which would fundamentally influence their everyday lives. Finally, Bismarck joined the campaign, incongruously arguing that the authority and prestige of the Reichstag should be defended against the government's attempts to encourage the decline of that body.[14]

Bismarck's involvement in this campaign was self-evidently opportunistic and seems to have been highly unpopular in Reichstag circles. The SPD clearly entertained doubts about allying with Bismarck and the extreme agrarians on this issue; as Franz Mehring later said, Bismarck's only interest in the matter was to deny Hohenlohe the prestige of being Chancellor when the Code was completed. Nevertheless, Bismarck still had influence among important sections of the German political nation. Moreover, his involvement was significant in that he tended to direct his attacks at the weakest point of the governmental coalition—the difficult negotiations concerning marriage law and the law of associations, on whose outcome the successful completion of the work rested.[15] As for the other participants in the campaign against an over-hasty consideration of the Code, it seems likely that they felt that their views had not previously been heard adequately. To that extent, the dispute was indicative of the limitations of the Reich's policy of including outside interests in the second commission in order to head off less manageable debates later on.

[13] *Kölnische Zeitung*, 17 June 1895.

[14] *Freisinnige Zeitung*, 21 July 1895; *Deutsches Volks-Recht*, 9 Oct. 1895; *Deutsche Tageszeitung*, 8 Dec. 1895; *SBRT*, 4 Feb. 1896, pp. 742A-B, 749B (Stadthagen); 19 June 1896; pp. 2721D-2723C (Singer); *Hamburger Nachrichten*, 9 Jan. 1896.

[15] Schicker, report of 7 May 1896, HStA Stuttgart, E 74 I, no. 87; F. Mehring, 'Hasenrechtliches', *Neue Zeit*, xiv/2 (1895-6), 417.

The government's response to these multiple threats showed all the tactical skill which Nieberding had displayed when steering the Code through the Bundesrat. As a compromise, he was willing to accept a proposal by the Conservatives that the Code should be debated mainly in a Reichstag committee. On 22 or 23 January, the representatives of the Reichstag parties eventually accepted Spahn's suggestion that this committee should only consider the most contentious parts of the Code. In practice, this procedure was not followed and committee debates took place whenever a motion was proposed. That method gave the Social Democrats and others the opportunity to slow things down by proposing and debating motions at length. Nevertheless, it did allow most questions to be dealt with relatively quickly, and had the added advantage of undermining claims that the government was 'whipping through' the Code.[16]

Nieberding also took care to prime the National Liberal press, through Planck and Bennigsen about Bismarck's schemes.[17] In the spring of 1896 a strident campaign within sections of the Conservative party against the Code's inclusion of obligatory civil marriage led Nieberding to redouble his efforts to complete the code before the summer. By May he was afraid that mounting agitation among the Centre party's supporters on the same issue would make it impossible for them to adhere to a compromise. The next month saw other important figures, particularly Boetticher and Hohenlohe's son, negotiating with the party leaders to try to find some way out of the political impasse. Until early June, however, the success of Nieberding's attempts to find a compromise to bring together a parliamentary coalition based on the National Liberals and the Centre party was still in doubt.[18]

The history of the debates in the Reichstag has been the subject of a number of recent studies,[19] and for that reason this account will not

[16] *Die Post*, 24 Jan. 1896; Jagemann, reports of 25 Jan. and 14 Mar. 1896, GLA Karlsruhe, Abt. 233/13996; see the various materials in HA Cologne, Bachem Papers 7.

[17] Nieberding to Bennigsen, 28 May 1896, ZStA Potsdam, Bennigsen Papers 119, fo. 1; Planck to Bennigsen, 22 May 1896, reprinted in H. Oncken, *Rudolf von Bennigsen. Ein deutscher Liberaler nach seinen Briefen und hinterlassenen Papieren*, ii (Stuttgart/ Leipzig, 1910), 599.

[18] Minutes of the Prussian ministry of state, 8 May 1896, reprinted in Schubert, *Materialien*, p. 403; on the negotiations in May, see Jagemann, report of 2 June 1896, GLA Karlsruhe, Abt. 233/13996; *Staatsbürger-Zeitung*, 13 May and *Allgemeine Zeitung*, 14 May 1896.

[19] Above all Brandt, 'Die politischen Parteien'; cf. Schubert, *Materialien*, pp. 64-8; R. Köhne, *Nationalliberale und Koalitionsrecht. Struktur und Verhalten der nationalliberalen Fraktion, 1890-1914* (Frankfurt, 1977), 181-90; M. Martiny, *Integration oder Konfrontation?*

attempt a detailed, clause-by-clause analysis of the parties' views. Rather, it will follow the practice of previous chapters in concentrating on certain politically important issues, in particular the convoluted debates concerning the law of associations and marriage law. However, the first plenary reading, which took place between 3 and 6 February, was also very revealing about the attitudes of the parties to the general question of legal unity. This opening debate was the subject of great interest on the part of the press, as it revealed considerable support for a positive attitude towards the task of revising the Code. On the other hand, there were already worrying signs of the problems that were to come, both within the Conservative party and more importantly in the Centre.

As expected, the spokesman for the National Liberals, Ludwig von Cuny, emphasized the national importance of the Code and rejected 'social' and Germanist criticisms. For the Conservatives, Gerhard von Buchka announced his party's support for the integrative function of the Civil Code and opposed radical Germanist criticisms. The Free Conservative spokesman, Ernst Leuschner, read out the decision of a party meeting that it would support the acceptance of the code as it stood, if that had any chance of success. Despite reservations about parts of the Code, especially the law of associations, the representatives of the two left-liberal parties showed their concern for the final establishment of legal unity and even suggested that the Reichstag committee be empowered to accept whole sections of the Code without debate.[20]

This support was encouraging for the government but was not sufficient to guarantee a majority. Nor did it preclude serious problems on specific issues. The left-liberals were likely to press their claims on the law of associations, and it became rapidly clear that the Conservatives were divided on the question of obligatory civil marriage. Obligatory civil marriage had become Reich law in 1875 but the Conservatives had never been fully happy with it. While Buchka—the only professional lawyer in the party—openly opposed any fundamental change in the law, Manteuffel declared his opposition in principle to existing Reich

(Bonn/Bad Godesberg, 1976), 55–71; T. Vormbaum, *Sozialdemokratie und Zivilrechts-kodifikation* (Berlin/New York, 1977); id., *Die Rechtsfähigkeit der Vereine im 19. Jahrhundert. Ein Beitrag zur Enstehungsgeschichte des BGB* (Berlin/New York, 1976), pp. 183 ff.; P. Kögler, *Arbeiterbewegung und Vereinsrecht. Ein Beitrag zur Enstehungsgeschichte des BGB* (Berlin, 1974) 108–15.

20 *SBRT*, 3 Feb. 1896, pp. 717A–718D (Cuny), 719A–723A (Buchka), 723A–725C (Schröder), 725D–726B (Leuschner); 4 Feb. 1896, pp. 728D–736A (Kauffmann).

legislation, though he did state that he would not let the Code fail on this issue.[21] In that situation the attitude of the Centre party, which was expected to oppose anything which undermined the sacramental nature of marriage, was clearly going to be crucial. At the beginning of the previous year, Spahn had suggested in the Reichstag that the law of marriage be excluded from the Code in order to make it easier for Roman Catholic deputies to vote for it.[22] That was not, however, a practical possibility given the Code's desire to secure the foundations of the law of marriage. In any case, obligatory civil marriage had been part of German law for over twenty years and was regarded as an article of faith by liberals. On the other hand, the Centre was the largest party in the Reichstag and would obviously have a substantial influence on the negotiations which would precede the conclusion of a parliamentary coalition.

The Centre's first spokesman was the deputy for Trier, Viktor Rintelen. Rintelen was something of a maverick figure in the Centre party. He was allowed to speak on behalf of the party as compensation for his exclusion from the Reichstag committee to discuss the Code; the party leaders feared that his obstinacy would wreck the committee stage of the parliamentary debates, just as it had done the previous year with the reform of penal procedure. At this stage, the party's policy was to attack the Code's marriage law strongly, but also to avoid any commitment relating to the final vote—a policy which was obviously related to the hope that concessions might be gained from the government and National Liberals.[23] Rintelen's speech was thus something of a surprise. Like other commentators, he announced his party's support for a Code as 'a great, important national work'. He then proceeded to attack the revised Code, claiming that it was unsystematic, contributed to the 'mobilization' of landed property, and weakened the family. Most important of all, the Code's law of marriage was contrary to Christian views on the subject and he concluded:

If it is not possible to remove these clauses from the Code or to revise them in such a way as to take away the doubts of Catholic consciences, we shall be forced to vote not only against these clauses but also against the Code as a whole.[24]

---

[21] Ibid., 3 Feb. 1896, pp. 721D-722A (Buchka); 6 Feb. 1896, p. 781B-C (Manteuffel).

[22] Ibid., 21 Mar. 1895, pp. 1633 ff.

[23] HA Cologne, Bachem Papers 7, 'Meine Verhandlungen mit den Grafen Roon' (cited hereafter as 'Verhandlungen').

[24] *SBRT*, 3 Feb. 1896, pp. 710D-717A (quotation, p. 717A).

This speech clearly exceeded Rintelen's brief and the Centre's leaders were horrified. Spahn felt it necessary to make a much more measured speech two days later, reaffirming the party's interest in legal unity. The Socialist newspaper, *Vorwärts*, was quick to note the lack of support for Rintelen within the party, and a few other papers were inclined to see his speech as a relatively unimportant statement of principle.[25] Others were not, however, so perceptive. The Kaiser voiced his irritation with the Centre, and had to be reassured by Hohenlohe that Rintelen's views were not representative of his party. That opinion was not, however, entirely accurate, in that Rintelen's speech gave the signal for a bitter debate within the Catholic press about the leadership's tactics. The description of his speech as 'a masterful statement' in one of the Catholic newspapers was only the beginning of a mounting campaign against the Centre's leadership.[26]

Another party to voice serious criticisms of the code was the SPD. That was hardly surprising in view of its hostility to bourgeois society, and *Vorwärts* had already announced that the Code was unacceptable and would be rejected as a whole by the party.[27] The first socialist spokesman, Arthur Stadthagen, announced that the party would be devoting considerable attention to the reform of the Code in the interests of the working classes. True legal unity was not, he said, 'the codified injustice of exploitation', but rather an attempt to follow the trend of modern legislation, which sought to protect the weaker elements in society.

Despite the radicalism of Stadthagen's tone, however, it was not the case that the Social Democrats were altogether opposed to the Code. Both he and his colleague, Karl Frohme, emphasized that the working class had a deep interest in legal unity, and promised that the SPD would participate positively in the revision of the Code. In Frohme's words:

It can only be good for us, and can only promote our interests and endeavours, if the civil law is unified in Germany. The working classes will not gain anything as such; nevertheless, this development is to be seen as an important step forward, in so far as its effects are to be seen in many areas of politics.

[25] HA Cologne, Bachem Papers 7—'Verhandlungen'; *Vorwärts*, 4 Feb. 1896; *Hamburgischer Correspondent*, 4 Feb. 1896.
[26] Wilhelm II to Hohenlohe, 4 Feb., and Hohenlohe to Wilhelm II, 5 Feb. 1896, in Hohenlohe, *Denkwürdigkeiten aus der Reichskanzlerzeit*, ed. K. A. v. Müller (Stuttgart/ Berlin, 1931), 164 f.; *Deutsche Reichszeitung*, 5 Feb. 1896.
[27] *Vorwärts*, 23 Jan. 1896.

Both speakers accepted the standard Second International Marxist view
that the law could do no more than reflect the level of economic
development of a society. They seem to have believed that the party
could intervene to give the working class the type of legislation which
its role in the economy required. Stadthagen thought that any attempt
to pursue the socialist 'goal' in these debates was 'childish', and was
instead concerned to bring in a unified law governing all labour contracts
and to end the exclusion of the old 'feudal laws' which contributed to
the continued subjection of the propertyless classes. As he concluded,
'[w]hat I have proposed recently and today is not specifically socialist,
but merely something which can be carried out now.' To Frohme, legal
progress was the 'progress towards greater social and political justice'.
There was thus absolutely no reason to oppose the Code in principle.
Despite Bachem's comments about the 'silly' tone of Stadthagen's first
speech, the message was not lost on the Reichstag. As the German
Reform party deputy, Dr Paul Förster, put it, the participation of the
Social Democrats was assured and that was to be welcomed.[28]

On the other hand, there were hidden dangers for the government
in the main parties' refusal to pursue a policy of outright rejection.
There was always the possibility that the Centre, left-liberals, and Social
Democrats might ally to produce a code whose provisions on the law
of associations would be too liberal for the Bundesrat. Baron von Stumm
had already declared that the Free Conservatives' support of the Code
was dependent on the rejection of the principal Centre and SPD
demands.[29] It seemed only too possible that the Reichstag might split
into two broad camps on the right and left, with the Centre perhaps
straddling the divide. Such an outcome offered little hope of a politically
acceptable Code emerging in the summer. It was against this uncertain
background that the Reichstag's committee began its deliberations.

The Reichstag committee began its debates on 17 February and
completed them after fifty-three sessions on 11 June.[30] The first problem

[28] *SBRT*, 4 Feb. 1896, pp. 741B–749C and 6 Feb. 1896, p. 792D (quotation)
(Stadthagen); ibid., 6 Feb., pp. 781D–788A (displayed quotation, p. 787C) (Frohme); HA
Cologne, Bachem Papers 7—'Verhandlungen'; *SBRT*, 5 Feb. 1896, p. 764D (Förster).

[29] *SBRT*, 5 Feb. 1896, pp. 761D–762A; for another expression of this fear, see J.
Petersen, 'Der Entwurf zu einem bürgerlichen Gesetzbuch vor dem Reichstage', *Die
Grenzboten*, lv/1 (1896), 115–29, esp. 116.

[30] The committee's exact membership fluctuated, but there were 6 representatives of
the Centre, 3 Conservatives, 3 National Liberals, 2 Free Conservatives, 2 representatives
each from the SPD and Freisinnige Volkspartei and 1 each from the Poles, anti-Semites,
and Freisinnige Vereinigung; see the membership lists in Schubert, *Materialien*, p. 65.

arose over the chairmanship of the commission, a post for which Bennigsen had originally been envisaged. The National Liberals predictably coveted this post, but Ernst Lieber of the Centre began to campaign hard for Spahn to be chairman in early 1896. At the time, Bachem explained this in terms of the Centre's desire to protect Catholic religious interests, given Buchka's presence as the main Conservative representative on the committee.[31] Such an explanation would have rung true to many contemporaries. However, Bachem was attempting to explain his party's actions to the papal nuncio in Munich, and might have been expected to have emphasized religious considerations. In view of Spahn's subsequent style of leadership, a rather more convincing explanation was that advanced by the National Liberal Friedrich Hammacher—that the Centre wanted the prestige of having successfully guided the Code through the Reichstag.[32] As we shall see, such an explanation is fully consonant with the main drift of Lieber's and Spahn's policy towards the government in 1896.

The assiduity with which different politicians approached the committee's work naturally varied. Bennigsen, for example, was considered by one observer to be a member of the committee only in an honorary capacity, and by April his absences had become so frequent that he had to rely on Cuny to tell him what had happened. On the other hand, Stadthagen and Gröber deluged the committee with motions and conducted lengthy debates in support of them, to the considerable annoyance of others present. In Gröber's case this aroused great hostility within his own party, the Centre, and on several occasions open arguments with Bachem were only averted by Spahn's skilful conciliation.[33] Many of these motions were quickly rejected, and were either abandoned there and then or met a similar fate when they were revived during the second plenary reading of the Code. On the other hand, the major political problems facing the Code—the law of associations and civil marriage—produced extremely significant debates, which led after a great deal of difficulty to the eventual compromise.

[31] Buchka, it will be remembered, was a much keener supporter of obligatory civil marriage than other elements in his party.

[32] Jagemann, report of 21 Oct. 1895, GLA Karlsruhe, Abt. 233/34801, fo. 203; cf. Spahn's note to Bachem's memorandum of 7 Jan. 1900, HA Cologne, Bachem Papers 7; Bachem to Ajuti, 19 Feb. 1896, HA Cologne, Bachem Papers 6; Hammacher to Bennigsen, ZStA Potsdam, Bennigsen Papers 77, fo. 17.

[33] A. Langfeld, *Mein Leben. Erinnerungen* (Schwerin, 1930), 142; Hammacher to Bennigsen, 18 Apr. 1896, ZStA Potsdam, Bennigsen Papers 77, fo. 18; on Gröber see the frequent references in HA Cologne, Bachem Papers 7 and Lerchenfeld, report of 8 Mar. 1896, BHStA Munich, MA 76730.

The private law of associations was first debated by the commission on 26 February.[34] The most radical reform proposals, which called for a system of completely 'free creation of corporations', came predictably from the SPD. Nobody seems to have taken this idea particularly seriously, and the government spokesmen did not even bother to reply. In the end, they gained the support of only one non-socialist deputy, the anti-Semite Georg Vielhaben.

A more serious problem was posed by the Centre and left-liberal parties, whose similar motions aimed to abolish the power of the authorities to remove the juristic personality of an association because of the nature of its activities. That power (the so-called *Einspruchsrecht*) was to be retained only for those associations whose goals were either economic, illegal, or immoral. Both Gröber and Gustav Kauffmann of the Freisinnige Volkspartei called for the removal of the last remnants of the 'concessionary system' from the Code; the administration could not, they said, be relied upon to administer the law impartially. In the case of the Centre party at least, however, it is highly probable that this motion was designed to secure a bargaining counter for later debates on the law of marriage.[35]

Despite strong objections from Nieberding and the representatives of the various states, the Centre party's motion was accepted by thirteen votes to eight, with the Conservatives, the Free Conservatives, and the National Liberals in the minority. Thus, the feared Centre-left-liberal-Social Democrat alliance against the Bundesrat had come into being.[36] That was not however the end of the story, for, as *Vorwärts* noted, many of the supporters of the motion seemed likely to change their minds before the second reading.[37] The Bundesrat's opinion that the decision was unacceptable was very clear; if the Reichstag upheld its decision, the whole of this section of the law would be omitted from the Code. In view of the fact that the revised Code as accepted by the Bundesrat constituted an undoubted improvement of the existing law

---

[34] The following details are derived from *Bericht der Reichstags-Kommission über den Entwurf eines Bürgerlichen Gesetzbuchs* (Berlin, 1896), pp. 9 ff.; Heller, reports of 26 and 27 Feb. 1896, BHStA Munich, MA 76730.

[35] As was later admitted by Bachem; see his memorandum 'Zum Bürgerlichen Gesetzbuch' of 11 June 1907, HA Cologne, Bachem Papers 7; cf. Lerchenfeld, report of 8 Mar. 1896, BHStA Munich, MA 76730.

[36] Heller, report of 26 Feb. 1896, BHStA Munich, MA 76730.

[37] *Vorwärts*, 28 Feb. 1896, 1. Beilage; one of those who was certainly likely to change his mind was Hugo Schröder of the Freisinnige Vereinigung—see Heller, report of 26 Feb. 1896, BHStA Munich, MA 76730.

in most of Germany, it is difficult to believe that a majority would have continued to defy the government to the bitter end.

This view is confirmed by the outcome of the committee's second reading of the Code in June. By this stage the whole issue had become much more complicated because of the connection with the question of obligatory civil marriage. In early March there were a large number of rumours suggesting that the Conservatives planned to introduce a motion proposing *optional* civil marriage—a response to growing demands within the Conservative camp, which centred on the newspaper *Die Reichsbote*. By 6 March at the latest, such a motion did exist, and the pressure within the Conservative party in the country continued to grow.[38] The Centre party was predictably surprised by this after Buchka's comments in the Reichstag and, equally predictably, saw in it a possible way of breaking the principle that marriage was an essentially secular act. Negotiations with the Conservatives and anti-Semites were then begun.[39]

The political dangers of this campaign were not lost on Nieberding, especially after the two Free Conservatives on the committee declared themselves in favour of the motion. This meant that there was almost certainly a majority in favour of a measure to which the Reich government would never agree. Nor was the danger over when a meeting of the Free Conservative party on 12 March disavowed the views of its representatives, who promptly resigned from the committee. When the matter was discussed by the committee in April, the Centre was sure of a majority and there was dark talk of a Centre–Conservative alliance against the code.[40]

That majority was not, however, forthcoming. Strong opposition to the proposal was voiced by Schröder, Cuny and Bennigsen, and the anti-Semite Vielhaben was also rather surprisingly opposed. Moreover, the Conservatives had failed to replace Buchka in the committee, which they had promised to do during the preceding negotiations. Bachem's arguments about the sacramental nature of marriage were to no avail, and the motion was defeated against the votes of the Centre party, the Pole, and two of the three Conservatives. The Centre's leaders now

[38] *Berliner Neueste Nachrichten*, 11 Mar.; *Hannoverscher Courier*, 10 Mar.; *Die Reichsbote*, 11 and 12 Mar.; Heller, report of 6 Mar., BHStA Munich, MA 76730.
[39] The source material for the following is to be found in HA Cologne, Bachem Papers 7, especially 'Verhandlungen'.
[40] Heller to Leonrod, 8 Mar. 1896, BHStA Munich, MA 76730; *Die Post*, 12 Mar.; *Kölnische Zeitung*, 12 Mar.; *Deutsche Sonntags-Post*, 26 Apr. 1896.

agreed that any attempt to revive the proposal was utterly hopeless. By failing to replace Buchka, the Conservatives had demonstrated that they were not totally committed to the success of their motion. When Count Roon proposed the same motion again on 30 May, Bachem insisted that the Conservatives made the success of their motion a necessary precondition for voting for the Code as a whole. When Roon refused to do this, Bachem came to the conclusion that his colleagues, Spahn and Lieber, were right in seeing the matter as hopeless. When the question was debated again in the committee on 9 June, it secured only four votes.[41] The Centre party had found a better and more reliable way of securing its goals.

That way was through negotiations with Nieberding and the National Liberals, which were decided upon immediately after the breakdown of talks with Roon. This decision was by no means easy, and was preceded by lengthy consultations with Rome and with a Jesuit theologian, Father August Lehmkuhl. The basis for negotiation lay in the possibility that the revised Code might contain a statement to the effect that the religious side of marriage was in no way touched by the institution of obligatory civil marriage. During the discussions of the committee Nieberding had hinted that such an arrangement might be possible, and Lehmkuhl advised the Centre party to take the opportunity. It was actually Lehmkuhl who proposed the formulation of the vital clause which removed the religious side of marriage from the Code. Bennigsen was apparently very dubious about the proposal, which he believed involved 'discrediting civil marriage', but was won over by Nieberding in the first week of June. The compromise involved the National Liberals' acceptance of Lehmkuhl's formulation and of the introduction of the Roman Catholic concept of separation as an alternative to divorce. In return, the Centre agreed to fall in with the National Liberals over the law of association. This entailed a return to the system adopted by the second commission, which allowed the state to deny juristic personality to associations pursuing political, social, or religious goals. Last minute attempts by Roon to win the Centre party back failed, and the committee accepted the compromise without great difficulty on 8 June.[42]

[41] HA Cologne, Bachem Papers 7—'Verhandlungen'; Heller, reports of 25 Apr. and 9 June, BHStA Munich, MA 76730.

[42] For Bachem's lengthy correspondence with Lehmkuhl, see HA Cologne, Bachem Papers 8; details of the negotiations with Nieberding and the National Liberals are to be found in Bachem Papers 7; cf. the published material in H. Conrad, 'Der parlamentarische Kampf um die Zivilehe bei Einführung des Bürgerlichen Gesetzbuches für das Deutsche Reich', *Historisches Jahrbuch*, 62 (1952), 474-93, and K. Bachem, *Vorgeschichte, Geschichte*

As might be expected, this compromise was somewhat unpopular. As long as it held, the parliamentary success of the Code was assured, and those groups which desired substantial reforms were outmanœuvred. The newspapers began to talk scathingly of 'horse-trading', and *Vorwärts* claimed that the compromise 'documented the moral and intellectual depths of our bourgeois society'. Those, like Eugen Richter and the anti-Semites, who opposed the compromise renewed the campaign to delay the final decision until the autumn.[43] By this time, however, the majority on the other side was too strong, and the way was clear for the Code to be accepted with one or two minor amendments on 1 July.

By early June, Nieberding seems to have won his battle to instil in the parties the necessary 'resignation' so that an admittedly imperfect Code might be accepted. In any case, the parties were remarkably circumspect in their criticisms, with only the Social Democrats attempting anything more than piecemeal improvements. As Spahn pointed out, the Reichstag committee raised no issue which had not already been considered in the second commission. One informed commentator considered that the Code had come back from the Reichstag very much in the form it possessed when it was presented, and that this said a great deal about its qualities. Very few supporters of the work of the second commission considered that the Reichstag had amended too much or actually worsened matters.[44] As we have seen, this state of affairs was largely the product of the successful completion of a compromise which headed off effective further debate. On the other hand, the debates which did take place suggest answers to a number of important questions. Why, for example, was the influence of the Code's major critics and their followers in the pressure groups so slight? How susceptible to pressure from below were the power-brokers in the party leaderships? How constrained were the parties by inherited ideological traditions?

Of all the parties in the Reichstag, the National Liberals were, of course, the most closely associated with the campaign for legal unity. By the 1890s the party was finding it difficult to cope with the demands of national politics, and seemed in acute danger of losing more and more

und Politik der Deutschen Zentrumspartei, v (Cologne, 1929), ch. 5.; Heller, report of 8 June 1896, BHStA Munich, MA 76730.

[43] *Vorwärts*, 9 June 1896, 1. *Beilage*.

[44] *SBRT*, 19 June 1896, p. 2726C-D (Spahn); G. v. Buchka, 'Das Bürgerliche Gesetzbuch nach den Beschlüssen des Reichstages', *DJZ* 1 (1896), p. 308; for one critical view, see M. Stenglein, 'Epilog zur Beratung des Bürgerlichen Gesetzbuches', *DJZ* 1 (1896), pp. 264 f.

sections of its electorate to opponents on the right and left. Its problems lay, above all, in the social and regional heterogeneity of that electorate, and by the mid-1890s the party seemed to be irrevocably split into factions representing different interests. The response of the party leadership to this problem tended to emphasize the party's nationalist credentials, and to deny any exclusive association between the party and particular social or economic interests. Such sentiments were a standard feature of National Liberal politics in these years.[45]

One recent writer has correctly pointed to the integrative function of nationalism in a party that was increasingly unable to agree on material issues.[46] Support for the Civil Code was obviously well suited to perform this function. When making preparations for the Delegates' Congress in February 1896, the party secretary suggested a debate on the Code and added, '[i]f the Code has been passed by then, the Reichstag can be proud of its co-operation. If it is not yet completed, our party must once more place great emphasis on its necessity for the nation.' In July, a memorandum from the same official made the point even more clearly. The party's role as the representative of the national interest, both in the past and in the future, must be recognized. However matters of detail were to be judged, both the Civil Code and the stock exchange law must be recognized as important contributions to the strengthening of the Reich. At the same time, he could not avoid referring to doubts within the party about the alliance with the Centre which, some feared, had strengthened political Catholicism at the expense of liberalism.[47]

The National Liberals were therefore keen to grasp the political opportunities offered by the debates on the Code, which offered a welcome distraction from their normal internal disagreements. The two main spokesmen (Enneccerus and Cuny) were both academic lawyers with particular interests, Enneccerus being concerned mainly with the common law and Cuny with the French law, which still operated in his native Rhineland. On the few occasions when these spokesmen proposed

[45] On the problems faced by the party in the mid-1890s, see especially A. J. O'Donnell, 'National Liberalism and the Mass Politics of the German Right, 1890-1907', Ph.D. thesis (Princeton, 1974), pp. 226 ff.; for other examples of the typical National Liberal response to these divisions, see J. J. Sheehan, *German Liberalism in the Nineteenth Century* (Chicago/London, 1978), 248-53.

[46] H. A. Winkler, 'Vom linken zum rechten Nationalismus. Der deutsche Liberalismus in der Krise von 1878/79', *Geschichte und Gesellschaft*, 4 (1978), 27 f.

[47] Carl Patzig to Marquardsen, 10 Feb. 1896 and Patzig's 'Memorandum betr. Delegirtentag 1896', 30 July 1896, ZStA Potsdam, Marquardsen Papers 45, fos. 38 f., 46 f.

reforms, they were almost always concerned with these special legal interests and devoid of party political significance.[48] For the most part, however, the party saw itself as the main defender of the Code in the form accepted by the government. Enneccerus in particular played a leading role in fighting proposed amendments, particularly those suggested by the Social Democrats. So keen was he in this task that Bennigsen had to intervene to cut short his frequent speeches.[49]

The National Liberals were thus likely to vote for virtually any code that would be acceptable to the Reichstag and Bundesrat. There was, however, a further feature of National Liberalism, which made it easier for them to find agreement with the Centre party, namely the strength in the party of the Christian, moral conception of marriage. To be sure, the party was among the keenest defenders of obligatory civil marriage, a standpoint rooted in the politics of the 1860s and 1870s. Yet this had far more to do with the party's interest in denying the church forms of temporal power than with any deep-seated belief that marriage was in essence a purely temporal, civil phenomenon which was subject to the same principles as any other legal contract. This emerged very clearly in connection with the question of divorce. In September 1895, the *National-Zeitung* argued that liberals must accept the validity of divorce under certain circumstances, but continued: '[o]ne can be liberal and still take very seriously the idea of marriage as a moral institution, which should be able to withstand powerful shocks.' Gottlieb Planck, the National Liberal lawyer who was more than anyone else responsible for the Code's family law, agreed wholeheartedly with that point of view. His drafts of Book 4 of the code (family law) were based on the fundamental principle of the 'moral nature of marriage', which was superior to the private wills of the individuals concerned. Thus he argued that, '[w]ith regard to divorce, the Code is based on the view that marriage is a moral order superior to the arbitrary wills of the married couple and thus can never be broken by a contract between them.' On that basis he proceeded to produce a divorce law which has been described as 'the most restrictive that was politically conceivable'.[50]

[48] F. Hartung, *Jurist unter vier Reichen* (Berlin, 1971), 12; P. Spahn, 'Cuny, Ludwig von', *ADB* xlvii (Leipzig, 1903), p. 578; cf. their opposition to each other on the question of the law of property in marriage in the committee meeting on 8 May; Heller, report of 8 May, BHStA Munich, MA 76730.

[49] Jagemann, report of 25 Feb. 1896, GLA Karlsruhe, Abt. 233/13996.

[50] *National-Zeitung*, 27 Sept. 1895; G. Planck, *Die rechtliche Stellung der Frau nach dem Bürgerlichen Gesetzbuch* (Göttingen, 1899), 6; D. Blasius, 'Scheidung und Scheidungsrecht im 19. Jahrhundert. Zur Sozialgeschichte der Familie', *HZ* 241 (1985),

There was in fact considerable National Liberal support for moderate Catholic demands in the sphere of family law. Cuny and Planck had unsuccessfully attempted to find a compromise on the question of divorce in the second commission, and Spahn later wrote of Cuny's accommodating attitude towards Catholic feelings about the law of marriage. Cuny clearly came quickly to the opinion that an understanding between the National Liberals and the Centre was essential to the success of the Code. He informed Spahn in late 1895 or early 1896 that his party might accept the Roman Catholic concept of separation but was very dubious about breaking with obligatory civil marriage. When Bachem proposed a motion introducing separation as an alternative to divorce, Cuny supported it as a return to pre-1875 Rhenish law, and Bennigsen was prepared to agree in order to ease the passage of the Code through the Reichstag.[51]

It seems very likely that the emphasis on marriage as a Christian, moral institution helped to justify concessions to Catholic views on family law in the National Liberal party. In the end, the Centre party obtained what Spahn had originally considered to be the minimum acceptable concessions. Indeed, it is quite possible that the compromise might have been hammered out much earlier, had it not been for the hopes aroused in some Catholic circles by the Conservatives' campaign for optional civil marriage. The basis of the eventual compromise lay in the willingness of men in both the National Liberal and Centre parties—particularly Cuny and Spahn—to moderate surviving antagonisms between the main protagonists of the *Kulturkampf* in order to take credit for the rapid completion of the Code. As has been seen, there were many within the National Liberal camp who were distinctly uneasy about these concessions. That unease was something that Bismarck's supporters attempted to play on when attacking the government in the spring and early summer. Yet, on the whole, the National Liberals had far too much at stake in the completion of the Code to have allowed minor concessions to the Catholics to stand in their way.

p. 345. See in general H. Dörner, *Industrialiserung und Familienrecht* (Berlin, 1974), pp. 89 ff., 108 ff. and especially E. Kauffmann, 'Das "sittliche Wesen der Ehe" als Massstab für die inhaltliche Bestimmung der Normen bei der Kodifizierung des Bürgerlichen Gesetzbuches', in *Rechtsgeschichte und Kulturgeschichte. Festschrift für Adalbert Erler* (Aalen, 1976), pp. 649-62.

51 Jacubezky, report no. 113, n.d. (Feb. 1894), BHStA Munich, MJu 16115; for Spahn's views about Cuny, see *ADB* xlvii, p. 578; see Spahn's note on his conversation with Cuny and the record of a conversation between Bachem and Nieberding on 7 Dec. 1895, in which the latter said much the same thing about Cuny; HA Cologne, Bachem Papers 7; Heller, report of 6 May 1896, BHStA Munich, MA 76730.

The same was not necessarily true of the Centre. Writing in the impeccably Protestant *Preussische Jahrbücher* in July, Hans Delbrück astutely commented on what had taken place:

> The Centre has done even more for the Civil Code than the National Liberals because it had many more obstacles to overcome in its own camp. What the National Liberals did was their duty and obligation in line with the best inherited traditions of the party. The Centre, on the other hand, has played for high political stakes and has brilliantly carried it off.[52]

Sources normally more sympathetic to Catholic interests came to very much the same conclusion. Looking back a decade later, Spahn's son considered the Code to have been 'an extraordinary test of the political character of the party' and regarded it as Ernst Lieber's greatest success.[53] For Lieber's supporters in the party, the Code provided the first major sign that the party was capable of operating responsibly as a party of government. Nor was the political significance of the completion of the Code lost on contemporaries. As Wilhelm von Kardorff said in his last speech on the Code: 'The Centre is now the decisive party in the Reichstag and will remain so all the while the Right can agree more easily with it than with the Left, and while the Left can agree with the Centre more easily than with us.'[54] As the subsequent history of the Reich showed, this feature of Reichstag politics was to make it very difficult for successive chancellors to rule without the support of the Centre.

Modern historians agree that Lieber, Spahn, and Karl Bachem were the major representatives of a new generation of middle-class Catholic leaders who came to power after a brief skirmish with the aristocratic old guard after Windthorst's death in March 1891. The policies dear to these men reflected very different preconceptions from those which had dominated the 1870s and 1880s. In particular, the pursuit of *Parität*—equality of opportunity in public employment for Catholics—became the hallmark of the policies of this new generation of leaders in the 1890s. In some senses, of course, this was a confessional issue, though not one that concerned the power of the Catholic church as such. Lieber's policy was geared towards overcoming the pariah status

[52] H. Delbrück, 'Politische Korrespondenz', 24 July 1896, *Preussische Jahrbücher*, 85 (1896), 397 f.
[53] M. Spahn, *Das deutsche Zentrum* (Mainz/Munich, 1906), 101 f.; id., *Ernst Lieber als Parlamentarier* (Gotha, 1906), p. 49.
[54] *SBRT*, 30 June 1896, p. 3042C.

enjoyed by middle-class Catholics in the eyes of the establishment and, not least, the Kaiser. Implicit in such a programme was the down-playing of purely confessional interests and a concern to prove that Catholics were as capable, as national, etc. as their Protestant counterparts. It was this concern which led Lieber to pursue a pro-government line on such matters as Caprivi's trade treaties. Lieber was also the first of the Centre's leaders to see the political potential of supporting the Kaiser's beloved fleet plans. None of this was uncontroversial within the Centre party, and trouble repeatedly flared up over economic and taxation issues in the Rhineland, Westphalia, and Bavaria. It was in this atmosphere of acute disunity over the party's true goals that Lieber, Spahn, and Bachem had to develop the Centre's policy towards the Civil Code.[55]

David Blackbourn has shown that the Centre was vulnerable to many of the same pressures as its Protestant counterparts. This was particularly true with regard to two of the great issues of the 1890s—the Russian trade treaty and the plan to build a battle fleet. The first issue saw the mobilization of the party's agrarian factions in the Rhineland and Bavaria in favour of renewed protection; the second aroused the hostility of many sections of the party on account of the implied rise in taxation. The years between 1894 and 1896 saw major battles between the party's leadership and an increasingly strident agrarian movement, whose most threatening manifestation originated in the Rhineland. Particular difficulties for the leadership were created by the Rhenish Peasants' Association, led by Baron Felix von Loë-Terporten.[56]

These party difficulties did not lead the Centre to espouse agrarian demands in relation to the Civil Code, in order to head off men like Loë. It is true that Gröber did raise the question of the multiplicity of mortgage forms in the committee, which would, he claimed, lead to greater indebtedness and 'mobilization' of landed property. But Gröber's

---

[55] In general, see D. Blackbourn, *Class, Religion and Local Politics in Wilhelimine Germany. The Centre Party in Würtembertg before 1914* (New Haven/London, 1980), ch. 1; R. Morsey, 'Die deutschen Katholiken und der Nationalstaat zwischen Kulturkampf und dem ersten Weltkrieg', *Historisches Jahrbuch*, 90 (1970), 48–59; J. K. Zeender, *The German Center Party 1890–1906* (Philadelphia, 1976), chs. 3–5; W. Loth, *Katholiken im Kaiserreich. Der politische Katholizismus in der Krise des wilhelminischen Deutschlands* (Düsseldorf, 1984), 51 ff.; J. C. Hunt, ' "Die Parität in Preussen" (1899): Hintergrund, Verlauf und Ergebnis eines Aktionsprogramms der Zentrumspartei', *Historisches Jahrbuch*, 102 (1982), 418–34.

[56] See in general Blackbourn, *Class, Religion and Local Politics*, pp. 44–7; D. W. Hendon, 'The Center Party and the Agrarian Interest in Germany, 1890–1914', Ph.D. thesis (Emory University, Atlanta, 1976), pp. 53 ff., 371 ff., 395 ff.

motion was largely the product of south German hostility to the extreme complexity and innovativeness of the Code's mortgage law, and he certainly did not adopt the views of the radical agrarians with regard, for example, to annuity charges.[57] Rather, the effect of the rise of Catholic agrarianism was to place confessional issues at the centre of political debate within the party. Thus, at the Catholic Congress in 1893 Loë called for the Centre to be an openly Roman Catholic party— a move which was correctly interpreted by the 'Cologne group' around Bachem as an attempt to restrict party unity to religious issues. In the following years this became a major feature of the politics of Catholic agrarianism in the Rhineland. By 1895–6 there were clearly drawn battle-lines between those like Bachem and Lieber, who were convinced that the Centre had to move beyond the defence of immediate Catholic interests, and those like Loë, who saw the defence of those interests as the essence of the Centre party. The implication of the latter position was, of course, that the party could have a free vote on social and economic questions.[58]

The relevance of these developments to the Civil Code lay in the response of sections of the Roman Catholic community to the Centre leadership's policy of compromise on family law. In particular, the acceptance of obligatory civil marriage was seen by many as a betrayal of Catholic principles. As the Bavarian centre party leader, Franz Schädler, put it to Lieber, 'even sensible people want to create a scandal about civil marriage.' Newspapers connected with Loë, such as the *Deutsche Reichszeitung* and the *Rheinische Volksstimme*, began a vigorous campaign against the Centre's participation in the compromise on this vital issue. When it became clear that they had been outmanœuvred, they concentrated their attacks on the speed with which the Code had been rushed through the Reichstag. Interestingly, they joined Bismarck in castigating this as making 'a mockery of parliamentarism' through blatant opportunism.[59]

[57] *Bericht der Reichstags-Kommission*, pp. 75 ff.; Heller, report of 22 Apr. 1896, BHStA Munich, MA 76730.
[58] Hendon, 'Center Party and the Agrarian Interest', p. 359; K. Müller, 'Zentrumspartei und agrarische Bewegung im Rheinland 1882–1903', in K. Repgen and S. Skalweit (eds.), *Spiegel der Geschichte. Festgabe für Max Braubach zum 10. April 1964* (Münster, 1964), 828–57; R. J. Ross, *Beleaguered Tower. The Dilemma of Political Catholicism in Wilhelmine Germany* (Notre Dame, 1976), 43 f.
[59] Schädler to Lieber, 28 May 1896, HA Cologne, Bachem Papers 8; *Deutsche Reichszeitung*, 10, 20 June and 17 July 1896; *Westfälischer Merkur*, 23 June 1896; *Rheinische Volksstimme*, 23, 27, and 30 June 1896 (quotation from the last of these).

The opposition to the leadership's policies came from two directions: the Catholic fundamentalist groups in Mainz and Bonn, whose views found expression in *Die Katholik* and the *Deutsche Reichszeitung* respectively, and the agrarians around Loë, whose organ was the *Rheinische Volksstimme*. Bachem's constant fear was that they would attempt to open separate negotiations with the papacy, and he was consequently keen to secure the Vatican's agreement to the party's policies. In fact, Bachem had already secured the agreement of the papal nuncio in Munich that Catholic interests in Germany were best protected by a party whose political activities were not merely restricted to the confessional sphere.[60] Nevertheless, the attitude of the Vatican was clearly of some importance; the Centre would have found it practically impossible to vote for the Code against the explicit opinion of the papacy.

Both the Prussian and Bavarian governments approached the Curia in the spring of 1896. Cardinal Rampolla told the Prussian ambassador that the papacy would support a certain 'toning down' of the clauses relating to the law of marriage. On two separate occasions, the Bavarian ambassador gained the impression that divorce was the principal issue as far as the papacy was concerned. Both the Pope himself and Rampolla avoided any reference to the thorny issue of obligatory civil marriage, and the Bavarian government was not keen to push the matter. Meanwhile, direct negotiations had begun between the Centre and Ajuti, the papal nuncio in Munich. By March, the Papacy seems to have come to the view that, while the duties of Catholics with regard to marriage were quite clear, it had no intention of attempting to influence the Centre's final vote on the Code. A key intermediary was Cardinal Kopp, a churchman renowned for his 'nationalism', who advised Rampolla against making any official pronouncement on the code for fear that the Vatican would be accused of interfering in the worldly affairs of a foreign country. He also emphasized the positive advantages of the new Code for Germany's Catholics.[61]

Bachem's principal concern in his correspondence with Ajuti was to

[60] Bachem to Ajuti, 15 July 1896, HA Cologne, Bachem Papers 6; on the press controversies in general, see Bachem's scathing comments in *Zentrumspartei*, v, pp. 443 f.; on the party going beyond confessional interests, see the notes on a conversation between Bachem and Ajuti on 29 Aug. 1895, HA Cologne, Bachem Papers 15.

[61] Bülow, reports of 28 Feb. and 2 Mar. 1896, GStA Berlin-Dahlmen, Rep. 84a 11834, fos. 603 ff.; Cetto, reports of 1 March and 4 Apr. 1896, BHStA Munich, MA 76728; Ajuti to Bachem, 11 Mar. 1896, HA Cologne, Bachem Papers 6; Kopp to Lieber, 14 May 1896, Bachem Papers 8. On Kopp, see M. L. Anderson, *Windthorst. A Political Biography*

make the political aspects of the question clear. In late May and early June, he took care to explain the political necessity of completing the Code rapidly, especially in view of the increasing feud over the matter between Bismarck and the Kaiser. He had no doubts that the political strength of the Centre party hung in the balance:

> If the Code is not rapidly completed, the Centre will be held responsible. The Kaiser, who has hitherto had to consider our views, will attempt to carry out his policies with the aid of other parties; he will be provoked by others to oppose the Centre. In the country, Prince Bismarck will revive his old accusations about the weakness of this Reichstag and the inability of the Centre to take the lead, and the position of Baron von Buol as President of the Reichstag will become untenable. If, on the other hand, the Code is completed this summer, the position of the Centre and of Buol will be greatly reinforced and the Kaiser will always look to the Centre for support.[62]

Meanwhile Bachem consulted August Lehmkuhl for help with the production of a theological justification for the Centre's stance. As we have seen, Lehmkuhl played an important role in formulating a compromise acceptable to the Centre, and he was later to give the party valuable support in the Catholic press. In return, Bachem attempted to intercede with both Hohenlohe and Bennigsen to secure the repeal of the legislation which had expelled the Jesuits from Germany. However, Bachem's protestations about the undoubted patriotism of the Jesuits as exemplified by Lehmkuhl fell on deaf ears.[63]

The support of the papacy and prominent theologians was clearly important in defeating the leadership's opponents. Some, like Rintelen, refused to be mollified and, as Lieber was later to admit, the Centre's policies led him to be considered 'a deliberate heretic' in Mainz. Nevertheless, all the Centre deputies who attended the party meeting on the subject in early June accepted the leadership's views, with the exception of Rintelen. The agrarian opposition had effectively been tamed and the fundamentalists outmanœuvred by the papacy's refusal

(Oxford, 1981), 300, 324 f., and Morsey, 'Die deutschen Katholiken und der Nationalstaat', pp. 46 f.

[62] Bachem to Ajuti, 14 June; see also Bachem to Ajuti, 27 May 1896, HA Cologne, Bachem Papers 6.

[63] See the correspondence between Bachem and Lehmkuhl in HA Cologne, Bachem Papers 8; A. Lehmkuhl, 'Das neue Bürgerliche Gesetzbuch des Deutschen Reiches und seine bürgerliche Eheschliessung', *Stimmen aus Maria-Laach* (1896), Heft 7, 125–39; Bachem to Hohenlohe, 6 July 1896, reprinted in Hohenlohe, *Denkwürdigkeiten aus der Reichskanzlerzeit*, pp. 241 f.; Bachem to Bennigsen, 6 July 1896, reprinted in Oncken, *Bennigsen*, ii. 600 f.

to give them a lead.[64] The evidence is that a majority of prominent Catholics supported the leadership's view that as much had been achieved as possible, and that the Code marked a substantial improvement on existing law from a Catholic point of view.[65]

To this line of argument was added the endless assertions of the great contribution the Centre had made to the strength of the Reich, which filled the pages of the *Kölnische Volkszeitung* and similar newspapers in July 1896 and again in January 1900, when the Code came into force.[66] And why not? Given the political situation in 1896, it is highly unlikely that the government's policy of hurrying the Code through the Reichstag before the summer recess would have been practicable without the agreement of the Centre party. Moreover, Catholics had played a disproportionately important role in the preparation of the Civil Code. As one contemporary put it to Planck: '[it is] remarkable that the work was concluded under a Catholic Chancellor, a Catholic minister of justice and a Catholic president of the Reichstag.'[67] He might have added the names of Pape and Spahn as well. The irony was, of course, that the completion of the great national work whose origins lay in the period of the *Kulturkampf* should have owed so much to the political and legal skills of Germany's Catholic middle classes.

The problems experienced by the leadership of the Centre party were undoubtedly greatly exacerbated by the proposal of part of the Conservative party to introduce optional civil marriage. The Conservatives had a reputation in Berlin for 'indifference' to the success of the Code, and it may well have been this that convinced National Liberals like Cuny that a deal would have to be done with the Centre.[68] In the end, Nieberding's early prediction that the Conservative's internal divisions might prove to be an advantage to the government were justified. The party's vacillations over civil marriage and its seeming incapacity to proceed in a politically responsible way destroyed the only

---

[64] Lieber to Brentano, 4 Sept. 1896, quoted in Zeender, *German Center Party*, p. 59 n. 97; Bachem to Ajuti, 14 June 1896, HA Cologne, Bachem Papers 6; cf. Hendon, 'Center Party and the Agrarian Interest', pp. 406 f.

[65] See the resolution to this effect which was drafted by Bachem and accepted by the Catholic Congress at Dortmund in Sept. 1896, HA Cologne, Bachem Papers 16.

[66] *Kölnische Volkszeitung*, 2 July 1896 and 2 Jan. 1900.

[67] G. Claussen to Planck, 3 July 1896, NSUUB Göttingen Planck Papers IV/3, fo. 112. The reference to the Catholic minister of justice may have meant either Schönstedt or (more probably, but inexactly) Nieberding; both were Roman Catholics. See also Bachem, *Zentrumspartei*, v. 440.

[68] See Spahn's note to this effect in HA Cologne, Bachem Papers 7; cf. Nieberding's comments in the Prussian ministry of state on 18 May, Schubert, *Materialien*, p. 406.

prospect that its policies might win the day—i.e. through an alliance with the Centre.[69]

The debates on the Civil Code revealed that the Conservatives were deeply divided on the question of optional civil marriage. As we have seen, Buchka was a firm opponent of any fundamental change in the law, and he was not alone. When Roon's motion finally went to a vote in the Reichstag plenum, thirteen members of the party, including the editor of the *Kreuzzeitung*, Hermann Kropatschek, voted against it. Why then should influential elements in the party have repeatedly campaigned for a proposal which had no chance of support from the government, the other Protestant parties, or even from all of its own members?

The simple answer is, of course, the Conservatives' devotion to the cause of religion, especially the Lutheran church. Men like Roon and Pastor Martin Schall (the deputy for Potsdam-Ost Havelland) emphasized that obligatory civil marriage was 'an outgrowth of the heathen state', not to mention the French Revolution. On the basis of a number of devout speeches in the Reichstag, one author has concluded that Roon's motion was an expression of Prussian Protestant hostility to the Catholic Centre.[70] If that were the case, it would be difficult to explain the successive Conservative attempts to win the support of the Centre, and the well-documented willingness of some of the party's spokesmen to tailor their motions in accordance with Catholic wishes.

A more convincing explanation is suggested by the Conservatives' internal difficulties with the Christian-Social group around Stoecker. These difficulties had been present in latent form for years, but came to a head in 1895-6. The problem essentially lay in the irreconcilability of the Christian-Socials' demand for social reform on behalf of the lower orders and the interests of the landowners who made up the backbone of the Conservative party. Divisions became unreconcilable after 1894, when the Evangelical Social Congress, under the influence of Max Weber and Paul Göhre, drew attention to the situation of rural workers on East Elbian estates. The following year saw a Conservative pastor calling for the clergy to help with the organization of rural workers so

---

[69] Nieberding's speech to the justice committee of the Bundesrat, 7 Oct. 1895, reported on the same day by Heller, BHStA Munich, MA 76729; see the many vituperative comments about the Conservatives' unreliability and lack of political principle in HA Cologne, Bachem Papers 7.

[70] *SBRT*, 24 June 1896, pp. 2870D-2875A, 2880D-2886A; Brandt, 'Die politischen Parteien', p. 74.

as to allow them to escape from the influence of the Junkers.[71] These
developments were predictably unwelcome to the Junkers in the
Conservative party.

There is strong evidence that these difficulties led some Conservatives
to the view that optional civil marriage might be a means of limiting the
damage to the party. Stoecker and many of his followers left the party
in February, and it was precisely at this point that the campaign for
the Conservative motion was stepped up. Among the party newspapers
it was Heinrich Engel's *Reichsbote*, an organ which had since the 1880s
been closely connected with conservative social reform, which did most
to publicize the campaign. Significantly, the *Kreuzzeitung* opposed the
proposal on 1 March, but then supported it four days later. The editor
told Bosse that the only reason for the motion was to ensure the support
of the pastors for the party. The principal supporters of the motion,
especially Schall, were clearly close to Stöcker and the Christian-Socials,
and keen to win back the support of the pastors. Similar interpretations
of these events appeared in the non-Conservative press in the early
weeks of March. Moreover, the Conservative representatives on the
committee seem to have openly admitted to Nieberding that this was
the reason, and Manteuffel later reportedly said exactly the same thing
to Bachem.[72]

The question of optional civil marriage was thus closely linked to the
death-throes of the so-called Stoecker-Hammerstein group in the
Conservative party. This group had emerged in the 1880s around the
then editor of the *Kreuzzeitung*, Wilhelm von Hammerstein, in opposition
to the governmentalism of men like Helldorf and Manteuffel. In its call
for the creation of a conservative Volkspartei through a blend of
Christian social reform, radical *Mittelstandspolitik*, and anti-Semitism,

[71] See W. R. Ward, *Theology, Sociology and Politics. The German Protestant Social
Conscience* (Berne, 1979), 64-8; cf. P. W. Massing, *Rehearsal for Destruction. A Study of
Political Antisemitism in Imperial Germany* (New York, 1949), 118-34 and Düding, *Der
Nationalsoziale Verein. Der gescheiterte Versuch einer parteipolitischen Synthese von
Nationalismus, Sozialismus und Liberalismus* (Munich/Vienna, 1972), 22-6.
[72] On Engel and the *Reichsbote*, see J. N. Retallack, *Notables of the Right. The
Conservative Party and Political Mobilization in Germany, 1876-1918* (Boston, 1988), 57;
Kreuzzeitung, 1 and 5 Mar. 1896; on the campaign in general, see the large number of
press cuttings in ZStA Potsdam, RJM 3828; for Bosse, see minutes of the Prussian
ministry of state, 25 Mar. 1896, in Schubert, *Materialien*, p. 398; for Schall, see his
speech to the parish association of the commune of St Thomas, reported in *Deutsche
Tageszeitung*, 21 Mar. 1896; for other newspapers, see *Kölnische Zeitung*, 9 Mar. 1896;
Hamburgischer Correspondent, 14 Mar. 1896; Jagemann, report of 7 Mar. 1896, GLA
Karlsruhe, Abt. 233/13996; for Manteuffel, see HA Cologne, Bachem Papers 7,
'Verhandlungen'.

this group represented an attempt to break with the old traditions of governmental conservatism which had found expression in the *Kartell* of 1887. The years 1895–6, which saw the imprisonment of Hammerstein for fraud and the departure of the Christian-Socials, marked a painful turning-point in the internal history of the Conservative party, but there is evidence of continuing sympathy within the party for the views expounded by Stoecker and his followers. Prominent exponents of such views included Roon and Robert von Puttkamer, the former Prussian minister of the interior, who was reported to have signed a petition in favour of the restoration of optional civil marriage in early 1896.[73]

The Conservatives' attitude to agrarian questions strengthens the view that the party was only interested in the Code in so far as it impinged on the party's internal problems. The Conservatives were, of course, the main parliamentary representatives of the interests of agriculture. As we have seen, the Code had aroused a considerable amount of adverse comment in agrarian circles in the previous years. Yet the party was noticeably reticent on the subject of agrarian demands in the Reichstag. The *Kreuzzeitung*, which had given great support to Gierke's views in the years before 1896, became remarkably quiet on this subject once the parliamentary debates actually began. In the committee meeting of 22 April, when the multiplicity of mortgage forms came under attack, Buchka defended the Code's provisions so as not to create any difficulties for the government in the Reichstag.[74] This issue was, however, revived on the last day of debate by Bernhard von Ploetz, who proposed the abolition of the land charge (*Grundschuld*) This was only the second time that the language of the agrarian critics of the Code was heard in these debates. The land charge was, according to Ploetz, a Roman institution which was likely to further the 'mobilization' of landed property. The Code had failed to consider the many recent studies of the problems faced by landowners. In this area of the law, above all, he said, 'we would have wished that the Code had paid attention to the contemporary *Zeitgeist* and that it had not been merely a codification of existing laws'. Ploetz then announced that he would vote against the Code. This was too much for the Conservative establishment. The next speaker, Count von Mirbach-Sorquitten, declared his sympathy with the motion, which he had mysteriously

[73] See in general Retallack, *Notables of the Right*, ch. 9; for Roon's and Puttkamer's involvement, see ibid. 40; for Puttkamer's support of the petition, see the minutes of the Prussian ministry of state, 25 March 1896, in Schubert, *Materialien*, p. 400.

[74] Heller, report of 22 May 1896, BHStA Munich, MA 76730.

forgotten to propose in the second reading. He then withdrew the motion in order to avoid difficulties at this late stage. With this feeble attempt to lend support to the radical agrarians, the Conservative opposition to the Code ended.[75] In the end, Ploetz was one of only three Conservatives to vote against the code.

This evident lack of concern with the promotion of the broader interests of agriculture stood in ludicrous contrast to the amount of attention the Conservatives gave to the question of liability for damage caused by game animals. The main subject of a lengthy debate on 23 June was the question of whether or not hares should be included in the list of animals covered by the Code. Encouraged by the Prussian minister of agriculture, most Conservatives and Free Conservatives would have preferred the matter to have been left to the individual states. It was scarcely surprising that the debate was greeted by scorn and sarcasm from the left; when a compromise motion to remove the infamous hares was accepted by 178 votes to 69, *Vorwärts* commented that 'hares thus have almost three times as many friends in this Reichstag as do people'.[76]

On this and other issues, the Free Conservatives showed themselves to be divided. Their original representatives on the Reichstag committee, Baron von Gültlingen and Count Bernstorff, had both supported optional civil marriage and had therefore been replaced. The debate on Roon's motion on 24 June saw Bernstorff once again supporting the measure. In the end, two members of the party voted for it and four abstained, after Wilhelm von Kardorff had been forced to admit that the party's official stance was determined by the desire to avoid introducing problems for the Code. A similar argument had been used by Stumm on the subject of the liability for damages caused by game.[77]

Both Conservative parties were thus dissatisfied with certain features of the Code, but were nevertheless eventually prepared to accept the work despite its imperfections. This 'resignation' was easier for some

[75] *SBRT*, 1 July 1896, pp. 3072A–3073A; the only previous attempt to press for the demands of the agrarian critics of the Code came on 27 June, when Mirbach proposed that agricultural land be exempted from the operation of the 'compulsory portion'—i.e. the part of inheritance law which guaranteed financial payments out of the estate to certain designated relatives. This motion found support from the Free Conservatives but was dismissed without a formal division; *SBRT*, 27 June 1896, pp. 3015A–3016D.

[76] *Vorwärts*, 24 June 1896; cf. Mehring, 'Hasenrechtliches', pp. 420 f.; for the debates, see *SBRT*, 23 June 1896, pp. 2821C–2852C.

[77] *SBRT*, 24 June 1896, pp. 2876D–2877C, 2887A–C, 2899A–2900D; ibid., 23 June 1896, pp. 2843D–2844A.

than for others but, with the exception of the two Conservatives who
followed Ploetz into opposition, all either succumbed to the government's pressure, abstained, or stayed away on 1 July.[78] Whenever the
government threatened to allow the Code to fail if the Reichstag
persisted in pushing for unacceptable amendments, it was successful in
pulling enough deputies round. As Buchka had put it in the first
reading, 'we would not wish to take on the historical responsibility for
the failure of the Civil Code'.[79]

The importance of this sort of political calculation was apparent to
the left as well as the right. Eugen Richter, the leader of the Freisinnige
Volkspartei, was a renowned opponent of compromises on what he
believed to be liberal principles; in the words of one contemporary, he
was 'liberal doctrine in flesh and blood'.[80] Yet, in line with that lifelong
doctrinaire liberalism, he was also a supporter of the principle of legal
unity through codification. Thus the only real question was how far his
party would compromise in order to secure the Code's completion. Put
another way, the main question was not whether the Code would be
completed, but when it would be completed.[81]

As we have seen, Richter was among those who were opposed to the
restriction on the rights of the Reichstag implicit in the 'whipping
through' of the Code. As early as 1892 he had begun to develop a set
of left-liberal criticisms of the Code, which concentrated on the agrarians'
attempts to secure special treatment for their interests. In particular he
was hostile to the tendency of the codifiers to leave these problematic
areas of the law to the individual states. To Richter, equality and unity
were very much the same thing: '[t]he attempt to create special laws for
individual sections of the population not only removes the equality of
the civil law, but also the concept of unity.' True legal unity could, he
said, have no respect for differences of social class. The party thus
concentrated on the Code's propensity to ignore 'all the remnants of
feudal law [which survive] in the states' legislation'. In the words of
Julius Lenzmann, the party's principal spokesman in the Reichstag
committee, the Introductory Law, which enumerated these areas of the
law, constituted a 'list of the losses to the cause of legal unity'.[82]

---

[78] Among the Conservatives, there were 2 abstentions and 28 members were absent;
among the Free Conservatives, there was 1 abstention and 14 absentees—see Brandt,
'Die politischen Parteien', p. 165.   [79] *SBRT*, 3 Feb. 1896, p. 723A.

[80] F. Rachfahl, 'Eugen Richter und der Linksliberalismus im neuen Reiche', *Zeitschrift
für Politik*, 5 (1912), 372.   [81] As Richter said, *SBRT*, 23 June, p. 2846A.

[82] E. Richter, *Politisches ABC-Buch* (7th edn., Berlin, 1892), 62 ff.; ibid. (8th edn.,
Berlin, 1896), 96; Heller, report of 11 June 1896, BHStA Munich, MA 76730.

Such views linked the Freisinnige Volkspartei with the radical liberal tradition in Germany, which saw legal unification as a means of completing the destruction of archaic, 'feudal' elements in the legal system. Another issue in which this connection was apparent was the private law of associations, which Lenzmann described as the most important part of the Code as far as his party was concerned. The party campaigned in vain for the extension of the system of normative conditions to all associations, including those representing occupational groups. In this the left-liberals found a certain amount of common ground with the Social Democrats. On the other hand, attempts by the latter party to include domestic servants within the system of compulsory sickness insurance found no support from the Freisinnige Volkspartei, which saw in the proposal an example of the 'state socialism' which it had always abhorred.[83]

In general the Freisinnige Volkspartei stayed true to its radical traditions. On only one issue—the restoration of the right of divorce on account of the incurable insanity of one of the partners in a marriage—were the party's proposals accepted. Yet, despite this lack of success, it eventually voted unanimously in favour of the Code. On one issue—the liability of the state for the actions of its employees—it even deserted its traditional principles after an appeal by Nieberding. As with the conservative parties, reservations were eventually overcome by the overall advantages of legal unity and an insistence that 'the Code was not the end but the beginning of the reform of our modern law'.[84]

This tendency to accept the advantages of legal unification was even more pronounced in the other left-liberal party, the Freisinnige Vereinigung. Its main spokesmen—Hugo Schröder and Heinrich Rickert—expressed doubts about the Code's law of association, supported the women's movement on the law of marriage, and rejected Germanist criticisms of the Code. However, Schröder eventually accepted the compromise on the law of association and was prepared to vote for the introduction of the Roman Catholic separation as an alternative to divorce. This greater pliability led Franz Mehring to accuse the party of leaning towards the National Liberals.[85]

[83] *SBRT*, 19 June 1896, pp. 2735B–2737D; *Bericht der Reichstags-Kommission*, pp. 47 ff.

[84] *SBRT*, 24 June 1896, pp. 2860C–2863A; cf. Heller, reports of 15 April and 6 June 1896, BHStA Munich, MA 76730 and *Bericht der Reichstags-Kommission*, pp. 64 ff.; *Freisinnige Zeitung*, 3 July 1896.

[85] *SBRT*, 3 Feb. 1896, pp. 723A–725C; Heller, report of 8 June 1896, BHStA Munich, MA 76730; F. Mehring, 'Hasenrechtliches', *Neue Zeit*, xiv/2 (1895–6), 419.

The reasons for the party's approach to the Code emerged clearly from Rickert's closing speech on 30 June. Denying that laws were the proper way of developing new *Weltanschauungen*, he revealed the extent to which Nieberding had won the day with his emphasis on legal unity as a good in itself, coupled with minor improvements in the existing law:

legal unity is now the first priority; afterwards the battle for improvements will be far easier than if we had several dozen codes to contend with. It is precisely this unification of existing law which is the great step forward, especially in view of the numerous small improvements which it contains.[86]

With that, the government had succeeded in gaining the support of all three liberal parties, the Centre party, and most of the two conservative parties for the Code. All of these groups recognized the advantages of legal unity, and the Code was in any case generally seen as an improvement on existing law. In that context, the response of the Social Democrats could have no real bearing on the eventual outcome.

In contrast to the other parties, the Social Democrats attempted to use the opportunity to push through major revisions of the work of the second commission, particularly in the field of labour law. However, as we have seen, the party consistently emphasized its willingness to participate positively in the completion of the Code and the flood of motions proposed by Stadthagen and Frohme testified to their seriousness of purpose. The time-consuming nature of the debates on these motions exasperated men like Bachem, and competent (if undoubtedly prejudiced) observers such as Langfeld considered that the Social Democrats were attempting to introduce a socialist law. Yet this was constantly denied by the party's spokesmen. Other commentators, such as Rudolf Stammler, noted that the party had constant recourse to arguments concerning 'justice' (*Gerechtigkeit*), a concept which was hardly the invention of Second International historical materialism.[87] Nor was the Social Democratic party immune from the sort of calculations which helped to determine the attitudes of the other parties. The party's spokesmen were well aware of the benefits to the working classes of a Civil Code, however imperfect. Yet in the end the Social Democrats were the only sizeable party to vote against the Code.

[86] *SBRT*, 30 June 1896, p. 3045A.
[87] Langfeld, *Mein Leben*, p. 142; R. Stammler, *Die Bedeutung der deutschen Bürgerlichen Gesetzbuches für den Fortschritt der Kultur* (Halle, 1900), 10 f.

One prominent school of thought with regard to the evolution of the Social Democratic party has emphasized the dichotomy between its theory and practice. On the one hand, the party held fast to a theory which stressed the inevitability of the coming socialist revolution, and its rhetoric was tailored accordingly. On the other, the party in practice pursued increasingly reformist goals, especially as the weight of the trade union movement and the party bureaucracy grew. In a sense, this distinction between revolutionary theory and reformist practice corresponded to the two halves of the Erfurt Programme of 1891. According to this line of argument, the function of the party's Marxist rhetoric was integrative, in that it sought to overcome the severe disagreements between the different strands of thought within the party.[88]

At first sight, the views expressed by the party's spokesmen seem to fit very well into this type of analysis. The speeches of Stadthagen and Bebel in particular were full of rhetorical assertions of the inevitability of the revolution and of the limited, class-bound, 'bourgeois' nature of the Code. They then proceeded to concentrate, as did the principal socialist newspapers, on practical improvements to the Code from the point of view of the working classes. The final rejection of the Code might then be the result of the fact that only six out of a possible ninety-four socialist proposals were adopted. An alternative possibility would be that the party repeatedly attempted to amend government legislation, while voting against it on principle in the end.

Closer consideration of the proposals put forward by the Social Democrats reveals the debt they owed to the radical liberal tradition. On the law of associations, they attempted to institute the system of 'free creation of corporations', abolish the restrictions on the right of political associations to join together, and remove the law relating to trade unions from the legislative competence of the individual states. Needless to say, all these proposals were rejected. The party then supported the more moderate Centre party/left-liberal motion, which for

[88] Among the classic works which adopt this argument are E. Matthias, 'Kautsky und der Kautskyanismus. Die Funktion der Ideologie in der deutschen Sozialdemokratie vor dem ersten Weltkriege', in I. Fetscher (ed.), *Marxismusstudien*, ii (Tübingen 1957), 151–97; G. A. Ritter, *Die Arbeiterbewegung im Wilhelminischen Reich* (Berlin, 1959); S. Miller, *Das Problem der Freiheit im Sozialismus* (Frankfurt, 1964); H.-J. Steinberg, *Sozialismus und deutsche Sozialdemokratie. Zur Ideologie der Partei vor dem 1. Weltkrieg* (Bonn/Bad Godesberg, 1967).

a time offered the possibility of an alliance with other parties. When that was overturned by the compromise of early June, the Social Democrats were once more isolated. The party's approach to the law of associations was obviously a reflection of its self-interest. Hostility to this aspect of the legal system was only to be expected, given the government's tendency to manipulate the law against the labour movement, whose lack of the right to own property seems to have caused considerable problems for socialist organizations.[89] However, Stadthagen went on to boast that the labour movement would be quite capable of coming to terms with unfavourable legislation. The real point was, he said, that the law was an indication that the state regarded its citizens as politically immature and refused to recognize their true social and economic interests.[90] On a range of other issues—the liability of the state for the actions of its officials, the legal position of women, and the breaches of the principle of legal unity contained in the 'reservations' of areas of the law to the individual states—the Social Democrats adopted positions which reflected this debt to the radical liberal tradition. On occasion, as with the proposal to remove the indivdual's right to use force in defence of personal rights, the party attempted to justify its position in terms of the workers' interests. On the other hand, many of these proposals went far beyond what was demanded by the immediate interests of the workers.[91] This emerged most clearly in the discussions on family law.

The Social Democrats were among the most determined opponents of any attack on the principle of obligatory civil marriage. Bebel attempted to give the argument a socialist twist by connecting civil marriage (*bürgerliche Ehe*) to bourgeois society (*bürgerliche Gesellschaft*), but most of his speech was devoted to an attack on Conservative tactics. Furthermore, when the debate turned to the law of property in marriage he was forced to admit that the labour movement had no direct interest in the question at all, arguing that working-class women had no interest in the fate of the property which they brought into the marriage. Rather, the party's reform proposals were motivated by the general interest in justice for all, and the desire to remove personal inequalities and

---

[89] *Vorwärts*, 13 Aug. 1895; in general, see A. Hall, 'By Other Means: The Legal Struggle against the SPD in Wilhelmine Germany', *Historical Journal*, 17 (1974), 365–86.

[90] *SBRT*, 19 June 1896, pp. 2745A–2746B.

[91] The party's proposals are discussed in detail in Brandt, 'Die politischen Parteien', pp. 16–52; cf. Martiny, *Integration oder Konfrontation?*, pp. 64 ff.

relations of dependence.[92] Clara Zetkin insisted that the establishment of legal equality for women was a valuable step towards political change, but it is difficult to believe that this was the really decisive consideration for the party leadership.[93] As was the case in the debate on the law relating to damages done by game, the party showed itself to be far closer to the traditions of radical liberalism than were any of the liberal parties, with the possible exception of Richter's Freisinnige Volkspartei.

There was, however, another side to the coin. In the field of labour law, the Social Democrats were concerned to introduce extensive changes in the interests of the workers. These proposals included the introduction of a comprehensive set of clauses governing all types of labour contract, including those which regulated the conditions of domestic servants, agricultural workers, and miners. The motions involved radical reform of the system adopted by the Code, in that the law relating to such categories of worker had been deliberately excluded from the Code by the various commissions. Such exclusions had been justified either because of regional variations (as in the case of the law of domestic servants) or because of the distinction between public and private law (as in the case of the miners). When Frohme called for the inclusion of certain areas of the Industrial Code (*Gewerbeordnung*), the Social Democrats' attack on the Code's minimalist definition of the civil law was apparent. Needless to say, the proposals were rejected with two minor exceptions. Most of the Reichstag deputies believed that the protection of the working classes had no place in the nation's Civil Code. In the case of the law relating to domestic servants, even those like Gröber who were sympathetic saw special legislation as a much better way of achieving this goal.[94]

Gröber's views on this matter were in line with the general theory of legislation, which we have encountered repeatedly in this account—

---

[92] *SBRT*, 24 June 1896, pp. 2877D-2880C, and 25 June 1896, pp. 2923D-2926C. The SPD's proposals on family law are discussed from a Marxist perspective in W. Plat, 'Die Stellung der deutschen Sozialdemokratie zum Grundsatz der Gleichberechtigung der Frau auf dem Gebiet des Familienrechts bei der Schaffung des Bürgerlichen Gesetzbuches des Deutschen Reiches', Jur. Diss. (Berlin-GDR, 1966).

[93] See Zetkin's speech to the party congress at Breslau in 1895, *Protokolle über die Verhandlungen des Parteitages der SPD zu Breslau* (Berlin, 1895), 89 ff. Zetkin's views are discussed in R. J. Evans, *Sozialdemokratie und Frauenemanzipation im deutschen Kaiserreich* (Berlin/Bonn, 1979), 98 ff.

[94] *SBRT*, 22 June 1896, pp. 2799B-C; cf. T. Vormbaum, *Politik und Gesinderecht im 19. Jahrhundert (vornehmlich in Preussen)* (Berlin, 1981), ch. 10. Gröber's views had changed, however, since the committee had discussed the code in early March; see Heller, report of 13 Mar. 1896, BHStA Munich, MA 76730.

i.e. that special legislation was the proper place for contentious reforms. Although the Social Democrats' proposals were on the whole extremely moderate and had as their goal the establishment of equal rights for employers and their workers, the fact that they contradicted this widely accepted principle of legislation condemned them to failure. On these issues, which Stadthagen regarded as the most important of the whole debate, the party did not essentially come into conflict with liberal political ideology. The party's position with regard to the law of domestic servants was very similar to that advanced by Lasker in the early 1870s.[95] What was really at stake was the validity of the dominant theory of the tasks and duties of the civil law. As Baden's ambassador in Berlin put it when commenting on Gröber's and Stadthagen attacks on the Code's labour law:

Instead of civil law, the law of association, freedom of conscience, industrial law, sickness insurance, and the law of domestic servants are constantly discussed, and all these complaints are turned into amendments to the code . . .[96]

Previous chapters have shown that this definition of the civil law and the conservative, compilatory conception of codification which went with it were seriously challenged in the 1890s. Here, as elsewhere, there were many points of contact between the socialist and non-socialist critics of the Code. Very few if any of the Social Democrats' specific proposals were uniquely socialist and there was a certain plausibility in the party's claim that they could all be fitted into the existing Code. Most of the proposed amendments were rooted in the liberal intellectual tradition. The rejection of the strict separation of public and private law and the demand for greater protection against usury showed considerable similarities with the views of the Code's 'social' critics. The government and its supporters were stuck with the traditional conception of the limited role of the civil law and its social functions. It was this above all which cut off any real possibility that the relatively moderate proposals of the Social Democrats might be accepted.

Towards the end of the debate, the party was in something of a dilemma. On the one hand, the party had always stressed the importance of the Code to the working classes and through conscientious participation had brought about a few improvements. On the other hand, the party's most important motions had been rejected, and the Code had failed to introduce true legal unity for the working classes. At the

[95] See above, p.57.
[96] Jagemann, report of 14 Mar. 1896, GLA Karlsruhe, Abt. 233/13996.

end of June, *Vorwärts* published a long article in which the party's indecision was clearly indicated. The Code was 'an undeniable political improvement', but it was also 'a class law directed against the working class', as was particularly revealed by those clauses which left the areas of the law of greatest interest to the poor to the individual states.[97]

The Social Democrats' opposition to the Code in the final vote was anything but inevitable. In the last week of June, the Reichstag delegation voted by fourteen to nine in favour of supporting the Code. The majority included noted 'reformists' such as Frohme and pragmatic party tacticians such as Ignaz Auer. But it also included 'radicals' such as Stadthagen. In the minority Bebel named himself and Paul Singer, the latter having taken no part in the debates on the Code. Despite this initial defeat, Bebel announced his intention of taking the matter up in the press 'on account of the fundamental importance of this vote for our parliamentary activities'.[98] In a second meeting on 30 June or 1 July, the party duly came round behind Bebel and voted unanimously against the Code in the Reichstag. It is very doubtful that Bebel would have achieved this success had it not been for the fact that the party knew the Code was going to be accepted anyway. The luxury of opposition without open division was thus the product of the successful conclusion of compromises between the non-socialist parties.[99]

The presence of Stadthagen in the majority opposed to Bebel on 28 June suggests that the party's differences cannot be explained in terms of a division between reformists and radicals. Nor, despite the claims of one historian to the contrary,[1] can differences in the degree of adherence to Marxist ideology explain the party's divisions. All of the party's spokesmen adhered to a rather crudely formulated materialist theory of law, and they all seem to have agreed in putting forward essentially non-socialist proposals. It is true that Bebel's polemics about the legislative incapacities of the German bourgeoisie and the decadence of liberalism were somewhat sharper than Frohme's, with Stadthagen standing somewhere between the two. However, these differences concerned style and tone more than principle, and were hardly the true source of division.

[97] *Vorwärts*, 30 June 1896; on the party's indecision, see also Frohme's comments, *SBRT*, 30 June 1896, p. 3050B.
[98] Bebel to Victor Adler, 28 June 1896, in V. Adler, *Briefwechsel mit August Bebel*, (Vienna, 1954), 210.
[99] See the comments of Martiny in *Integration oder Konfrontation?*, p. 69.
[1] Plat, 'Die Stellung der deutschen Sozialdemokratie', pp. 160 ff.

The Civil Code was, of course, not a typical piece of legislation for the Social Democrats. Until very late in the day, the party was willing to leave the debates entirely in the hands of Stadthagen and Frohme. Only when the discussions turned to the legal position of women in late June did Bebel enter the lists, and no other member of the party played any significant role. Thus both of the party's specialists agreed that the party should vote for the Code. In view of the fact that the Code's life was destined to be short (according to the party's ideology), it should not be allowed to fail, as it constituted a definite improvement of existing law. Bebel differed on this point because he saw the issue in terms of the broader question of the party's parliamentary strategy.

This emerged quite clearly when Bebel fulfilled his promise to carry the debate into the press. He agreed that the party had no interest in rejecting the Code out of hand, and that it should never adopt a purely negative attitude to legislation. However, the Code's treatment of hunting law, the unsatisfactory position of women, and the large areas of the law left to the individual states made it impossible for the party to vote for the Code. His defence of the party's negative vote was essentially self-contradictory. The code had been rejected because of the failings of the bourgeois society that had produced it. The resignation of the bourgeois parties towards an unacceptable code was part of 'the *Götterdämmerung* of the bourgeois world'. On the other hand, the Code was unacceptable because crucial Social Democratic amendments of a liberal variety had not been taken up, implying that such amendments were possible. The responsibility for the party's negative vote must therefore lie with those 'who were in the first place obliged to struggle for a good Civil Code.'[2] At the subsequent party congress at Gotha, special emphasis was placed on the unacceptable amount of legislation which had remained intact as a result of the survival of the rights of the individual states. Meanwhile, party spokesmen such as Stadthagen spoke frequently at public meetings about the Code's 'nature as a class law'.[3] The party seemed torn between implacable hostility towards the existing social order and the desire to participate positively in legislation. The speeches and writings of the party's spokesmen in the Civil Code constantly reflected that ambivalence.

[2] See Bebel's 2 articles, 'Das Bürgerliche Gesetzbuch und die Sozialdemokratie', *Neue Zeit*, xiv/2 (1895–6), 554–9, 577–85. For a good analysis of these articles see Martiny, *Integration oder Konfrontation?*, p. 69 n. 74.

[3] *Protokolle ... des Parteitages der SPD zu Gotha* (Berlin, 1896), 58. Stadthagen gave 10 talks on this subject in Württemberg in Oct.; see Plat, 'Die Stellung der deutschen Sozialdemokratie', p. 205.

Bebel's position is probably explained most adequately in terms of what has been called his 'political deficit'—i.e. his failure to develop a coherent political strategy in which the radical possibilities of sections of the bourgeoisie might have been realized.[4] Bebel was only too willing to accept the prima-facie evidence of the liberals' rejection of their own heritage as symbolic of the bourgeoisie's essential bankruptcy. Yet even that view was crossed with bitter disappointment at the apostasy of the party's potential allies. The Social Democrats had deliberately pitched their demands low in order to create an alternative to the Conservative–National Liberal–Centre party alignment, which eventually brought through a relatively unchanged Code. As late as 1903, the bitterness about the role of Richter's Freisinnige Volkspartei in particular was quite evident.[5] As far as Bebel was concerned, the other parties had failed to accept the Social Democrats' open invitation—sincere co-operation in return for moderate concessions. That refusal underlined the continuing pariah status of the Social Democrats in Wilhelmine politics, and for that reason Bebel insisted on a negative stance in the final vote.

The conclusion of the Civil Code was a political event of great importance, and contemporaries recognized it as such. Both Friedrich Naumann and Ernst Lieber were later to compare it to the first Navy Law of 1898 as a major piece of legislation and an honour to both the nation and the Reichstag.[6] It was indeed an honour to the much reviled parliament, whose leading parties had succeeded in overcoming serious internal differences and considerable pressures from outside. The high degree of party unity in the final division suggests the ability of the Reichstag parties to overcome their members' other loyalties, for example to interest groups. With very few exceptions, those who continued to oppose the Code chose to stay away rather than defy their parties and vote according to their beliefs. As recent research has shown, this supremacy of party over other connections was in fact quite normal in the period after 1898.[7] It may be time to reconsider the customary view

---

[4] On this, see R. Walther, »... aber nach der Sündflut kommen wir und nur wir.« »Zusammenbruchstheorie«, Marxismus und politisches Defizit in der SPD, 1890-1914 (Frankfurt, 1981), 52-9, 80 ff.

[5] Eugen Richters Sozialistenspiegel (Berlin, 1903), 25, 39.

[6] Die Hilfe, 3 Apr. 1898, quoted in Düding, Der Nationalsoziale Verein, p. 113; SBRT, 7 Dec. 1897, p. 87D.

[7] W. Smith and S. A. Turner, 'Legislative Behaviour in the German Reichstag, 1898-1903', Central European History, 14 (1981), 3-29.

that this period saw the dominance of party politics by battles between organized economic groups.

That is not to say that the debates provide unequivocal evidence of the Reichstag's strength. The outcome was dependent on a high propensity to compromise on important points with the government. Nieberding was well aware that the advantages of legal unity were so great that no party would willingly take the responsibility for the Code's failure. But that was also true of the states in the Bundesrat. The secretary of the Reich justice office was directly responsible for the encouragement of expressions of support for the national significance of the Code in 1895-96. He was also able to force the Bundesrat to accept unwelcome revisions which constituted the minimum that was likely to be acceptable to the Reichstag.

That minimum was generally defined as being what was necessary in order that the main political parties would come to see the final version of the Code as an improvement of existing law in Germany. This was a basic feature of the consensus in favour of legal unity on the basis of the Code in 1896. The government's call for 'resignation' on the part of sectional interests so that a national goal could be achieved was almost always accompanied by an insistence on the improvements which had been introduced into the Code. As we have seen, the concept of the national interest was by no means unproblematic in the 1890s. The victory of the government and its supporters over the Germanist opposition was in no small part the result of their willingness to accept some of the more moderate criticisms of the draft code. The rhetoric of national unity and strength was therefore important, but not enough on its own. The other component of the argument—that *this* Code rather than any conceivable code improved the legal system—was vital to the government's case. By May 1896 there was strong evidence that that case was beginning to win the day. The press began to report a weakening of resistance to the rapid completion of the Code in the Reichstag. Even the *Kreuzzeitung* began to recommend acceptance, on the basis that this was the best code that could be achieved and that the work would constitute 'a lasting memorial for a thankful posterity'.[8]

The difficulties experienced by the Social Democrats suggest strongly that this type of argument found considerable support outside the 'bourgeois' parties. Inside those parties, it seems clear that nobody of any significance doubted the desirability of the completion of the Code

---

[8] *Hamburgischer Correspondent*, 26 May 1896; *Kreuzzeitung*, 27 May 1896.

by 1896. Where problems arose, they did so for reasons which had little to do with any fundamental doubts about the desirability of legal unity on the basis of the work as it stood in 1896. The voice of the agrarian opposition was scarcely heard, and Gierke's criticisms fell on deaf ears. Richter's opposition to the government was rooted in his belief in the Reichstag's constitutional right to free debate. Bismarck was clearly opposing the government for his own opportunistic reasons. Even in the case of the law of marriage, which was perhaps the most contentious part of the Code, the divisions within the Conservative and Centre parties had more to do with factional infighting than with a real attempt to overturn the work of the codifiers. It is difficult to believe that any serious politician ever thought that the Bundesrat would accept the abolition of obligatory civil marriage, which had been Reich law for twenty-one years. Rather, the question revolved around the presentation of the parties to their electorates. For the Centre, this meant a battle between the party leadership and dissident elements like Rintelen and Loë. For the Conservatives, it was related to the desire to retain the support of Christian-Social sympathizers. In both cases, the problem lay essentially in the difficulties the parties had in adjusting their rhetoric to the reality of the mobilization of the masses.

The Centre's decision on obligatory civil marriage meant that the old liberal fear of a Conservative-Centre party coalition was ruled out. In its place emerged a National Liberal-Centre party coalition, which provided the framework for many government majorities in the following years. There can be very little doubt that the overwhelming majority in favour of the Code helped to stabilize the Hohenlohe ministry after the traumas of 1894–5. For all the Chancellor's complaints that he was not being given the credit for the passage of the Code, he seems to have derived considerable (if transient) political strength from the Code's acceptance. As Philipp Eulenburg put it in July, Hohenlohe could now afford to compromise on other issues with the Kaiser. In the typical hyperbole of the summer of 1896, he added that the acceptance of the Civil Code marked 'a great victory which goes beyond the boundaries of this life'.[9]

---

[9] On the government's problems in 1894–95, see J. C. G. Röhl, *Germany Without Bismarck. The Crisis of Government in the Second Reich, 1890–1900* (London, 1967), ch. 4; for Hohenlohe's complaints, see E. v. Jagemann, *Fünfundsiebzig Jahre des Erlebens und Erfahrens (1849–1924)* (Heidelberg, 1925), 140; P. Eulenburg to Hohenlohe, 5 July 1896, in J. C. G. Röhl (ed.), *Philipp Eulenburgs politische Korrespondenz*, iii (Boppard, 1983), 1700.

8.

Conclusion

A RECURRING theme in this account has been the relationship between legal codification and the major political questions of the nineteenth century. From 1815 until 1896, the campaign for a Civil Code always depended on answers to those broader questions—the nature of the nation, the location of sovereignty, the definition of the proper role of the state *vis-à-vis* the different interests which made up 'civil society', and so on. As the contours of the debates about these questions shifted in the course of the century, so too did the way in which Germans approached the problems associated with the legal system. At every stage, the positions adopted by participants in the discussions concerning legal codification only acquired meaning in connection with these broader political matters.

This primacy of the political element emerges quite clearly from the history of attempts at codification, which spanned the nineteenth century. Without the formation of the *Zollverein* in 1834, it is difficult to see how the unified law of bills of exchange of 1847 or the Commercial Code of 1861 could have come into being. Whatever its effects on the development of German nationalism in the middle of the nineteenth century, there can be no doubt that the *Zollverein* and its legal counterparts were the products of bureaucratic initiatives which cannot be adequately explained as a response to pressures from below. The other nineteenth-century codes had to await the settlement of the German question in 1866-71, when the political and constitutional hindrances to unified legislation were removed by Bismarck's 'revolution from above'. As we have seen, the major feature of the debates about legal unity in the 1860s and 1870s was the controversial nature of that 'revolution'.[1]

This political emphasis is, at first sight, paradoxical in that nineteenth-century attitudes to legal codification were heavily influenced by

---

[1] See H.-U. Wehler, *Deutsche Gesellschaftsgeschichte*, ii (Munich, 1987), 125-39; L. Gall, *Bismarck. Der weisse Revolutionär* (pbk. edn., Frankfurt, 1983), 373-455.

Savigny's work from the period of the Wars of Liberation. Savigny was in part motivated by a hatred of the French Revolution. His emphasis on the *Volksgeist* as the true source of law also had obvious political implications in that it downgraded the role of legislation as a source of valid law. This was important in the first half of the nineteenth century precisely because of the extent to which the state bureaucracies were attempting to solve the political problems of the post-revolutionary period by extensive use of their legislative powers. Yet in the long run these political aspects of Savigny's work had far less influence than the jurisprudential, technical aspects—the insistence on an historical approach to the law, the *Volksgeistlehre*, and so on. It was here that the Historical School won its decisive victory over alternative intellectual traditions concerning the law. By the 1840s it was becoming clear that the historical approach to the law was, in a sense, an empty vessel which was capable of being filled with a variety of different political attitudes. The Romanist/Germanist controversy of the 1840s provided the first signs of this change, which was largely completed by the 1860s. As a result, Savigny's theory of the origins of the law tended to be separated from his hostility to codification, and Savigny was gradually transformed into a supporter of national codes. By the mid-1860s it would be fair to say that support for codification on the basis of historical legal traditions was the position adopted by most of the German political nation and was by no means limited to those who considered themselves liberals. The debates concerning the Lasker-Miquel motions showed few signs of opposition in principle to the idea of codification. The political and constitutional implications of those motions were what really mattered.

The widespread acceptance of the *Volksgeistlehre* was important in undermining fears that codification would involve the introduction of radical legal reforms. It also had important consequences for the way in which the Civil Code was prepared, where emphasis was placed on lengthy historical research, respect for regional peculiarities, and systematic precision in the formulation of legal norms. The work of the first codifying commission between 1874 and 1888 provides much evidence to support another of the general themes of this study—the connection between the procedures adopted in the preparation of legislation and the eventual contents of that legislation. Here, once again, political considerations were paramount. The approach to codification adopted in 1874 not only allayed conservative fears about the potential radicalism of the work, but also entrenched the interests of the larger non-Prussian states in the commission, thus undermining the objection that the Code was a means of extending Prussian hegemony at the expense of the states' sovereignty. The origins of the Civil Code were determined by this complex of political fears. To overcome those fears and their own internal differences, the supporters of the Lasker–Miquel motions emphasized the 'state-forming' aspects of the work. The Code was to be a systematic compilation of existing law and was to respect regional variations. On that basis, the new Reich had the right to unify its legal system, a view which had clear conservative implications. This then formed the basis of the liberal–conservative alliance in favour of legal unity in 1873–4.

The decisions made in 1874 effectively consigned the preparation of the Code to the ministerial bureaucracy, which, together with influential outsiders such as Windscheid and Planck, dominated the first codifying commission. As we have seen, this exclusion of the political parties served to isolate the commission from the changes in the nature of politics which were becoming apparent in the mid-1880s. The 'state-forming' priorities of the bureaucrats and the conceptual jurisprudence of the 1860s and 1870s combined to produce a draft code which was vulnerable to attack in the new political circumstances of the late 1880s. The Code was attacked for its neglect of the 'social' duties of the legislator, for its formalism, and for its reliance on 'foreign', Roman law. As always, these attacks derived their importance from developments in the wider political sphere. The expansion of the political nation and the mobilization of sectional interest groups provide the essential explanation for the power of the campaign against the Code.

One important feature of these developments was that they attacked the symmetrical relationship between mainstream private-law jurisprudence and liberal political thought. This symmetry found a number of different expressions in the liberal doctrine of the *Rechtsstaat* with its emphasis on the formal attributes and limitations of sovereignty, the basic dichotomy between public and private law, and above all in a common conception of the individual and his freedoms. Conceptual jurisprudence posited the formal equality before the law of all private individuals in their possession of untrammelled freedoms of contract, disposition of property, and inheritance. The claims of that jurisprudence to social and political neutrality were increasingly undermined as it became clear that social change was limiting the range of citizens who could meaningfully exercise those freedoms. Of what use were contractual and property freedoms to those who were vulnerable to exploitation because of their lack of economic power? Liberalism faced problems which were in many ways analogous. In its heyday, liberalism claimed to speak for a united *Volk*, but the 1870s already saw disquieting symptoms of the problem which bedevilled the liberal parties—their inability to surmount the socio-economic differences within their electorate and their vulnerability to hostile popular mobilizations. As the National Liberals' electoral position weakened, their doubts about the wisdom of universal suffrage broadened into a growing distaste for this institution. As became increasingly obvious after 1871, the connection between liberalism and conceptual jurisprudence lay in their common association of full membership of the political and legal nations with property ownership.[2]

It was the attack on this implicit definition of the nation, which gave the debates concerning the draft code their significance. The revival of Germanism by Gierke and others gave groups which were becoming increasingly alienated from liberal politics an ideal 'national' justification. The draft code was very much the product of the era of liberal predominance in the 1870s, and was perceived to have failed to fulfil the duties of a truly 'German' code, just as liberalism had failed to promote the interests of many of its erstwhile supporters. Both liberalism and conceptual jurisprudence were thus vulnerable to attacks on their 'national' credentials. The Germanists' campaign against the Code derived much of its force from its ability to exploit that vulnerability in ways which linked political, social, and ethical concerns to an alternative conception of the national interest. Thus 'Germanness' came to mean a complex of beliefs involving the protection of the weak, the moral authority of the family, the special status of landownership, and the restriction of the freedom of action of the individual for the sake of the common good. Roman law, on the other hand, was increasingly equated with negative moral attributes—selfish egotism, the exercise of rights without duties, the promotion of the interests of the strong at the expense of the weak through the operation of a capitalist economy, and so on. This sort of rhetoric won the moral high ground in the debates studied here, as is shown by the subtle shifts in the ways in which the Code's defenders framed their arguments in the 1890s. By

---

[2] See W. J. Mommsen, 'Der deutsche Liberalismus zwischen "klassenloser Bürgergesellschaft" und "Organisiertem Kapitalismus": Zu einigen neueren Liberalismusinterpretationen', *Geschichte und Gesellschaft*, 4 (1978), 77–90; on the liberals and universal suffrage, see W. Gagel, *Die Wahlrechtsfrage in der Geschichte der deutschen liberalen Parteien 1848–1918* (Düsseldorf, 1958).

1896, it was no longer possible merely to emphasize the Code's contribution to national unity and legal certainty. All sections of the political nation had had to recognize the permanent nature of the new 'social' demands.

That having been said, the effects of those demands were relatively slight, and the reasons for that lay once again in the political sphere. If the controversy about the draft code of 1888 showed all the signs of a popular mobilization from below, the government's response showed the possibilities of manipulation from above. The connection between legal unification and nationalism lay so deep in the nineteenth-century political tradition that it did not simply disappear overnight in the political changes of the 1880s and 1890s. The government's ability to use the 1870s' 'state-forming' conception of national codification as a propaganda vehicle to head off the likes of Gierke is evidence of the survival of these older traditions. By the late 1880s these traditions were becoming problematic, but they had not been supplanted.

This type of manipulation was important, but it was not enough on its own. The strength of the government's case was that such manipulation was one of a number of different approaches to the question of the nation's legal system. A vitally important role was played here by the way in which the revision of the Code was approached, which involved broadening the decision-making machinery while keeping effective control in the hands of the bureaucracy and professional lawyers. This gave the impression that 'the whole nation' was being consulted, while excluding any serious possibility that the demands of the more radical reformers would be heeded. But even that would not have been sufficient had it not been the case that the Reich government was willing in the end to accede to a limited number of reforms which were clearly supported by most of the political nation. The development of the government's policies concerning the private law of associations provides the clearest evidence of this willingness to give in where the pressure was great enough.

The consequence was that, for all the power of the campaign for legal reform in the 1890s, it failed to generate sufficient pressure on the government to force a fundamental change of attitude. Once again, the reasons for this failure were complicated, but lay essentially in the difficulties the interest groups had in arriving at unity concerning important parts of the Code. The breadth and complexity of the Code made it difficult for the interest groups to consider it in a systematic way, a problem which tended to be reinforced by their frequent refusal to consider parts of the work which were not directly relevant to 'their' sections of the economy. The schemes of men like Gierke required an evaluation of the Code as a whole, which the interest groups steadily refused to attempt. This feature of interest group activity and the evidence of disunity concerning detailed policy proposals allowed the government to exploit the divisions in the opposition. Calls for reform could often be diverted with the promise of special legislation, at either a national or a state level. In this way the relatively small group of radical critics, who insisted that their proposals should be incorporated in the Code rather than in other parts of the legal system, were isolated.

This suggests a great deal about the conditions for successful manipulation of nationalist opinion by the government. As we have seen, most commentators outside the radical agrarian camp agreed by 1896 that the Code was a great national achievement and an improvement of existing law—two aspects of the work which could not be separated. The fact was that the Code did improve existing law from a number of different perspectives. Catholics could find some solace in the final formulation of the law of marriage. As the Social Democrats recognized, the Code was inadequate but the working classes had nevertheless gained from its acceptance. The introduction of the annuity charge had at least gone some way towards meeting agrarian demands. Finally, it is difficult to see how any major group in German society could actually lose by the establishment of legal unity *per se*. There are reasons for believing that these modest gains provided the essential foundations for the success of Nieberding's nationalist appeals. The Code did serve real social interests, albeit in ways which failed to satisfy the radicals. In that sense, calls for 'resignation' were really calls to accept the advantages that the code had to offer, while not pressing for major reforms that the political system could not deliver in 1896. There is every reason to think that the reception of these arguments would have been very much less favourable if the advantages of the Code had not been real.

Moreover, we have seen repeated examples of the way in which the debates were characterized by overblown rhetoric and hyperbole. By any sober evaluation, the Code was neither the completion of German unification nor the most powerful unifying force in German society. Nor, however, did it provide incontrovertible evidence that the destruction of the German social fabric was imminent because of the law's failure to protect endangered social groups within the *Mittelstand*. Gustav Roesicke's comments at least reveal an understanding of one basic fact—that radical agrarian demands simply could not be realized through the Civil Code. However, the way in which the Farmers' League proceeded is instructive in that it was merely the most extreme version of a common occurrence in the 1890s. This was the tendency of different groups to propose radical reforms of the Code in highly apocalyptic language because of the Code's importance as a symbol of national unity. This involved no real feeling that the Code was the best way of realizing these demands. Rather, radical opponents saw the inclusion of their reforms in the Code, rather than in a less significant part of the legal system, as being tantamount to a statement of intent by the government. What was really being demanded here was a *national* commitment that Germany would henceforth be ruled in the interests of the *Mittelstand* or the agrarians. In view of the nature of Germany's economy and political system in the 1890s, no government could make such a commitment. Agrarian groups and artisans could exert enough pressure to gain concessions in the form of special legislation, however cosmetic that may have been in terms of its effects. But any realistic analysis of the balance of forces in German society makes it clear that they could never hope to exert hegemony over the legal system as a whole. The recasting of the Civil Code in their interests would have been tantamount to the creation of such a hegemony and was thus never possible.

This aspect of the debate had consequences which the government could turn to its advantage. By concentrating on the Code as a symbol of the nation, the radicals were bolstering the claims of the Reich justice office and its parliamentary allies. Despite the threat of an alternative 'Germanist' nationalism, the interest groups were in practice helping the government by putting the Code's nationalist credentials at the centre of the debate. That nationalist emphasis helped to undermine other possible objections, for example from the particularist camp. Secondly, by combining rhetorical excess with a lack of precision about policy details, the opponents allowed the government to play on doubts that their plans really promoted the interests of the social groups they claimed to represent. Gierke was an exception here, in that he did attempt a detailed review of the Code as a whole. However, his influence was most significant in providing an idiom in which agrarian and other criticisms of the legal system might be expressed, and he tended to find far less support on matters of detail. All of this points to the weakness of interest groups as a means of bringing overwhelming pressure to bear on the government, at least with regard to the Civil Code. The Code's supporters could thus plausibly claim that the satisfaction of the more radical demands of the interest groups would have consequences very different from those intended.

Throughout the nineteenth century, codification had been a favourite method of political integration for the state bureaucracies. Indeed, it would be correct to suggest a certain consonance between the bureaucrats' drive towards rationalization of the law and the liberals' campaign for codification. That connection existed in the Restoration period but reached its height in the mid-nineteenth century. Both bureaucrats and private citizens found the endless variations in the application of the law a hindrance to their activities. The development of conceptual jurisprudence provided an ideal means of realizing the desires of bureaucratic and liberal reformers. As we have seen, there was a close relationship between the 'social models' of liberalism and conceptual jurisprudence. For the bureaucrats, conceptual jurisprudence constituted the only available set of legislative techniques which could satisfy their drive for rationalization of the legal system. Furthermore, the liberals and the bureaucracy had an overlapping interest in the establishment of 'legal certainty'. If, as has been argued, German political culture was characterized by its bureaucratic, non-participatory form of liberalism, there is every reason to see the Civil Code as the classic expression of that culture. In fact, it is difficult to think of a more bureaucratic and non-participatory way of preparing a major liberal reform than that adopted by the first codifying commission.

The idea of a consonance between bureaucratic and liberal reforms, mediated by conceptual jurisprudence, is a fundamental aspect of the development of German politics in the nineteenth century. We have repeatedly seen how the bureaucracy developed its own priorities and imperatives, which cannot be reduced to the level of functional responses to pressures arising out of economic or social change. Those pressures did of course exist, and the bureaucracy was never acting in a political vacuum, least of all in the 1890s. At the root of the process of modernization lay the economic changes associated with the transition to an industrial society. Those changes naturally created their own imperatives, some of which have been discussed here. No return to unfree tenures was conceivable, for example, and the refusal of reformers like Gierke and Miaskowski to overturn testamentary freedom reflects a recognition of that fact. But these socio-economic imperatives cannot fully explain the ways in which the legal system developed.

This account has sought to emphasize the powerful influence of a specifically German jurisprudential tradition on the ways in which bureaucrats and lawyers considered the legal system. The importance of German jurisprudence in the shaping of the attitudes of bureaucrats is difficult to assess accurately but was certainly very great. The codifying commissions provided many examples of agreements between legally trained bureaucrats and professional lawyers, and it is this connection which was more than anything else responsible for the frustration of most of the proposed 'social' reforms after 1890. Further evidence for this contention is provided by the apparent willingness of the government to agree to reforms which had the overwhelming support of the community of professional lawyers, as in the case of the law of associations. Finally, the 1895 Lawyers' Congress saw very great enthusiasm for the rapid acceptance of the revised Code—a position which was exactly the same as that adopted by the Reich justice office. Throughout the 1890s, Gierke's general criticisms of the Code (as opposed to his views on a few specific points) never attracted the support of more than a tiny minority of Germany's professional lawyers.

Like any social group, lawyers were of course divided on many issues. But the overwhelming majority of them accepted certain basic propositions: that a Civil Code must attempt to create 'legal certainty' and to provide a fair balance between different social interests; that Roman law elements could not simply be excluded from the nation's Code; that conceptual jurisprudence provided the best techniques for the creation of 'legal certainty', and so on. These basic principles harmonized exactly with those adopted by the bureaucracy, and the alliance of lawyers and bureaucrats on that basis constituted an insuperable barrier to radical reforms of the Code.

There was, however, another side to this question. As was seen in Chapter 6, the bureaucracy was anything but a monolithic entity. Despite the similarities in the educational backgrounds of officials from different sections of the government, immediate departmental considerations did much to divide them over the question of legal reform. The departmental priorities of the Reich justice office and the Prussian ministry of justice involved an emphasis on clarity and systematic precision which successfully worked against demands from other ministries for social and economic reforms through the civil law. As the cases of Schelling and Bosse suggest, these priorities were emphasized irrespective of the ministers' political views. Schelling was highly sympathetic to the agrarians and Bosse was willing to press the case of the master builders. Neither could succeed in bringing their opinions into harmony with the technical requirements of the legal system. This combination of a high degree of sympathy for reform proposals and insuperable jurisprudential objections to their incorporation in the Civil Code was exactly the approach adopted by many of the professional lawyers in the second commission.

Moreover, an analogous type of division arose outside the government and its commissions. The reliance of the interest groups on professional lawyers undoubtedly moderated the hostility of those groups and concentrated attention on limited aspects of the Code. It was significant that the Farmers' League considered that a lawyer would not be capable of expressing its fundamental hostility to the Code's ideological foundations.[3] The same process occurred within the Reichstag parties. On the one hand, there were lawyers such as Spahn and Buchka, who were concerned with what was practically achievable within the context of the successful passage of the Civil Code. In some ways, Stadthagen might be categorized in this way as well, although he eventually voted against the work. On the other hand, there were those like Roon, Bebel, and the Centre party agrarians, who viewed the Code principally as a means of forcing a particular set of tactical priorities on their parties. In general, the main participants in the debates about the Code—who were by definition trained lawyers and often professionally involved in the legal system—tended to share many of the features of Germany's jurisprudential culture.

The process of transition to an industrial society has tended to throw up similar problems all over Europe. The legal system must attempt to cope with the development of a situation in which the most important economic actors are characteristically not private individuals. All economically advanced states in the twentieth century have been forced to recognize that formal legal equality is not enough to ensure equitable treatment, and that some attempt to make allowances for social and economic inequalities must be made. Fundamental changes have taken place with regard to contractual transactions, property and inheritance rights, and family relationships. In all these respects the basic principles of the Code locate it firmly in the nineteenth century; it was the final statement of the doctrines of the period of unification rather than a 'creative' attempt to deal with problems which were already clearly emerging. The very fact that that sort of code was conceivable in the 1890s suggests a great deal about the 'peculiarities' of German

---

[3] Suchsland to Roesicke, 11 June 1895, ZStA Potsdam, Roesicke Papers 19, fo. 211.

development. This study has attempted to suggest that that development is incomprehensible without a consideration of the complex bundle of intellectual traditions and political practices which we have termed 'political culture'.

It seems clear that without these traditions and practices—without the mediating function of politics—the reasons why bureaucratic policy-making took the direction it did will remain indistinct. David Blackbourn may be correct in seeing the Civil Code as evidence for the power of 'bourgeois' values in late nineteenth-century Germany. He is surely, however, incorrect in following Dirk Blasius' arguments concerning the essential unity of the German bourgeoisie over such matters as contractual and testamentary freedom and the untrammelled exercise of property rights.[4] As has been seen, the debates about the Civil Code reveal high levels of disagreement within Germany's property-owning classes about precisely these 'bourgeois' freedoms. To be sure, nobody was seriously arguing for a return to the *ancien régime*, which would have been an absurd suggestion in the last decade of the nineteenth century. But the question of how far personal freedoms might legitimately be restricted in the public interest was now firmly on the agenda. In a sense, the divisions within the German property-owning classes revolved around the question of who was going to foot the bill for modernization. Put another way, the controversies revealed the deepening divisions between creditor and debtor, town and country, financial interests and agrarian landowners, all of which returned to plague the legal system after 1918. Where is the evidence of Blasius' 'bourgeois identity' here?

In one sense, however, this is a question of definition. If the term 'bourgeois' refers solely to a legal order based on the exercise of liberal property rights in a general nineteenth-century sense, it is probable that most of Germany's civil law was 'bourgeois' by about 1860. When work on the Code began this characteristic of the legal system was not seriously challenged, and this helps to explain why liberals should have been largely content with a unification of existing law. Where the bourgeoisie did have a seeming unity of interests was in its demand for

---

[4] See D. Blackbourn and G. Eley, The *Peculiarities of German History. Bourgeois Society and Politics in Nineteenth-Century Germany* (Oxford, 1984), 190–4; D. Blasius, 'Bürgerliches Recht und bürgerliche Identität. Zu einem Problemzusammenhang in der deutschen Geschichte des 19. Jahrhunderts', in H. Berding *et al.* (eds.), *Vom Staat des Ancien Regime zum modernen Parteistaat. Festschrift für Theodor Schieder zum 70. Geburtstag* (Munich/Vienna, 1978), 213–24; I have developed these arguments in much greater detail in M. John, 'The Peculiarities of the German State: Bourgeois Law and Society in the Imperial Era', *Past and Present*, 119 (1988), 105–31.

formal unification of different legal systems whose material contents were definitely converging in the decades before unification. It is this emphasis which emerges most strongly from the debates considered in this study.

Assertions about the 'bourgeois' nature of the Code abound in the scholarly literature and form an essential part of Wieacker's influential investigations of the 'social model' of the German legal system. The main point at issue, however, is not whether such assertions are 'right' or 'wrong' but how much they actually tell us about the legal system. The case of England, which so fascinated Max Weber because of its demonstration of the possibility of an industrial revolution in a country whose law retained 'archaic' elements,[5] suggests that industrial capitalism can come to terms with a wide variety of legal systems. The common contention that certain types of legal system are 'functional' for capitalist development is notoriously difficult to prove. Even more so is the implicit suggestion that the law actually develops *because* it is functional for economic activity. Yet if that type of functional argument is rejected, the advantage to be gained from describing the legal system as 'bourgeois' is unclear.

There is, however, a final important aspect of this question. Most of those who are concerned to highlight the Code's 'bourgeois' nature consider the law as an expression of social values. It is striking, for example, that Blackbourn places his discussion of the legal system in the context of the economy and society (in which the bourgeoisie was relatively united and successful) rather than in the political sphere (in which it was not).[6] This prompts certain reflections about the difficulties of transposing German linguistic categories into common English usage. The German word *bürgerlich* with its double meaning of 'civil' and 'bourgeois' is an important case in point, especially as Blackbourn's argument seeks to develop the connections between the two. The German term *bürgerliche Gesellschaft* (civil society) is generally used to mean a society whose fundamental values are formal equality before the law and a substantial measure of private autonomy for the state's citizens—i.e. exactly the type of social values that Blackbourn characterizes as 'bourgeois'. There can be no doubt that this type of society had developed in the late nineteenth century and that the Code sought to give expression to those values. But to place these matters in the

---

[5] D. M. Trubek, 'Max Weber on Law and the Rise of Capitalism', *Wisconsin Law Review*, 3 (1972), 746 ff.

[6] See in general Blackbourn and Eley, *Peculiarities*, pp. 176–237.

arena of civil society, in which the bourgeoisie was strong and united, is to underestimate the political divisions with which the legislators had to contend.

On the other hand, the equivalent of the English term 'law' in most Continental languages has the double meaning of statute laws and the normative legal order.[7] Ideally, positive laws (statutes) seek to give expression to the normative values which develop in society, and it was this emphasis which gave Savigny's arguments against eighteenth-century legislation their force of conviction. But modern states have repeatedly shown that the relationship between statute laws and normative law can be highly problematic. Difficulties in this relationship have tended to arise for a number of reasons. Perhaps the most obvious is the likelihood of a 'time-lag' between changes in social mores and values and the expression of those changes in positive law. In some cases the jurisprudential traditions of a country may prove an obstacle to the solution of new legal problems, and the German Civil Code seems to provide many examples of this. In others, delay may be caused by the problems legislators face in drafting suitable legislation or by difficulties in creating the political will necessary to push through reforms.[8] All of these obstacles seem to be greatest at times of rapid change, when social and economic relationships are in a state of flux.

These comments concerning problems in the creation of political will point to an arguably more important source of problems in the relationship between social values regarding the legal order and positive law. For all that nineteenth-century German liberals and lawyers liked to talk of a united *Volk* or *Volksgeist* (of which they believed themselves to be the principal expression), there must be serious doubts about the existence of such unity in modern societies. The very fact that twentieth-century democracies frequently refer to themselves as pluralist societies suggests difficulties with any belief in a unitary social order. The transition to mass politics in the late nineteenth century in Germany meant the expression in politics of a large number of divergent and often contradictory claims by different interests. This study has presented many examples of the way in which a strident rhetoric of national unity concealed bitter disputes about what 'Germanness' actually meant. These problems may well be an inevitable fact of life for modern Western

---

[7] Hence the German distinction between *Recht* and *Gesetz*, the French *droit* and *loi*, etc.

[8] A case in point is the story of English land law reform in the nineteenth century; see A. W. B. Simpson, *A History of the Land Law* (2nd edn., Oxford, 1986), 273 ff.

societies, but the German case seems to present them in an extreme form.

The relevance of this to the relationship between the legal norms of a society and its positive laws is fairly obvious. Even if the development of beliefs about the ethical basis of a desirable legal order in the realm of 'civil society' occurs outside the structure of formal politics, the expression of those beliefs in statute law does not. In constitutional states, statutes have to receive the assent of parliamentary majorities— a process which automatically places them in the political arena and exposes them to all the divisions that characterize that arena. Parliamentary assent is by no means inevitably the result of a widespread belief that the proposed statute accurately expresses public opinion with respect to the ethics of the legal order. Rather, as we have seen in the case of the Civil Code, majorities often have to be created by a mixture of propaganda, tactical manœuvres, and political horse-trading. The frequency of the government's appeals to 'resignation' on the part of sectional interests might suggest that the Code only imperfectly represented the views of the political nation.

These aspects of the story prompt some concluding reflections about the problems facing liberalism in Germany. As we have seen, liberalism had most to fear from the division of politics into sectional interests coupled with the mobilization of subordinate groups in society to pursue such interests. The liberals' response to the problems inherent in the transition to mass politics was to re-emphasize their commitment to a form of politics which stood 'above' the clashes between sectional groups and the divisions of party politics. The Civil Code was an ideal vehicle, perhaps the last ideal vehicle in domestic policy, for the expression of their yearning for a form of national and social unity which transcended economic divisions. Both that yearning and those divisions were present in heightened form during the Weimar Republic, and both were exploited to the full by the emerging Nazi movement. But the seeds of that exploitation lay in patterns of liberal thought and political practice which were established in the last three decades of the nineteenth century.[9]

Liberalism's difficulties in the 1920s confirm much of what has been said here about the connections between private-law jurisprudence and liberal politics. A major reason for the electoral decline of liberalism

---

[9] See the brilliant analysis of these connections in R. Koshar, *Social Life, Local Politics and Nazism. Marburg 1880–1935* (Chapel Hill/London, 1986).

was the fact that the hyper-inflation of 1923 drove a wedge between different sections of the liberal electorate, and produced divisions that could never be bridged within the framework of Weimar democracy. Equally, no consensus between creditor and debtor groups within the property-owning classes could be established by judicial application of the relevant sections of the Civil Code. The alienation from Weimar of so many groups within the liberal electorate cruelly exposed the declining legitimacy of the existing political and legal order and provided a necessary, if not sufficient, condition for the subsequent electoral successes of the Nazi party. At this point, the failure of liberalism and German private law to take social divisions seriously as an ineluctable feature of modern life, and to come to terms adequately with the development of aggregate, non-individual forms of power, deprived both types of thought of meaningful answers to the problems of the post-war world.[10]

If Nazism could exploit the liberals' desire for national unity at a time of acute polarization, it also found fertile ground in their concern with the formal attributes of legality. As has often been pointed out, the Nazis' legitimacy in the early years after the 'seizure of power' in January 1933 was vitally conditioned by their willingness to work through the existing formal provisions of the law. Here, the contradiction between normative *Recht* and positive *Gesetz* appeared with a vengeance and, as in so many areas, Nazism succeeded in turning liberalism inside out. The formal structures of positive law were frequently used to destroy the ethical content of a liberal political order. However much the principles of the legal order were to come into conflict with the Nazi system of rule,[11] the government believed, with some justification, that a substantial degree of legitimacy might be gained by the correct application of formal legislative procedures inherited from the past, irrespective of the ethical content of new legislation.

An emphasis on formalism was, as has often been noted, a central feature of German legal positivism. The connection of such formalism with the failure of liberalism to provide more effective resistance to

---

[10] See L. E. Jones, 'The Dying Middle: The Fragmentation of the Bourgeois Parties', *CEH* 5 (1972), pp. 23–54; T. Childers, 'Inflation, Stabilization, and Political Realignment in Germany 1924–1928', in G. Feldman *et al.* (eds.), *Die deutsche Inflation: Eine Zwischenbilanz* (Berlin/New York, 1982), 409–31; D. B. Southern, 'The German Judiciary 1918–1933', D. Phil. thesis (Oxford, 1975), ch. 8; M. E. Hughes, 'Private Equity, Social Inequity: German Judges React to Inflation, 1914–1924', *CEH* 16 (1983), pp. 76–94.

[11] See the general comments in M. Broszat, *Der Staat Hitlers* (8th edn., Nördlingen, 1979), ch. 10.

Nazism is a principal explanation for the negative reaction to the positivist tradition after the war. As we have seen, the debates about the Civil Code were very much concerned with the extent to which formalist arguments were valid. This leads to the possibility that the Civil Code marked an important stage in the weakening of liberal values in the German political system, through its role in cementing formal rather than material conceptions of individual liberty at the heart of Germany's political and legal culture. This is what the famous English journalist Wickham Steed meant when he told an astonished Sebastian Haffner during the Second World War that the Code bore a major responsibility for the 'collective crimes' of the German people; its pursuit of scientific, formal precision had allegedly destroyed the Germans' intuitive feeling for the law.[12]

But to accept this view is surely excessively pessimistic and fails to do justice to German liberalism. The continuities in language and rhetoric between the 1890s and the 1920s mask basic differences in the meanings attached to the language of politics. Hitler's *Volk* was not that of the liberals in the Bismarckian era; nor was it that of the Germanists in the 1890s. When they talked of national unity and legal certainty, the men of the 1890s reflected the survival of long-term liberal aspirations which still retained certain aspects of their original emancipatory nature. And when nineteenth-century German liberals talked about the law in formal terms, they meant something far removed from the cynical opportunism which allowed so many civil servants and lawyers to salve their consciences while coming to terms with the destruction of the liberal political system in 1933. If that were not the case, why should the left have agreed that the Code's formal unification of most of Germany's civil law constituted a progressive step? It is far from clear that liberalism as a set of political values was dead in Germany before 1914. As far as the quite different question of the electoral fortunes of parties which called themselves liberal was concerned, there were ominous signs for the future in developments before the First World War. With hindsight, Hans Delbrück was right to conclude that, although the passage of the Code was a triumph for the National Liberals, it would not prevent the party's steady electoral decline. Nevertheless, it required the 'second mobilization' of important sections

---

[12] This conversation is reported in Schubert, 'Der Ausbau der Rechtseinheit unter dem Norddeutschen Bunde: Zur Enstehung des Strafgesetzbuchs von 1870 unter besonderer Berücksichtigung des Strafensystems', in A. Buschmann *et al.* (eds.), *Festschrift für Rudolf Gmür am 70. Geburtstag 28. Juli 1983* (Bielefeld, 1983), pp. 188 f.

of the electorate, as a result of the war and its aftermath, to finish the liberal parties off.[13] There is much to be said for the view that German liberalism—as a theory and as a set of political practices—failed because of the intolerable strains arising out of the First World War. The complex traditions which made up its inherited political culture were ill-suited to the demands placed upon them in the Weimar republic. Those traditions must, however, be judged against their true background— the framework of notable politics, in which an élite of educated property-owners held sway, and the political priorities of the period of national unification. The Civil Code was the final product of that culture and was perhaps already out of date by the time it was introduced. But, as with so many of the features of this story, the explanation for that out-of-date quality lies firmly in the sphere of German politics.

[13] H. Delbrück, 'Politische Korrespondenz', 24 July 1896, *Preussische Jahrbücher*, 85 (1896), 397; see J. Osmond, 'A Second Agrarian Mobilization? Peasant Associations in South and West Germany, 1918–1924', in R. G. Moeller (ed.), *Peasants and Lords in Modern Germany* (Boston, 1986), 168–97.

BIBLIOGRAPHY

PRIMARY SOURCES

(*i*) *Archival Sources*
Archiv der Hansestadt Lübeck
Senatsakten
Bayerisches Hauptstaatsarchiv, Munich
Ministerium des Aussern   MA
Ministerium der Justiz   MJu
Gesandtschaft Berlin
Gesandtschaft Dresden
Gesandtschaft Stuttgart
Bundesarchiv Koblenz
Prince Chlodwig zu Hohenlohe-Schillingsfürst Papers
Kleine Erwerbungen 303, 319
Geheimes Staatsarchiv Preussischer Kulturbesitz, Berlin-Dahlem
Justizministerium   Rep. 84a
Staatsministerium   Rep. 90
Generallandesarchiv Karlsruhe
Staatsministerium   Abt. 233
Justizministerium   Abt. 234
Hessisches Staatsarchiv Marburg
Ludwig Enneccerus Papers
Hauptstaatsarchiv Stuttgart
Staatsministerium   E 130a
Justizministerium   E 74I
Gesandtschaft Berlin   E 73
Gesandtschaft München   E 75
Historisches Archiv, Cologne
Karl Bachem Papers
Niedersächsische Staats- und Universitätsbibliothek Göttingen
Gottlieb Planck Papers
Niedersächsisches Staatsarchiv Wolfenbüttel
Kanzlei des Staatsministeriums   12 A Neu
Staatsministerium   19 B Neu
Staatsarchiv Bremen
Senatsakten
Staatsarchiv Dresden
Aussenministerium

Gesandtschaft Berlin
Gesandtschaft München
Gesandtschaft Stuttgart
Staatsarchiv Hamburg
Senatsakten
Senatskommission für die Justizverwaltung
Akten des Bevollmächtigten zum Bundesrat
Staatsarchiv Schwerin
Ministerium der Justiz
Gesandtschaft Berlin
Zentrales Staatsarchiv Merseburg
Königliches Civil-Cabinet   2.2.1
Justizministerium   2.5.1
Ministerium der geistlichen, Unterrichts- und Medicinal-Angelegenheiten
    Rep. 76
Ministerium des Innern   Rep. 77
Ministerium für die landwirtschaftlichen Angelegenheiten   Rep. 87B
Handelsministerium   Rep. 120
Gesandtschaft Dresden
Gesandtschaft Stuttgart
Friedrich Althoff Papers
Robert Bosse Papers
Adalbert Falk Papers
Zentrales Staatsarchiv Potsdam
Reichsjustizamt/-ministerium   RJM
Reichskanzlei   Rkz
Rudolf von Bennigsen Papers
Eduard Lasker Papers
Heinrich von Marquardsen Papers
Gustav Roesicke Papers

(*ii*) *Printed Sources*

(*a*) *Contemporary Periodicals.*
Archiv des deutschen Landwirthschaftsraths, 1889-90, 1893.
Deutsche Juristenzeitung, 1896-1900, 1909.
Frei-Land. Zeitschrift für friedliche Sozialreform, 1892-4.
Preussische Gerichts-Zeitung (from July 1861 *Deutsche Gerichts-Zeitung*), 1860-3.
Schriften des Vereins für Sozialpolitik, 1882-1900.
Zeitschrift für deutsches Recht und deutsche Rechtswissenschaft, 1839-48.

(b) *Printed Primary Sources*

'Aus den Briefen Carl von Gerbers vom konstituierenden Reichstag des Norddeutschen Bundes', *Neues Archiv für Sächsische Geschichte*, 60 (1939), 224–79.

BÄHR, O., *Der Rechtsstaat. Eine publicistische Skizze* (Cassel/Göttingen, 1864).

—— *Das bürgerliche Gesetzbuch und die Zukunft der deutschen Rechtssprechung* (Leipzig, 1889).

—— *Erinnerungen aus meinem Leben* (Cassel, 1898).

BAUMGARTEN, H. and JOLLY, J., *Staatsminister Jolly. Ein Lebensbild* (Tübingen, 1897).

BEKKER, E. I., *Die Reform des Hypothekenwesens als Aufgabe des Norddeutschen Bundes* (Berlin, 1867).

—— *System und Sprache des Entwurfs eines Bürgerlichen Gesetzbuchs für das Deutsche Reich* (Berlin/Leipzig, 1888).

Bemerkungen der Grossherzoglich Mecklenburg-Schwerinschen Regierung zu den Entwürfen eines Bürgerlichen Gesetzbuchs für das Deutsche Reich und eines Einführungsgesetzes zu diesem Gesetzbuch. Als Manuskript gedruckt (2 vols., Schwerin, 1891/2).

Bemerkungen zum Entwurf eines Bürgerlichen Gesetzbuchs für das Deutsche Reich. Bemerkungen des Königlich Preussischen Justizministers über die in dem Rundschreiben des Reichskanzlers vom 27. Juni 1889 hervorgehobenen Punkte. Als Manuskript gedruckt (Berlin, 1891).

Bericht der Reichstags-Kommission über den Entwurf eines Bürgerlichen Gesetzbuchs und Einführungsgesetzes nebst einer Zusammenstellung der Kommissionsbeschlüsse (Berlin, 1896).

Bericht über die Verhandlungen der XIV. General-Versammlung der Vereinigung der Steuer- und Wirtschaftsreformer (Berlin, 1889).

Bericht über die Verhandlungen der XX. Haupt-Versammlung des Congresses Deutscher Landwirthe zu Berlin am 26. Februar 1889 (Berlin, 1889).

BESELER, G., *Volksrecht und Juristenrecht* (Leipzig, 1843).

—— *Erlebtes und Erstrebtes, 1804–1859* (Berlin, 1884).

BETHMANN-HOLLWEG, M. A. v. *Ueber Gesetzgebung und Rechtswissenschaft als Aufgabe unserer Zeit* (Bonn, 1876).

Bismarck-Erinnerungen des Staatsministers Freiherrn Lucius von Ballhausen (4th edn., Stuttgart/Berlin, 1921).

BLUM, H., *Auf dem Wege zur deutschen Einheit. Erinnerungen und Aufzeichnungen eines Mitkämpfers aus den Jahren 1867 bis 1870*, i (Jena, 1893).

BLUNTSCHLI, J. C., *Die neueren Rechtsschulen der deutschen Juristen* (Zurich/Frauenfeld, 1841).

—— 'Der bayerische und sächsische Entwurf eines bürgerlichen Gesetzbuchs', *Kritische Vierteljahrsschrift für Gesetzgebung und Rechtswissenschaft*, 3 (1861), 421–46.

—— *Denkwürdiges aus meinem Leben* (3 vols., Nördlingen, 1884).

BRUNNER, H., 'Die Rechtseinheit' (1877), in K. Rauch (ed.)., *Abhandlungen zur Rechtsgeschichte. Gesammelte Aufsätze von Heinrich Brunner*, ii (Weimar, 1931), pp. 361–77.

BUECK, H. A., *Der Centralverband deutscher Industrieller, 1876–1901* (3 vols., Berlin, 1902–5).

BÜRKEL, H., 'Ueber die Erzielung der Einheit des Privatrechts im deutschen Reiche', *AcP*, 55 (1872), 145–66.

BUSCH, M., *Bismarck. Some Secret Pages From His History* (3 vols., London, 1898).

CHRIST, A., *Ueber deutsche Nationalgesetzgebung* (Karlsruhe, 1842).

—— *Die Verwirklichung der deutschen Nationalgesetzgebung* (Stuttgart/Tübingen, 1850).

CONRAD, J., *Lebenserinnerungen. Aus seinem Nachlass herausgegeben von Else Kesten-Conrad und Herbert Conrad. Als Manuskript gedruckt* (Berlin, 1917).

DAMASCHKE, A., *Aus meinem Leben*, i (Berlin, 1928).

—— *Zeitenwende. Aus meinem Leben*, ii (Leipzig/Zurich, 1925).

DELBRÜCK, R. v., *Lebenserinnerungen 1817–1867*, ii (Leipzig, 1905).

DERNBURG, H. v., *Persönliche Rechtsstellung nach dem Bürgerlichen Gesetzbuch* (Berlin, 1896).

DOVE, A. and WIEDEMANN, T. (eds.), *Leopold von Ranke's Sämtliche Werke*, li/lii (Leipzig, 1888).

ENNECCERUS, L., *Friedrich Carl von Savigny und die Richtung der neueren Rechtswissenschaft nebst einer Auswahl ungedruckter Briefe* (Marburg, 1879).

—— 'Die parlamentarischen Aussichten des Bürgerlichen Gesetzbuchs', *DJZ*, 1 (1896), 6–8.

Der Entwurf eines Bürgerlichen Gesetzbuchs für das Deutsche Reich und der Rheinische Bauernverein (Cologne, 1890).

FISCHER, L. W., *Die teutsche Justiz. Für die Freunde des Rechts und der nationalen Einheit, auch zur Verständigung über Zweck und Ziel der bevorstehenden Mainzer Advocatenversammlung* (Stuttgart, 1844).

—— 'Ueber die Reformfrage', *AcP*, 31 (1848), 33–62.

FITTING, H., 'Ueber die Mittel zur Erzielung der Einheit des Privatrechts im deutschen Reich', *AcP*, 54 (1871), 263–79.

FRIESEN, R. v., *Erinnerungen aus meinem Leben. Aus dem Nachlass herausgegeben von H. v. Freisen*, iii (Dresden, 1910).

FULD, L., 'Das Erbrecht des code civil und der bäuerliche Grundbesitz', *Jahrbuch für Gesetzgebung, Verwaltung und Volkswirthschaft*, 12 (1888), 999–1027.

—— 'Der Entwurf eines bürgerlichen Gesetzbuches und das bäuerliche Erbrecht', *Zeitschrift für Agrarpolitik*, 1 (1888), 145–64.

—— 'Das bürgerliche Gesetzbuch und die Sozialpolitik', *Gruchots Beiträge zur Erläuterung des Deutschen Rechts*, 35 (1891), 635–57.

GEIB, G., *Die Reform des deutschen Rechtslebens* (Leipzig, 1848).

263

263ography**263

GIERKE, O. v., 'Die Stellung des künftigen bürgerlichen Gesetzbuches zum Erbrecht im ländlichen Grundbesitz', *Jahrbuch für Gesetzgebung, Verwaltung und Volkswirthschaft*, 12 (1888), 401-36.

—— *Der Entwurf eines bürgerlichen Gesetzbuchs und das Deutsche Recht* (Leipzig, 1889).

—— 'Georg Beseler', *ZRG GA*, 10 (1889), 1-24.

—— *Personengemeinschaften und Vermögensinbegriffen in den Entwurf eines Bürgerlichen Gesetzbuchs für das Deutsche Reich* (Berlin/Leipzig, 1889).

—— *Das Bürgerliche Gesetzbuch und der deutsche Reichstag. Sonderabdruck aus der Täglichen Rundschau* (Berlin, 1896).

—— *Die historische Rechtsschule und die Germanisten* (Berlin, 1903).

—— 'Die soziale Aufgabe der Rechtswissenschaft', in E. Wolf (ed.), *Quellenbuch zur Geschichte der deutschen Rechtswissenschaft* (Frankfurt, 1949), pp. 478-511.

GOLDSCHMIDT, L., *Die Nothwendigkeit eines deutschen Civilgesetzbuches. Sonderabdruck aus 'Im neuen Reich'* (Berlin, 1872).

GÖNNER, N. T. v., *Ueber Gesetzgebung und Rechtswissenschaft in unsrer Zeit* (Erlangen, 1815).

HACHENBURG, M., *Lebenserinnerungen eines Rechtsanwalts* (Düsseldorf, 1927).

HATTENHAUER, H. (ed.), *Thibaut und Savigny. Ihre programmatischen Schriften* (Munich, 1973).

HEYDERHOFF, J. and WENTZCKE, P., *Deutscher Liberalismus im Zeitalter Bismarcks: Eine politische Briefsammlung*, ii (Bonn/Leipzig, 1926).

HINSCHIUS, P., *Suarez, der Schöpfer des preussischen Landrechts und der Entwurf eines bürgerlichen Gesetzbuches für das Deutsche Reich* (Berlin, 1889).

HOHENLOHE-SCHILLINGSFÜRST, Prince C. ZU, *Memoirs*, ed. F. Curtius (2 vols., London, 1906).

—— *Denkwürdigkeiten aus der Reichskanzlerzeit*, ed. K. A. v. Müller (Stuttgart/ Berlin, 1931).

HÖLDER, E., *Savigny und Feuerbach, die Koryphäen der deutschen Rechtswissenschaft. Ein Vortrag gehalten in Erlangen* (Berlin, 1881).

JAGEMANN, E. v., *Fünfundsiebzig Jahre des Erlebens und Erfahrens (1849-1924)* (Heidelberg, 1925).

JAKOBS, H. H. and SCHUBERT W., *Die Beratung des Bürgerlichen Gesetzbuches in systematischer Darstellung der unveröffentlichen Quellen* (Berlin/New York, 1978-).

JAKUBEZKY, K., *Bemerkungen zu dem Entwurfe eines Bürgerlichen Gesetzbuches für das Deutsche Reich* (Munich, 1892).

KETTELER, W. E. Frhr. v., *Die Centrums-Fraction auf dem ersten Deutschen Reichstag* (2nd edn., Mainz, 1872).

LABAND, P., 'Zum 18. Januar', *DJZ*, 1 (1896), 21-2.

LANGFELD, A., *Mein Leben. Erinnerungen* (Schwerin, 1930).

LANGEWIESCHE, D. (ed.), *Das Tagebuch Julius Hölders 1877-1890* (Stuttgart, 1977).

264 *Bibliography*

LASKER, E., 'Einheitliches bürgerliches Recht. Eine Festrede Eduard Laskers und eine Preisaufgabe', in G. Hirth (ed.), *Annalen des Deutschen Reiches*, 7 (1874), 743–8.
—— *Fünfzehn Jahre parlamentarischer Geschichte (1866–1880)*, ed. F. Hertnech (Berlin, 1901).

LEHMKUHL, A., 'Das neue Bürgerliche Gesetzbuch des Deutschen Reiches und seine bürgerliche Eheschliessung', *Stimmen aus Maria Laach* (1896), Heft 7, pp. 125–39.

LERCHENFELD-KOEFFERING, H. Graf, *Erinnerungen und Denkwürdigkeiten 1843 bis 1925* (Berlin, 1935).

LISZT, F. v., *Die Grenzgebiete zwischen Privatrecht und Strafrecht* (Berlin/Leipzig, 1889).

MARQUARDSEN, H. v., 'Die nationale Bedeutung des Reichscivilgesetzbuchs', *DJZ*, 1 (1896), 325–8.

MENGER, A., *Das bürgerliche Recht und die besitzlosen Volksklassen* (5th edn., Tübingen, 1927).

MIASKOWSKI, A. v., *Das Erbrecht und die Grundeigenthumsvertheilung* (2 vols., Leipzig, 1882/4).

MINNIGERODE, L., *Bemerkungen über den Stand der Gesetzgebung und Jurisprudenz in Deutschland* (Darmstadt, 1836).

MITTERMAIER, K. J. A., 'Ueber die nothwendigen Vorarbeiten zur Verwirklichung einer allgemeinen deutschen Gesetzgebung mit besonderer Beziehung auf die Bearbeitung eines allgemeinen Gesetzes über eheliche Güterrechte', *AcP*, 31 (1848), 109–39.
—— 'Die neuesten Gesetzgebungsarbeiten auf dem Gebiete der Civilgesetzgebung ...', *AcP*, 36 (1853), 94–119.

MOHL, R. v., *Lebenserinnerungen. 1799–1875* (2 vols., Stuttgart/Leipzig, 1902).

MUGDAN B. (ed.), *Die gesammten Materialien zum Bürgerlichen Gesetzbuch für das Deutsche Reich* (5 vols., Berlin, 1899).

NOELLNER, F. *Die deutschen Einheitsbestrebungen im Sinne nationaler Gesetzgebung und Rechtspflege* (Leipzig, 1857).

OECHSLI, W. (ed.), *Briefwechsel Johann Kaspar Bluntschli mit Savigny, Niebuhr, Leopold Ranke, Jakob Grimm und Ferdinand Meyer* (Frauenfeld, 1915).

OPITZ, H. G. *Gutachten über den Entwurf eines Bürgerlichen Gesetzbuchs für das Deutsche Reich. Erstattet für den Landeskulturrath des Königreichs Sachsens* (Leipzig, 1889).

Papst Leo XIII, Feldmarschall Graf Moltke und ihre Bekämpfung der Sozialdemokratie durch Sicherung der Heimstätte (Dresden, 1892).

PETERSEN, J., 'Der Entwurf zu einem bürgerlichen Gesetzbuch vor dem Reichstage', *Die Grenzboten*, 55 (1896), 115–29.

PFEIFFER, D. B. W., *Ideen zu einer neuen Civil-Gesetzgebung für Teutsche Staaten* (Göttingen, 1815).

PFIZER, G., 'Was erwartet Deutschland von dem bürgerlichen Gesetzbuch?', *Deutsche Zeit- und Streitfragen*, Neue Folge, 4, Heft 55 (Hamburg, 1889).

PLANCK, G., 'Zur Kritik des Entwurfes eines bürgerlichen Gesetzbuches', *AcP*, 75 (1889), 327-429.

—— *Die rechtliche Stellung der Frau nach dem Bürgerlichen Gesetzbuch* (Göttingen, 1899).

—— 'Die soziale Tendenz des Bürgerlichen Gesetzbuches', *DJZ*, 4 (1899), 181-4.

—— 'Das bürgerliche Recht und die arbeitenden Klassen', *DJZ*, 14 (1909), 23-8.

—— 'Windscheid als Mitarbeiter am Bürgerlichen Gesetzbuch', *DJZ*, 14 (1909), 951-4.

Protokolle über die Verhandlungen des Parteitages der SPD zu Breslau (Berlin, 1895), *Gotha* (Berlin, 1896).

PURGOLD, F., *Das nationale Element in der Gesetzgebung. Ein Wort zur deutschen Rechtseinheit* (Darmstadt, 1860).

REYSCHER, A. L. (ed.), *Vollständige, historisch und kritisch bearbeitete Sammlung der württembergischen Gesetze*, i (Stuttgart/Tübingen, 1828).

RICHTER, E., *Politisches ABC-Buch. Ein Lexikon parlamentarischer Zeit- und Streitfragen* (7th, 8th, 9th edns., Berlin, 1892, 1896, 1899).

RIEPENHAUSEN-CRANGEN, K. v., *Gesicherte Familienheimstätten im Deutschen Reich* (Berlin, 1890).

RODBERTUS-JAGETZOW, J. C. v., *Zur Erklärung und Abhülfe der heutigen Creditnoth des Grundbesitzes* (2nd edn., Berlin, 1893).

RÖDINGER, F., *Nationale Rechtserzeugung und Rechtsbildung in Deutschland. Ein Vortrag für die Versammlung der Advokaten in Mainz bestimmt* (Stuttgart/ Tübingen, 1844).

RÖHL, J. C. G. (ed.), *Philipp Eulenburgs politische Korrespondenz*, iii (Boppard, 1983).

ROTH, P. v., 'Unifikation und Kodifikation', *Hauser's Zeitschrift für Reichs- und Landrecht*, 1 (1873), 1-27.

RUHLAND, G. and KROIDL, N., 'Zur Kritik des Entwurfes eines BGB. Vorträge und Aufsätze herausgegeben vom Bund der Landwirthe', *Stimmen aus dem agrarischen Lager*, 1 (1896), 16-36.

RUNDE, C. L. *Patriotische Phantasien eine Juristen* (Oldenburg, 1836).

SCHUBERT W., *Materialien zur Entstehungsgeschichte des BGB. Einführung, Biographen, Materialien* (Berlin/New York, 1978).

—— *Die deutsche Gerichtsverfassung (1867-1877)* (Frankfurt, 1980).

—— *Die Vorlagen der Redaktoren für die erste Kommission zur Ausarbeitung des Entwurfs eines Bürgerlichen Gesetzbuches* (15 vols., Berlin/New York, 1980-).

SCHWARTZ, E. 'Die Geschichte der privatrechtlichen Kodifikationsbestrebungen in Deutschland und die Entstehungsgeschichte des Entwurfs eines bürgerlichen Gesetzbuchs für das Deutsche Reich', *Archiv für bürgerliches Recht*, 1 (1889), 1-189.

SEITZ, C. J., *Das praktische Bedürfniss der Rechtsreform gegenüber der historischen Schule* (Erlangen, 1865).

SINTENIS, C. F. F., *Zur Frage von den Gesetzbüchern. Ein Votum in Veranlassung des Entwurfs eines bürgerlichen Gesetzbuchs für das Königreich Sachsen* (Leipzig, 1853).

SOHM, R., 'Die deutsche Rechtsentwicklung und die Codificationsfrage', *Zeitschrift für das Privat- und öffentliche Recht der Gegenwart*, 1 (1874), 245-80.

—— *Ueber den Entwurf eines bürgerlichen Gesetzbuches für das Deutsche Reich in zweiter Lesung. Ein Vortrag* (Berlin, 1895).

—— 'Die Entstehung des deutschen Bürgerlichen Gesetzbuchs', *DJZ*, 5 (1900), 6-9.

—— and WACH, A., 'Arnold Nieberding', *DJZ*, 14 (1909), 1345-8.

SPAHN, M., *Ernst Lieber als Parlamentarier* (Gotha, 1906).

—— *Das deutsche Zentrum. Kultur und Katholizismus* (Mainz/Munich, 1906).

STAMMLER, R., *Die Bedeutung des deutschen Bürgerlichen Gesetzbuches für den Fortschritt der Kultur* (Halle, 1900).

Stenographische Berichte über die Verhandlungen des Reichstags, 1867-1896.

STOERK, F., 'Das Bürgerliche Gesetzbuch und der Gesetzgebungsapparat des deutschen Reiches', in *Festgabe der Greifswalder Juristenfakultät für Ernst Immanuel Bekker zum 17. Februar 1899* (Greifswald, 1899), pp. 85-154.

THORNDIKE, A., *Zur Rechtsfähigkeit der deutschen Arbeiterberufsvereine* (Tübingen, 1908).

VARRENTRAPP, C., 'Briefe von Savigny an Ranke und Perthes', *HZ*, 100 (1908), 330-51.

Verhandlungen der Germanisten zu Frankfurt am Main am 24., 25. und 26. September 1846 (Frankfurt, 1847).

Verhandlungen der Germanisten zu Lübeck am 27., 28. und 30. September 1847 (Lübeck, 1848).

Verhandlungen der Neunten, Neunzehnten, Zwanzigsten, Dreiundzwanzigsten Deutschen Juristentage (Berlin, 1871, 1888, 1889, 1895).

Verhandlungen der Königlich Landes-Oekonomie-Kollegiums über den Entwurf eines bürgerlichen Gesetzbuches für das Deutsche Reich und andere Gegenstände. III. Session der IV. Sitzungsperiode vom 11. bis 22. November 1889 (Berlin, 1890).

Verhandlungen des Westfälischen Bauernvereins über den Entwurf eines Bürgerlichen Gesetzbuchs für das Deutsche Reich (Münster, 1890).

VIERHAUS, F., *Die Entstehungsgeschichte des Entwurfs eines Bürgerlichen Gesetzbuchs für das Deutsche Reich in Verbindung mit einer Uebersicht der privatrechtlichen Kodifikationsbestrebungen in Deutschland* (Berlin, 1889).

WÄCHTER, C. G., 'Die neuesten Fortschritte der Civilgesetzgebung in Württemburg', *AcP*, 23 (1840), 33-111.

—— *Der Entwurf eines bürgerlichen Gesetzbuches für das Königreich Sachsen. Ein Beitrag zur Beurtheilung desselben.* (Leipzig, 1853).

—— 'Gesetzgebung', in C. T. v. Welcker, *Staatslexikon*, vii (3rd end., Leipzig, 1862), pp. 482-517.

WÄCHTER, O. v., *Carl Georg von Wächter. Leben eines deutschen Juristen.* (Leipzig, 1881).

WENTZCKE, P. and KLÖTZER, W. (eds.), *Deutscher Liberalismus im Vormärz. Heinrich von Gagerns Briefe und Reden 1815-1848* (Göttingen/Berlin/ Frankfurt, 1959).

WIGARD, F. (ed.), *Stenographische Berichte über die Verhandlungen der deutschen constituirenden Nationalversammlung* (9 vols., Leipzig, 1848/9; Frankfurt, 1849/50).

WINDSCHEID, B., *Gesammelte Reden und Abhandlungen*, ed. P. Oertmann (Leipzig, 1904).

WYDENBRUGK, O. v., *Briefe über deutsche Nationalgesetzgebung* (Jena 1848).

ZITELMANN, E., 'Zur Begrüssung des neuen Gesetzbuches', *DJZ*, 5 (1900), 2-6.

Zur Kritik des Entwurf eines Bürgerlichen Gesetzbuches für das Deutsche Reich. Ergänzungsheft der Juristischen Rundschau für das katholische Deutschland, herausgegeben durch den katholischen Juristen-Verein zu Mainz (2 vols., (Frankfurt/M., 1890/1).

Zusammenstellung der gutachtlichen Aeusserungen zu dem Entwurf eines Bürgerlichen Gesetzbuchs gefertigt im Reichsjustizamt. Als Manuskript gedruckt (6 vols., Berlin, 1890/91).

Zusammenstellung der Aeusserungen der Bundesregierungen zu dem Entwurf eines Bürgerlichen Gesetzbuchs, gefertigt im Reichsjustizamte. Als Manuskript gedruckt (2 vols., Berlin 1891).

Zusammenstellung der Aeusserungen der Bundesregierung zu dem Entwurf eines Bürgerlichen Gesetzbuchs zweiter Lesung (5 vols., Berlin, 1895).

SECONDARY SOURCES

ALBRECHT, W., *Fachverein—Berufsgewerkschaft—Zentralverband. Organisationsprobleme der deutschen Gewerkschaften 1870-1890* (Bonn, 1982).

ANDERSON, M. L., *Windthorst. A Political Biography* (Oxford, 1981).

—— 'The Kulturkampf and the Course of German History', *CEH*, 19 (1986), 151-96.

—— and BARKIN, K. D., 'The Myth of the Puttkamer Purge and the Reality of the *Kulturkampf*: Some Reflections on the Historiography of Imperial Germany', *JMH*, 54 (1982), 647-86.

BACHEM, K., *Vorgeschichte, Geschichte und Politik der Deutschen Zentrumspartei*, v (Cologne, 1929).

BÄHR, U., 'Die berufsständischen Sonderinteressen und das BGB: Ein Beitrag zur Entstehungsgeschichte der Kodifikation', Jur. Diss. (Heidelberg, 1973).

BARK, T., *Vertragsfreiheit und Staat im Kapitalismus* (Berlin, 1978).

BARKIN, K. D., *The Controversy over German Industrialization, 1890–1902* (Chicago, 1970).

BEHMEN, M., *Das Preussische Wochenblatt (1851–1861)*. *Nationalkonservative Publizistik gegen Ständestaat und Polizeistaat* (Göttingen, 1971).

BEHN, M., 'Der Generalbericht der Badischen Kommission zur Begutachtung des Entwurfs eines Bürgerlichen Gesetzbuches für das Deutsche Reich: Ein Beitrag zur Mitwirkung der Bundesländer bei der Ausarbeitung des Bürgerlichen Gesetzbuches', *ZRG GA*, 99 (1982), 113–219.

BENÖHR H.-P., 'Konsumentenschutz vor 80 Jahren. Zur Entstehung des Abzahlungsgesetzes vom 16. Mai 1894', *Zeitschrift für das gesamte Handelsrecht und Wirtschaftsrecht*, 138 (1974), 492–503.

—— 'Politik und Rechtstheorie: Die Kontroverse Thibaut-Savigny vor 160 Jahren', *JuS*, 14 (1974), 681–4.

—— 'Die Grundlage des BGB: Das Gutachten der Vorkommission von 1874', *JuS*, 17 (1977), 79–82.

—— 'Wirtschaftsliberalismus und Gesetzgebung am Ende des 19. Jahrhunderts', *Zeitschrift für Arbeitsrecht*, 8 (1977), 187–218.

—— 'Das Gesetz als Instrument zur Lösung sozialpolitischer Konflikte: Das Beispiel des Bauforderungssicherungsgesetz von 1909', *ZRG GA*, 95 (1978), 221–8.

BINDER, H.-O., *Reich und Einzelstaaten während der Kanzlerschaft Bismarcks, 1871–1890. Eine Untersuchung zum Problem der bundesstaatlichen Organisation* (Tübingen, 1971).

BLACKBOURN, D., 'The *Mittelstand* in German Society and Politics, 1871–1914', *Social History*, 4 (1977), 409–433.

—— *Class, Religion and Local Politics in Wilhelmine Germany. The Centre Party in Württemberg before 1914* (New Haven, Conn.,/London, 1980).

—— 'Between Resignation and Volatility: The German Petite Bourgeoisie in the Nineteenth Century', in G. Crossick and H.-G. Haupt (eds.), *Shopkeepers and Master Artisans in Nineteenth-Century Europe* (London, 1984), pp. 35–61.

—— and ELEY, G., *The Peculiarities of German History. Bourgeois Society and Politics in Nineteenth-Century Germany* (Oxford, 1984).

BLASIUS, D., 'Der Kampf um die Geschworenengerichte im Vormärz', in H.-U. Wehler (ed.), *Sozialgeschichte Heute. Festschrift für Hans Rosenberg zum 70. Geburtstag* (Göttingen, 1974), pp. 148–161.

—— 'Bürgerliches Recht und bürgerliche Identität: Zu einem Problemzusammenhang in der deutschen Geschichte des 19. Jahrhunderts', in H. Berding *et al.* (eds.), *Vom Staat des Ancien Regime zum modernen Parteistaat. Festschrift für Theodor Schieder zum 70. Geburtstag* (Munich/Vienna, 1978), pp. 213–24.

—— 'Scheidung und Scheidungsrecht im 19. Jahrhundert: Zur Sozialgeschichte der Familie', *HZ*, 241 (1985), 329–60.

BLESSING, W. K., 'Staatsintegration als soziale Integration: Zur Entstehung einer bürgerlichen Gesellschaft im frühen 19. Jahrhundert', *Zeitschrift für bayerische Landesgeschichte*, 41 (1978), 633-700.

BOLDT, H., *Rechtsstaat und Ausnahmezustand. Eine Studie über den Belagerungszustand als Ausnahmezustand des bürgerlichen Rechtsstaates im 19. Jahrhundert* (Berlin, 1967).

BONHAM, G. J., 'Bureaucratic Modernizers and Traditional Constraints: Higher Officials and the Landed Nobility in Wilhelmine Germany 1890-1914', Ph.D. thesis (Berkeley, CA, 1985).

BORNKAMM, H., 'Die Staatsidee im Kulturkampf', *HZ*, 170 (1950), 41-72, 273-306.

BRANDT, D., 'Die politischen Parteien und die Vorlage des Bürgerlichen Gesetzbuches im Reichstag', Jur. Diss. (Heidelberg, 1975).

BREUILLY, J., 'Civil Society and the Labour Movement, Class Relations and the Law: A Comparison between Germany and England', in J. Kocka (ed.), *Arbeiter und Bürger im 19. Jahrhundert* (Munich, 1985), pp. 287-318.

BUCHHOLZ, S., *Abstraktionsprinzip und Immobiliarrecht. Zur Geschichte der Auflassung und der Grundschuld* (Frankfurt, 1978).

BULLOCK, N. and READ, J., *The Movement for Housing Reform in Germany and France 1840-1914* (Cambridge, 1985).

BÜTTNER, S., *Die Anfänge des Parlamentarismus in Hessen-Darmstadt und das du Thilsche System* (Darmstadt, 1969).

CARONI, P., 'Savigny und die Kodifikation: Versuch einer Neudeutung des "Berufes" ', *ZRG GA*, 86 (1969), 97-176.

COHN, E. J., *A Manual of German Law* i (London, 1968).

COING, H., 'Bemerkungen zum überkommenen Zivilrechtssystem', in E. v. Caemmerer *et al.* (eds.), *Vom deutschen zum europäischen Recht. Festschrift für Hans Dölle*, i (Tübingen, 1963), pp. 25-40.

—— (ed.), *Handbuch der Quellen und Literatur der neueren europäischen Privatrechtsgeschichte* (3 vols., Frankfurt, 1973-82).

—— and WILHELM, W. (eds.), *Wissenschaft und Kodifikation des Privatrechts im 19. Jahrhundert* (6 vols., Frankfurt, 1974-82).

CONRAD, H., 'Der parlamentarische Kampf um die Zivilehe bei Einführung des Bürgerlichen Gesetzbuches für das Deutsche Reich', *Historisches Jahrbuch*, 62 (1952), 474-93.

—— 'Der Deutsche Juristentag', in E. v. Caemmerer *et al.* (eds.), *Hundert Jahre Deutsches Rechtslebens. Festschrift zum hundertjährigen Bestehen des Deutschen Juristentages, 1860-1960*, i (Karlsruhe, 1960), pp. 1-36.

DANN, O. (ed.), *Vereinswesen und bürgerliche Gesellschaft* (*HZ*, Beiheft 9 Neue Folge; Munich, 1984).

DILCHER, G., 'Genossenschaftstheorie und Sozialrecht: ein 'Juristensozialismus' Otto v. Gierkes?', *Quad. fior.*, 3/4, t. 1 (1974/5), 319-65.

—— 'Der rechtswissenschaftliche Positivismus: Wissenschaftliche Methode,

270   *Bibliography*

Sozialphilosophie, Gesellschaftspolitik', *Archiv für Rechts- und Sozialphilosophie*, 61 (1975), 497-528.

DILCHER, G., and KERN, B.-R., 'Die juristische Germanistik des 19. Jahrhunderts und die Fachtradition der Deutschen Rechtsgeschichte', *ZRG GA*, 101 (1984), 1-46.

DÖLEMEYER, B., 'Einflüsse von ALR, Code Civil und ABGB auf Kodifikationsdiskussionen und -projekte in Deutschland', *Ius Commune*, 7 (1978), 179-225.

DÖRNER, H., *Industrialisierung und Familienrecht. Die Auswirkungen des sozialen Wandels dargestellt an den Familienmodellen des ALR, BGB und des französischen Code Civil* (Berlin, 1974).

DÜDING, D., *Der Nationalsoziale Verein. Der gescheiterte Versuch einer parteipolitischen Synthese von Nationalismus, Sozialismus und Liberalismus* (Munich/Vienna, 1972).

ELEY, G., *Reshaping the German Right. Radical Nationalism and Political Change after Bismarck* (New Haven, Conn.,/London, 1980).

—— 'State Formation, Nationalism and Political Culture in Nineteenth-Century Germany', in R. Samuel and G. Stedman Jones (eds.), *Culture, Ideology and Politics. Essays for Eric Hobsbawm* (London, 1983), pp. 277-301.

—— *From Unification to Nazism. Reinterpreting the German Past* (London, 1986).

ELSENER, F., 'Carl Georg von Wächter (1797-1880) und die Bemühungen Württembergs um eine Vereinheitlichung des Privat- und Prozessrechtes in der Zeit des Deutschen Bundes (1847/8)', in K. Ebert (ed.), *Festschrift Herrmann Baltl* (Innsbruck, 1978), pp. 193-209.

EPSTEIN, K., *The Genesis of German Conservatism* (Princeton, NJ, 1966).

ERDMANN, M., *Die verfassungspolitische Funktion der Wirtschaftsverbände in Deutschland, 1815-1871* (Berlin, 1968).

EVANS, R. J. (ed.), *Society and Politics in Wilhelmine Germany* (London, 1978).

—— *Sozialdemokratie und Frauenemanzipation im deutschen Kaiserreich* (Bonn, 1978).

FABER, K.-G., *Die Rheinlande zwischen Restauration und Revolution. Probleme der rheinischen Geschichte von 1814 bis 1848 im Spiegel der zeitgenössischen Publizistik* (Wiesbaden, 1966).

FEHRENBACH, E., *Traditionale Gesellschaft und revolutionäres Recht. Die Einführung des Code Napoleon in den Rheinbundstaaten* (Göttingen, 1974).

—— 'Zur sozialen Problematik des rheinischen Rechts im Vormärz', in H. Berding et al. (eds.), *Vom Staat des Ancien Regime zum modernen Parteistaat. Festschrift für Theodor Schieder zu seinem 70. Geburtstag* (Munich/Vienna, 1978), pp. 197-208.

FENSKE, H., 'Reich, Bundesrat und Einzelstaaten 1867-1914. Ein Literaturbericht', *Der Staat*, 13 (1974), 265-79.

FISCHER, W., *Wirtschaft und Gesellschaft im Zeitalter der Industrialisierung. Aufsätze—Studien—Vorträge* (Göttingen, 1972).

FRICKE, D. *et al.*, *Die bürgerlichen Parteien in Deutschland. Handbuch der Geschichte der bürgerlichen Parteien und anderen bürgerlichen Organisationen vom Vormärz bis zum Jahre 1945* (2 vols., Leipzig, 1968, Berlin-GDR, 1970).

FRENSDORFF, F., *Gottlieb Planck, deutscher Jurist und Politiker* (Berlin, 1914).

GALL, L., 'Die partei- und sozialgeschichtliche Problematik des Kulturkampfs', *Zeitschrift für die Geschichte des Oberrheins*, 113 (1966), 151-96.

—— *Der Liberalismus als regierende Partei. Das Grossherzogtum Baden zwischen Restauration und Reichsgründung* (Wiesbaden, 1968).

—— 'Liberalismus und "bürgerliche Gesellschaft": Zur Charakter und Entwicklung der liberalen Bewegung in Deutschland', *HZ*, 220 (1975), 324-56.

—— *Bismarck. Der weisse Revolutionär* (pbk. edn., Frankfurt/Berlin/Vienna, 1983).

GETZ, H., *Die deutsche Rechtseinheit im 19. Jahrhundert als rechtspolitisches Problem* (Bonn, 1966).

GRIMM, D., 'Bürgerlichkeit im Recht', in J. Kocka (ed.), *Bürgerlichkeit im 19. Jahrhundert* (Göttingen, 1987), pp. 149-88.

GRUNER, W. D., 'Die Würzburger Konferenzen der Mittelstaaten in den Jahren 1859-1861 und die Bestrebungen zur Reform des deutschen Bundes', *Zeitschrift für bayerische Landesgeschichte*, 36 (1973), 181-253.

GUGEL, M., *Industrieller Aufstieg und bürgerliche Herrschaft. Sozioökonomische Interessen und politische Ziele der liberalen Bürgertums zur Zeit des Verfassungskonflikts 1857-1867* (Cologne, 1975).

HABERMAS, J., *Strukturwandel der Öffentlichkeit. Untersuchungen zu einer Kategorie der bürgerliche Gesellschaft* (11th end., Darmstadt/Neuwied, 1980).

HALL, A., 'By Other Means: The Legal Struggle Against the SPD in Wilhelmine Germany, 1890-1900', *Historical Journal*, 17 (1974), 365-86.

HARRIS, J. F., 'Eduard Lasker and Compromise Liberalism', *JMH*, 42 (1970), 342-60.

HARTMANNSGRUBER, F., *Die Bayerische Patriotenpartei 1868-1887* (Munich, 1986).

HEDEMANN, J. W., *Der Dresdner Entwurf von 1866. Ein Schritt auf dem Wege zur deutschen Rechtseinheit* (Berlin, 1935).

—— *Die Fortschritte des Zivilrechts im 19. Jahrhundert. Ein Überblick über die Entfaltung des Privatrechts in Deutschland, Österreich, Frankreich und der Schweiz*, i (Berlin, 1910), ii/1 (Berlin, 1930), ii/2 (Berlin, 1935).

HENDON, D. W., 'The Center Party and the Agrarian Interest in Germany, 1890-1914', Ph.D. thesis (Emory University, Atlanta, Ga., 1976).

HERZFELD, H., *Johannes von Miquel. Sein Anteil am Ausbau des Deutschen Reiches bis zum Jahrhundertwende* (2 vols., Detmold, 1938).

HÖRNER, H., *Anton Menger. Recht und Sozialismus* (Frankfurt, 1977).

ISELE, H. G., 'Ein halbes Jahrhundert deutsches bürgerliches Gesetzbuch', *AcP*, 150 (1949), 1-27.

JOHN, M., 'Liberalism and Society in Germany, 1850-1880: The Case of Hanover', *English Historical Review*, 102 (1987), 579-98.

JOHN, M., 'The Peculiarities of the German State. Bourgeois Law and Society in the Imperial Era', *Past and Present*, 119 (1988), 105-31.

KAELBLE, H., 'Industrielle Interessenverbände vor 1914', in W. Ruegg and O. Neuloh (eds.), *Zur soziologischen Theorie und Analyse des 19. Jahrhunderts* (Göttingen, 1971), pp. 180-192.

KÄSTNER, K. H., *Anton Menger (1841-1906). Leben und Werk* (Tübingen, 1974).

KANTOROWICZ, H., 'Volksgeist und historische Rechtsschule', *HZ*, 108 (1912), 295-325.

KAUFFMANN, E., 'Das, sittliche Wesen der Ehe' als Massstab für die inhaltliche Bestimmung der Normen bei der Kodifizierung des Bürgerlichen Gesetzbuches', in *Rechtsgeschichte und Kulturgeschichte. Festschrift für Adalbert Erler zum 70. Geburtstag* (Aalen, 1976), pp. 649-62.

KERN, B.-R., *Georg Beseler. Leben und Werk* (Berlin, 1982).

KIEFNER, H., 'Der Einfluss Kants auf Theorie und Praxis des Zivilrechts im 19. Jahrhundert', in J. Blühdorn and J. Ritter (eds.), *Philosophie und Rechtswissenschaft. Zum Problem ihrer Beziehung im 19. Jahrhundert* (Frankfurt, 1969), pp. 3-25.

—— 'Thibaut und Savigny. Bemerkungen zum Kodifikationsstreit', in A. Buschmann *et al.* (eds.), *Festschrift für Rudolf Gmür zum 70. Geburtstag 28. Juli 1983* (Bielefeld, 1983), pp. 53-85.

KLEINE, G. H., *Der Württembergische Ministerpräsident Freiherr Herrmann von Mittnacht (1825-1909)* (Stuttgart, 1969).

KLEINE, H., *Die historische Bedingtheit der Abstraktion von der causa* (Berlin-GDR, 1953).

KNEMEYER, F.-L., *Regierungs- und Verwaltungsreform in Deutschland zu beginn des 19. Jahrhunderts* (Cologne/Berlin, 1970).

KÖGLER, P., *Arbeiterbewegung und Vereinsrecht. Ein Beitrag zur Entstehungsgeschichte des BGB* (Berlin, 1974).

KÖHNE, R., *Nationalliberale und Koalitionsrecht. Struktur und Verhalten der nationalliberalen Fraktion, 1890-1914* (Frankfurt, 1977).

KRAEHE, E. E., 'Practical Politics in the German Confederation. Bismarck and the Commercial Code', *JMH*, 25 (1953), 13-24.

KRIEGER, L., *The German Idea of Freedom. History of a Political Tradition* (Chicago/London, 1957).

KROESCHELL, K., 'Zur Lehre vom "Germanischen" Eigentumsbegriff', in *Rechtshistorische Studien. Hans Thieme zum 70. Geburtstag zugeeignet von seinen Schülern* (Cologne/Vienna, 1977), pp. 34-71.

KUNTSCHKE, H., 'Zur Kritik Otto v. Gierkes am BGB', in A. Csizmadia and K. Kovacs (eds.), *Die Entwicklung des Zivilrechts in Mitteleuropa (1848-1914)* (Budapest, 1970), pp. 153-64.

KUCZINSKI, J., *Studien zu einer Geschichte der Gesellschaftswissenschaften*, vi (Berlin-GDR, 1977).

LAUFKE, F., 'Der Deutsche Bund und die Zivilgesetzgebung', in P. Mikat (ed.), *Festschrift der Rechts- und Staatswissenschaftlichen Fakultät der Julius-Maximilians-Universität Würzburg zum 75. Geburtstag von Hermann Nottarp* (Karlsruhe, 1961), pp. 1–57.

LAUFS, A., 'Die Begründung der Reichskompetenz für das gesamte bürgerliche Recht', *JuS*, 12 (1973), 740–4.

LEBOVICS, H., ' "Agrarians" versus "Industrialisers": Social Conservative Resistance to Industrialism and Capitalism in late 19th-century Germany', *International Review of Social History*, 12 (1967), 31–65.

LEE, L. E., *The Politics of Harmony. Civil Service, Liberalism and Social Reform in Baden, 1800–1850* (Cranbury, N.J., 1980).

LENZ, M., *Geschichte des königlichen Friedrich-Wilhelms-Universität zu Berlin*, ii/1 (Halle, 1910), ii/2 (Halle, 1918).

LOTH, W., *Katholiken im Kaiserreich. Der politische Katholizismus in der Krise der wilhelminischen deutschland* (Düsseldorf, 1984).

MARTINY, M., *Integration oder Konfrontation? Studien zur Geschichte der sozialdemokratischen Rechts- und Verfassungspolitik* (Bonn/Bad Godesberg, 1976).

MATTHIAS, E., 'Kautsky und der Kautskyanismus. Die Funktion der Ideologie in der deutschen Sozialdemokratie vor dem ersten Weltkriege', in I. Fetscher (ed.), *Marxismusstudien*, ii (Tübingen, 1957), 151–97.

MERTENS, H.-G., *Die Entstehung der Vorschriften des BGB über die gesetzliche Erbfolge und das Pflichtteilsrecht* (Berlin, 1970).

—— 'Heinrich Eduard Pape (1816–1888)', in R. Stupperich (ed.), *Westfälische Lebensbilder*, xi (Münster, 1975), 153–71.

MOELLER, R. G., 'The Kaiserreich recast? Continuity and change in modern German historiography', *Journal of Social History*, 17 (1984), 655–83.

MOMMSEN, W. J., 'Der deutsche Liberalismus zwischen "klassenloser Bürgergesellschaft" und 'organisiertem Kapitalismus'. Zu einigen neueren Liberalismusinterpretationen, *Geschichte und Gesellschaft*, 4 (1978), 77–90.

MORSEY, R., *Die oberste Reichsverwaltung unter Bismarck 1867–1890* (Münster, 1957).

—— 'Die deutschen Katholiken und der Nationalstaat zwischen Kulturkampf und dem ersten Weltkrieg', *Historisches Jahrbuch*, 90 (1970), 31–64.

MÜLLER, E., *Anton Mengers Rechts- und Gesellschaftssystem* (Berlin, 1975).

MÜLLER, K., 'Zentrumspartei und agrarische Bewegung im Rheinland, 1882–1903', in K. Repgen and S. Skalweit (eds.), *Spiegel der Geschichte. Festgabe für Max Braubach zum 10. April 1964* (Münster, 1964), pp. 828–57.

NIPPERDEY, T., 'Interessenverbände und Parteien in Deutschland vor dem ersten Weltkrieg', in id., *Gesellschaft, Kultur, Theorie. Gesammelte Aufsätze zur neueren Geschichte* (Göttingen, 1976), pp. 319–37.

—— *Deutsche Geschichte, 1800–1866. Bürgerwelt und starker Staat* (Munich, 1983).

NOLL, A., *Sozio-ökonomischer Strukturwandel des Handwerks in der zweiten Phase der Industrialisierung unter besonderer Berücksichtigung der Regierungsbezirke Arnsberg und Münster* (Göttingen, 1975).

O'DONNELL, A. J., 'National Liberalism and the Mass Politics of the German Right 1890-1907', Ph.D. thesis (Princeton, 1974).

OERTMANN, P., 'Bauforderungen, Sicherung der', *Handwörterbuch der Staatswissenschaften*, ii (4th edn., Jena, 1924), 417-30.

OFFERMANN, T., *Arbeiterbewegung und liberales Bürgertum in Deutschland, 1850-1863* (Bonn, 1979).

ONCKEN, H. *Rudolf von Bennigsen. Ein deutscher Liberaler nach seinen Briefen und hinterlassenen Papieren*, ii (Stuttgart/Leipzig, 1910).

ORRÙ, G., ' "Idealismo" e "Realismo" nel socialismo di Menger', *Quad. fior.*, 3/4, t. 1 (1974/75), 182-272.

PERKINS, J. A., 'The Agricultural Revolution in Germany 1850-1914', *Journal of European Economic History*, 10 (1981), 71-118.

PFEIFFER-MUNZ, S., *Soziales Recht ist deutsches Recht. Otto von Gierkes Theorie des sozialen Rechts untersucht anhand seiner Stellungnahmen zur deutschen und schweizerischen Privatrechtskodifikation* (Zurich, 1979).

PLAT, W., 'Die Stellung der deutschen Sozialdemokratie zum Grundstaz der Gleichberechtigung der Frau auf dem Gebiet des Familienrechts bei der Schaffung des Bürgerlichen Gesetzbuches des Deutschen Reiches', Jur. Diss. (Berlin-GDR, 1966).

POLLEY, R., *Anton Justus Friedrich Thibaut (A.D. 1772-1840) in seinen Selbstzeugnissen und Briefen* (3 vols., Frankfurt, 1982).

PUHLE, H.-J., 'Parlament, Parteien und Interessenverbände, 1890-1914', in M. STÜRMER [ED.], *Das kaiserliche Deutschland. Politik und Gesellschaft, 1870-1918* (Düsseldorf, 1970), pp. 340-78.

—— *Agrarische Interessenpolitik und preussischer Konservatismus im wilhelminischen Reich (1893-1914). Ein Beitrag zur Analyse des Nationalismus in Deutschland am Beispiel des Bundes der Landwirte und der Deutsch-Konservativen Partei* (2nd edn., Bonn/Bad Godesberg, 1975).

RACHFAHL, F., 'Richter und der Linksliberalismus', *Zeitschrift für Politik*, 5 (1912), 261-374.

RAUH, M., *Föderalismus und Parlamentarismus im Wilhelminischen Reich* (Düsseldorf, 1973).

RETALLACK, J. N. *Notables of the Right. The Conservative Party and Political Mobilization in Germany, 1876-1918* (Boston, 1988).

REXIUS, G., 'Studien zur Staatslehre des Positivismus', *HZ*, 107 (1911), 513-33.

RIEDEL, M., 'Bürger, Staatsbürger, Bürgertum', in O. Brunner *et al.* (eds.), *Geschichtliche Grundbegriffe*, i (Stuttgart, 1972), 702-25.

—— 'Gesellschaft, bürgerliche', in O. Brunner *et al.* (eds.), *Geschichtliche Grundbegriffe*, ii (Stuttgart, 1975), 719-800.

RITTER, G. A., *Die Arbeiterbewegung im Wilhelminischen Reich. Die Sozial-demokratische Partei und die freien Gewerkschaften 1890-1900* (Berlin, 1959).

RÖHL, J. C. G., 'Higher Civil Servants in Germany, 1890-1900', *Journal of Contemporary History*, 2 (1967), 101-21.

—— *Germany without Bismarck. The Crisis of Government in the Second Reich, 1890-1900* (London, 1967).

ROSENBERG, H., *Grosse Depression und Bismarckzeit. Wirschaftsablauf, Gesellschaft und Politik in Mitteleuropa* (pbk edn., Frankfurt, 1976).

ROSS, R. J., *Beleaguered Tower. The Dilemma of Political Catholicism in Wilhelmine Germany* (Notre Dame, Indiana, 1976).

RÜCKERT, J., *August Ludwig Reyschers Leben und Rechtstheorie, 1802-1880* (Berlin, 1974).

—— *Idealismus, Jurisprudenz und Politik bei Friedrich Carl von Savigny* (Edelsbach, 1984).

SCHMIDT, F., The German Abstract Approach to Law. Comments on the System of the Bürgerliches Gesetzbuch', *Scandinavian Studies in Law*, 9 (1965), 131-58.

SCHMIDT, G., 'Die Nationalliberalen—eine regierungsfähige Partei? Zur Pro-blematik der inneren Reichsgründung, 1870-1878', in G. A. Ritter (ed.), *Die deutschen Parteien vor 1918* (Cologne, 1973), pp. 208-223.

SCHRÖDER, R., *Abschaffung oder Reform des Erbrechts. Die Begründung einer Entscheidung des BGB-Gesetzgebers im Kontext sozialer, ökonomischer und philosophischer Zeitströmungen* (Ebelsbach, 1981).

SCHUBERT, W., *Die Entstehung der Vorschriften des BGB über Besitz und Eigen-tumsübertragung. Ein Beitrag zur Entstehungsgeschichte des BGB* (Münster, 1966).

—— 'Der Code Civil und die Personenrechtsentwürfe des Grossherzogtums Hessen-Darmstadt von 1842 bis 1847', *ZRG GA*, 88 (1971), 110-71.

—— 'Franz von Kübel und Württembergs Stellung zur Erweiterung der Reichskompetenz für das gesamte bürgerliche Recht', *Zeitschrift für würt-tembergische Landesgeschichte*, 36 (1977), 167-98.

—— 'Windscheids Briefe an Planck und seine für Planck bestimmte Stel-lungnahmen zum Schuldrecht und zum Besitzrecht der 1. BGB-Kommission', *ZRG RA*, 95 (1978), 283-326.

—— 'Preussens Pläne zur Vereinheitlichung ders Zivilrechts nach der Reichs-gründung', *ZRG GA*, 96 (1979), 243-56.

—— 'Der Ausbau der Rechtseinheit unter dem Norddeutschen Bunde: Zur Entstehung des Strafgesetzbuchs von 1870 unter besonderer Berücksichtigung des Strafensystems', in A. Buschmann *et al.* (eds.), *Festschrift für Rudolf Gmür am 70. Geburtstag 28. Juli 1983* (Bielefeld, 1983), pp. 149-89.

SCHWAB, D., 'Eigentum' in O. Brunner *et al.* (eds.), *Geschichtliche Grundbegriffe*, ii (Stuttgart, 1975), 65-115.

SCHWARZ, A., *Rechtsgeschichte und Gegenwart. Gesammelte Schriften zur Neueren Privatrechtsgeschichte und Rechtsvergleichung*, ed. H. Thieme and F. Wieacker (Karlsruhe, 1960).

SHEEHAN, J. J., *German Liberalism in the Nineteenth Century* (Chicago/London, 1978).

SIEMANN, W., *Die Frankfurter Nationalversammlung 1848/49 zwischen demokratischem Liberalismus und konservativer Reform. Die Bedeutung der Juristendominanz in den Verfasssungsverhandlungen des Paulkirchenparlaments* (Frankfurt, 1976).

SMITH W. and TURNER, S. A., 'Legislative Behaviour in the German Reichstag', *CEH*, 14 (1981), 3-29.

STOLL, A., *Friedrich Karl v. Savigny. Ein Bild seines Lebens mit einer Sammlung seiner Briefe*, ii (Berlin, 1929).

STRUVE, W., *Elites against Democracy. Leadership ideals in bourgeois political thought in Germany, 1890-1933* (Princeton, NJ, 1973).

STÜHLER, H.-U., *Die Diskussion über die Erneuerung der Rechtswissenschaft von 1780-1815* (Berlin, 1978).

STÜRMER, M., *Regierung und Reichstag im Bismarckstaat 1871-1880. Cärismus oder Parlamentarismus* (Düsseldorf, 1974).

THIEME, H., 'Aus der Vorgeschichte des Bürgerlichen Gesetzbuches. Zur Gesetzgebung des Positivismus', *DJZ*, 39 (1934), 968-71.

THIEME, J., Zur Entstehung der Konkursordnung', in *Einhundert Jahre Konkursordnung* (Cologne, 1975), pp. 42-75.

TOEWS, J. E., *Hegelianism. The path toward dialectical humanism, 1805-1841* (Cambridge, 1980).

TRUBEK, D. M., 'Max Weber on Law and the Rise of Capitalism', *Wisconsin Law Review*, 3 (1972), 720-53.

UNGER, R. M., *Law in Modern Society. Towards a Criticism of Modern Social Theory* (New York/London, 1976).

VOLKOV, S. A., *The Rise of Popular Antimodernism in Germany. The Urban Master Artisans 1873-1896* (Princeton, NJ, 1978).

Vom Reichsjustizamt zum Bundesministerium der Justiz. Festschrift zum 100-jährigen Gründungstag des Reichsjustizamt am 1 Januar 1877 (Cologne, 1977).

VORMBAUM, T., *Die Rechtsfähigkeit der Vereine im 19. Jahrhundert. Ein Beitrag zur Entstehungsgeschichte des BGB* (Berlin/New York, 1976).

—— *Sozialdemokratie und Zivilrechtskodifikation. Berichterstattung und Kritik der sozialdemokratischen Partei und Presse während der Entstehung des Bürgerlichen Gesetzbuchs* (Berlin/New York, 1977).

—— *Politik und Gesinderecht im 19. Jahrhundert (vornehmlich in Preussen)* (Berlin, 1981).

WADLE, E., 'Der Zollverein und die deutsche Rechtseinheit', *ZRG GA*, 102 (1985), 99-129.

WALTHER, R., »...aber nach der Sündflut kommen wir und nur wir.« »Zusammenbruchstheorie«, *Marxismus und politisches Defizit in der SPD, 1890-1914* (Frankfurt, 1981).

Wegner, K., *Theodor Barth und die Freisinnige Vereinigung. Studien zur*

Bibliography 277

Geschichte des Linksliberalismus im wilhelminischen Deutschland (1893-1910) (Tübingen, 1968).

WEHLER, H.-U., *The German Empire 1871-1918* (Leamington Spa, 1985).

—— *Deutsche Gesellschaftsgeschichte* (2 vols., Munich, 1987).

WESENBERG, G., 'Die Paulskirche und die Kodifikationsfrage. (Zu para 64 der Paulskirchenverfassung)', *ZRG RA*, 72 (1955), 359-65.

WHITE, D., *The Splintered Party. National Liberalism in Hessen and the Reich, 1867-1918* (Cambridge, Mass., 1976).

WIEACKER, F., 'Aufstieg, Blüte und Krisis der Kodifikationsidee', in *Festschrift Gustav Boehmer* (Bonn, 1954), pp 34-50.

—— *Privatrechtsgeschichte der Neuzeit unter besonderer Berücksichtigung der deutschen Entwicklung* (2nd edn., Göttingen, 1967).

—— *Industriegesellschaft und Privatrechtsordnung* (Frankfurt, 1974).

—— 'Vom linken zum rechten Nationalismus. Der deutsche Liberalismus in der Krise von 1878/79', *Geschichte und Gesellschaft*, 4 (1978), 5-28.

WINKLER, H. A., Der rückversicherte Mittelstand: Die Interessenverbände von Handwerk und Kleinhandel im deutschen Kaiserreich', in W. Ruegg and O. Neuloh (eds.), *Zur soziologischer Theorie und Analyse des 19. Jahrhunderts* (Göttingen, 1971), pp. 163-79.

WINDELL, G. G., 'The Bismarckian Empire as a Federal State 1866-1880: A Chronicle of Failure', *CEH*, 2 (1969), 291-311.

WROBEL, H., Rechtsgeschichte, Wirtschaftsgeschichte, Sozialgeschichte: die Thibaut-Savigny Kontroverse', *Kritische Justiz*, 6 (1973), 149-57.

ZEENDER, J. K., *The German Center Party 1890-1906* (Philadelphia, 1976).

ZWEIGERT, K. and KÖTZ, H., *An Introduction to Comparative Law*, i (2nd edn., Oxford, 1987).

INDEX